SERVING A GREAT AND NOBLE ART

Serving a Great and Noble Art

Howard Hanson and the Eastman School of Music

Vincent A. Lenti

MELIORA PRESS
An Imprint of the University of Rochester Press

First published 2009

Meliora Press is an imprint of the
University of Rochester Press
668 Mt. Hope Avenue, Rochester, NY 14620, USA
www.urpress.com

and Boydell & Brewer, Ltd.
P.O. Box 9, Woodbridge, Suffolk IP12 3DF, UK
www.boydellandbrewer.com

Library of Congress Cataloging-in-Publication Data

Lenti, Vincent.
    Serving a great and noble art : Howard Hanson and the Eastman School of Music / Vincent A. Lenti.
        p. cm.
    Includes bibliographical references and index.
    ISBN-13: 978-1-58046-280-8 (cloth : alk. paper)
    ISBN-10: 1-58046-280-4 (cloth : alk. paper)
    ISBN-13: 978-1-58046-054-5 (pbk. : alk. paper)
    ISBN-10: 1-58046-054-2 (pbk. : alk. paper) 1. Eastman School of Music.
I. Title.
    MT4.R6E245 2009
    780.71'174789--dc22

                                                                2009019558

British Library Cataloguing-in-Publication Data
A catalogue record for this item is available from the British Library

Printed in the United States of America
This publication is printed on acid-free paper

To Jon Engberg,
Associate Director of the Eastman School of Music 1975–95
In recognition of his dedication to the school,
its students, and its faculty
and in sincere appreciation for the honesty and integrity
he consistently demonstrated
in fulfilling his administrative responsibilities.

Contents

Figures

Figure

Preface

This book recounts the second part of the history of the Eastman School of Music. The narrative begins in 1932 following the death of George Eastman and ends in 1972 with the resignation of the school's third director, Walter Hendl. The first chapter presents a retrospective summary of the school's establishment and its earliest years through the end of the 1931–32 school year. Those who want a more complete treatment of the subject are referred to my first book, *For the Enrichment of Community Life: George Eastman and the Founding of the Eastman School of Music*, published in 2004 by Meliora Press (an imprint of the University of Rochester Press). Selecting the events to include in the present volume and choosing the individuals who deserve mention has been a formidable task, since the story related encompasses a forty-year time span. It has been my intent to choose material that appropriately conveys a clear picture of the Eastman School of Music as it developed during the four decades following the death of the school's founder and benefactor while at the same time not burdening the reader with unnecessary detail.

This book is very much about Howard Hanson, who served as director of the school from 1924 until his retirement in 1964. Few leaders in any field enjoy the privilege of such a long tenure. Long tenures, however, produce failings as well as accomplishments, and I hope that I have presented a balanced portrait of this remarkable man who led the school for so many years. Hanson appointed me to the Eastman School of Music faculty in 1963, the year before his retirement. I knew him well and, frankly, admired him greatly. It has been my privilege to have served as a faculty member under all but the first of the school's six directors, the two most recent incumbents bearing the title "dean of the Eastman School of Music."

Hanson's successor as director, Walter Hendl, had a far less happy tenure at Eastman. The story of his resignation in response to pressure from the student body was reported in Rochester newspapers at the time and was a topic for editorial comment in the *Campus Times*, the University of Rochester's student newspaper. The 1972 Eastman

School of Music student yearbook similarly devoted much space to the circumstances behind Hendl's resignation. Much of what was written was, at best, an incomplete account of the events. Therefore, the story now needs to be told—perhaps for the first time with complete accuracy and fairness to everyone involved, especially Walter Hendl. I am deeply grateful to Walter and his wife, Barbara, for their hospitality on two occasions when I visited with them at their home in Erie, Pennsylvania. Material they graciously shared with me has assisted me in relating the events with more accuracy and clarity than any previous account has been able to achieve. I had a very deep respect for Walter Hendl, who was a musician of great stature and one of the most talented conductors of his generation. He treated me with much kindness and friendship during the years we worked together at Eastman. The fact that his time at the Eastman School of Music ended with great unhappiness and personal struggles is to be deeply regretted. Those circumstances, however, do nothing to diminish the respect and admiration he deserved.

I owe a debt of gratitude to many people who have helped and encouraged me. My first obligation is to the administration of the Eastman School of Music, which charged me with the responsibility of writing the school's history. A third volume remains to be written to complete the project. I also gratefully acknowledge the assistance of Nancy Martin, manuscript librarian and archivist at the University of Rochester's Rush Rhees Library, and the immeasurable help provided by David Peter Coppen, special collections librarian at the Sibley Music Library and Eastman School archivist. This book could not have been written without the continual assistance of David and his staff, especially Mathew Colbert, special collections assistant. When mentioned in the notes, collections at Rush Rhees Library and the Sibley Music Library are abbreviated as RRL and SML, respectively. I owe a particular debt of gratitude to three former Eastman School of Music students who have given the Sibley Music Library their written accounts and recollections of the Eastman Philharmonia tour to Europe and the Middle East during the 1961–62 school year. This information—provided by Clifford Spohr, Richard Kilmer, and Richard Rodean—has made it possible for me to provide a fairly detailed account of the orchestra's itinerary and activities during its absence from Rochester from November 24, 1961, to February 25, 1962.

I also acknowledge the cooperation of Matt Dudek, assistant managing editor at the Rochester *Democrat & Chronicle;* Edwin Blomquist Jr. at the *Christian Science Monitor;* Francis McBeth, publisher of Frederick Fennell's *The Wind Ensemble;* Anne Welsbacher, editor of *The Flutist Quarterly;* William Scharnberg, editor of *The Horn Call;* Beverly Holmes, administrator of the William Schuman Music Trust; Russell A. James from the *Washington Post Writers Group;* and Thomas M. Hampson, executor of the Estate of David L. Diamond. A special thanks is extended to Bonnie O'Leary, who provided a wealth of information concerning her mother, Henrietta Schumann. I would like to acknowledge my continuing friendship with Timothy Madigan, who served as editor for the 2004 publication of my initial volume on the history of the Eastman School of Music and who proved an excellent and encouraging mentor for a first-time author. I am most grateful to his successor at the University of Rochester Press, Suzanne Guiod, as well as to Tracey Engel, with whom I worked on the final preparation of the manuscript. A special word of appreciation is owed to copyeditor Cheryl Carnahan, whose previous association as a student at the Eastman School of Music provided unique insight and many valuable suggestions. Finally, I once again express heartfelt thanks to my wife and daughter, who have shown exemplary patience and understanding throughout the writing and production of this book.

All photographs and illustrations, unless otherwise indicated, are from the Eastman School of Music Archives, Eastman School of Music, University of Rochester, and are used by permission.

Vincent A. Lenti
January 2009

Introduction

When Howard Hanson retired at the end of the 1963–64 school year, he had been director of the Eastman School of Music for forty years—a tenure that encompassed all but the first three years of the school's history. After forty years under Hanson's guidance, the Eastman School of Music was a near-perfect reflection of the values and ideals of its long-term director. A composer, educator, and conductor, Howard Hanson was a man of many talents. As an educator he had a consistent and well-defined philosophy that guided him throughout his many years at the school. Hanson was thoroughly committed to the comprehensive education of the total musician, a philosophy that continues to characterize the education the school provides to its students. Under Hanson's leadership, the Eastman School of Music became widely known as an institution that welcomed the performer and the scholar, the composer and the educator. It was a school committed to the development of musical leadership, and above all it was an institution that was thoroughly American in its outlook, methods, and goals.

When Hanson arrived in 1924, the Eastman School's bachelor of music curriculum was already in place. During the school's earliest years, however, the majority of students were enrolled in a certificate program rather than pursuing an academic degree. Hanson had little sympathy for the certificate program, and from the beginning of his tenure he was committed to making the academic degree the norm for undergraduate music students. Under Howard Hanson's direction, the Eastman School exerted much influence throughout the country—not only as a result of the school's leadership in the development of undergraduate and graduate programs and curricula but also through Hanson's long association with the National Association of Schools of Music (NASM), an organization that became the professional accrediting agency for music schools and music departments throughout the United States. Hanson had attended the first meeting of NASM in October 1924, shortly after he assumed the director's position at Eastman. He held the all-important position of chairman of NASM's commission on curriculum from 1924 until 1933 and later served a number of consecutive terms as the association's president. His influence in the professional training of musicians at the undergraduate and graduate levels through his role at NASM was strongly felt throughout the country.

No cause aroused Hanson's interest more than that of American composers, and no American musical leader of his generation worked as tirelessly on their behalf. His passionate advocacy for American music led him to provide an annual forum at the Eastman School of Music for the works of American composers, an activity that began in 1927 and continued for the next forty-five years—including seven years following his retirement in 1964. He encouraged the publication of works by American composers and also recorded American music when few, if any, others were doing so. In addition, he conducted pieces from the American repertoire when he appeared as a guest conductor with orchestras such as the Boston Symphony, the New York Philharmonic, the Philadelphia Orchestra, and the Berlin Philharmonic.

By the time Howard Hanson retired, the school had been shaped into an institution that represented his philosophy of education, his commitment to American music, and his vision for the future. The school's degree programs and curricula were a reflection of his leadership. Only two members of the active faculty could trace their appointment to his predecessor; everyone else had been appointed by Hanson. The indelible stamp Hanson left on the Eastman School of Music created a terrible burden for his successor. In truth, one might speak of the "Hanson Years" and the "Post-Hanson Years" to describe the period between his arrival in 1924 as Eastman's second director and the arrival of Robert Freeman as the fourth director in 1972. His immediate successor, Walter Hendl, was burdened not only with his predecessor's legacy but also with dealing with an institutional inertia that was an inevitable outcome of a leadership tenure that had lasted four decades.

In providing leadership for the school as well as for the music profession in general, Howard Hanson was ably assisted by a great talent for public speaking. He was a master of the art of persuasive speaking and was frequently an inspiring orator. His style perhaps reflected his generation more than it did the present day, and it certainly had something in common with the great public speakers in the religious and political spheres at the time. His effectiveness in communicating with his listeners came not only from his rhetorical skills but also from his fervent belief that the art of music was a sublime expression of the human spirit. He undoubtedly believed music was the greatest of all the arts, and it was in these terms that he frequently spoke to the faculty and students.

Hanson's address at the school's opening convocation in September 1945 was typical of the message he so often preached from the stage of Kilbourn Hall, but it was perhaps delivered with more than his usual passion and eloquence. The convocation took place shortly after the surrender of Japan, which brought an end to World War II. Therefore, he may have had a particularly receptive audience as he spoke to the students:

> We are serving a great and noble art. We as men and women should be worthy of the art we serve. My hope for each of you is that you will be worthy apostles of an art whose beauty passes understanding, whose blessings pour forth on a wave of sound to a weary, heartsick, beauty-starved world. My hope is that you will be strong yet compassionate, magnificently gifted yet filled with a spirit of humility, technically skilled but emotionally warm and understanding, men and women born to serve through your art a world which greatly needs your gifts; men and women filled with the spirit of revelation which teaches you that all that you have, your talents, your vitality, your youth, your enthusiasm, are gifts from the Almighty for which you are the steward, the custodian.[1]

These words provide a vivid picture of Howard Hanson and his leadership of the Eastman School of Music. Hanson was a complex person. Like many strong leaders, he was a man of strong opinions and deeply held convictions. He was not a person to seek out the opinions and advice of others—especially the Eastman faculty—and at times one might discern a self-serving aspect to his decisions and priorities. As the years passed, he became more set in his ways and more resistant to change. Yet throughout his forty-year tenure as director of the school—even when he was promoting his own music and agenda—he always remained in the service of the great and noble art of music to which he was so thoroughly devoted. What follows is the story of his leadership beginning in 1932 and ending with the opportunities and challenges the school faced in the years immediately following his retirement in 1964.

---

[1] Howard Hanson, "Convocation Address," *Alumni Bulletin of the Eastman School of Music* 17, nos. 1–2 (November 1945): 16.

Part One

The Hanson Years

Chapter 1

1932

A Funeral in Rochester

George Eastman, whose vision and generosity had led to the founding of the Eastman School of Music, was dead. Alice Whitney Hutchison, his faithful secretary for forty years, was downstairs at Eastman's home on East Avenue when she heard a gunshot. It was 12:50 P.M. on Monday, March 14, 1932. Moments earlier George Eastman had finished smoking a cigarette, taken off his glasses, and laid down on his bed. Carefully folding a wet towel over his chest, he had calmly pointed the muzzle of a Luger automatic pistol at his chest and pulled the trigger. George Eastman died of a self-inflicted gunshot wound, leaving a note addressed to his friends that simply stated, "My work is done—Why wait?" His personal physician, Audley Stewart, was immediately summoned, as was the Reverend George Norton from nearby St. Paul's Episcopal Church. Although not a religious man, Eastman had befriended Norton and his late wife and counted them among his closest friends.

Suffering from declining health, the millionaire philanthropist had committed suicide rather than face an uncertain future that he feared would leave him an invalid, increasingly dependent upon others for his daily needs. Word of his death quickly spread throughout Rochester and beyond. Financial news tickers carried the announcement within about an hour of Eastman's death, although Wall Street did not know until after the stock market closed at 3:00 P.M. that it had been a suicide. There was apparently fear that the market might react very negatively to the knowledge that he had taken his own life. The mere news of his death produced a five-point drop in the price of a share of Kodak stock. Newspapers the following morning paid tribute to Eastman's many contributions to photography and industrial philosophy, as well as to his philanthropic generosity. Personal tributes were made by many of the country's business leaders. Adolph S. Ochs (1858–1935), longtime publisher of *The New York Times*, said "his loss is a national calamity,"[1] while Will H. Hayes (1879–1954), president of the Motion Picture Producers and Distributors of America, spoke of Eastman as "a great humanitarian, intent on developing whatever he touched to the greatest possible usefulness for the world's millions."[2]

Although the general public had little idea that Eastman was ill, those closest to him were well aware of his declining health. Specialists at the Mayo Clinic and in Rochester had confirmed that he was suffering from what they described as a hardening of the cells in his lower spinal cord, a condition Dr. Stewart called atherosclerosis. He was in considerable pain, walked with difficulty, and suffered from increasingly deep depression. Withdrawing more and more to his home on East Avenue, George Eastman was becoming somewhat of a recluse, spending much of his time in his second-floor bedroom suite. The Wednesday evening dinners, once the centerpiece of Rochester social life, had come to an end; and the regular Sunday musicales, which at one time had attracted as many as 150 guests each week, now took place in a house that was essentially empty except for Eastman and his household staff. He had debated the ethics of suicide with Norton, and when the clergyman had suggested that we owe it to others to live as long as we can, he retorted, "I don't owe any man a damned thing."[3]

George Eastman's funeral took place on the afternoon of March 17, 1932, at St. Paul's Episcopal Church. At the time, a suicide victim was normally barred from having a funeral service in an Episcopal church and from having a Christian burial, but George Eastman was no ordinary Rochesterian. Therefore, the usual expectations in such a situation were conveniently set aside. George Norton officiated at the service, assisted by the Reverend Murray Bartlett, former rector at St. Paul's and now president of Hobart College in nearby Geneva, New York, and by the Right Reverend David Lincoln Ferris, bishop of the Rochester Episcopal Diocese. Rush Rhees, president of the University of Rochester, read the scripture lesson.

Admittance to St. Paul's that afternoon was strictly by invitation only. A special section was reserved for distinguished friends and associates of the deceased. Colleagues from Kodak—notably Charles Hutchison and Albert K. Chapman—were there, as was Carl Ackerman (1890–1970), Eastman's first biographer who was

[1] "Eastman Charted Path for Industry," *The New York Times*, March 15, 1932: 14. Copyright © 1932 by The New York Times Co. Reprinted with permission.
[2] Ibid.
[3] George Norton, "My Friend George Eastman," *University of Rochester Library Bulletin* 23, no. 1 (Fall 1967): 3–14.

Figure 1. George Eastman, benefactor and founder of the Eastman School of Music. (Photograph by Alexander Leventon.)

then dean of the Pulitzer School of Journalism at Columbia University. Several members of the family of Thomas Edison, who had predeceased Eastman by six months, were in attendance, as was President Karl Compton from Massachusetts Institute of Technology—a school that had been the recipient of George Eastman's generosity in the past. Among the pallbearers were three doctors: his physician Audley Stewart, George Hoyt Whipple, and Albert Kaiser. Whipple had been selected several years earlier as the first dean of the university's new medical school, another institution that owed much to Eastman's generous support.[4] Dr. Kaiser, a pediatrician who had once served as tutor for Eastman's grandnephew, had often joined Eastman on his travels, including his second African safari in 1928. Eastman's two safaris to Africa had been made with Osa Johnson (1894–1953) and Martin Johnson (1884–1937), famous explorers and photographers of African wildlife, and the Johnsons were among Eastman's many friends who traveled to Rochester to be among the mourners at St. Paul's Episcopal Church.

The local radio station WHAM broadcast the service nationwide. Massachusetts Institute of Technology and the University of Rochester, both recipients of large gifts from George Eastman, canceled classes for the afternoon. In a somewhat theatrical gesture, the lights in Rochester's many movie houses were dimmed for one minute at precisely 3:30 P.M., and the bell in Rochester's city hall tolled seventy-seven times, one for each full year of Eastman's life. After the service at St. Paul's, the funeral cortege slowly made its way to Mount Hope Cemetery. George Norton led the committal service, and Eastman's body was then cremated. The ashes were later carried to Kodak Park, a large industrial complex located about two miles from downtown Rochester, where they were interred and marked with a large stone memorial.

George Eastman had contributed very generously to many causes and institutions, giving away a considerable part of his fortune. As a bachelor he had no direct heirs and had no interest in establishing a charitable foundation to carry on his philanthropic work after his death. He simply wanted to enjoy giving away his considerable fortune while he was still living. Of all his philanthropic endeavors, however, none meant more to him personally than the Eastman School of Music. He had not merely provided the funds for the construction and endowment of the school and its adjacent theater, but he had been deeply involved in all aspects of the planning, including some of the smallest and seemingly inconsequential finishing details. Moreover, his involvement did not lessen once the school opened. If anything, it intensified. The story of how this man, who was musically uneducated and often described as musically quite ignorant, came to establish a major institution of musical learning that would bear his name is a fascinating tale.

Twenty-seven years before his death, George Eastman had celebrated the opening of his beautiful new home on East Avenue with a formal housewarming. The guest list was entirely male, since

---

[4]   George Hoyt Whipple (1878–1976) later shared the 1934 Nobel Prize in medicine.

Eastman's mother—who would have been the hostess for the evening—had recently broken her hip and was indisposed. Social conventions of the time more or less required the presence of a hostess for mixed social events, so Eastman invited only men to the housewarming. Dinner was served at tables set up in the arcade that ran from the dining room to the palm house, and a male vocal quartet provided entertainment. Had anyone suggested during dinner that George Eastman, Rochester's newest millionaire and most influential citizen, would someday provide millions of dollars for the construction and endowment of a music school and an adjoining 3,000-seat theater, it would have provoked either polite laughter or stunned silence. Yet only fifteen years later that seemingly absurd suggestion was in the early stages of becoming a reality.

Many influences were at work that would eventually turn Eastman's interests toward music. Among the earliest was his friendship with Mary Durand Mulligan, the wife of Dr. Edward Mulligan, his personal physician at the time. She was an intelligent and cultured woman with considerable musical talent, and she organized not only the musical evenings at Eastman's home but also most of his social life. Her influence lasted beyond the time when he began to take charge of his own entertaining, and her death from pneumonia while traveling in Europe in 1927 was a blow from which he never recovered. The death of Edward Mulligan the following year only deepened his sense of loss. Eastman's most important friendship, however, was with Rush Rhees, president of the University of Rochester. When appointed to that post in 1900, Rhees had few credentials except for being an ordained Baptist minister, a prerequisite for the job in those days. The University of Rochester, founded by American Baptists about a half-century earlier, was little more than a small liberal arts college at the time, but the university's trustees had chosen their new president with uncanny wisdom. When Rhees retired in 1935, the institution had grown enormously in stature and reputation and could boast of having become the fifth most heavily endowed university in America—a credit to both Rhees's leadership and Eastman's generosity.

George Eastman initially had little interest in supporting higher education, but in 1904 he gave $77,000 to the University of Rochester for the construction of a new biology/physics building. This gift, a relatively substantial sum of money at the time, was accompanied by a note saying it would be the last gift Rush Rhees could expect from him. This was an inaccurate prediction, and Eastman eventually lavished tens of millions of dollars on the University of Rochester. Credit for this belongs largely to Rhees, who cultivated

Figure 2. Rush Rhees, president of the University of Rochester. (Photograph by Alexander Leventon.)

his friendship with George Eastman with exemplary patience. Theirs was perhaps an unlikely friendship: a Baptist minister who was now a university president and a self-made millionaire whose beliefs probably categorized him as an agnostic. Rhees was heavily involved in supporting many local cultural and philanthropic endeavors, and he often found himself working closely with Eastman. One of the musical organizations that attracted both men's attention was the Dossenbach Orchestra, the first attempt at organizing a professional symphony orchestra in Rochester. Founded by

Hermann Dossenbach, a local musician with perhaps more vision than ability, the orchestra was later reorganized as the Rochester Orchestra and did much to cultivate an interest in orchestral music among Rochesterians.

Dossenbach had been introduced to George Eastman's mother by Adelaide Hubbell, the wife of Eastman's attorney, Walter Hubbell, and he soon began to provide chamber music for Eastman on a regular basis. Dossenbach therefore became very much of a musical presence, both through the orchestra as well as through the music he was providing at Eastman's home. In 1912 Dossenbach also became involved in a new endeavor: the establishment of a new music school in Rochester. His partner in this enterprise was Alf Klingenberg, a Norwegian pianist who had come to Rochester the previous year to teach at the Rochester Conservatory of Music, founded several years earlier. Dossenbach and Klingenberg opened their own school on Prince Street, adjacent to what was then the University of Rochester campus, and they appropriately called their institution the Dossenbach-Klingenberg School of Music.

In 1913 the two men brought in a third partner, Oscar Gareissen, and the educational enterprise was renamed the D.K.G. Institute of Musical Art. Within a short time the "D.K.G." (as it was known to local Rochesterians) absorbed the operations of the older conservatory and became an increasingly important part of the local musical scene. A music school, however, is expensive to run, and the D.K.G. continually struggled to meet its financial obligations. Dossenbach and Gareissen abandoned the project in 1917, leaving Klingenberg the sole owner of the institute, which faced a questionable future. The institute's board of advisers was headed by Rush Rhees, and there is evidence that George Eastman had been providing financial assistance from time to time to keep the school in operation. But Klingenberg's school now faced ever-increasing problems that would require a bolder initiative if it were to survive.

During the years of their increased involvement in supporting cultural endeavors, George Eastman and Rush Rhees had come to strongly believe that music had a particular capacity to enrich the life of the community. They understood that music in Rochester would be dealt a severe blow if Klingenberg's school was forced to close. Therefore, in 1918 the two men agreed that Eastman would purchased the D.K.G. Institute of Musical Art from Alf Klingenberg and give it to the University of Rochester in an effort to find a more permanent solution to the school's recurring financial difficulties. Accordingly, Eastman purchased the institute's property and corporate rights for $28,000 on July 8, 1918. The transfer to the university was delayed for nearly a year because of difficulties with the university's charter, but the university eventually acquired the institute and its property on June 12, 1919, by paying George Eastman the sum of one dollar.

Five months later Rochester newspapers announced that George Eastman was going to provide the university with a new building for the institute as well as an adjoining theater, facilities that would be surpassed by no others in the world. Eastman's decision to do this had been formalized with the signing of a memorandum of agreement with the university in July. Land was acquired on the city's east side, architects were chosen, and preliminary plans were prepared—all under the close scrutiny and supervision of the millionaire philanthropist who was going to finance this ambitious undertaking. The site was quickly cleared of existing buildings, and construction began with the expectation that instruction would begin in the new school in September 1921. In the meanwhile, the university would maintain current instruction at its newly acquired Institute of Musical Art on Prince Street.

Eastman had originally contributed $1 million toward construction of the new facilities, and the university had agreed to relieve him of any further obligation should costs exceed this amount. During the construction period, however, he found it necessary to increase his gift to a total of $3.5 million, and by the completion of construction he had further increased his support to a total of about $5.5 million. Within a few years the amount grew to $12 million, including provision of an endowment. The best estimate of Eastman's eventual support would be about $17.5 million, about five times his original commitment to the project.

In spite of intense activity at the construction site, the new school building was not completed by its target date of September 1921. Only the third and fourth floors were ready for the new school year. Therefore, the new Eastman School of Music opened its doors to students while construction proceeded on its lower floors. The old institute building on Prince Street continued to be used until all facilities at the new building were completed at the end of February 1922. The school was finally opened to the public on Friday, March 3, 1922, and its lovely recital hall—named Kilbourn Hall in honor of the founder's late mother, Maria Kilbourn Eastman—was formally dedicated the following evening. Music for the dedication was provided by the Eastman School's resident string quartet, appropriately named the Kilbourn Quartet, which performed Beethoven's String Quartet in B-flat Major, Op. 18, No. 6. The quartet was then joined by the school's director, Alf Klingenberg, for a performance of Christian Sinding's Piano Quintet. Meanwhile, construction continued at a rather feverish pace to finish the 3,000-seat auditorium, which was being built adjacent to the new school and was scheduled to open in about six months.

George Eastman's commitment to the music school and its adjoining theater went far beyond supporting the education and training of professional musicians. Personally convinced that music could be a positive and enriching experience for the people of Rochester, he envisioned the school and theater working in partnership toward the betterment of community life. The new Eastman School of Music, the successor to Klingenberg's Institute of Musical Art, would therefore serve two distinct student constituencies: a collegiate program committed to the training of professional musicians and offering both a diploma program and an undergraduate degree, and a preparatory and special program providing music instruction for children and adults from the community. Even this, however, was inadequate for his purposes. Therefore, Eastman envisioned the new theater as also part of his commitment toward "building musical capacity on a large scale from childhood."[5] His goal, therefore, was to build an audience for music, not just to train musicians. To help accomplish this, he proposed to utilize the popular medium of motion pictures as a means of increasing musical awareness and appreciation, devoting his theater to showing movies six days a week and reserving only one day each week for concerts and recitals.

To support his musical goals, he provided the theater with what was reported to be the largest theater organ in the world, and he organized a theater orchestra that would accompany the silent movies of the day and also provide high-class musical entertainment as part of the movie shows. Eastman hoped that movie patrons, by being exposed to good music as part of the Eastman Theatre shows, would return to hear concerts and recitals. Therefore, each show began with an overture and included scenes from ballets or operas or selections by vocalists or instrumentalists, intermingled with somewhat lighter musical fare.[6] Eastman eventually underwrote the expenses of a resident opera company and a ballet corps. Among the many people involved in these early days of the Eastman Theatre were Martha Graham (1894–1991), later the most famous

---

5 William L. Chenery, "Philanthropy under a Bushel," *The New York Times,* March 21, 1920: XXX8. Copyright © 1920 by The New York Times Co. Reprinted with permission.

6 The Eastman Theatre Orchestra played the "deluxe" shows scheduled mid-afternoon and twice in the evening. The other movie presentations were accompanied by one of the theater organists.

name in American dance, and Rouben Mamoulian (1897–1987), who went on to a highly distinguished career as a producer/director on Broadway and in Hollywood.

In addition, Eastman built upon the work Hermann Dossenbach had painstakingly undertaken in developing an audience for orchestral music by augmenting his theater orchestra with additional players so it could present full symphonic concerts. The Eastman Theatre Orchestra, therefore, periodically became the Rochester Philharmonic Orchestra, and its early artistic development was placed in the very capable hands of people such as Albert Coates (1882–1953) and Eugene Goossens (1893–1962). The two men shared conducting responsibilities through the 1924–25 season, after which Coates left and Goossens remained to become the first permanent conductor of the Rochester Philharmonic Orchestra. Philharmonic concerts, however, were only part of the musical presentations in the new theater. The world's most famous artists regularly appeared in recitals, as did several of the finest American orchestras. In addition, the Metropolitan Opera presented various operas in an annual series of visits to Rochester that extended for many years.

The Eastman Theatre opened with a flurry of publicity in September 1922. The initial show featured the movie *The Prisoner of Zenda* and opened with the Eastman Theatre Orchestra performing Tchaikovsky's *1812 Overture*. Artistic entertainment was provided by dancer Ester Gustavson and by soprano Marion Armstrong, both accompanied by the orchestra, and the show ended with a spectacular exit performed on the mighty Austin theater organ. Despite the large crowds that attended the movie shows, however, the enterprise was relatively short-lived. Many factors contributed to the failure of the dream of using the theater as a culturally focused movie palace, not the least of which was the advent of talking pictures, a development that made the large theater orchestra and lavish shows somewhat of an anachronism. More important, however, was the difficulty of coping with the increasing competition from theaters operated by large production and distributing companies. Independent operations, such as the Eastman Theatre, found it impossible to secure the better movies for their shows.

Even the size and grandeur of the Eastman Theatre were insufficient to secure its future in the movie industry. The Rochester Theatre (later known as Loew's Rochester), which opened on South Clinton Avenue in 1928, was even larger, with a seating capacity of 4,000; and most observers considered the RKO Palace, built on North Clinton Avenue and also opened in 1928, a far more beautiful and opulent movie palace. Concurrent with the opening of these two new rivals, the decision was reached to abandon the movie business and to lease the Eastman Theatre to Paramount Pictures. But even Paramount was not able to make a profit with the enterprise, especially when faced with the financial hardships of the deepening economic depression, and the theater's career as a movie palace ended in April 1931. Henceforth, the Eastman Theatre would be used principally as a concert hall.

If the theater somehow failed to fulfill George Eastman's expectations and dreams, the school that bore his name quickly began to establish itself as an important center of musical learning by virtue of its exemplary facilities and excellent faculty. Alf Klingenberg had been retained as director of the Institute of Musical Art after it was acquired by the University of Rochester in 1919, and he then became the director of the newly opened Eastman School of Music in 1921. But on June 22, 1923, he received a letter from George Eastman proposing that he be given a year's leave of absence with full salary with the understanding that he would submit his resignation as director. In spite of his many accomplishments, not the least of which was his participation in the planning for the opening of the Eastman School of Music, the prevailing feeling was that he lacked sufficient vision and leadership qualities to lead the school.

Raymond Wilson, a member of the school's piano department, was appointed acting director for the 1923–24 school year, and the search for Klingenberg's successor began. Authority at the school had been vested in a board of managers, which consisted of the now-departed Klingenberg plus George Eastman, Rush Rhees, and George Todd, a Rochester businessman. Eastman and Rhees, however, controlled all decision making. Their choice for Alf Klingenberg's successor was bold and far-reaching. Howard Hanson was only twenty-eight years old when he arrived in Rochester to become the second director of the Eastman School of Music. He remained the school's leader for the next forty years, transforming the institution into one of the most influential music schools in the world. In later years Hanson commented on the challenges he faced upon accepting the director's position at Eastman:

> The problems were very real. The faculty was largely of foreign birth and training. . . . The student body was small and, with some exceptions, not very good. . . . All the classes in history and theory were taught by a wonderful old gentleman, George Barlow Penny, whose passion was numerology and who puzzled his students with the presentation of diagrams in various colors depicting the history of "musicke." Few of the famous teachers had students worthy of their

teaching and to build a student body worthy of the faculty was an immediate and pressing problem.[7]

Born in Wahoo, Nebraska, on October 28, 1896, Howard Hanson was the son of Swedish immigrants. He was first taught music by his mother and decided on a music career early in life. Hanson began his formal training in music at Luther College in his hometown and earned a diploma from that institution when he was only fifteen. He continued his studies with Percy Goetschius (1853–1943) at the Institute of Musical Art (later the Juilliard School) in New York City, then earned a bachelor of music degree from Northwestern University in 1916, where he also served as an assistant teacher of music theory.

After graduation from Northwestern, Hanson taught theory and composition at the College of the Pacific in San Jose, California, where he became dean of the Conservatory of Fine Arts in 1919 at age twenty-three. He soon began to attract widespread attention and critical acclaim as a composer and was awarded the Prix de Rome in 1921, becoming a Fellow of the American Academy in Rome for the next three years. Hanson's name was first mentioned to George Eastman by the English conductor Albert Coates, upon whom Eastman relied heavily for advice. He was quietly invited to meet with Eastman and Rush Rhees in January 1924, returning two months later as a result of an invitation to conduct his Symphony No. 1 ("Nordic") with the Rochester Philharmonic Orchestra. The following month Rhees sent Hanson a letter offering him the Eastman directorship. Hanson immediately responded by sending a telegram that simply read, "Accept position/Writing."[8]

While these events were transpiring, the school had opened a new building—a five-story annex—to provide much-needed space for preparing the Eastman Theatre shows and had also made plans for dormitories that would open in the fall of 1925. The expansion of the school's facilities continued in 1927 with the opening of a twelve-story building that contained 109 practice rooms, 9 classrooms, 8 offices, and a fully equipped gymnasium complete with dressing rooms and showers. The practice rooms and additional classrooms were much needed in view of the growing enrollment of collegiate students, including those who enrolled in the school's new graduate department, which opened in 1927.

---

[7] Howard Hanson, Autobiography (unpublished manuscript, Sibley Music Library, © 1969), 131.
[8] Howard Hanson, telegram to Rush Rhees, May 9, 1924. RRL.

While increasing numbers of students were coming to the Eastman School of Music during its first years of operation, the majority were from Rochester or the surrounding area. Entrance requirements were initially rather modest, and the general level of accomplishment among incoming students was nowhere near what it would eventually become. Yet, there were some exceptional students, perhaps none more so than Henrietta Schumann. Henrietta, who had been born in Lithuania in 1909, came to the United States from Russia in 1924, accompanying her father who settled in Syracuse, New York, as a music teacher. Ilya Schumann had been his daughter's only piano teacher, and her progress had been nothing short of remarkable, as illustrated by the fact that she had learned and memorized all thirty-two Beethoven piano sonatas by the time she was fifteen.

Henrietta started attending the Eastman School in November 1925, studying with Max Landow. Landow, a former teacher at the Stern Conservatory in Berlin, had begun to teach at Eastman in 1922 and must have been somewhat overwhelmed by his young student's precociousness. She made her debut in the Eastman Theatre with Eugene Goossens and the Rochester Philharmonic Orchestra on February 16, 1928, playing the Rachmaninoff Second Piano Concerto. The performance was a stunning success, and she was re-engaged as a soloist the following season, playing the Chopin First Piano Concerto on January 29, 1929, with Artur Rodzinski (1892–1948) on the podium. Shortly before the Rochester performance, Henrietta had made her debut in Detroit, performing Liszt's *Totentanz* with the Detroit Symphony under the direction of Ossip Gabrilowitsch (1878–1936).

Henrietta then went to Paris to study with Alfred Cortot (1877–1962), returning to America in the early 1930s. She made numerous concert appearances, including a performance of the Rachmaninoff Third Piano Concerto with the Rochester Philharmonic Orchestra in 1933. The following year she became the featured piano soloist on the weekly Radio City Music Hall broadcasts and in this capacity performed perhaps as many as eighty different piano concertos over the next dozen years or so. Her repertoire eventually included all of the Rachmaninoff concertos, and she may have been the first pianist other than the composer to perform them all.

While the radio broadcasts provided the main venue for Henrietta's performing career, she also appeared as a frequent recitalist and soloist, including at least two Carnegie Hall recitals that were well-received by New York music critics. In 1946 she was signed to play the leading role in the forthcoming Hollywood movie *Carnegie*

Figure 3. Publicity flyer for Eastman alumna Henrietta Schumann's
Carnegie Hall debut. (Collection of the author.)

Hall[9] but was forced to withdraw from the contract when she and her husband learned that she was pregnant. Nonetheless, her career continued until her sudden death in 1949. During the twenty-one years since her debut with the Rochester Philharmonic, Henrietta had proven to be a brilliant performer, and the future would surely have held even greater successes on the concert stage.

While Henrietta Schumann may have been the most spectacularly talented student at Eastman during its earliest years, the number of gifted young musicians who chose to attend the school increased on a yearly basis. The university's commencement ceremonies on June 15, 1925, featured the graduation of the first group of Eastman students who had spent all four years studying at the school. The first graduates of the Eastman School of Music had been Marion Eccleston and Roslyn Weisberg in 1922. Weisberg had come to Eastman as a transfer student from Syracuse University in the fall of 1921, while Eccleston had completed her course work at the old Institute of Musical Art and then spent the 1921–22 academic year enrolled at the University of Rochester to complete requirements for the bachelor of music degree.

The reputation of the Eastman School of Music began to spread more rapidly after Howard Hanson arrived in 1924. He quickly gave the school a sense of identity and purpose as a truly American institution, dedicated to American ideals. In addition, he was committed to the concept of a professional school within the context of a university. A passionate and tireless advocate for American music, in 1925 Hanson inaugurated a series of orchestral concerts to showcase the works of American composers. These annual concerts led to the establishment in 1931 of a yearly Festival of American Music. In presenting the works of American composers, Hanson was performing an invaluable service while also placing the Eastman School of Music in the forefront of such activities.

George Eastman, who had been deeply involved in the school's early development both as benefactor and as the most important member of the board of managers, began to quietly withdraw from the everyday operations of the school as the 1920s drew to a close. This was simply a reflection of his advancing years as well as his growing confidence in the leadership and direction of the institution. Yet it was comforting for Howard Hanson and Rush Rhees to

[9] *Carnegie Hall* was released by United Artists in 1947, starring Marsha Hunt and William Prince. The movie featured appearances by some of the most prominent artists of the day, including Bruno Walter (1876–1962), Lily Pons (1898–1976), Gregor Piatigorsky (1903–76), Rise Stevens (b. 1913), Jan Peerce (1904–84), Ezio Pinza (1892–1957), Leopold Stokowski (1882–1977), and Artur Rubinstein (1887–1982).

know that the school's benefactor and founder was always at hand to deal with any difficulties that required his assistance. Despite his continued presence, however, it was obvious to those close to him that Eastman was aging and in declining health. Yet his death on that fateful day in March 1932—and the fact that he had taken his own life—was a complete shock. Several hours before his suicide Eastman had signed a codicil to his will, leaving the bulk of his estate to the University of Rochester and revoking bequests to Cornell University, Massachusetts Institute of Technology, and the Young Women's Christian Association (YWCA) of Rochester. Three representatives from Cornell were present when the will was later offered for probate, but they made no objection after hearing the interrogation of the witnesses who all testified that Eastman was perfectly rational when he asked them to sign the codicil. Everyone also recalled Eastman jesting about income tax and asking questions about his new Ford automobile just before he went to his bedroom and took his own life. Howard Hanson later reflected on Eastman:

> It is difficult to write of George Eastman without emotion. To those of us who knew him well and who had the inestimable privilege of working in close contact with him he was a veritable superman—the type of leader to whom one gives unquestioning loyalty and devotion. To me he was not only an inspiring guide but a beloved friend. Though by nature a reserved and essentially shy and modest man, he possessed qualities of genuine sympathy and understanding that called forth in those who knew him best an admiration and loyalty that approached idolatry.[10]

The path George Eastman took toward becoming a generous benefactor and enthusiastic supporter of the art of music was gradual and probably not without occasional hesitation and doubt. The initial contribution to the University of Rochester in 1904 plus his growing involvement in community cultural and charitable causes marked his first steps on this path. The influence of his dear friend Mary Durand Mulligan was another step, as was his developing collaboration with President Rush Rhees. If his relatively modest contributions to Dossenbach's orchestra and Klingenberg's school were cautious in nature, all of these tiny steps led him eventually to an act of unparalleled generosity in establishing one of the great musical institutions in the world, a school that even today proudly bears his name—the Eastman School of Music.

[10] Howard Hanson, "George Eastman and Music," *Alumni Bulletin of the Eastman School of Music* 3, no. 3 (May 1932): 3–4.

Chapter 2

1932–33

A Portrait of the
Eastman School of Music

The death of the Eastman School's founder and benefactor was an event of the past, and Howard Hanson and his faculty faced the new school year and its many challenges in September 1932. The economic hardships affecting all facets of life in America were somewhat softened by the generous endowment George Eastman had provided to the school that proudly bore his name. The endowment had been little affected during the first two years immediately following the collapse of the stock market in 1929, but it had shown a more recent decline of about 7.5 percent between June 1931 and June 1932. Yet its value remained above $3 million. During the period 1927–32, the endowment provided an average of $178,000 in usable income each year. The amount needed from the endowment would more than double within the next several years as income from tuition and fees fell rather precipitously. Notwithstanding the seriousness of the economic situation, the Eastman School of Music was more fortunate than many other institutions in having ample financial resources that could help it meet its obligations to its faculty and students.

Howard Hanson addressed these issues in a statement to the school's alumni in the fall of 1932, pointing out that the school began the 1932–33 academic year with the largest enrollment of collegiate students in its history; total enrollment was 467, of whom 369 were candidates for the bachelor of music degree. The school had done everything possible through its scholarship and loan funds to allow for the continued study of students who found themselves in a distressed financial situation. A total of 192 students were being assisted by scholarships from the institution. Hanson's message included a strong statement concerning the importance of music in the face of current economic hardships:

In these years of disturbing economic conditions, the importance of music is being more fully recognized than perhaps ever before. I believe that the alumni of the Eastman School are fully aware of the place that music must take in the social life of every community if it is to fulfill its real purpose. Indeed this socialization of music, if it may be so termed, is the first duty of music education. I know that every Eastman School student, whether he be an alumnus or under-graduate, will labor in his or her sphere to the end that music may more and more contribute to the world that spiritual rejuvenation which the world so badly needs and which only things of the spirit can provide.[1]

All entering students in 1932 were requested to be present for an opening session in the school's Kilbourn Hall at 9:00 A.M. on Monday, September 19, at which time they received instructions for the week. The schedule for the next several days consisted of tests and auditions designed to properly assign students to sections of classes as well as to their primary studio teacher. Many students at the time, and well into the future, entered the school without benefit of a formal audition because of the difficulties in requiring such auditions from students who lived a considerable distance from Rochester. Therefore, admission was often based on high school transcripts and teacher recommendations. Students also competed for scholarships in auditions scheduled during the period Thursday, September 15, through Tuesday, September 20.

Yearly tuition at the school was $300, and the cost of room and partial board was $405. Miscellaneous fees and expenses made the total cost of attending the Eastman School of Music about $800 per year. There were many concessions because of the harsh economic times, including lower fares offered by American railroads for students returning to educational institutions. The Eastman School provided twenty-nine rooms at a reduced rate in one of its dormitories. These rooms, located on one floor of Foster Hall, functioned on a cooperative basis, with students obliged to clean both their own rooms and a small section of the general corridor. In spite of the financial difficulties, the school was not in favor of students seeking employment to earn all or part of their school expenses, especially not during the freshman year.

---

[1] Howard Hanson, "The New School Year," *Alumni Bulletin of the Eastman School of Music* 4, no. 1 (November 1932): 4.

The Eastman faculty in 1932 numbered about eighty, although that total included a number of teachers who primarily taught in the school's preparatory department. Unlike the collegiate program, the preparatory department suffered a precipitous decline in enrollment as a result of the Great Depression, with the number of students in the department declining to an all-time low of 417 in 1933–34. Several years earlier the school's administration had decided that 1,600 preparatory and special students, or about four times the number attending lessons in 1933–34, would be an ideal enrollment. The figure of 1,600 students was perhaps somewhat unrealistic, although the number of preparatory and special students rose to almost 1,100 by the 1943–44 school year, and the school was able to sustain an enrollment of between 1,100 and 1,200 students until the late 1960s.

The largest group of faculty members was made up of the piano teachers, a total of twenty-two in 1932. Included in this group was Mabel Cooper, one of the original members of the faculty in 1921. The more important members of the piano faculty were Cecile Genhart, Max Landow, Sandor Vas, and Raymond Wilson. Genhart had joined the faculty in 1926, and her illustrious career at the school lasted nearly a half-century. She had studied in Europe first with her father, who taught at the conservatory in Zurich, and then with Emil Frey (1889–1946), who had been a student of Louis Diémer (1843–1919) at the Paris Conservatory. Diémer was perhaps the most influential French piano teacher of his generation. Genhart went to Berlin in 1921 and studied for three years with Edwin Fischer (1886–1960), making her debut with the Berlin Philharmonic on December 16, 1922, performing the Beethoven Piano Concerto No. 1 and the Brahms Piano Concerto No. 2. In 1924 she married Herman Genhart,[2] who had been her father's student in Zurich and was now working part-time at the Eastman School of Music. In September 1925 she accepted some part-time teaching at Eastman, becoming a full-time faculty member the following year.

Max Landow had come to the Eastman School in 1922, after having taught for eight years at the Peabody Conservatory in Baltimore. He had studied in Paris with Eduard Risler (1873–1929), widely considered one of the finest pianists of his generation, and then continued his piano studies in Germany with Liszt's student Karl Klindworth (1830–1916). Prior to coming to the United States in 1914, he had taught for a number of years at the famous Stern

---

[2]   Cecile and Herman Genhart were divorced in 1943.

Conservatory in Berlin. Sandor Vas arrived at the Eastman School of
Music a year after Landow and also had impressive credentials. His
professional studies had been at the Leipzig Conservatory where
he studied with Liszt's student Alfred Risenauer (1863–1907), but
he was also an accomplished cellist, a serious composer, and a fine
conductor. He soon directed all his energies to the piano, however,
and pursued additional study with Terresa Carreño (1853–1917)
before embarking on a successful concert career. Before the outbreak
of World War I he was appointed professor at the Lodz Conservatory in Poland, and after the war he began teaching at the Fodor
Conservatory in Budapest.

Vas and Landow, very different pianists and certainly very different personalities, both enjoyed long and successful careers at
Eastman, as did their colleague Raymond Wilson. Wilson was an
American who had attended the Peabody Conservatory, where he
was a special student of Ernest Hutcheson (1871–1951). He subsequently studied with Rudolph Ganz (1877–1972) and eventually
began teaching at Syracuse University. He was teaching at Syracuse
in 1921 when he was invited to become a member of the faculty at
the new Eastman School of Music in Rochester. In addition to his
work in Eastman's piano department, Wilson became the first director of the preparatory department when the department was formally organized in 1927. Other piano teachers who were Wilson's
colleagues in 1932 included Marie Erhart, Ernestine Klinzing, Donald Lidell, George McNabb, Gladys Metcalf Leventon, and Harry
Watts, all of whom enjoyed long teaching careers at the school.

There were eight members of the voice department in 1932,
including Lucy Lee Call and Adelin Fermin, both among the
school's original faculty members. Call had studied in Prague,
Dresden, and Milan and had been a member of the Metropolitan
Opera Company. Fermin, who had completed several recital tours
in Europe and America, had taught at the Peabody Conservatory in
Baltimore before joining the faculty at the newly opened Eastman
School of Music. Jeanne Woolford, who began her Eastman teaching career in 1922, had been Fermin's student in Baltimore. Thomas
Austin-Ball joined the Eastman voice faculty a year after Woolford.
An Irishman, Austin-Ball had enjoyed a successful career in opera,
oratorio, and recital work in England after completing his studies at
the Royal Academy in London. Before coming to Eastman he had
been head of the voice department at Skidmore College in Sara-
toga Springs, New York. Nicholas Konraty, another member of the
voice faculty, had received his musical training at the Moscow Conservatory and also earned a degree from the Moscow Institute

of Economics. He joined the Eastman faculty in 1929 after having enjoyed success as an opera singer in Russia, France, Spain, and the United States. Other members of the voice faculty included Richard Halliley, Frederick Haywood, and LeRoy Morelock.

Two men taught organ in 1932. Harold Gleason had originally come to Rochester in 1919 to serve as organist at George Eastman's home and to teach at the Institute of Musical Art. A student of Edwin Henry Lamare (1865–1934), W. Lynwood Farnam (1885–1930), and Joseph Bonnet (1884–1944), Gleason became one of the most influential members of the Eastman faculty—not only as a teacher of organ but also in establishing the graduate department and later in developing the school's music literature courses. Gleason's colleague in the organ department was Abel Marie Decaux, a Frenchman who had been organist at Sacré-Coeur in Paris. A student of the famous Charles-Marie Widor (1844–1937), Decaux had joined the Eastman faculty in 1923, succeeding another French organist, Joseph Bonnet.

The principal members of the string faculty since the Eastman School opened in 1921 had been the four men who comprised the Kilbourn Quartet, which had regularly performed in George Eastman's home and now served as the school's resident quartet. The four men were also principals in the Rochester Philharmonic Orchestra and therefore were expected to be teachers, chamber music performers, and orchestral musicians. The first violinist in 1932 was Gustave Tinlot, who had come to the Eastman School of Music in 1925. Trained at the Paris Conservatory, Tinlot came to the United States to become concertmaster of Walter Damrosch's New York Symphony in 1918. He then spent a year as concertmaster in Minneapolis before accepting his appointment in Rochester. The cellist in the Kilbourn Quartet was Paul Kéfer, a fellow member of the New York Symphony with Tinlot. The two men had also played together as members of the Franco-American String Quartet. Kéfer had previously played chamber music with Pierre Monteux (1885–1964), the famous French conductor, when both were members of the Modern Quartette. He was also the founder and a member of the Trio di Luctece with flutist Georges Barrère (1876–1944) and harpist Carlos Salzedo (1885–1961). Kéfer had arrived in Rochester in October 1924 to replace Joseph Press, who had just died of complications from pneumonia.

The violist of the Kilbourn Quartet, Samuel Belov, was a member of the original Eastman School of Music faculty. Born in Russia, Belov had played in the Philadelphia Orchestra and had taught both violin and viola at the Philadelphia Conservatory of Music. In addition to teaching viola at Eastman, Belov conducted the school orchestra. Gerald Kunz, who had been the quartet's second violinist since its inception, had resigned at the end of the 1931–32 school year. He was replaced for the next two years by Alexander Leventon, the second concertmaster in the Rochester Philharmonic. However, Leventon did not join Tinlot, Belov, and Kéfer on the Eastman faculty. Leventon was one of the most interesting and gifted musicians in Rochester at the time, but he is principally remembered as a photographer, especially for his portrait photography.[3] Born in Russia and trained at the Moscow Conservatory, he subsequently studied in Vienna with Otakar Ševčik (1852–1934). Placed in an internment camp during World War I because he was classified as an enemy noncombatant, Leventon learned English from a fellow prisoner and eventually made his way to the United States. His talent as a photographer was widely recognized, and this special interest may have contributed to his reluctance to accept teaching responsibilities at the school. His involvement with the quartet was relatively short-lived; he left the group after only two years.

Tinlot, Belov, and Kéfer, therefore, were the three main string teachers at the school in 1932. Among their colleagues were violinists Paul White and Karl Van Hoesen and the bass teacher Nelson Watson. White had been a student of the famous Belgian violinist Eugène Ysaÿe (1858–1931) and was therefore connected to the great tradition of violin performance extending back to Henryk Wieniawski (1835–80) and Henry Vieuxtemps (1820–81), with whom Ysaÿe had studied. White succeeded Kunz as principal second violin in the Rochester Philharmonic, and he eventually took Leventon's place in the Kilbourn Quartet. Van Hoesen had earned a bachelor of arts degree in English literature from Cornell University but had also studied violin with Ševčik in Ithaca when the great violin pedagogue was teaching at the Ithaca Conservatory. Van Hoesen enjoyed a forty-year tenure at Eastman. Watson was an Englishman who had trained at Trinity College in London as well as at the Royal College of Music. He had come to Eastman from the Philadelphia Orchestra in 1924 and served the school with great distinction until his death in 1945.

White, Van Hoesen, and Watson were members of the Rochester Philharmonic Orchestra, as were all of the principal woodwind, brass, and percussion teachers in 1932. The policy of hiring members of the orchestra to also teach at the school was already firmly in

---

[3]   A fine collection of photographs was donated to the Eastman School of Music by his widow, Gladys Leventon.

place by 1932, and it would continue for more than three decades. Orchestral playing had provided these musicians with full-time employment when the Eastman Theatre opened in 1922, with responsibilities including the heavy demands of performing in the Eastman Theatre Orchestra plus the more professionally satisfying experience of playing in Rochester Philharmonic concerts. Teaching at Eastman was hardly a full-time occupation for many of these musicians at the time, initially limited to providing lessons for only a handful of students.

The convenience of this system, however, was rudely interrupted when the Eastman Theatre was leased to Paramount in 1928. The new operator of the movie enterprise would only guarantee continuation of the Eastman Theatre Orchestra through June 1929. This created an immediate threat to continued employment for these musicians, by both the philharmonic and the school. The Rochester Philharmonic Orchestra had been founded on the premise that its members would be fully employed by the Eastman Theatre Orchestra. The continued existence of the philharmonic was now called into question because it played too few concerts to be able to offer its members an adequate salary when they were no longer also engaged to play the movie shows.

The collapse of the Rochester Philharmonic might, in turn, deprive the Eastman School of Music of the availability of orchestral players needed for the faculty. However, the Rochester community rallied around an imaginative plan that called for the creation of a new orchestra named the Rochester Civic Orchestra, consisting of forty-eight players. The new orchestra would perform as many as sixty concerts each year at local high schools and then be properly augmented to form the full-sized Rochester Philharmonic Orchestra, which would continue to present symphonic programs in the Eastman Theatre. As in the past, members of the orchestra would be available for teaching responsibilities at the school.

Funding for the new Rochester Civic Orchestra came from a variety of sources, including an annual campaign that asked for assistance from citizens of Rochester. The Eastman School of Music also contributed $75,000, effectively subsidizing the orchestra in an attempt to secure the continued presence of orchestral musicians needed to provide instruction at the school. The $75,000 became a very necessary part of the orchestra's annual operating income. But while the school viewed this as a subsidy, the orchestra saw it as a contribution, a difference in perspective that would lead to difficulties in the future. The musicians employed by both the school and the orchestra became victims of exploitation, since the financial management of the orchestra and the school was vested in the same person—namely, Arthur See. While this situation planted the seeds for serious problems in the future—problems not satisfactorily addressed for another three decades—in 1932 these musicians were probably grateful for steady employment and a regular paycheck, which may have been the envy of many others during this period of high unemployment and economic hardships.

The principal players in the Rochester Philharmonic Orchestra who taught at Eastman in 1932 included flutist Leonardo DeLorenzo, oboist Arthur Foreman, clarinetist Rufus Arey, and bassoonist Vincent Pezzi. DeLorenzo was the school's first flute teacher and had come to America from his native Italy in 1910 to become principal flutist in the New York Philharmonic. Foreman was English by birth and training and had taught at the Guildhall School in London while also serving as principal oboist in the Royal Philharmonic Orchestra. He began his Eastman career in 1926, replacing Louis Catalano, the first oboe teacher at the school. Pezzi was also a European and was new to the orchestra and the school in 1932. Trained in Italy, Pezzi had moved to the United States in 1908 and had been an orchestral player in St. Paul and Detroit prior to coming to Rochester. Unlike De Lorenzo, Foreman, and Pezzi, clarinetist Rufus Arey was an American. He had been trained in Boston and had performed as a member of the Detroit Symphony and the Philadelphia Orchestra before coming to Rochester in 1927.

Other members of the Rochester Philharmonic Orchestra who were teaching at Eastman in 1932 included Edward Mellon and Frederick Remington, who taught trumpet. Mellon, who had studied at the Bush Conservatory of Music in Chicago and at Chicago Musical College, had been a member of both the school's faculty and the Rochester Philharmonic since 1929. His orchestral colleague, Frederick Remington, had started teaching at Eastman in 1930. But the more significant member of the Remington family was Emory, the school's trombone teacher for nearly fifty years. Emory Remington, called "The Chief" by his friends, students, and colleagues, had no impressive résumé, but he developed into one of the most influential and successful teachers in the history of music education in America. In the future, former Remington students could be found as members of many of the country's most prominent symphony orchestras.

And then there was Arkady Yegudkin, affectionately known as "The General" to the many young people who studied French horn with him during his long career at Eastman. Yegudkin had been among the many Russian musicians who had fled to Western

Europe and the United States following the Bolshevik Revolution. A colorful character with a heavy Russian accent that never lessened during his many years in America, he combed his hair from back to front to cover his bald spot and apparently even held it in place with bobby pins. He was known to tell his new students that he was quite simply the best horn teacher in the world, and many believed him. But as Gene Coghill has written, "He was, to say the least, controversial: a pain in the neck to some (notably the school administration), a good friend to many, outspoken antagonist of others and, above all, a *character* the likes of which had to be seen to be believed."[4]

The Eastman School could boast of two harp teachers in 1932, both of whom were members of the Rochester Philharmonic. Lucile Johnson Bigelow (now Lucile Johnson Harrison following her marriage to conductor Guy Fraser Harrison) had been the school's first harp teacher as well as the original harpist with the philharmonic. She was joined in the orchestra and on the faculty by her young student Eileen Malone. While the date of Malone's initial appointment to the faculty is variously given as 1931 or 1932, the date of her retirement in 1989 is quite certain. Her tenure of fifty-seven or fifty-eight years is probably the longest of anyone who ever taught at the school.

Two other members of the Rochester Philharmonic were also on the Eastman faculty in 1932: Paul Schmidt and William Street. Schmidt, who played the tuba, was a German by birth and training, and he performed and taught in Germany before joining the orchestra and the Eastman School faculty in 1929. Street, who had started teaching percussion at Eastman in 1927, became another legend among faculty members. Born in Hamilton, Ontario, he and his brother Stanley, also a percussionist, had played in a number of Rochester's movie theaters before joining the new Eastman Theatre Orchestra in 1922. His forty-year career at the Eastman School of Music was an especially distinguished one, and when he retired in 1967 he was succeeded on the faculty by one of his students, John Beck. Beck described Street as "a unique guy, someone who didn't have much schooling but had an insight for always doing the right thing."[5] Like Emory Remington, William Street lacked an impressive résumé, but his success and influence as a teacher became legendary.

---

[4] Gene Coghill, "My First Teacher, Arcady Yegudkin," *The Horn Call* 15, no. 1 (October 1984): 15 (original emphasis).
[5] John Beck, interviewed by the author, Rochester, NY, May 20, 2005.

Figure 4. Arkady Yegudkin, teacher of French horn, 1926–53.

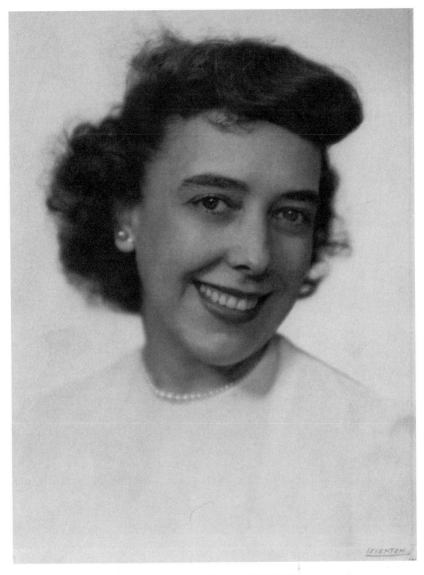

Figure 5. Eileen Malone, teacher of harp, 1931–89.

Figure 6. William Street, teacher of percussion, 1927–67.
(Photograph by Alexander Leventon.)

The composition faculty consisted principally of Howard Hanson and Bernard Rogers. Rogers had joined the faculty in 1929 after having had a Guggenheim Fellowship the previous two years. A composer who had studied with Ernest Bloch (1880–1959), Percy Goetschius (1853–1943), Frank Bridge (1879–1941), and Nadia Boulanger (1887–1979), Rogers was a perfect choice as someone who could work and survive amid Hanson's increasingly larger-than-life presence at the Eastman School, and he served the institution and its students with exemplary dedication until his retirement in 1967. Allen Irvine McHose, who also joined the faculty in 1929, had been appointed chair of the theory department in 1931. Well-known to generations of Eastman students, especially in later years among those for whom his textbook became a memorable part of their undergraduate experience at the school, McHose was an energetic and influential presence at Eastman for the next thirty-six years.

McHose's colleagues in 1932 included two highly effective theory teachers, Ruth Northup Tibbs and Elvira Wonderlich. Tibbs and Wonderlich were both graduates of the Eastman School, where they had majored in piano, and both quickly developed a reputation for thoroughness and toughness. Jon Engberg, who later served the school as associate director, studied with Tibbs and recalled that she was a "wonderful teacher, extremely energetic," adding, however, that it was a "frightening experience to be in her class."[6] Wonderlich was no less thorough in her classroom manner and was known to give a low grade on an assignment simply because she did not like it. Richard Thorell (BM '63, MA '73) recalled the familiar scene in Wonderlich's theory classes when she would ask everyone to gather around the piano while she played through their part-writing assignments.

> I handed her my paper. She placed it on the music rack and played through it in a rather perfunctory manner. She stopped, looked at it, adjusted her spectacles, and played it through a second time, ever so slowly and deliberately. She stopped, turned, and in a tone of utter disbelief said in that inimitable Wonderlich way, "Why Dick, that's really quite good!" I was on music theory cloud 9 for a grand total of about 2 seconds before the fuller meaning of both her words and her tone managed to sink in. Uncompromising and meticulous she was, but she compelled us to at least recognize the existence of such a standard, and if we lived up to her expectations—be it only once—we knew that there just might be a glimmer of hope for those of us so decidedly average.[7]

In spite of both Wonderlich's and Tibbs's sometimes arbitrary nature and strictness, students were generally very devoted to them, recognizing the dedication and skill they brought to their teaching. Joining them as a member of the teaching staff in September 1932

---

[6] Jon Engberg, telephone interview by the author, January 11, 2005.
[7] Richard Thorell, letter to the author, October 27, 2004.

was Donald White. He enjoyed a long career at Eastman, eventually serving for several years as chair of the theory department prior to his retirement. Yet another theory teacher of note was Gustave Soderlund. Born and educated in Sweden, he had subsequently studied and taught at the University of Kansas, then earned a master of music degree at the Eastman School. He immediately joined the faculty and taught counterpoint for the next twenty-six years.

Music history had been taught by George Barlow Penny since 1921. Penny, born in 1861 during Abraham Lincoln's first term as president, must have been the oldest member of the Eastman School of Music faculty in 1932. He was very much a "university" man, having graduated from Cornell in 1885 with a bachelor of science degree. However, his background also included theory and organ study at Syracuse University, and he later studied with Percy Goetschius in New York. His academic career had included a thirteen-year tenure as dean of the School of Fine Arts at the University of Kansas, but he had come to Rochester to teach at the Rochester Conservatory of Music in 1910, later affiliating himself with the D.K.G. Institute of Musical Art. He became a charter member of the Eastman School faculty in 1921.

Musicology was not yet a subject being taught at the Eastman School of Music in 1932, although there was a master's degree curriculum that allowed students to earn a degree with a major in musicology. The curriculum, however, had little to do with musicology and included six credits for a thesis, eight credits in composition, orchestration, and/or counterpoint, plus sixteen credits elected from areas such as pedagogy, psychology, or applied music study (i.e., instrumental or vocal lessons). Soon, however, the school would become an important center for the study of musicology, largely because of a decision in 1932 to hire a young man as a part-time teacher of psychology. That teacher was Charles Warren Fox, a 1926 graduate of Cornell University. Although his official field of study was psychology, Fox had also studied musicology at Cornell, working with Otto Kinkeldy (1878–1966), the first musicology professor in the United States. Kinkeldy suggested to Howard Hanson in 1934 that the study and teaching of musicology could confidently be entrusted to Fox. Initially, however, he was the new psychology teacher in 1932, joining a small staff of others who provided instruction in "non-music" disciplines such as history, English, French, and German.

The teacher of French and French diction was Anne Theodora Cummins, who had joined the Eastman School faculty in 1924. Educated in England, she later went to Paris to study at the Sorbonne and to pursue private study of diction, dramatics, and phonetics. Her subsequent teaching career took her to India, where she taught at the diocesan high school in Darjeeling and later became head of a government high school in nearby Kurseong. This area is in northeastern India, just south of China, with Nepal to the west and Bhutan to the east. Surely, no other Eastman faculty member ever taught in such a remote and exotic part of the world. Her career as a teacher at the Eastman School of Music extended for forty-two years, and she came into contact with countless numbers of students, especially from the voice and opera departments. She was an unforgettable character at the school, with her quaint accent and distinctively British manner. Howard Hanson later praised her as one of the greatest teachers he had ever known, adding that "her somewhat formal attitude and her clipped English speech only partially disguised a pixie sense of humor which endeared her to students and faculty alike."[8]

Joining the faculty seven years after Cummins was the young Jessie Hoskam (Jessie Kneisel after her marriage to Viennese-born Karl Kneisel), who was hired to teach German. Kneisel earned undergraduate and graduate degrees from the University of Rochester, attended the University of Bonn on a German-American exchange stipend, and later earned a doctorate at Columbia University. She taught at Eastman for forty-two years and brought her great love of German art and culture to countless numbers of students who eagerly enrolled in her classes. Her effectiveness as a German teacher resulted not only from her knowledge of the subject but even more from the great affection she had for her students. She shared with many of her students a deep appreciation and knowledge of opera and German lied, which made her all the more wonderful to those studying with her.

Other members of the Eastman School faculty in 1932 included five people who taught music education or, as it was then known, public school music. The school differed from many other conservatories in having a strong commitment to training elementary and secondary school music teachers, a commitment consistent with the vision of the school's founder, George Eastman. Faculty members in this area of study were part-time at the school and were also employed by the Rochester City School District. Prominent among them was Charles Miller, who had joined the faculty in 1923, and Sherman Clute, appointed in 1924. Karl Van Hoesen, already mentioned as a member of the string faculty, also taught public school music, as did Ellen Hatch Beckwith and Carlotta Ward Greene.

---

[8] Quotation from a University of Rochester news release on the occasion of the death of Anne Theodora Cummins, December 12, 1977. SML.

Figure 7. Jessie Hoskam Kneisel, teacher of German, 1932–76.
(Photograph by Josef Schiff.)

The opera department, which involved the services of a number of the voice faculty members, was directed by Emanuel Balaban, an exceptionally fine pianist—one of the best at Eastman—as well as an excellent opera director. He had studied piano with Zygmunt Stojowski (1870–1946) at the Institute of Musical Art in New York and later continued his piano studies with Artur Schnabel (1882–1951). He studied conducting in Dresden with Fritz Busch (1890–1951) while serving as an assistant conductor at the Dresden Opera House. In addition to considerable subsequent experience as a conductor, Balaban served as a piano accompanist for such artists as Mischa Elman (1891–1967) and Efrem Zimbalist (1889–1985). He originally came to Rochester in 1925 as an opera coach, soon became assistant to Eugene Goossens in the school's operatic training program, and was appointed opera director to succeed Goossens when the conductor left Rochester for Cincinnati.

Serving as chorus master in the opera department, as well as conductor of the Eastman School Chorus, was Herman Genhart. Educated in Zurich, Leipzig, and Munich, Genhart had come to the Eastman School as an opera coach but had been promoted to conductor of the chorus in 1926. He will be best remembered as conductor of the Eastman School Chorus by those who were at Eastman during his forty years at the school. Students had a variety of reactions and opinions concerning Genhart, who was among the most unforgettable and controversial characters in the school's history. His choral rehearsals were run with strict discipline, and no mistake or lack of attention on the part of a singer escaped his notice. Whether berating the orchestra at a rehearsal or shouting at the chorus in his frequently incomprehensible German accent, Genhart was a presence in the lives of a great many Eastman students.

While his faculty was busily providing for the educational needs of the students, Howard Hanson maintained a busy professional schedule. In late October he went to Cincinnati to chair meetings of the commission on curriculum organized by the National Association of Schools of Music (NASM). He had been the chair since 1924 and was highly influential in the development of standards for professional degrees in music, as well as the accreditation of such degrees. Hanson then traveled to New York in November to attend a meeting of the music committee of the Carnegie Foundation. The following month the Eastman School's busy young director was in Washington, D.C., to preside as chair at a banquet for the Music Teachers National Association (MTNA). On December 20 he left Rochester again, this time for Germany. That trip was sponsored and funded by the Oberlander Trust of the Carl Schurz Foundation as an effort to foster greater mutual understanding and cooperation in the musical endeavors of Germany and the United States. On January 6, 1933, Hanson was guest conductor of the Berlin Philharmonic in a program of American music, and he subsequently conducted in Leipzig before returning to Rochester in early February.

While Hanson was advancing the cause of music education and championing American music, the students pursued their studies at the school. The severity of the economic downturn undoubtedly diminished opportunities for leisurely pursuits, but there were still ample concerts and recitals to satisfy the desire for live music. Central among them were the ten Rochester Philharmonic Orchestra concerts scheduled during the 1932–33 school year. The orchestra had lost its first conductor at the end of the 1930–31 season when Eugene Goossens left to become conductor of the Cincinnati Symphony Orchestra. For the next five seasons the Rochester players performed without a permanent conductor and enjoyed a wide range of guest conductors. The opening two concerts of the 1932–33 season were conducted by Arturo Bodanzky (1877–1939), the Austrian maestro who had succeeded Arturo Toscanini at the Metropolitan Opera in 1915. He was known as much for his fiery temperament as for his conducting of Wagner. Bodanzky chose an all-Wagner program for his first appearance with the Rochester Philharmonic Orchestra, while the featured work on his second program was the Beethoven Seventh Symphony.

Fritz Reiner (1888–1963), who had just stepped down from the conductor's post in Cincinnati, conducted three times during the season. Reiner served as an adviser to the Rochester Philharmonic over the next several years. His program on January 19, 1933, included the first Rochester performance of Ravel's Concerto for Piano and Orchestra in G Major, with Sandor Vas as piano soloist. The piece had premiered only a year earlier in Paris with the composer as conductor and Marguerite Long (1874–1966), to whom the work was dedicated, as soloist. Eugene Goossens, who had replaced Reiner in Cincinnati, returned twice during the season as a guest conductor, sharing the podium on his second visit with Howard Hanson who had just returned from Germany. Guy Fraser Harrison (1894–1986), the talented conductor of the Rochester Civic Orchestra, conducted one of the orchestra's concerts, as did Sir Hamilton Harty (1879–1941), who was in his final year as conductor of the Hallé Orchestra. Harrison's program included a performance of the Tchaikovsky Violin Concerto with Alexander Leventon as soloist. Included on Harty's program was the Brahms Concerto in D Minor, featuring Eastman School faculty member Max Landow at the piano. The last of the guest conductors for the 1932–33 season was Walter Damrosch (1862–1950), the man who had persuaded Andrew Carnegie to build Carnegie Hall and the brother of Frank Damrosch (1859–1937), the founder and longtime director of the Institute of Musical Art in New York City.

The Civic Music Association, the managing organization and legal entity for the Rochester Philharmonic, also presented a series of ten major artist recitals in the Eastman Theatre. These artist recitals had been a major part of musical life in Rochester since 1922 when the theater first opened its doors, and the 1932–33 lineup was impressive indeed. The first recital of the season, on October 28, 1932, was by the famous young American baritone Lawrence Tibbett (1896–1960). His appearance was followed two weeks later by a recital featuring the Spanish lyric soprano Lucrezia Bori (1887–1960), who would soon retire from opera performance after a long and distinguished career. Fritz Kreisler (1875–1962), often billed as "the world's greatest violinist," performed on November 18, 1932, prior to the school's Thanksgiving recess. Kreisler was justifiably regarded as one of the most popular artists of the time and had performed to enthusiastic audiences in the Eastman Theatre on two previous occasions. He would return for five more Eastman Theatre recitals. The fourth recital of the season was provided on December 16 by the sensational American soprano Lili Pons (1898–1976). Trained in Paris, she had made her Metropolitan Opera debut in 1931. Highly popular with audiences throughout the country, Pons returned to Rochester for recitals in 1943 and 1944.

The new year began with an appearance in the Eastman Theatre by the Hall Johnson Negro Choir on January 6, 1933. Hall Johnson (1888–1970) was an early advocate for African American spirituals and had formed his choir in 1925. It enjoyed outstanding success for many years. Vladimir Horowitz (1903–89), the electrifying Russian-born pianist, appeared in a recital on January 13, 1933, followed a week later by the famous Irish tenor John McCormack (1884–1945). Horowitz's program was very interesting, illustrating the wide range of repertoire he performed throughout his career. His recital included music of Bach (as arranged by Busoni), Schumann, Ravel, Debussy, Poulenc, and Saint-Saëns (the latter represented by his *Danse Macabre* as arranged by Liszt), but it also included a performance of Beethoven's Sonata in A Major, Op. 101. About the only Beethoven Horowitz consistently programmed throughout his career was the C Minor Variations, but at this particular time he was playing both the Op. 101 and Op. 81A sonatas. His recital in Rochester, therefore, was a somewhat rare occasion to hear late Beethoven played by this extraordinary Russian virtuoso.

On February 10, 1933, Yehudi Menuhin (1916–99) presented an Eastman Theatre recital. Menuhin was still promoted as a "boy violinist," but his days as a child prodigy were coming to an end. He would soon withdraw from public performing to spend considerable time in further study before reemerging as an important adult concert artist. A week after Menuhin's concert, Mary Wigman (1886–1973) and her dancers made an appearance in the Eastman Theatre. Wigman, a major pioneer in German modern dance, was a noted dancer, choreographer, and teacher. Her appearance on the artist series reflected widespread interest in modern dance among Rochester audiences. The tenth and final program of the 1932–33 artist series was a recital by Sergei Rachmaninoff (1873–1943), a familiar figure to Rochester audiences and an artist who was probably at the peak of his performing abilities at the time. He returned to Rochester on five more occasions for Eastman Theatre recitals.

For those on a limited budget who might have found the Eastman Theatre concerts a little expensive, the Eastman School of Music also offered a smaller series of eight concerts in Kilbourn Hall. Two of these were chamber music performances, the first by the school's own Kilbourn Quartet on January 3, 1933, and the second by the famed Budapest String Quartet on March 13, 1933. The program presented by the Budapest String Quartet included Beethoven's String Quartet in F Major, Op. 135; Schubert's Quartett-Satz in C Minor; Hugo Wolf's *Italian Serenade in G Major;* and Smetana's Quartet in E Minor, Op. 116. A completely different kind of presentation was a dance recital by Anga Enters (1907–??), a versatile dancer popular at the time who was also an accomplished painter, writer, and mime. She appeared in Kilbourn Hall on October 24, 1932, the opening event of the Kilbourn series, followed one week later by a recital by the African American baritone Edward Matthews (1905–54). Several years later, Matthews sang the role of Jake in the original production of Gershwin's *Porgy and Bess* and subsequently enjoyed a fine career until his untimely death in 1954.

A somewhat more unusual concert was provided by the Aguilar Lute Quartet on December 6, 1932. The lute players were three brothers—Eziquiel, Pepe, and Paco—with their sister Elisa, all from Madrid. They had previously performed in Kilbourn Hall in 1929. Another concert with special appeal to those interested in early music was presented on January 23, 1933, by the Society of Ancient Instruments. The leader of this pioneering early music ensemble was Henri Casadesus (1879–1947), an uncle of the noted French pianist Robert Casadesus (1899–1972), and the group included several members of the Casadesus family. The program performed by the

Society of Ancient Instruments consisted of music by Jean-Joseph Mouret (1682–1788), François Francoeur (1698–1787), Edmund Ayrton (1734–1808), Domenico Cimarosa (1749–1801), and Jean-François Le Sueur (1763–1837).

A more traditional evening was a joint recital by two Eastman faculty members, pianist Raymond Wilson and baritone Nicholas Konraty, on February 20, 1933. Konraty, however, was accompanied that evening by Emanuel Balaban, not by Wilson. But the highlight of the Kilbourn series may have been a recital by English pianist Myra Hess (1890–1965) on January 31, 1933. Hess, now regarded as one of the greatest pianists of the twentieth century, had yet to achieve the kind of reputation that would have justified an invitation to perform in the Eastman Theatre, although that invitation would come in 1939. Those in attendance at her 1933 recital were surely not disappointed by her performance that evening. Her program consisted of Mozart's Fantasy and Fugue in C Major, K. 394; Beethoven's Sonata in A-flat Major, Op. 110; Brahms's *Klavierstücke,* Op. 119; and the Chopin Preludes, Op. 28.

The enriching schedule of concerts and recitals added much to everyday life at the Eastman School of Music during this, its twelfth year of existence. It was still a very young institution, but it could boast of an energetic and dynamic director, exemplary facilities, a faculty growing in stature and reputation, and—perhaps most important because of economic realities of the time—the financial resources that could sustain its development. Increasing numbers of talented students would turn their attention to the school when deciding upon the course of their education, and the dream of establishing in Rochester a school of music that would have far-reaching influence and a reputation for excellence was fast becoming reality.

Chapter 3

1933–41

The Pre-War Years

The new school year opened in September 1933 with forty-two fewer students than the previous year enrolled in undergraduate and graduate programs. In spite of efforts to assist students with scholarships and loans, the effects of the Great Depression were being felt at the Eastman School of Music. The U.S. unemployment rate reached about 25 percent in 1933. Half of all households were affected either by unemployment or reduced wages and/or hours of work. The harsh economic realities American families were facing in the mid-1930s led to inevitable enrollment declines in colleges and universities throughout the country, and the Eastman School was no exception.

The downward trend at Eastman continued the following year when forty-three fewer students enrolled for collegiate study. These figures meant a loss in enrollment of about 9 percent in September 1933 and an additional 10 percent in September 1934. Although enrollment started to recover beginning in September 1935, operating income from tuition and fees continued to decline through the 1935–36 academic year while operating expenses rose on a yearly basis. Therefore, it was necessary to draw larger and larger amounts from the endowment, reaching about $393,000 for the 1936–37 fiscal year. Tuition and fees provided only about 40 percent of necessary operating income that year. Although the school had been given a generous endowment by its founder, there were limits as to how much could be utilized to meet expenses on an annual basis without jeopardizing the institution's future financial security.

Howard Hanson addressed new and returning students at the annual opening convocation in September 1933, ending his remarks with these comments:

> I cannot close my talk to you without saying that it is my earnest prayer that your study at the Eastman School will develop not

only your musical talents but that indescribable thing that we call your character. If at the end of your student life here you come out able musicians but small men and women I shall not be happy. For life is all-encompassing, and music is but part of life. If you develop qualities of meanness, pettiness, jealousy, envy, conceit, selfishness, I shall consider your education a failure regardless of your musical accomplishments. If, on the other hand, you develop a philosophy of living which includes the divine qualities of love, sympathy, self-sacrifice, humility, and unselfishness, I shall consider that you have wrought well and that the Lord has crowned our labors with success.[1]

These kinds of thoughts, including the reference to the Almighty, were very typical of Hanson throughout his forty years as the school's leader.

Among the new freshmen listening to Howard Hanson in Kilbourn Hall that day was a young percussion student from Cleveland named Frederick Fennell. He would make important contributions to the school as a student and have an even more influential role in later years as a member of the faculty. When Fennell entered Eastman in 1933, it had no band, and there was no particular interest in forming one. But the eighteen-year-old freshman had been brought up in the tradition of John Philip Sousa (1854–1932) and other great bands of the era, and he felt that band music was one of the most eloquent forms of music making. While growing up in Cleveland, Fennell had the good fortune of attending John Adams High School, which had an exceptional school music program. In 1931 he started attending the National Music Camp at Interlochen (then called the National High School Orchestra and Band Camp). The director of the high school band at Interlochen was Albert Austin Harding from the University of Illinois. He offered Fennell a scholarship to Illinois, but the young percussionist had set his sights on attending the Eastman School of Music.

Nineteen years later, Fennell would conduct the first rehearsal of the newly established Eastman Wind Ensemble, an event that transformed the performance of wind music throughout the country. That brilliant achievement was in the future, but the young man from Cleveland was not going to wait to show initiative in promoting band music. Therefore, he marched out to the university's River Campus to ask the director of athletics if he could audition for the position of drum major in the marching band.

[1]   Howard Hanson, "Convocation Address," *Alumni Bulletin of the Eastman School of Music* 5, no. 1 (November 1933): 1–2, 10–12.

Figure 8. Frederick Fennell, orchestral and wind ensemble conductor, 1940–62.

I told him that my purpose in coming was to try out for the drum majorship of the University of Rochester's marching band. For one of the few times I can remember, he paused before talking, but blandly informed me that the U. of R. had no marching band and as far as he knew [had] never had one. The words were out of my mouth before I could stop them: "I can get one for you, Dr. Fauver." For another of the few times I can remember, he smiled—but it was a smile of incredulity!—accompanied by a single retort—"How?"[2]

Fauver need not have worried. Fennell quickly organized a group to form the first University of Rochester marching band, with the personnel drawn from Eastman students who were his friends from summers at Interlochen, others who were friends from Cleveland, and still more who were ineligible to play in the orchestra at Eastman and were looking for an opportunity to perform in some sort of ensemble. One of Fennell's biggest supporters was trombonist Gordon Pulis (BM '35), Emory Remington's star student, whom Fennell described as "a very-big-man-on-campus."[3] With the help of Pulis and others, Fennell was able to recruit fifty-six players for the first meeting of the marching band, an ensemble he conducted through November 1943.

Attending the National High School Orchestra and Band Camp in Interlochen, Michigan, had greatly influenced Fennell's decisions concerning his future in music, an experience shared by countless other young people throughout the years since the camp was founded. The idea for such a summer program came from Joseph E. Maddy (1891–1966), one of the first public school instrumental music teachers in the United States. Maddy wrote the first instrumental music method book, as well as many arrangements for youth orchestras and bands. He eventually became professor of music at the University of Michigan in Ann Arbor and in that capacity exerted much influence on the course of elementary and secondary music education in the United States. But he will always be best remembered for founding the camp in Interlochen, an institution for which he served for many years as president and music director.

The National High School Orchestra and Band Camp opened its doors for the first time in June 1928. Among the people associated with Maddy's great experiment was Howard Hanson, who became a regular visitor to Interlochen each summer. It was the

[2] Frederick Fennell, *The Wind Ensemble* (Arkadelphia, AK: Delta Publications, 1988), 8–9.
[3] Ibid., 9.

beginning of a long association between the Eastman School of Music and Interlochen, an association that would involve a number of important Eastman faculty members as camp teachers during the summer months. Each freshman class at the school would include a number of young musicians, like Frederick Fennell, who had been "campers" at Interlochen. Hanson was deeply committed to the summer goals of Interlochen and enjoyed a warm friendship with "Joe" Maddy, for whom he had great admiration: "Dr. Maddy was a dreamer, a visionary, but at the same time a man of volcanic energy and—in the best sense—a 'salesman of ideas' the likes of whom I have never met. His ideas came so fast that it was almost impossible for his speech to keep up with them."[4]

It was at Interlochen that Hanson wrote part of his Symphony No. 2 ("Romantic"), first conducting it at the camp in the summer of 1931. This was only a year after the work had received its official premiere in Boston, with Serge Koussevitzky (1874–1951) conducting the Boston Symphony Orchestra. The symphony's connection with Interlochen was assured when Hanson presented the theme of the work to the camp for use as a theme and broadcast signature.

Hanson's "Romantic Symphony" was perhaps his best-known work, and part of its widespread recognition can be traced to the countless number of "campers" who came to know that theme. It is interesting that several years before Hanson's death in 1981, this symphonic composition suddenly received a wide audience of new listeners because of a Hollywood film—the science-fiction thriller *Alien*, produced by 20th Century Fox and directed by Ridley Scott. The score for the movie was written by Jerry Goldsmith, but the studio was dissatisfied with the music he had provided for the finale and end credits. Therefore, the studio substituted music from the slow movement of Hanson's symphony to conclude the movie, a decision that caused a surge of interest in the work as well as high demand for Hanson's own recording of the symphony on the Mercury label.

Fifty years earlier, Howard Hanson did not need a science-fiction movie to elicit interest in his compositions. He was considered one of America's most important young composers, even though he wrote in a clearly romantic style. He was frequently in demand as a guest conductor, and his works were widely performed. The conductor of the Boston Symphony, Serge Koussevitzky, was among those who admired Hanson's works, and even the great Italian maestro, Arturo Toscanini (1867–1957), conducted the "Romantic

---

4   Hanson, Autobiography, 149.

Symphony" when he led the New York Philharmonic in a Carnegie Hall concert on May 1, 1933. Hanson was invited to attend the final rehearsal before the concert and later wrote about his encounter with the fiery Italian maestro:

> After the rehearsal maestro Toscanini beckoned me to the conductor's stand and asked me what I would like to change. I replied that I had no suggestions, that I was delighted with the performance. His reply was, "Non mi faccia complimenti" (Don't make compliments), and [he] demanded that I tell him what changes I wanted.
>
> When I replied again that I had no suggestions to offer, he looked at me with disapproval. Suddenly he said, "Young man, three bars after letter A, in the first movement, you conduct it too fast." I replied, "Maestro, how do you know how I conduct it?" Came the reply, "Last year you conducted this symphony in Berlin with the Berlin Philharmonic. It was broadcast, and I was sitting before the radio in Milan with the score. Three bars after letter A you conduct it too fast. Remember, young man, always conduct the composition the way the composer wrote it!" It took me several minutes to remember that I was the composer![5]

The concert performance was well received by an enthusiastic audience. Olin Downes, the noted music critic for *The New York Times*, raised some questions about the work, but he also commented favorably on "the straightforwardness of this music and its perfectly obvious and unconcealed sentimentalism," adding that "the symphony deserves the welcome it received whatever its ultimate value may be."[6]

An even larger accomplishment awaited Howard Hanson the following year when the Metropolitan Opera Company gave the first performance of his new opera *Merry Mount* on February 10, 1934. The libretto by Richard Stokes took as a point of departure Nathaniel Hawthorne's tale, *The Maypole of Merry Mount*. The lead role of Pastor Wrestling Bradford was sung by Lawrence Tibbett (1896–1960), and the nationally broadcast performance was conducted by Tullio Serafin (1878–1968). Serafin, who had been principal conductor at La Scala in Milan immediately preceding the outbreak of World War I, conducted premieres of several new American works while at the Metropolitan Opera during the years 1924–34. Tibbett

---

[5] Ibid., 179.
[6] Olin Downes, "Toscanini Gets a Warm Welcome," *The New York Times,* March 2, 1933: 21. Copyright © 1933 by The New York Times Co. Reprinted with permission.

had made his debut at the Metropolitan Opera in 1923 and was featured in leading roles for the next twenty-seven seasons.

Joining Howard Hanson in his box at the Met were Rush Rhees
and his wife, Harriet Seeyle Rhees, plus Arthur See, Nicholas
Konraty, and Emanuel Balaban. The performance was a triumph
for Hanson, obviously also attracting attention to the Eastman
School of Music. Olin Downes reported that the opera "had the
most enthusiastic reception given any native music drama that
has been produced in New York in ten years—and probably in a
much longer period."[7] Lawrence Gilman of *The New York Herald Tribune* pronounced the work "impressive in its security and ease of
workmanship, its resourcefulness, and maturity of technique" but
added that it was "unequal in musical value."[8] Winthrop P. Tryon,
writing in the *The Christian Science Monitor,* commented that Hanson's scoring for the brass instruments "is sheer nineteenth century
romanticism, though something different from Schumannesque,
Wagnerian, or Straussian sort."[9]

The Metropolitan Opera premiere was a stunning success for
Hanson. Any critical comment made at the time was buried in
an avalanche of audience enthusiasm. The performance resulted
in fifty curtain calls, still a house record. The Metropolitan Opera
Company did a full production of *Merry Mount* in the Eastman
Theatre on April 12, 1934. This was the eleventh consecutive year
the opera company had appeared in Rochester, surely a highlight
each year for local music lovers.

Rochester could boast of a particularly rich concert life at the
time, which included chamber music and solo recitals by major
artists, as well as symphonic programs by the Rochester Philharmonic Orchestra. The philharmonic was still without a permanent
conductor, and it depended upon a number of well-chosen guest
conductors until 1936, when José Iturbi (1895–1980) became the
orchestra's second permanent conductor. The Spanish-born Iturbi
was best known at the time as a concert pianist with a special flair
for the music of his native country, but he became an effective and
respected orchestral conductor during his years in Rochester. Among
the soloists he engaged were pianist Josef Hofmann (1876–1957),

[7]   Olin Downes, "Merry Mount Gets a Stirring Ovation," *The New York Times,* February 11, 1934: N1. Copyright © The New York Times Co. Reprinted with permission.
[8]   Lawrence Gilman, "Merry Mount World Premiere Is Acclaimed at Metropolitan," *The New York Herald Tribune,* February 11, 1934. SML (news clipping).
[9]   Winthrop P. Tryon, "Hanson's Merry Mount," *The Christian Science Monitor* (Boston), February 17, 1934: 6. Quotation used courtesy of The Christian Science Monitor (www.csmonitor.com).

harpist Carlos Salzedo (1885–1961), the Rumanian composer and violinist Georges Enesco (1881–1955), the noted German pianist Walter Gieseking (1895–1956), and violinist Mischa Elman (1891–1967).

Meanwhile, the Artist Series in the Eastman Theatre was presenting many of the world's most famous artists during this period. The Boston Symphony Orchestra, which had previously performed in the Eastman Theatre in 1922, 1927, and 1928, played eighteen more concerts in Rochester between the years 1935 and 1961. The famous Ballet Russe of Monte Carlo appeared in the Eastman Theatre on January 12, 1934, and returned to Rochester five more times during the next seven years. Pianists who presented Eastman Theatre recitals included Sergei Rachmaninoff (1873–1943), Josef Hofmann, and Artur Schnabel (1882–1951). Violinists included Fritz Kreisler (1875–1962), Georges Enesco (1881–1955), and Jascha Heifetz (1901–87), while the singers who performed Eastman Theatre recitals included soprano Lotte Lehmann (1888–1976), contralto Marian Anderson (1897–1993),[10] and soprano Kirsten Flagstad (1895–1962). Complementing the Eastman Theatre concerts was a series of programs presented by the school in Kilbourn Hall. Although these events often featured members of the Eastman School of Music faculty, they also included a number of important visiting ensembles such as the Budapest String Quartet, the Gordon String Quartet, the Roth Quartet, the Stradivarius Quartet, and the Salzedo Trio.

During this period, which featured such exciting and enriching opportunities to hear some of the world's greatest ensembles and solo artists, the quality of students graduating from the Eastman School consistently improved. Among the graduates in the Class of 1934, for example, were three composers—Wayne Barlow (1912–96), Kent Kennan (1913–2003), and Gail Kubik (1914–84)—who subsequently enjoyed considerable professional success. Barlow later joined the Eastman School faculty, becoming chair of the composition department in 1968 and dean of graduate studies in 1973. Kennan enjoyed a long career as a composer and teacher at the University of Texas at Austin, and Kubik's many accomplishments included winning the 1952 Pulitzer Prize for Music for his *Symphonie Concertante.* Among the other students receiving degrees at the 1934 ceremonies was Ruth Hannas, the first person to be awarded a PhD in music from Eastman. Hannas had earned her bachelor of arts degree from the University of California in 1914 and a master of arts degree from the same institution in 1928.

[10] Anderson listed her birth year as 1902, although official records clearly show that she was born in 1897.

The graduate program at Eastman was growing significantly and would continue to do so in the coming years. Hannas had been one of forty graduate students during the 1933–34 school year, and within five years the number of graduate students had more than doubled. Meanwhile, an important development in the undergraduate program arose from a suggestion Hanson made to his faculty at their final meeting of the 1934–35 school year. He suggested that some form of recognition in addition to the bachelor's degree be given to students graduating as performers. At this time a student majoring in an instrument, such as piano or violin, graduated either as a "performer" or a "teacher."[11] Those recommended to graduate in performance were exempted from some of the methods courses in the curriculum but were required to present a senior recital.

Hanson's suggestion for some official recognition of graduation in performance was approved by the faculty and also by the school's board of managers. This new form of recognition was known as the "performer's certificate." In later years it became something of a competitive honor, but its origins were simply to recognize those students graduating as "performers." Apparently no one thought of recognizing the "teachers" with a similar certificate, but Hanson did ask the faculty to consider the possibility of granting an "artist's diploma," which would represent work significantly beyond the requirements for graduation as a performer. The faculty responded enthusiastically, and the following year three students—violinists Millard Taylor and Joseph Fortuna and pianist Irene Gedney—applied for the new artist's diploma, eventually becoming the first graduates of the Eastman School thus honored.

While all these developments were transpiring, a number of important changes in the school's faculty were occurring. Leonardo DeLorenzo, the school's first flute teacher and principal flutist in the Rochester Philharmonic, retired at the end of the 1934–35 school year and was replaced in both positions by Joseph Mariano, who had completed his studies at Curtis two years earlier. Mariano, who enjoyed an immensely successful career at the school for the next thirty-nine years, had been born in Pittsburgh on March 17, 1911. He grew up with a special love for opera and initially learned to play the flute on an instrument given to him by his father, a worker for the Pittsburgh Railroad who had received it as payment for a job. After graduation from high school he entered Curtis, where he

[11] Students graduating as "teachers" should not be confused with those undergraduates who were majoring in public school music and preparing to teach in elementary and secondary schools.

Figure 9. Eastman School faculty members (from left to right) Joseph Mariano, Rufus Arey, and Vincent Pezzi.

studied for three years with William Kinkaid (1895–1967) and also with Marcel Tabuteau (1887–1966), who tried to convince Mariano to switch to oboe. After graduation he joined the National Symphony Orchestra as principal flute for the 1934–35 season, a position from which Hanson recruited him to the Eastman School.

Although Mariano later received several offers from major symphonies—including NBC, Chicago, and Philadelphia—he chose to remain in Rochester, playing in the Rochester Philharmonic Orchestra until 1968 and teaching at the school until 1974. Albert Tipton, one of his first students and later principal flute in Detroit and St. Louis, commented that Mariano's "sound sailed above the entire orchestra in all registers."[12] Another former student, James Walker, who played with the San Francisco Opera, described Mariano's sound in these words: "'The Mariano Sound' was legendary by the time I arrived at Eastman. But . . . it was more than just a warm, generous tone that held me. There was a completeness, a totality to

[12] Quoted in Leone Buyse, "Joseph Mariano: The Man, the Artist, the Teacher," *The Flutist Quarterly* 10, no. 4, Royal Oak, Michigan (Summer 1985): 6.

his playing that was enormously satisfying."[13] Even his colleagues stood in awe of his sound, including bassoonist David Van Hoesen, who commented that the sound was so beautiful that one would wonder, "How the heck did he do that?"[14]

Joining Mariano in the orchestra and at the school in 1937 was oboist Robert Sprenkle, who similarly enjoyed a long and distinguished career in Rochester. Sprenkle had come to the Eastman School to study with Arthur Foreman in the fall of 1932, after having decided against attending the Carnegie Institute of Technology as a scholarship student in engineering. He was not especially happy with Foreman as a teacher, however, and decided to transfer to Curtis. Howard Hanson was able to persuade him to remain at Eastman, and Foreman retired at the end of the 1935–36 school year. Foreman's replacement, who arrived in time for Sprenkle's senior year, was the young Robert Bloom, who selected Sprenkle to play second oboe in the Rochester Philharmonic. When Sprenkle asked his teacher why he had chosen him instead of another student, Bloom replied that Sprenkle had fewer bad habits than the other students.[15] After only one year at Eastman, Bloom was offered the solo oboe position with the NBC Symphony under Arturo Toscanini, an offer he could hardly refuse. Sprenkle, who had graduated with a bachelor's degree only a year earlier, presumably free of his former bad habits, succeeded Bloom at the Eastman School and in the Rochester Philharmonic.

Other new faculty members from this period included Pattee Evenson, Arthur Kraft, Allison MacKown, and Catherine Crozier. Evenson, a graduate of the University of Michigan and a former member of the Minneapolis Orchestra, started teaching trumpet at Eastman in 1935 following the departure of Frederick Remington. Kraft had begun his notable singing career in New York City, where he was tenor soloist for ten years at St. Bartholomew's Church, and he was also tenor soloist for seven consecutive seasons at the Bach Festival in Bethlehem, Pennsylvania. In 1931 he had accepted the presidency of the Columbia School of Music while continuing performing in and around the Chicago area. His long Eastman teaching career began in September 1936. MacKown came to Rochester after having been appointed first cellist of the Rochester Philharmonic and

---

13 Quoted in ibid., 11.
14 Quoted in Stuart Low, "Joseph Mariano, Flutist," [Rochester] *Democrat and Chronicle*, February 26, 2007: 4B.
15 Daniel Stolper, "Remembering Robert Sprenkle," *The Double Reed* 14, no. 1, Idaho Falls (1991): 15.

the Rochester Civic Orchestra following the resignation from both orchestras of Paul Kéfer, who wanted to devote himself entirely to teaching. MacKown joined the Eastman faculty in September 1937 when George Finkel, who had been teaching at the school since 1928, resigned to accept a position in Chicago. Finkel had occupied a role that was somewhat secondary to Kéfer's, but many observers regarded him as a superb cellist.

Catherine Crozier, who later became an internationally known concert organist and teacher, joined the faculty in 1938.[16] She had received her bachelor's degree and performer's certificate at Eastman in 1936, studying with Harold Gleason, and earned an artist's diploma in 1938 and a master's degree in 1941. Crozier's debut at the 1941 national convention of the American Guild of Organists marked the beginning of a highly successful and distinguished performing career. Her teaching career at Eastman was similarly marked with great success. She and Harold Gleason were later married, following his divorce from his first wife. Crozier co-edited several editions of the *Method of Organ Playing*, the highly popular and almost indispensable method book written by her husband and first published in 1937, and served as editor of the seventh and eighth editions following Gleason's death in 1980.

Retiring at the end of the 1937–38 academic year was Charles Miller, who had been director of music for twenty-one years in the Rochester city schools and a member of the public school music faculty at Eastman since 1924. Succeeding Miller in the Rochester City School District was Alfred Spouse, who also became head of the voice teaching class at Eastman. Joining Spouse the same year in teaching public school music at Eastman were Howard Hinga, assistant director of music in Rochester's elementary and junior high schools, and Marlow Smith, newly appointed as supervisor of music in Rochester's high schools. The Eastman School additionally placed Smith in charge of practice teaching in the high schools. These changes were the result of a reorganization of Eastman's department of public school music, which was now under the leadership of William Larson. Each phase of pedagogy in the school's curriculum was to be under the supervision of the corresponding department in the public school system.

---

[16] All official printed material concerning Crozier indicates that she joined the faculty in 1939. However, the minutes from the Eastman School of Music faculty meeting in September 1938 show that Howard Hanson introduced her at that time as a new member of the faculty.

Larson had originally come to Eastman in 1929 as the school psychologist, responsible for maintaining, administering, and preserving the "Seashore Tests" administered to all incoming Eastman students (as well as throughout the city's public schools) in an attempt to measure aspects of musical capacity such as pitch, rhythm, and tonal memory. These tests were given to entering Eastman students long after they had any practical application. Larson had earned a bachelor of fine arts degree from the University of Nebraska, a master of arts degree in music education from Columbia University, and a doctor of philosophy degree in the psychology of music from the University of Iowa.

At the time of the reorganization of the public school music department, Eastman's enrollment had climbed to a total of 507 collegiate students, a dramatic improvement compared with four years earlier when the total enrollment had been only 382. The economic hardships of the 1930s were definitely lessening, although the amount of income needed from endowment sources remained high in spite of improving enrollment. It was at this time of tight budgetary constraints that the Eastman School of Music faced the absolute necessity of providing new space for the Sibley Music Library.[17] The library traced its origins to an important collection donated to the University of Rochester in 1904 by Hiram W. Sibley, material he intended as a circulating music library for the people of Rochester. Sibley was a member of one of Rochester's most influential and affluent families, and his gift was housed on campus in the university's library building, which had been dedicated in 1876 as Sibley Hall. The largest donor of funds for the building had been Hiram Sibley, Hiram W. Sibley's father.

There had initially been no concrete plans for the music collection when the Eastman School of Music building was under construction, but it soon seemed logical that the collection should reside at the new music school rather than in the library building on the Prince Street campus. There was, however, hesitation in approaching Mr. Sibley and Mr. Eastman concerning the prospect that the former's library reside in the latter's school. A carefully arranged meeting between the two philanthropists secured agreement that the music collection should indeed be moved from its present location to an appropriate space in the school building. Since the original architectural plans had made no provision for a library, the space originally intended as the director's office and studio on the

---

[17]   The collection was known at the time as the Sibley Musical Library.

east side of the main floor was hastily redesigned to accommodate the music collection. The resulting amount of available space was deemed sufficient at the time for about 40,000 volumes, perhaps an overly optimistic assessment.

By the mid-1930s it was generally recognized that the library was in need of additional space. Alan Valentine, who had succeeded Rush Rhees as president of the University of Rochester, conveyed the urgency of the matter to the university's board of trustees in June 1936:

> The very success of the Eastman School of Music raises new problems. One of them is largely of a physical nature. The Sibley Musical Library, which serves both the University and the community, has so increased in size and general use that the present arrangements for its accommodations are clearly inadequate. Your Committee on Building and Grounds, in collaboration with administrative officers, has given much thought during the past year to alterations or additions to the physical plant which would house the Sibley Musical Library in a manner appropriate to its importance and usefulness. No solution has yet been reached, but the committee is well aware that the problem is a pressing one, and hopes with the coming year to present definite proposals.[18]

An announcement was made the following March that a new building for the music collection would be constructed and available for use by September 1937. Its cost would be about $125,000, an amount that would provide a simple structure designed for convenience and efficiency. This cost would be met during those difficult economic times by setting aside funds on an annual basis for a number of years.

Construction of the building, however, was delayed as a result of the difficulty of obtaining steel because of labor troubles in the steel industry. Thus, the new building was not dedicated until February 10, 1938, five months later than originally anticipated. The dedicatory ceremonies were followed by an all-university convocation in the Eastman Theatre the same day. Speakers at the convocation included President Alan Valentine and Edward Minor, chair of the university's board of trustees. Also speaking at the convocation was Harper Sibley, son of Hiram W. Sibley (the original donor) who had

---

[18] Alan Valentine, *Annual Reports of the President and Treasurer to the Board of Trustees of the University of Rochester,* Rochester, NY (August 1936): 9–10.

Figure 10. Sibley Music Library reading room.

died in 1932. The library's former quarters in the school's main building were converted for use as faculty and student lounges, with their decoration supervised by Alan Valentine's wife.

The new Sibley Music Library building was a two-story structure on the east side of Swan Street, located between Annex I and Annex II. It was thought to be the first building ever constructed to house a music library. The main reading room on the ground floor was designed to seat about eighty people and had shelves for dictionaries, encyclopedias, and general reference books in addition to current issues of fifty music periodicals. Also located on the ground floor were the circulation desk, offices, and catalog room. Thirty cubicles on two levels and book stacks occupied the rear of the first floor. Located on the second floor of the new building were three large seminar rooms, two phonograph listening rooms, two piano rooms, and what was known as the "treasure room." The latter provided space for rare volumes and manuscripts, of which the library possessed an increasing number. At the rear of the second floor were two additional levels of stacks. The total capacity of all four levels of stacks was 100,000 volumes, more than adequate for the 35,000 volumes in the current collection and also, it was hoped, for future acquisitions for many years to come.

At about this time, the Eastman School community began to share the nation's apprehension concerning the deepening crisis in Europe. The German occupation of Austria occurred only a month after the dedication of the new Sibley Music Library, and the annexation of Sudetenland was accomplished just as the new 1938–39 school year was beginning. While the faculty and students may have wished that English prime minister Neville Chamberlain was correct in promising "peace for our time," there was a troubled mood and much apprehension as everyone feared the worst— namely, war in Europe. Those fears were realized in September 1939 with the German invasion of Poland and the outbreak of hostilities that marked the beginning of World War II. Yet there was hope that, even though war had come, perhaps the United States would avoid becoming a combatant.

It was at this troubling time that Howard Hanson announced an important new master's degree curriculum with a major in music literature. The new program was specifically designed to provide a graduate degree for people who had been performance majors on the undergraduate level. To underscore that point, Hanson announced to the faculty that only students previously recommended by the faculty as candidates for the performer's certificate could be admitted to candidacy for the master of music degree in music literature. The initial curriculum for this new graduate degree included eight credits in musicology, four credits in analytical technique, ten in applied music, and eight for a thesis. The required thesis was to be directly related to the student's field of performance and had to be accompanied by recordings and illustrative material. In addition, the candidate needed to pass an oral examination on the subject matter of the thesis. The first students to register for the degree began their studies in the fall of 1940.

The fall of 1940 also witnessed the appointment to the faculty of a young man who was already a very familiar figure at the Eastman School of Music. Frederick Fennell, who had entered the school as a percussion major in the fall of 1933, was now a member of the school's faculty. This energetic and talented musician, who had organized the marching band at the University of Rochester, had also organized and conducted the University of Rochester Symphony Band in January 1935, during his sophomore year at Eastman. Howard Hanson had attended the band's opening concert at the River Campus on January 18 and asked Fennell to repeat the concert in Kilbourn Hall. He also suggested that the group be renamed the Eastman Symphony Band the following year, a not unreasonable request given the number of Eastman students playing in the group. Furthermore, Hanson requested that the band have a rehearsal schedule that somehow fit both the fall football season at the University of Rochester and the winter concert season at the Eastman School of Music. Fennell happily complied, but the school paid him nothing for conducting the band. After all, he was merely a student at the time.

In the fall of 1937, following his graduation from Eastman, Fennell applied for the Salzburg International Prize in conducting and was awarded the prize in February 1938, only a month prior to Hitler's Anchluss of Austria. In spite of the threat of war in Europe, he went to Salzburg to study conducting at the Mozarteum. He described this experience in these words:

> Salzburg was a big thing in my life and pivotal in my career, not only for the travel exposure, a meeting at Strauss' house in Garmisch, daily rehearsals at the Festspielhaus, terrific classes at the Mozarteum, and the chance to be put alongside ten other young men from other countries and to draw the honor slot of closing the class *Schlusskonzert* with Dvorak IX and an invite to become conductor of the Mozart Orchestra of Salzburg—messed up by the Hitler, Daladier, Mussolini, Chamberlain thing at Berchtesgaden, just a few kilometers down the road on the red interurban car, when the State Department ordered me out fearing no peace settlement. But of greater importance at home in Rochester was the simple four-part action which took me up two gangplanks and down two others. *NOW* I could conduct an orchestra; I'd been *TO EUROPE!*[19]

Fennell returned to Rochester to complete his master's degree in 1939. A week after his return, the brothers of Phi Mu Alpha Sinfonia invited him to become conductor of their Little Symphony, the first orchestral conducting position Fennell had held. The following year he became a member of the Eastman faculty. The brilliant initiative known as the Eastman Wind Ensemble occurred more than ten years later, but Fennell was already an important influence at the school. His commanding and energetic presence on the podium, in spite of his somewhat diminutive five-foot one-inch stature, would lead to a mutually beneficial and fruitful relationship with his alma mater over the next twenty-two years.

---

[19]   Fennell, *The Wind Ensemble*, 13 (original emphasis).

Chapter 4

1932–41

Broadcasts, Festivals, and Recordings (I)

Among the more interesting developments during the Eastman School of Music's opening year in 1921–22 was the school's connection with the establishment of the Rochester radio station WHAM. An announcement was made on April 19, 1922, that the two leading local newspapers, the *Democrat and Chronicle* and the *Times-Union,* had agreed to establish and maintain broadcast equipment that would be located at the new music school. Space was provided at the southwest corner of the school's top floor, and a broadcasting tower was erected on the roof. The license to operate this new radio station was authorized on July 6, 1922, and five days later WHAM made its first broadcast—a short piano recital by Raymond Wilson, a member of the school's piano faculty. WHAM was among the earliest commercial radio stations, and the plan was for the station to broadcast recitals from the Eastman School of Music three times a day during the school year. There was a great demand for live music programs during the earliest days of the broadcast industry, and the school found itself in the enviable position of having the ability and necessary resources to contribute to this kind of programming.

In 1925 WHAM became a member of a larger New York State network, the other members of which were WGY in Schenectady (the anchor station), WJZ in New York City, WBFC in Syracuse, and WMAK in Lockport (near Buffalo). The first WHAM network broadcast was a concert from the Eastman School of Music by the Rochester Little Symphony conducted by Eugene Goossens on December 23, 1925. This concert reached an estimated audience of about 1 million people. A little more than a year after the network was formed, Stromberg-Carlson took over operation of WHAM and upgraded its equipment and operations to increase programming from a mere three hours to seven and a half hours per day.[1] The new management worked closely with the Eastman School of Music in the development of educational broadcasting, and it soon became the supplier of more symphonic programming than any other U.S. station outside of New York City and Chicago. This symphonic broadcasting, originating from the Eastman School, reached an ever-widening audience and was an extremely valuable tool in spreading and enhancing the young music school's reputation.

In September 1929 WHAM inaugurated a series of weekly concerts by the newly formed Rochester Civic Orchestra, becoming the first independent station in the country to produce a commercial program for distribution by the National Broadcasting Company. Sixteen months later the station began broadcasting a series of half-hour concerts on Wednesday afternoons at four o'clock that featured various Eastman School ensembles, including the Eastman School Orchestra, the Eastman School Chorus, and smaller chamber ensembles. Included among these concerts were two programs in March 1931 devoted to a complete performance of Beethoven's *Missa Solemnis.*

The 1932–33 school year began with an announcement that the Eastman School would sponsor thirty broadcasts over the National Broadcasting Company, a more comprehensive and ambitious endeavor than ever before. The first two of these broadcasts, on November 16 and November 23, were provided by students from the ensemble classes of Paul White. They were followed on November 30 with a performance of Howard Hanson's Symphony No. 1 ("Nordic") by the Eastman School Symphony Orchestra with the composer conducting. The Eastman School Little Symphony, conducted by Karl Van Hoesen, provided the next broadcast, which was followed by a program of orchestral music by Brahms, Haydn, and Rimsky-Korsakov performed by the Eastman School Symphony Orchestra under the direction of Samuel Belov, the orchestra's regular conductor.

Following several weeks of chamber music, the school's orchestra was featured on a January 11 broadcast devoted to a performance of the opening movement of the Tchaikovsky Piano Concerto in B-flat Minor. The soloist was Eastman School of Music senior Irene Gedney, who studied with Raymond Wilson. If Henrietta Schumann had been the outstanding talent of the 1920s, perhaps Gedney had a

---

[1] Stromberg-Carlson was an important maker of telecommunications equipment. Formed in 1894 by Alfred Stromberg and Androv Carlson, the firm was originally located in Chicago but was relocated to Rochester when it was purchased in 1904 by the Home Telephone Company.

similar reputation during the early 1930s. She was frequently in the spotlight during her years at the school, and in 1936 she was among the first students—and the first pianist—awarded the school's artist's diploma.

The Eastman School Symphony Orchestra was featured on seven additional radio broadcasts during the 1932–33 school year, including a performance of the Mozart Requiem on March 15, 1933, with Herman Genhart as conductor. Samuel Belov conducted the other performances, including an all-Wagner program broadcast on March 29, 1933. Other programming during the school year featured chamber music performances by students of Paul Kéfer and Sandor Vas, including a performance of the Schubert "Trout" Quintet. The thirty broadcasts of live music from the Eastman School provided a wonderful showcase for the student talent, and more than a handful of prospective students likely submitted applications to the school as a result of hearing some of the radio programs.

The WHAM broadcasts from Eastman had been shifted to Thursday afternoons, and this continued during the 1933–34 school year. Several of the radio programs presented performances by the Rochester Philharmonic Orchestra during its regular matinee concerts in the Eastman Theatre. Eastman School ensembles featured during 1933–34 included the Eastman School Symphony Orchestra on six occasions and the Kilbourn Hall Orchestra on three occasions, as well as various smaller ensembles and chamber groups. The broadcast on November 30, 1933, featured students from the quartet classes of Paul Kéfer playing Beethoven and Mozart. The first violinist for Mozart's Fugue in C Minor was the young John Celentano, who later joined the faculty and made an enormous contribution to the development of the art of chamber music during his many years at the school. There were two student soloists with the Eastman School Symphony Orchestra: Arlene Walton (BM '34) playing the Saint-Saëns Concerto No. 4 on February 1 and Thomas Marrocco (BM '34) playing the Chausson *Poem* on February 15.

The Rochester Philharmonic continued to be heard on a number of the broadcasts during the next several school years. Since the orchestra was without a permanent conductor, radio audiences were able to hear the group under the direction of a number of leaders. These included the conductor of the Rochester Civic Orchestra, Guy Fraser Harrison (1894–1986), plus Fritz Reiner (1888–1963), Sir Hamilton Harty (1879–1941), and José Iturbi (1895–1980) who subsequently became the orchestra's permanent conductor. During the same period, several students were featured as soloists with the school's orchestra, most notably Millard Taylor (BM '35) who performed the final two movements of the Beethoven Violin Concerto on December 6, 1934. This was Taylor's senior year at Eastman, and he would remain for an additional year to complete his artist's diploma and then return six years later to begin what would ultimately be a thirty-five-year career of distinguished teaching at the Eastman School. Among the other notable broadcasts was a performance on April 2, 1936, by the newly created University of Rochester Symphony Band conducted by Frederick Fennell, the first band music included in the WHAM series. Fennell led the group once again in a broadcast the following year on March 11, 1937, and again the year after with a performance broadcast on March 17, 1938. This time, however, the group was properly identified as the "Eastman School" Symphony Band.

In the fall of 1938 it was announced that Howard Hanson and Paul White would lead the Eastman School Symphony Orchestra in a series of Thursday evening broadcasts from 8:30 to 9:15 P.M. over the NBC blue network. There were sixteen dates for these evening presentations, and four were devoted to music by American composers. In addition to these more formal concert broadcasts, a series of Saturday morning programs over the NBC red network[2] from 11:30 A.M. to 12:00 noon would feature programs that illustrated the development of musical composition from the middle ages to the early nineteenth century. These performances were under Hanson's supervision and utilized the services of Harold Gleason, Paul White, Emanuel Balaban, Herman Genhart, and Frederick Fennell.

This innovative series of concert broadcasts was known as "Milestones in the History of Music." In its second year the series presented eighteen programs running from November 4, 1939, through March 16, 1940.

Program 1   Music at the Court of Frederick the Great
Program 2   Ballet in the 17th and 18th Centuries
Program 3   Modern Ballet
Program 4   Music at the Court of Louis XIV and Louis XV
Program 5   Music of the 15th Century
Program 6   Early Chamber Music
Program 7   Sacred Music of the 16th Century
Program 8   Music of George Frederic Handel

Program 9   The Concerto Grosso
Program 10   The Bach Family
Program 11   *Dido and Aeneas*—Henry Purcell
Program 12   Music One Hundred Years Before Bach
Program 13   Early Music in America
Program 14   The Overture
Program 15   Music of the Mass
Program 16   The Solo Concerto
Program 17   Modern Chamber Music
Program 18   Howard Hanson's *Lament for Beowulf*

The Milestones in the History of Music series, broadcast over the NBC red network, continued for another year. Hanson supervised the broadcasts, serving as musical director and commentator, while Harold Gleason was the series musicologist and Allen Irvine McHose the production manager. The school's full performing resources were involved in the broadcasts, including the orchestra, choir, and opera department, as well as the Little Symphony of Phi Mu Alpha and various vocal, string, and wind ensembles.

The Eastman School of Music's broadcast activities did a great deal to raise widespread awareness of the school and to enhance its reputation for excellence. But it was the commitment to the performance of music by American composers that gave the school its distinctive and important profile among music schools and conservatories throughout the country. That commitment was hardly surprising. When Rush Rhees and George Eastman began to look for a new director following the departure of Alf Klingenberg, they quickly decided that the institution would be best served if an American were selected to occupy the position. While this was not necessarily a total rejection or repudiation of the European conservatory model, the university president and his benefactor were obviously interested in charting a course for the school that was clearly different with respect to its identity and goals. Therefore, it is not surprising that from the earliest days of Howard Hanson's tenure as director, the school functioned not only within the context of a university setting—in itself a clear departure from the European model—but also as a distinctively American institution. Hanson had clearly identified this as a personal priority prior to his appointment when he told Rhees in a letter that the new Eastman director should have "tremendous sympathy for American music."[3]

---

[3]   Howard Hanson, memo to Rush Rhees, January 26, 1924. SML.

Howard Hanson was only in his fourth month as the school's director when he presented a plan calling for two concerts at the end of the spring semester that would consist entirely of works by American composers. Scores would be solicited from all over the country, from which the school's young director would select appropriate music for the programs. The proposal was eventually scaled back to one concert, which took place on May 1, 1925, with Hanson conducting the Rochester Philharmonic Orchestra in the Eastman Theatre. This was the first in a long series of American Composers' Concerts, and it featured music by Aaron Copland (1900–1990), Quincy Porter (1897–1966), Bernard Rogers (1893–1968), Mark Silver (1892–??), Donald Tweedy (1890–1948), and Adolph Weiss (1891–1971). Similar concerts were scheduled on an annual basis in subsequent years. In the spring of 1931 Hanson added a four-day festival in May featuring works by American composers, in commemoration of the school's tenth anniversary.

Response to the festival was enthusiastic, and a Festival of American Music continued as an annual event through 1971. During its long history, the Festival of American Music, in combination with the annual American Composers' Concerts, presented works by 497 American composers—a total of 1,470 different compositions. The importance of these concerts cannot be overemphasized, for Hanson provided a regular opportunity for the pubic performance of American music at a time when few others were willing to program the works of American composers. The list of composers whose works were performed on these concerts includes such prominent names as Samuel Barber (1910–81), Elliot Carter (b. 1908), Aaron Copland (1900–1980), Henry Cowell (1897–1965), Paul Creston (1906–85), Norman Dello Joio (1913–2008), David Diamond (1915–2005), Ross Lee Finney (1906–97), Charles Tomlinson Griffes (1884–1920), Roy Harris (1898–1979), Alan Hovhannes (1911–2000), Charles Ives (1874–1954), Otto Luening (1900–1996), Peter Mennin (1923–83), Vincent Persichetti (1915–87), Walter Piston (1894–1976), William Grant Still (1895–1978), and Randall Thompson (1899–1984).

The 1932–33 school year included American Composers' Concerts on December 9, 1932, and March 31, 1933, each featuring the Rochester Philharmonic Orchestra with Hanson conducting. Hanson included his Symphony No. 2 ("Romantic") on the latter program, commenting in the program notes that the work "represents my escape from the rather bitter type of modern musical realism which occupies so large a place in contemporary thought."[4] It is

---

[4] Howard Hanson, program notes for American Composers' Concert, March 31, 1933. SML.

interesting that even at age thirty-seven, Hanson could view his own works as a reaction to much contemporary music for which he had no sympathy whatsoever. The Festival of American Music took place on four days at the beginning of May. The opening concert was presented by the Eastman School Symphony Orchestra and Eastman School Chorus with music of Lawrence Powell (1899–1990), Charles Martin Loeffler (1861–1935), Horatio Parker (1863–1919), and John Alden Carpenter (1876–1951). The festival's second concert was presented by the Eastman School Little Symphony of Phi Mu Alpha under the direction of Karl Van Hoesen, and the program included a performance of Deems Taylor's *Portrait of a Lady* scored for strings, winds, and piano, with Irene Gedney as piano soloist. Howard Hanson and the Rochester Philharmonic were featured in the third program. The final event of the festival was a presentation of two ballets, *Princess and Puppet* by Burrill Phillips (1907–88) and *La Guiblesse* by William Grant Still.

Dancers for the ballets were students of Thelma Biracree, who maintained a ballet studio in Annex I, the five-story building on Swan Street that connected with the Eastman Theatre via a bridge. Biracree had been a member of the Eastman Theatre Ballet, founded in 1923 by Enid Knapp Botsford to provide ballet presentations for Eastman Theatre shows. She then associated herself with Martha Graham during the latter's brief time in Rochester, continuing to dance for the shows after Graham left. When the Eastman Theatre movie operation came to an end, Biracree (among many others) found herself essentially unemployed, but she was able to negotiate an opportunity to maintain her studio for teaching in the theater annex. Although not officially affiliated with the Eastman School of Music, Biracree supplied dancers for various school performances in return for the teaching space she was using. The presence of what amounted to a resident ballet corps at Eastman facilitated the inclusion of ballet productions during the yearly festivals, and a program involving Biracree and her students was typically the closing performance each year.

The combination of two American Composers' Concerts during the school year followed by a Festival of American Music near the end of the second semester continued for the next two years. An especially interesting concert took place on December 15, 1933, with the program devoted to music by composers who had been awarded the Guggenheim Fellowship—Quincy Porter, Randall Thompson, George Antheil (1900–1959), Robert Russell Bennett (1894–1981), and Robert Delaney (1902–56). Notable among the events at the Festival of American Music the following spring was a solo recital of American piano music offered by Irene Gedney on April 30, 1934. Gedney had been a featured soloist the previous year, and she would again be selected to perform two years later when she was the soloist in the first Rochester performance of the *Divertimento for Piano and Orchestra* by David Diamond on April 27, 1936, and in the *Concerto Grosso for String Orchestra and Piano* by Albert Stoessel (1894–1943) on April 30, 1936. Gedney had been seriously injured in an automobile accident in June the preceding year, sustaining injuries that forced her to remain in bed until December and then to use crutches until February 1936. Yet she was still able to perform the two works during the festival in April. Gedney returned one more time as a performer at a Festival of American Music when she presented a symposium of American piano music on April 28, 1937.[5]

A significant change was made during the 1936–37 school year when two of the American Composers' Concerts were replaced by symposia, one in the fall semester and one in the spring. The four-day fall symposium was devoted to reading works by composers from throughout the United States, while the four-day spring symposium was devoted to reading works by students, faculty, and graduates of the Eastman School. Both symposia involved the Rochester Civic Orchestra with Hanson conducting. Although these were essentially reading sessions rather than performances, the Rochester Civic Orchestra became very proficient at presenting the new works, much to the benefit of the young composers—especially students—who might not otherwise have had an opportunity to hear their work performed. Throughout the years, the symposia of student compositions were an important part of supporting the study of the school's composition students.

The annual American Music festivals in late April were fairly consistently focused on large orchestral scores, performed by the Eastman School Symphony Orchestra, the Rochester Philharmonic Orchestra, the Rochester Civic Orchestra, and the Eastman School Little Symphony of Phi Mu Alpha. Another ensemble made its festival debut on April 26, 1937, when Frederick Fennell led the University of Rochester Symphony Band in a program of American music. Fennell and his players returned the following year, this time identified as the Eastman School Symphony Band. During the same period, choral music was not neglected. The Eastman School Chorus participated in almost all the festivals, but the music was always large-scale choral works with orchestra. Among the more

---

[5] A little more than four months later, Gedney was once again seriously injured in an automobile accident.

unusual choral pieces performed on a festival concert was Hanson's arrangement for chorus and orchestra of Palestrina's *Missa Papae Marcelli*,[6] which was performed on April 27, 1937.

Various Eastman faculty members performed as soloists during American Composers' and Festival concerts. Sandor Vas was soloist for the Concertino for Piano and Orchestra by Edward Burlingame Hill (1872–1960) on May 4, 1933, and for Charles Martin Loeffler's *Pagan Poem* on November 1, 1934. Flutist Leonardo DeLorenzo was soloist on March 25, 1934, in a performance of Charles Tomlinson Griffes's *Poem for Flute and Orchestra*. DeLorenzo's successor at Eastman, Joseph Mariano, performed *Night Piece for Flute and Strings* by Arthur Foote (1853–1937) in an American Composers' Concert on February 24, 1938. The following year Cecile Genhart was the featured soloist in a festival concert on April 27, 1939, playing the Concertino for Piano and Orchestra by Walter Piston. Joseph Mariano appeared on the same program as soloist in Kent Kennan's *Night Soliloquy for Flute and Strings*. These are just a few examples of Eastman faculty members' participation in these concerts. Clearly, the full resources of the Eastman School of Music were utilized in trying to make each of these programs a success.

The selection of music for these concerts was, naturally, a decision that rested with Howard Hanson. Some people have suggested that he overlooked works of genuine merit and chose others of questionable merit because of his personal preferences and prejudices. Yet he included music of composers with whom he had less than cordial relations. The lack of friendly relations between Hanson and David Diamond is well-known, yet Hanson programmed seventeen different works by Diamond during the forty years of American Composers' Concerts and Festivals of American Music, including his Symphony No. 1, Symphony No. 2, Concerto for Chamber Orchestra, and Concerto for Cello and Orchestra.

Hanson also programmed the music of Aaron Copland, in spite of a misunderstanding dating back to the 1920s that had considerably cooled their relationship. In 1926 Copland had suggested in a speech that Hanson's music could not arouse enthusiasm among the "elite" but instead served a broader audience for new music. Hanson reacted angrily to the remark, replying that one cannot ever satisfy the elite New York establishment. His response was interpreted rather harshly, and the relationship between Hanson and Copland was anything but cordial from that time forward. Yet in spite of hurt

---

[6]   Palestrina's work is thought to date from the early 1560s and was first published in 1567.

feelings on both sides, Hanson continued to present performances of Copland's music at the American Composers' Concerts and the Festivals of American Music. Years later these two icons of American music were finally reconciled when the University of Rochester awarded an honorary doctorate to Copland in 1975, eleven years after Howard Hanson had retired. Although Hanson was unable to attend, he extended a personal gesture of friendship toward Copland, who responded in kind during the ceremonies in the Eastman Theatre acknowledging him as the "dean of American composers." His speech began with these gracious words:

> Ladies and gentlemen, I may be the Dean of American composers in other places, but not here at Eastman, where my friend and colleague Howard Hanson has established this most important school which has served American music perhaps better than any other institution of its kind. I gladly take second place to him.[7]

Serving American music better than any other institution of its kind is exactly what the Eastman School of Music was doing through the American Composers' Concerts and the subsequent festivals. It was therefore only natural that Hanson would seek an opportunity to record the works of American composers in an effort to bring American music to the larger audience recordings might reach. The pioneering effort in this regard arose following an agreement Hanson negotiated with RCA Victor, then one of the country's leading recording companies, to produce a series of 78 rpm recordings of American music. The first album was released on November 1, 1939, and it consisted of *Overture to Oedipus Tyrannus* by John Knowles Paine (1839–1906), *Night Soliloquy* by Kent Kennan (1913–2003), "Jubilee" from the *Symphonic Sketches Suite* by George W. Chadwick (1854–1931), the "Dirge" from the *Indian Suite* of Edward MacDowell (1860–1908), and *The White Peacock* by Charles Tomlinson Griffes.

It is obvious that, with the exception of the piece by Kennan, the remaining works were by American composers born in the mid-nineteenth century. A significant number of pieces on the regular annual concerts were similarly by the older generation. Hanson's intention with the recordings, as well as with the American Composers' Concerts and the annual Festivals of American Music, was to promote the cause of *American* music, not necessarily contemporary music. Quite naturally, however, the overwhelming majority

---

[7] Quote from Samuel Adler, http://www.newmusicbox.org/hymn/nov99/samueladler.html.

of the 1,470 works performed between 1925 and 1971 were by living composers, 551 of them receiving their first performance. That total does not include the hundreds (perhaps thousands) of student compositions that were heard for the first time in the Eastman Theatre or Kilbourn Hall. Yet none of this diminished Hanson's interest in performing and recording the works of the older generation of American composers.

Other repertoire Hanson recorded for RCA Victor included music of Wayne Barlow (1912–96), William Bergsma (1921–94), Robert Braine (1896–1940), George W. Chadwick, Aaron Copland, Charles Tomlinson Griffes, Homer Keller (1915–96), Charles Martin Loeffler,[8] Edward MacDowell, John Knowles Paine, Burrill Phillips, Bernard Rogers, Charles Skilton (1868–1941), Norman Spence, William Grant Still, Charles Vardell (1893–1962), and, of course, Howard Hanson himself.[9] Hanson chose four of his best-known works for these recordings—the early *Lament for Beowulf,* the Suite from the opera *Merry Mount,* Symphony No. 1 ("Nordic"), and Symphony No. 2 ("Romantic").

These recordings, combined with the school's extensive broadcast activities and the annual concerts and festivals featuring the works of American composers, did a great deal to enhance the Eastman School of Music's reputation throughout the country. It was an impressive set of accomplishments, all the more impressive since these important initiatives were taking place during depressed economic times in the United States, and it was because of Hanson's creative imagination and dedication that any of these events happened. In the ten years since the death of its founder and benefactor, the Eastman School of Music had developed into one of the foremost institutions of its kind in America. But new challenges were on the horizon as the 1941–42 school year opened in Rochester. Three months later America was at war.

---

[8] The composition by Loeffler that Hanson chose to record was the *Pagan Poem,* which he had performed with Sandor Vas as piano soloist several year earlier. Irene Gedney, however, was the pianist for the RCA Victor recording.

[9] A complete listing of the repertoire contained on the RCA Victor recordings can be found in Appendix 7.

Chapter 5

1941–52

The War Years and Beyond

The war in Europe had been raging for two years when students returned for the new school year in September 1941. Thoughts that America might still avoid becoming embroiled in the conflict were undoubtedly on everyone's mind. As usual, returning students were interested in changes that had occurred over the summer, especially the appointment of any new faculty members.

Of special interest that September was the appointment of cellist Luigi Silva. He was joining the faculty to replace Paul Kéfer, who had died of a heart attack the previous February. Silva came from a very musical family, his father having been a well-known teacher of voice and his mother a Viennese singer. After graduating from the music conservatory in Bologna (Conservatorio di Musica "G.B. Martini"), he became solo cellist in the opera orchestra in Rome, cellist in the Quartetto di Roma (Italy's leading chamber music group at the time), and a teacher at the conservatory in Florence (Conservatorio Statale di Musica "Luigi Cherubini"). Silva came to the United States in 1939 and settled in New York the following year. He now joined Allison MacKown, the principal cellist of the Rochester Philharmonic, in teaching cello at Eastman, but he also continued to teach students at the Mannes School of Music in New York. A rather small but dapper man, Silva was also an excellent pianist and could accompany his students at lessons. He had the added responsibility at Eastman of directing and supervising chamber music for the school's string students.

Another addition to the Eastman community in 1941 was the Gordon String Quartet, hired as guest instructors to present a symposium each semester on string quartet playing. The quartet had been founded by violinist Jacques Gordon, who had been born and trained in Odessa. Gordon had come to the United States when he was about seventeen to study with Franz Kneisel (1865–1926). In 1921 he became the concertmaster of the Chicago Symphony Orchestra. He organized his string quartet the same year, resigning from the Chicago position in 1930 so he could devote all his time and energy to chamber music. He had headed the violin department at the American Conservatory of Music in Chicago for nine years, then established the Gordon Musical Association at Falls Village, Connecticut, in 1930. In Falls Village Gordon founded "Music Mountain" as a permanent home for his quartet. While New England winter weather ended his dream of a year-round home for the quartet, Music Mountain became the base of operations for the group from April through October every year. The Gordon Quartet was widely regarded as one of the premiere chamber music groups in the United States, and countless numbers of students were attracted to Music Mountain for study each summer. Having the quartet available for symposia at the Eastman School of Music was exciting news for Eastman's string department.

The entry of the United States into the war in December 1941 following the Japanese attack on Pearl Harbor eventually affected many members of the Eastman School of Music student body. The first important war-related matter that needed to be addressed in the spring of 1942 was the status of seniors who had either volunteered or been drafted for military service prior to completion of their degree requirements. It was decided at a faculty meeting held on May 6, 1942, that four of these students[1] would be approved for graduation in June, even with some missing requirements.

Among the members of the graduating class that year were composers William Bergsma and John LaMontaine, who subsequently enjoyed particularly fine careers. Bergsma accepted a position at the Juilliard School in 1946, remaining there until 1963 when he went to the University of Washington as head of the music school. LaMontaine won the 1959 Pulitzer Prize for Music for his Piano Concerto No. 1, Op. 9 ("In Time of War"). Also receiving his degree was Lewis Van Haney. Four years later he and Gordon Pulis (BM '34) became the second and first trombonists, respectively, in the New York Philharmonic, evidence of the growing presence of former Emory Remington students in American symphony orchestras.

But such accomplishments lay in the future for many young men who now found their careers temporarily set aside by the war. Enrollment at Eastman in September 1942 showed no decline in numbers, but women comprised 80 percent of the total as opposed

---

[1]   Louis Van Haney, Ernest Harrison, Dan Hinger, and Ferdinand Pranzatelli.

to the more or less equal division of men and women that had been
the norm in recent years. The preponderance of women at the school
during the war years forced the Rochester Philharmonic to finally
admit eight women to the orchestra. Previously, only the harpists
had been female. During the summer, Howard Hanson had communicated with the male students concerning developing plans for
the Enlisted Reserve Corps:

> As you know, both the Army and the Navy are setting up a plan of
> enlistment in the Enlisted Reserve Corps. Acceptance . . . will auto-
> matically permit the student to remain in school until he has com-
> pleted his course. . . . In order to make it possible for our students in
> the Eastman School of Music to take advantage of this opportunity,
> we are setting up a course of study which meets the requirement of
> the Army and Navy.
>   The first year curriculum will substitute Mathematics 1–2 for
> the requirement in Historical Survey. English 1–2 remains a first
> year requirement. The second year will require a course in General
> Physics in place of the usual college elective. In the third year a
> course in the Principles of Radio is suggested as the academic elec-
> tive, with orchestration substituting for Counterpoint 101–102. In
> courses where a second academic elective is required in the junior
> year some course such as General and Educational Psychology is
> suggested. In the fourth year a three-hour course in Astronomy
> plus a two-hour course in Meteorology is suggested to take the
> place of the college elective, with Historical Survey substituting for
> the theory elective.[2]

At the beginning of the 1942–43 school year, Howard Hanson
appointed Jacques Gordon to the regular full-time faculty. He was
to replace Gustave Tinlot, the school's principal violin teacher since
1925, who had died unexpectedly on March 2, 1942, at age fifty-four.
Tinlot had resigned as concertmaster of the Rochester Philharmonic
in 1937, but he continued to teach at Eastman after his resignation
as well as continuing as first violinist of the Kilbourn Quartet. The
selection of Gordon to replace him was a significant decision by the
school's director. Tinlot's death created another problem, however,
with regard to the future of the Kilbourn Quartet. The quartet had
lost half its personnel, with the death of Kéfer in February 1941
and now Tinlot in March 1942. Faced with the prospect of having
to reconstitute the quartet by appointing a new first violinist and

---

[2] Howard Hanson, memo to Eastman School students, July 26, 1942. SML.

Figure 11. Jacques Gordon, teacher of violin and chamber music, 1942–48. (Photograph by Alexander Leventon.)

a new cellist, Hanson chose instead to name the Gordon String Quartet the resident quartet at the Eastman School of Music. Over the next several years, however, it was difficult to precisely define the quartet, since the group underwent numerous changes in personnel. The second violin position was held successively by William Nowinski, Samuel Weiss, Walter Hagen, Andor Toth, Michael Kuttner, and Urico Rossi, while the violists were Bernard Milofsky,

William Lincor, Morris Krackmalnik,[3] and David Dawson. Among the cellists were Luigi Silva and Gabor Rejto (who eventually replaced Silva on the faculty), as well as Fritz Magg, who was a quartet member in 1941 and returned to play with the group once again in 1946. Therefore, the Gordon Quartet was Jacques Gordon and whoever else happened to be playing with him at the time.

Meanwhile, more attention was directed in December 1942 to the question of students enlisting or being drafted for military service. The Board of Regents of the State of New York had recently authorized graduation for such students if they were within ten semester hours of completion of the requirements for a degree. The Eastman faculty approved this policy at a meeting on December 8, 1942. Among those thus approved for graduation was William Warfield (BM '43), who later achieved widespread fame and success as one of the country's preeminent singers. The same gathering of faculty approved a motion that, on a much sadder note, granted a degree posthumously to Marvin Lee, who had died in service on November 19. Nine Eastman students lost their lives in the service of their country, and their sacrifice should not be forgotten:

Sidney Archibald	*ex* 1933
Seth Chapin	BM 1944
James Deming	*ex* 1944
Thor Hamrin Jr.	*ex* 1942
Paul Husted	*ex* 1945
Earl Krumwiede	*ex* 1946
Marvin Lee	BM 1942
Robert Speas	*ex* 1942
Vernon Winton	BM 1943

Over five hundred students and alumni served in all branches of the services, including a number of women who enlisted with the Navy WAVES, the Army WACS, and the Red Cross. A large number of the men saw combat during the war, while others were assigned to various service bands.

During this time when so many of the Eastman community's young men and women were going to war, several former members of the Eastman community had recently died. Joseph Bonnet, the distinguished French organ virtuoso who had taught during the school's first two years, died in France on August 20, 1944. His

---

[3]   Morris Krackmalnik, also known as Kras Malno, was awarded his bachelor of music degree and performer's certificate at the Eastman School of Music in 1942 and received his artist's diploma in 1943.

countryman and successor at Eastman, Abel Decaux, had died on August 11 the preceding year. Another former Eastman organist, Dezo d'Antallfy, died on April 29, 1945. He had been one of the original Eastman Theatre organists in 1922 and had taught theater organ at the school for only a year before he left Rochester, later becoming organist for the New York Philharmonic and organist at Radio City Music Hall. Another former faculty member who died during this period was the voice teacher Thomas Austin-Ball. He passed away on October 3, 1944, only a little more than a year following his retirement from the faculty after twenty years of teaching at the school. Austin-Ball's longtime faculty colleague Adelin Fermin, an original member of the Eastman School faculty, had died three years earlier on May 9, 1941.

The passing that should have been noted with the greatest sadness was that of Alf Klingenberg, the school's first director. The Eastman School of Music owed much to Klingenberg. His departure in 1923 following George Eastman's request for his resignation must have been a bitter experience for him. In later life Klingenberg divided his time between France in the winter and Norway during the summer months, leading a modest and quiet life and surely finding time to reflect on his years in Rochester. He must have enjoyed some feelings of pride and accomplishment for his role in the events that led to the opening of the Eastman School in 1921, an institution he was able to lead for only two years. The older members of the faculty who remembered Klingenberg with special fondness noted his death in Oslo, Norway, on August 20, 1944, with particular sadness.

Hermann Dossenbach, Klingenberg's partner when they opened their music school on Prince Street in 1912, died about seventeen months later on January 28, 1946. Prior to the opening of the Eastman School of Music and the Eastman Theatre, Dossenbach had worked tirelessly to develop an audience for orchestral music. Although his Rochester Orchestra enjoyed considerable success, he was by-passed when the decision was made concerning who should lead the new Rochester Philharmonic Orchestra. Like Klingenberg, he had been essentially dismissed and had to watch the subsequent development of the school and the orchestra from the sidelines. Unlike Klingenberg, however, Dossenbach remained in Rochester and faced constant reminders that the musical aspirations and dreams of his youth were never fulfilled.

For many members of the Eastman community, the deaths of Dossenbach and Klingenberg were noted with only passing interest. They were figures from the school's origins more than two decades earlier, and the school was now represented by figures such as Luigi Silva and Jacques Gordon, distinguished additions to the faculty in 1941 and 1942, respectively. Their appointments did a great deal to strengthen the Eastman School's string department. In 1944 they were joined by Eastman alumnus Millard Taylor, who also became concertmaster of the Rochester Philharmonic Orchestra, succeeding Alexander Leventon who had resigned to pursue his talents as a photographer. Taylor had previously served for six years as concertmaster of the National Symphony and now began a teaching career at Eastman that would extend until his retirement in 1979. Also joining the faculty in 1944 was pianist José Echániz, whose colorful and outgoing personality made him a great favorite among students and faculty alike. Born in Havana, Cuba, on June 4, 1905, Echániz first studied piano with his father and then with several prominent teachers in Havana. He made his New York debut in Town Hall on January 4, 1922, when he was only seventeen and subsequently appeared as soloist with the Chicago, Philadelphia, St. Louis, and Minneapolis orchestras. Prior to his appointment to the Eastman faculty, Echániz had been teaching at the Conservatory of Music at James Millikin University in Decatur, Illinois, a post he had held for twelve years.

When the men who had gone off to war came back to Eastman to resume their studies—those fortunate enough to return from service to their country—a new set of problems needed to be addressed to accommodate them. As early as September 1945 the school felt it necessary to temporarily lift the existing enrollment restriction of 500 students in its regular courses to make room for returning servicemen. Hanson was also aware that readjustment to civilian life, especially among those who had seen combat or been prisoners of war, required thoughtful consideration and sympathy from the Eastman community. The following September he offered remarks concerning the difficulties of accommodating returning servicemen when he addressed the Eastman community at the opening convocation:

> I must confess that your return has not been without problems. First, we have had to expand the size of the student body beyond that which we would normally consider advisable. We have had to eliminate almost entirely the admission of students transferring from other institutions. We have had to cut the size of the freshman class to the smallest number possible without destroying completely the continuity of a four-year undergraduate program. We have had to refuse many hundreds of applications from qualified students for admission including

those of many servicemen who are not former students of the Eastman School of Music. We have, in addition, been rather vigorous in declining to permit to continue in the school those students who through lack of ability or application had not seemed to profit from their studies here, thereby creating additional room for veterans.[4]

As the veterans returned to Eastman, they found a new teacher of string bass at the school. Nelson Watson, who had joined the faculty in 1924, died on February 21, 1945, and was replaced by Oscar Zimmerman. Zimmerman was a member of the first graduating class at the Curtis Institute of Music and had been hired by the Philadelphia Orchestra when he was only nineteen. After playing with Philadelphia for six years, Zimmerman went to St. Louis as principal bass player before joining the NBC Orchestra as principal bass under Arturo Toscanini (1867–1957). When he came to Eastman, Zimmerman was replacing a fine player and exceptional teacher, but he quickly established his own reputation as one of the most important string teachers of his generation.

Among Zimmerman's many friends and admirers was Frederick Fennell, who later recalled their friendship:

> Oscar Zimmerman had come into my life in the summer of 1939 when I was invited by Joe Maddy to join the Interlochen faculty as teacher of percussion; he was to become a close and devoted friend and fabulous foil for my continual evolution as a conductor. At this time (1939) he was on the first stand of the basses in the NBC Symphony. I had not ever heard the bass played so fabulously, both solo and in the orchestra. He had graduated from Torello's class at the Curtis Institute and was a member of the Philadelphia Orchestra before he was 20. He knew Stokowski's conducting intimately and at NBC he was always sopping-up everything from Toscanini and his frequent distinguished guests. Oscar is a music madman, too, so we became close, quickly. . . . At Oscar's apartment he had the greatest pre-hi-fi set . . . and a huge living room full of record shelves. *He had everything* orchestral and operatic there was in the 78 days, probably took his Philadelphia checks in records![5]

Zimmerman's students eventually occupied important positions in many of the finest orchestras in America, and his appointment to the faculty in 1945 marked the beginning of a highly successful career as a teacher.

---

[4] Howard Hanson, "Convocation Address," *Alumni Bulletin of the Eastman School of Music* 18, nos. 1–2 (November 1946): 1–2.
[5] Fennell, *The Wind Ensemble*, 23 (original emphasis).

Figure 12. Nelson Watson, teacher of double bass, 1924–45.
(Photograph by Alexander Leventon.)

Figure 13. Oscar Zimmerman, teacher of double bass, 1945–76.

It was perhaps because of the increase in the undergraduate student population and the return of former servicemen that the Eastman School of Music appointed its first dean of students in 1945. Previously, there had only been an "adviser for women," with Marian Weed holding that position until 1938. She had been succeeded for a time by Jessie Hoskam Kneisel, the German teacher, but now the school would have a full-time dean of students. Selected for the position was Margaret Grant, a graduate of Sweet Briar College, with master of arts and doctor of philosophy degrees from Columbia University in sociology and economics. Grant had been associated with Twentieth Century Fox, the Carnegie Corporation, and the Social Science Research Council. More recently, she served as executive assistant to Serge Koussevitzky (1874–1951) in the Berkshire Music Center at Tanglewood and as secretary of the Koussevitzky Music Foundation. After only one year at Eastman, Grant resigned to join the Economic Affairs Department of the United Nations, to work directly with the assistant secretary-general. In seeking a replacement for Grant, Howard Hanson turned to Flora Burton, recently hired as director of the school's residence halls. Appointed acting dean in 1946, Burton was officially named Grant's successor in September 1947, beginning what would be a significant quarter century of increasing influence at the Eastman School of Music.

Also new in 1947 was Ruth Taiko Watanabe, who joined the faculty as a teacher of music history. Born in Los Angeles, Watanabe attended the University of Southern California, where she earned a bachelor of music degree in piano in 1937 and a bachelor of arts degree in English and literature two years later. This was followed by a master of arts degree in English in 1941 and a master of music degree in piano and musicology in 1942. Her family members were among the many Japanese Americans interned during the war, but Watanabe won an Eastman School fellowship in 1942 and a World Student Fund scholarship in 1943. At Eastman she worked in the library as a staff member in charge of circulation and served as a "house mother" at the student residence halls while pursuing studies that eventually led to completion of a doctor of philosophy degree in musicology. The year after her appointment to the faculty, Hanson named Watanabe to succeed Barbara Duncan as librarian at the Sibley Music Library, a position she held with great distinction for the next thirty-six years.

Joining the Eastman faculty the same year as Watanabe was Leonard Treash, who began his long association with the school as a teacher of voice. Treash was a graduate of the Cincinnati Conservatory and had pursued additional studies for several years at Curtis. He sang under such conductors as Fritz Reiner (1888–1963), Leopold

Stokowski (1882–1977), Artur Rodzinski (1892–1958), and Erich Leinsdorf (1912–93). Prior to coming to Eastman, he was head of the voice and opera department at Baldwin-Wallace College. That experience served him well when Hanson asked him to also become dramatic director and producer for the opera department. Emanuel Balaban had resigned, and his replacement in the fall of 1945 was Carl Fuerstner, trained at the Hochschule für Musik in Cologne. Hanson hired Fuerstner not only for the opera department but also as a member of the school's piano faculty. In 1947, however, Hanson divided the opera responsibilities, making Treash the dramatic director and Fuerstner the musical director. Two years later Treash became the sole director. Fuerstner was left with only opera conducting responsibilities and piano teaching, and he resigned the following year.

The postwar years also produced a number of additional changes in the string department. The first of these came as a result of the death of Jacques Gordon on September 15, 1948. Gordon had been in Massachusetts the previous day, visiting the American violinist Albert Spalding (1888–1953) in Great Barrington. Fritz Kreisler (1875–1962) was also a guest at the Spalding home, and the three distinguished violinists enjoyed a pleasant evening of friendship and discussing shared interests. Shortly after returning home, Gordon suffered a stroke, was rushed to the hospital, and died the following day. Although he was only forty-nine years old, he had been in ill health for some time, a condition that had forced him to reluctantly give up quartet playing at the end of 1947. Nonetheless, his death came as a profound shock to his friends, students, and colleagues at Eastman. Howard Hanson addressed the school's opening convocation on September 30 and spoke of Gordon:

> We have been saddened by the passing of a great artist and a great teacher to whom both the Eastman School of Music and many of us as individuals were deeply indebted. Jacques Gordon was my friend. I have known him for almost the entire span of my professional life. I knew him as the brilliant young concertmaster of the Chicago Symphony Orchestra—the youngest man ever to fill such a responsibility in the United States—and I knew him as a matured artist, a man who had known spiritual trial, suffering and sacrifice. To all of you who knew him I don't need to speak of his artistry and his musical integrity. Nor do I need to speak of his tremendous artistic self-discipline, his remarkable energy in pursuit of his ideals, nor his tireless labor.[6]

---

[6] Howard Hanson, "Convocation Address," Howard Hanson Papers, September 30, 1948. SML.

The person chosen to replace Gordon on the faculty was Andre de Ribaupierre. Born in Switzerland, de Ribaupierre had come to the United States to study with Eugène Ysaÿe (1858–1931) at the Cincinnati Conservatory. He subsequently taught in Cincinnati and then at the Cleveland Institute of Music. He then returned to his native Switzerland, where he taught at the conservatory in Geneva (Conservatoire de Musique de Genève) as head of the violin department.

Accepting an appointment to the string faculty in 1949 was Francis Tursi, who succeeded Samuel Belov as the principal viola teacher at Eastman. Tursi had received diplomas in viola and composition from Curtis before coming to Eastman to earn two bachelor degrees, one in composition in 1947 and the other in viola in 1948. Tursi was only twenty-seven when he joined the faculty. There was little in his background to suggest the extraordinarily gifted teacher he became during his years at Eastman. The selection of a young and relatively inexperienced person for an important faculty position was something for which Howard Hanson seemed to have either a special talent or extraordinary good fortune. Joseph Mariano and Robert Sprenkle were two other examples of his apparent ability to measure the potential of young people who would eventually contribute so much as teachers at the school.

Also new to the faculty in 1949 was the cellist Gabor Rejto, hired to replace Luigi Silva, who had resigned. Rejto was a graduate of the Academy of Music in Budapest and later studied for two years with Pablo Casals (1876–1973), first in Barcelona and then in Prades. Rejto toured Europe as a soloist and recitalist, coming to the United States in 1939. He had played with the Gordon Quartet and was a founding member of the Alma Trio. With Rejto's appointment came the reestablishment of an Eastman faculty quartet, which for the time being was still known as the Kilbourn Quartet. Joining Rejto in the newly reestablished ensemble were Andre de Ribaupierre, Paul White, and Francis Tursi.

Another person who joined the string department during the immediate postwar years was violinist John Celentano, initially hired in 1946. Celentano had served as Luigi Silva's assistant in chamber music teaching and was placed in charge of the program following Silva's resignation in 1949. Celentano's passion for chamber music, especially the string quartet literature, convinced him that quartet playing was not simply a pleasurable pastime but an essential part of the development of musicianship in string students. That philosophy guided him throughout his exceptionally long career, to the great benefit of his chamber music students.

Figure 14. John Celentano, teacher of violin and chamber music, 1946–80. (Collection of the author.)

No other single member of the faculty touched the lives of so many string students. His former students often felt deep gratitude for all Celentano had done for them in their development as musicians and artists, including the pianists who had studied chamber music with him and been positively traumatized by Celentano's insistence that they could, indeed, accurately sight-read the piano parts to Brahms trios and quartets. Even some people who never studied at Eastman had special memories of how their lives were touched by his devotion to the art of music. One such person wrote to Celentano in 2006, recalling a time forty years earlier when she had heard him play a recital. She later explained the reason for her note:

> So my hope was that my note would remind Mr. Celentano that all the good he has done in his life has a continuing impact, even among those whose lives he touched only in the briefest ways. Surely those who were his students and colleagues benefitted still more richly.[7]

Hanson's primary interest in faculty hiring was to find individuals who would be thoroughly loyal to the institution and completely devoted to their students. For this reason, he was usually unimpressed with long résumés and generally disinterested in those who had important performing careers, although Jacques Gordon was certainly an exception. If people came to Eastman with important performing careers, those careers were customarily somewhat in the past. What Hanson achieved with this philosophy was a faculty that was indeed dedicated primarily to the welfare of its students. Few Eastman faculty members during the Hanson administration had performing careers outside the school or, in the case of orchestral musicians, the Rochester Philharmonic Orchestra.

It has been suggested that Hanson was unable to have anyone at the Eastman School whose star shone more brightly than his own. This might explain, for example, his refusal to respond positively to the inquiry by Béla Bartók (1881–1945) about a possible piano faculty position at Eastman. He quickly dismissed the famous Hungarian as "not much of a pianist, and certainly not much of a teacher."[8] While we might try to give Hanson the benefit of the doubt by wondering if Bartók really could have been an effective member of the Eastman community, it is also perhaps undeniable that Hanson's self-image and ego would never have allowed anyone of Bartók's

---

[7]   Joan Covingtone, e-mail message to the author, November 21, 2006.
[8]   Howard Hanson, interview by the author, Rochester, NY, 1977.

stature to join the faculty. And Bartók was surely not the only famous musician who found the doors of the Eastman School of Music firmly closed.

A less famous pianist than Bartók, but one who contributed greatly to the graduate program, was Verne Thompson, who joined the faculty in September 1948. Thompson struck many observers as brilliant, yet quiet and unassuming, but his background as a musician was surprisingly rich and diverse. He had earned a bachelor of science degree in 1923 from Pacific Union College and a bachelor of music degree in 1929 from the American Conservatory in Chicago. He later earned a master of music degree from the American Conservatory and then pursued additional piano study with Josef Lhevinne (1877–1944) in New York. His piano skills were such that he served as accompanist for artists such as Tito Schipa (1888–1965), Lauritz Melchior (1890–1973), and Joseph Szigeti (1892–1973). At the same time, he was also a special correspondent for *Musical America* and had taught at various institutions throughout his career. His appointment to the Eastman faculty came while he was working on his PhD in musicology.

The new faculty appointments, combined with the influx of returning servicemen, were transforming the Eastman School of Music into a different institution in the late 1940s. There were some problems assimilating the former servicemen, as mentioned, especially since their numbers resulted in a disproportionate ratio of upper-division students. At the same time, however, they raised the student body's average maturity and technical proficiency to a much higher level than was the case before the war. In total numbers, the school's enrollment was growing. During the five-year period prior to the U.S. entry into the war, total collegiate enrollment at Eastman had averaged about 512 students per year; during the five-year period following the end of the war, enrollment averaged about 608 students. However, this increase was not necessarily only because of the returning servicemen, since during the next five-year period enrollment still averaged about 600 students. This upward trend troubled Howard Hanson, whose annual report in May 1949 included the cautionary note that "every additional student beyond 600 seems at least a triple burden on faculty and administration, and it is my feeling that a total of 550 students once set as the optimal registration is still valid."[9]

[9]   Howard Hanson, "Report of the Director of the Eastman School of Music," *Reports of the President and Treasurer 1948–1949*, Rochester, NY, 30.

The largest increase in students came in the school's preparatory department, where enrollment had been steadily recovering from the devastating effects of the Great Depression. From a low of 417 students in the 1933–34 school year, the number of preparatory department students grew to 1,249 by the 1946–47 school year and was exceeded nine years later when enrollment reached 1,445. Such numbers of students needed a large faculty, many of whom also taught collegiate students. These included some of the older generation of teachers, such as Marjorie Truelove MacKown (appointed in 1921), Marie Erhart Pearson (appointed in 1923), and Gladys Metcalf Leventon (appointed in 1928). But faculty members who taught preparatory students also included a group of relative newcomers, such as Wallace Gray (appointed in 1941), Blair Cosman (appointed in 1945), Harold Weiss (appointed in 1947), Abram Boone (appointed in 1947), and Anastasia Jempelis (appointed in 1949). Although none of these people ever taught collegiate performance majors, their contribution to the school and to their students should never be underestimated or minimized. They were among the school's most dedicated and loyal faculty members.

Most of the Eastman School of Music faculty members had relatively heavy teaching loads, but there was little expectation of any other responsibility toward the institution. There was no academic rank at the time and no tenure procedures. Expectations for publication or outside professional activity were essentially nonexistent. Even within the institution, there were few committees or opportunities for the faculty to have a part in the decision-making process. The officers of the administration of the Eastman School of Music were essentially in charge of everything, subject to the approval of the school's board of managers and the central administration of the University of Rochester.

Assisting Howard Hanson in running the school's affairs was Raymond Wilson, who served as assistant director, director of the summer session, and director of the preparatory department in addition to his responsibilities as an important member of the piano faculty. Flora Burton was, as noted, the dean of students, while Allen Irvine McHose served as "administrative assistant" to Hanson in addition to his responsibilities as chair of the theory department. Arthur Larson was the school's secretary-registrar as well as head of the placement bureau, and Arthur See was the financial secretary and concert manager. Wayne Barlow was secretary of the graduate committee in addition to his faculty responsibilities in the composition department, Marion Davis served as cashier, and Dorothy Vincent fulfilled responsibilities as the school's recorder. Arline Piper Putnam was the manager of Kilbourn Hall, Ruth Watanabe the librarian, and Jean Ancona the director of the concert bureau. These eleven individuals, four of whom also had significant teaching responsibilities, essentially ran the Eastman School of Music with the assistance of a very few secretaries. The school also provided a staff to run its dormitories and dining halls and provided access to two doctors: John Fletcher McAmmond, who served as medical adviser for men, and Jean Watkeys, medical adviser for women.

Within the school's administrative structure, however, Hanson reigned supreme, sometimes called by friends and foes alike "a benevolent dictator." He kept himself involved in all aspects of the school, yet still found time to pursue his own professional interests. In December 1943 he was in Boston as guest conductor for the premiere of his Symphony No. 4 ("Requiem") by the Boston Symphony Orchestra. The work subsequently received its radio premiere on January 2, 1944, with Leopold Stokowski leading the NBC Symphony, and had its Philadelphia premiere with Hanson conducting the Philadelphia Orchestra at the end of January. José Iturbi and the Rochester Philharmonic Orchestra introduced the work to Rochester audiences on February 3. These performances preceded the dramatic announcement on May 2, 1944, by the board of trustees of Columbia University that Hanson had won the coveted Pulitzer Prize for Music for his fourth symphony.

Hanson received many honors for his work as an educator and a composer, especially for his advocacy of American music. By 1946 he had received nine honorary doctorates, the most recent from Columbia University on June 4, 1946. The citation lauded Hanson as "conductor, director of the Eastman School of Music; founder and conductor of the American Composers' Concerts at Rochester; writer of music acclaimed for beauty, vitality and originality; brilliant conductor; versatile, touching the musical civilization of our nation at every point."[10] Adding a note of personal happiness to his professional triumphs, Hanson was married on July 24, 1946. His new wife was the former Margaret (Peggy) Nelson, whom he had met four years earlier when he was conducting in Chautauqua, New York. She was the daughter of the vice president and treasurer of the Gulf Oil Company. Officiating at the wedding, which took place in Chautauqua, was the Reverend John Nelson, brother of the bride. Hanson's best man was his longtime Eastman School colleague, Arthur Larson. A year later Howard and Peggy Hanson were the wedding attendants when Larson married Flora Burton on August 12, 1947.

[10] "Honorary Degree Awarded Dr. Hanson at Columbia University Exercises," *Alumni Bulletin of the Eastman School of Music* 17, nos. 3–4 (June 1946): 17.

Neither his marriage nor his professional successes, however, deterred Hanson from his primary preoccupation: the Eastman School of Music. Although Hanson never easily delegated authority, the school was growing in size and complexity and was very much in need of greater faculty participation in its affairs. One of the earliest efforts to stimulate more faculty advice and participation came in 1948 when Hanson suggested at an October faculty meeting that a number of departmental committees should be formed. These committees, with their faculty chairs, were as follows:

Academic	Flora Burton
Piano	Raymond Wilson
Strings	Millard Taylor
Orchestra	Paul White
Graduate	Wayne Barlow
Music Education	William Larson
Theory	Allen Irvine McHose

There had been an earlier effort in 1940 to form an "administrative committee" consisting of the department chairs, but securing faculty participation in the school's affairs proved an elusive goal. In his new plan for departmental committees, Hanson suggested that department meetings take place at the beginning of each quarter (i.e., four times a year), with matters of general interest referred to the entire faculty only after action had been taken by a department. This was the rather humble and perhaps inadequate beginning of faculty involvement in the affairs of the Eastman School of Music, and it would be many years before a newer generation of faculty members asserted their right to be part of the decision-making process of the institution at which they were teaching. For the most part, Hanson and his administrative colleagues still controlled the school's destiny, mainly by choice but also as a result of faculty disinterest in the process.

The 1951–52 school year began, as many other school years had done in the past, with welcoming the new freshmen. There was a Monday evening meeting in Kilbourn Hall to outline the week's events, followed by a pajama party for the girls in the dormitory. Tuesday evening was the occasion for a "boys' smoker" in the school lounge, and there was a square dance on Wednesday in the girl's dormitory recreation room. On Thursday a dinner and a coffee hour were provided for both boys and girls in the dormitory, and on Friday the students were subjected to a talk on the school's history by Arthur See. A Saturday tour of the campus, followed by a dance in the dormitory recreation hall and a picnic in Genesee Valley Park, concluded the planned activities for the week. On a less pleasant note, various placement tests were given during the first three days, and auditions were held on Thursday and Friday.

Classes and lessons began the following Monday, and the weekly cycle of lessons, classes, practicing, and rehearsals was under way for the thirty-first consecutive year at the Eastman School of Music. As in previous years, there were wonderful opportunities to hear concerts and recitals at the school and in the theater. The Rochester Philharmonic Orchestra was presenting its customary series of concerts on Thursday evenings in the Eastman Theatre. A new music director, Erich Leinsdorf, had been appointed in 1947 and was providing strong leadership from the podium. Soloists during the 1951–52 school year included Gabor Rejto and José Echániz from the Eastman faculty, as well as guest artists such as pianist Rudolf Firkusny (1912–94), violinist Szymon Goldberg (1909–93), and the famous American baritone Mack Harrell (1909–60). Leinsdorf had engaged some impressive soloists in recent seasons, including the gifted young French violinist Ginette Neveu (1919–49), who played with the orchestra on November 11, 1948, a year before her tragic and untimely death in an airplane crash on October 2, 1949. Pianist William Kapell (1922–53), who similarly died at a young age in an airplane accident, had been soloist with the Rochester Philharmonic on three occasions in the late 1940s.

The Artist Series in the Eastman Theatre, while perhaps losing some of its reputation for presenting the world's greatest artists in recitals, still offered an excellent selection of events. Among the eight concerts during the 1951–52 season were recitals by violinist Jascha Heifetz (1901–87), pianists Clifford Curzon (1907–82) and Alexander Brailowsky (1896–1976), and the American mezzo-soprano Risë Stevens (b. 1913). These artist events, plus the eight recitals in the Kilbourn Hall chamber music series, presented many opportunities for Eastman students and faculty to enjoy music making at its highest level.

The difficult times caused by World War II had subsided, and the school was settling into a more usual routine in September 1951. But if the new school year began with the tone of "business as usual," one item of business was decidedly new. At the end of the previous year, Howard Hanson had discussed with his faculty the feasibility of granting a doctor of music degree, a professional doctorate distinct from the existing doctor of philosophy degree already conferred. In later times such a suggestion would have called for the formation of a faculty committee, but in 1951 Hanson was content to ask that any suggestions be forwarded to him or to Wayne Barlow, the secretary of the graduate committee. On February 15, 1952, Hanson returned to the subject of a new doctorate in music, and the pertinent section of the minutes from the faculty meeting reads as follows:

> Dr. Hanson then reviewed the question of offering the Doctor of Music degree as a terminal, professional, earned degree. The increasing number of PhDs in musicology is not wise, said Dr. Hanson. College presidents are looking for administrators in music who have a doctor's degree. If only musicologists are available for these executive positions, it is not good for music. The time has come when there should be a terminal professional degree. It is not only desirable but necessary.
>
> The National Association of Schools of Music in November 1951 approved the degree. With over 200 schools represented there were only two or three objections. The question had been referred to the State Education departments that reported no objections if the degree is approved by the institutions. Dr. Hanson said the question was presented to the graduate committee of the Eastman School of Music and was unanimously approved. After some discussion by the faculty a motion was passed approving the establishment of a terminal professional degree of Doctor of Music.[11]

The degree Hanson was proposing and which the faculty approved was to be known as the doctor of musical arts degree, and the Eastman School of Music would thrust itself into the front ranks of schools offering this new doctorate. Those who might have wondered if Howard Hanson had been director for too many years to expect any exciting new initiatives from him were obviously mistaken.

[11] Minutes of the faculty meeting, February 15, 1952. SML.

Chapter 6

1952–64

Hanson: The Final Years

The opening of the new school year in September 1952 brought a number of new faces to the Eastman faculty. One of the most notable newcomers was the former Metropolitan Opera baritone Julius Huehn. Although born in Massachusetts, Huehn had grown up in Pittsburgh, where his father was an official at a local steel mill. His musical interests as a teenager centered upon playing the saxophone in various dance bands. After graduating from high school, Huehn started working in the steel mill making boilers, but he was then sent to Carnegie Institute of Technology to become an engineer. It was at this time that people took notice of his extraordinary vocal talent, and he went to Juilliard to study voice. His Metropolitan Opera debut took place on December 21, 1935, when he was the herald in Wagner's *Lohengrin.* He subsequently became the youngest baritone at the Met to sing the role of Wotan in *Die Walküre,* and he was soon frequently singing with famous operatic stars such as Kirsten Flagstad (1895–1962) and Lauritz Melchoir (1890–1973). Huehn joined the United States Marines in 1944 and was trained as a night fighter director, first serving on the West Coast and then in the Marshall Islands. At the end of the war he was assigned to Japan and was discharged from the service in the spring of 1946. Prior to his appointment at Eastman, Huehn was chair of the voice department at Jordan College of Butler University in Indianapolis, Indiana.

Within the next several years, two of Huehn's Metropolitan Opera colleagues joined him on the Eastman faculty. Josephine Antoine, a leading coloratura at the Met for about a dozen years, joined the faculty in September 1957 after having previously taught at Indiana University, the University of Colorado, the Los Angeles Conservatory, and the University of Texas. Antoine had studied at the Juilliard School with the famous coloratura Marcella Sembrich (1858–1935) and made her Metropolitan Opera debut on January 4, 1936, singing the role of Philine in a production of *Mignon* by Ambroise Thomas (1811–96). *The New York Times* gave her a very

Figure 15. Julius Huehn, teacher of voice, 1952–71.

favorable review, stating that "the future looms bright for Josephine Antoine" and adding that she "sang her music with such charm and animation that she scored an immediate hit with the large matinee audience."[1] Antoine resigned her Eastman position after only two years, but she returned in 1966 to again teach at the school.

Anna Kaskas, who had sung at the Metropolitan Opera for fourteen seasons, was hired at Eastman in 1959 when Antoine left. She had been a co-winner in 1936 of the Met's Auditions of the Air, which led to the opportunity to join the company. During the ensuing years she developed a reputation as a highly dependable contralto, singing a great variety of roles. In 1943 she substituted at the last moment for Bruna Castagna (1915–83) as Azucena in Verdi's *Il Trovatore* and was praised by Olin Downes in *The New York Times*, who declared that "the one singer of the evening whose performance was abreast of the qualities of the music was Anna Kaskas."[2] Kaskas, who would establish an amazing record as a voice teacher in Rochester, had previously taught at Indiana University and Florida State University.

Appointed to the piano faculty in 1952 were two relatively young men, Armand Basile and Orazio Frugoni. Basile had come to the Eastman School of Music to earn a master of music degree, and he was awarded the school's coveted artist's diploma at the end of the 1952–53 school year. A highly skillful pianist and gifted musician, he had first studied at the Carnegie Institute of Technology before earning a bachelor of music degree in 1949 at the Philadelphia Conservatory. Frugoni was Swiss-born of Italian parents and had been educated in Milan. His principal teacher was the noted Italian pianist and composer Alfredo Casella (1883–1947). Frugoni's musical career was interrupted during World War II, when he was forced to flee Italy and seek refuge in Switzerland because of his anti-Fascist activities. While in Switzerland, however, he was able to study with Dinu Lipatti (1917–50) at the conservatory in Geneva, where he was awarded the Prix de Virtuosité in 1945. Frugoni made his New York debut in Town Hall on October 11, 1947, for which he received a highly favorable review from *The New York Times*:

> The youthful artist's work was alike extraordinary for its blazing virtuosity, its vividness and dramatic force. The vitality of his playing, its

---

[1] "Mignon Presents New Coloratura," *The New York Times*, January 5, 1936: N6. Copyright © The New York Times Co. Reprinted with permission.
[2] Olin Downes, "Anna Kaskas Sings in Il Trovatore," *The New York Times*, February 5, 1943: 8. Copyright © The New York Times Co. Reprinted with permission.

bigness of line and brilliance would have been gripping in themselves but, in addition, there was a musical sincerity always in evidence that added to his remarkable hold on the audience's attention.[3]

In addition to his growing concert career, Frugoni regularly recorded for the Vox label. Several of his recordings were very highly regarded at the time of their release, especially his rendition of the two Liszt piano concertos, which he recorded with Hans Swarowsky (1899–1975) and the Pro Musica Symphony of Vienna. Frugoni's faculty colleague, José Echániz, was also recording during these years, releasing a number of fine performances on the Westminster label.

Frugoni, Basile, and Huehn were formally introduced at the first faculty meeting of the year, held on October 9, 1952. Further mention was made at this meeting concerning the proposal for a professional doctorate, which Hanson announced would be called the doctor of musical arts degree. The school's director stated that since the new degree had received approval from all appropriate officials and committees at the school and the university, it had been referred to the New York State Board of Regents for consideration. The school inaugurated the degree a year later, justifiably claiming to have been the first to promote such a degree and one of the very first schools to offer it. The degree was conferred for the first time in June 1955, awarded to Will Gay Bottje at the university's commencement ceremonies.

The Eastman School of Music had shown strong leadership among its peer institutions in promoting the professional doctorate in music. At the same time, it demonstrated unique leadership in promoting the concept of a symphonic wind ensemble, all because of the leadership, imagination, vision, and incredible energy of Frederick Fennell. The first rehearsal of the Eastman Wind Ensemble took place on September 20, 1952, and Fennell later recalled that historic occasion:

> Sitting in its straight/curved rows it blew its way into history. Everybody knew we had found something. I had selected the players myself from the best in the school. For the first time, seniority had no place in an Eastman group.[4]

---

[3] Noel Strauss, "Frugoni Impresses in Piano Program," *The New York Times*, October 12, 1947: 75. Copyright © The New York Times Co. Reprinted with permission.
[4] Fennell, *The Wind Ensemble*, 26.

Fennell had long recognized that a significant body of music for wind instruments was rarely performed because of the lack of an existing ensemble that might consider this music an essential part of its repertoire. He had long entertained doubts about large symphonic bands, doubts that were reinforced when returning servicemen during the immediate postwar years expressed open opposition to and disinterest in playing in such a group. Fennell became convinced that by eliminating unnecessary doublings of the players, he could create a group with genuine artistic credibility for the performance of wind music. It would be smaller than existing symphonic bands, resulting in fewer problems of intonation and far greater clarity of sound.

The debut performance of the Eastman Wind Ensemble took place in Kilbourn Hall on February 8, 1953. The program consisted of Mozart's Serenade No. 10 in B-flat Major (K. 361), *Nonet for Brass* by Wallingford Riegger (1885–1961), and the Symphony in B-flat Major by Paul Hindemith (1895–1963). The printed program that evening contained this statement from Fennell:

> The Eastman School of Music welcomes you to the premiere perfor-mance of the Eastman Wind Ensemble. In this, its first public con-cert, it will present three works written for wind instruments. This ensemble has been brought into existence to serve the cause of music through the presentation of original music for those instruments which are played by an embouchure.
>
> The development of wind playing has been one of America's great-est contributions to the art of musical performance, and in establish-ing this group we have arrived at a point where, by the process of elimination of multiple doubling of the players, we hope to present the vast bulk of music written for these instruments in which we believe to be a proper balance of the players.[5]

Prior to this debut, Fennell had taken the bold step of writing to four hundred composers requesting appropriate compositions for the new wind ensemble. Among the first to respond were Percy Grainger (1882–1961), Vincent Persichetti (1915–87), and Ralph Vaughan Williams (1872–1958). In the years that followed, Fennell's Eastman Wind Ensemble became the school's elite per-forming ensemble, involving the best available talent at Eastman. Similar wind ensembles were established elsewhere throughout the

---

[5]   Frederick Fennell, Program Notes, February 8, 1953. SML.

Figure 16. Frederick Fennell and the Eastman Wind Ensemble.

country, perhaps none quite like Fennell's original group from the fall of 1952 but all owing much to his inspiring example at the Eastman School of Music.

Less than two years after the Wind Ensemble's spectacular debut, a potentially catastrophic event occurred in the Eastman Theatre during a rehearsal on the afternoon of December 9, 1954. While Herman Genhart was leading a school orchestra and chorus in a rehearsal of the Bach *Magnificat,* a section of the theater's ceiling collapsed without any warning, destroying or damaging six rows of seats in the left and left-center sections of the auditorium. Mercifully, no one was sitting in the seats at the time of the accident. Genhart, always a strict disciplinarian in rehearsals, casually looked over his shoulder at the enormous cloud of dust and debris and continued to rehearse his rather startled students until he was finally urged to evacuate the theater as a matter of safety. Until repairs could be made, the Eastman Theatre was essentially unusable. Those repairs began in March 1955 with the installation of four newly cast ceiling panels and strengthening of the ceiling by more than three thousand steel wire hangers, iron bars, and I-beams. In addition, the ceiling was redecorated and the side walls were cleaned, all at a cost of about $100,000.

Several years earlier, there had been another incident in the Eastman Theatre, although benign in comparison with the collapse of a portion of the ceiling. Erich Leinsdorf was leading the Rochester Philharmonic Orchestra in a concert on Valentine's Day in 1952. Concluding the program that evening was Tchaikovsky's famous *1812 Overture,* and at the work's most climatic moment—with cannons roaring offstage, bells pealing, and the orchestra furiously playing—the audience was astonished to see a huge cloud of feathers slowly floating down from the ceiling. Some pranksters had gained access to the catwalks high above the auditorium and released this shower of feathers onto the audience, an event not terribly well received by the ladies in their fine velvet dresses, now liberally covered with duck feathers. The culprits who perpetrated this unusual event were assuredly Eastman students, but they were not identified or apprehended, which was fortunate since Dean Flora Burton was hardly noted for her sense of humor.

Among those playing in the orchestra at the time of the "feather incident" were several Eastman faculty members who would retire within the next several years. Vincent Pezzi, who had served as the school's bassoon teacher since 1932, retired at the end of the 1953–54 school year. His replacement at the school and in the Rochester Philharmonic Orchestra was his former student K. David Van Hoesen, the son of Karl Van Hoesen. He had previously taught at the Oberlin Conservatory of Music and the Cleveland Institute of Music while serving as a member of the Cleveland Symphony Orchestra following graduation from Eastman in 1950. Van Hoesen had studied the violin as a child but later joked that he was "no competition for Heifetz."[6] His father, a fine violinist, made the decision that young David would be best advised to play the bassoon instead of the violin. Therefore, he took his first bassoon lessons with Kenny Pasmanick, later the principal bassoon in the National Symphony, then started lessons with Pezzi through the Eastman School preparatory department.

The year after Van Hoesen's appointment to the faculty, Stanley Hasty was hired to teach clarinet at Eastman and to serve as principal clarinet in the orchestra. He had graduated from Eastman with a bachelor's degree in 1941. Among his classmates were William Osseck, who had started teaching clarinet and saxophone at Eastman

---

[6] K. David Van Hoesen, interview by the author, Pittsford, NY, March 12, 2004.

in 1946, and Sidney Mear, who had become the school's principal trumpet teacher in 1949, replacing Pattee Evenson with whom
he had studied at Eastman.[7] Prior to returning to his alma mater,
Hasty had served as principal clarinet in the Cleveland Orchestra,
the Pittsburgh Symphony Orchestra, the Indianapolis Orchestra,
and the Baltimore Symphony Orchestra. In addition, he had taught
at the Cleveland Institute, the Peabody Conservatory, Indiana University, Carnegie Institute, New England Conservatory, and the
Juilliard School of Music.

There were also changes in the French horn faculty. Arkady Yegudkin, one of the most colorful characters in the school's history, retired
in 1953 and then died at age sixty-eight on September 8, 1956. A few
months later Yegudkin's longtime faculty colleague, Fred Bradley,
also died. Bradley had retired from the Rochester Philharmonic two
years earlier but had continued teaching at Eastman. Bradley was
well-known among local music educators because he was the owner
of Tally-Ho Music Camp in Livonia, New York, a place that combined
musical training with outdoor activities long before the proliferation
of summer music camps throughout the country.

With Bradley and Yegudkin gone, Morris Secon, who had been
playing in the Rochester Philharmonic since 1944, became the principal horn teacher at Eastman. However, Secon's tenure at the school
was relatively brief. In 1959 he left Rochester for New York City,
where he helped his brother Paul manage the original Pottery Barn
store on Tenth Avenue. The Secon brothers had invested in a quantity of pottery products in 1949 and had opened the store in New
York, which soon attracted hordes of shoppers. When Paul Secon
started making long trips to Europe in search of new products, he
asked his brother to come to New York to manage the store, and
Morris Secon then left Eastman and the Rochester Philharmonic.
The Secon brothers eventually opened seven Pottery Barns, but
Paul left the business in 1966 and Morris sold it in 1968. The Pottery Barn subsequently became an important and highly successful retail chain in the United States, although Morris Secon often
quipped that they had called it the "Poverty" Barn when he and his
brother were the owners.

Secon's successor at Eastman and in the Rochester Philharmonic
was Verne Reynolds, a graduate of the Cincinnati Conservatory of
Music and the University of Wisconsin and the recipient of a Fulbright
grant for study at the Royal College of Music in England during the

---

[7] Another member of the Class of 1940 was Clyde Roller, who succeeded Frederick Fennell on the Eastman faculty in 1962.

1953–54 school year. Before coming to Eastman, Reynolds taught at the Cincinnati Conservatory, the University of Wisconsin, and Indiana University. Reynold's colleague in the horn department was Milan Yancich, appointed to the Eastman faculty two years earlier when Fred Bradley died. Yancich, who was Paul White's son-in-law, had been a member of the Chicago Symphony and the Cleveland Orchestra before joining the Rochester Philharmonic in 1954. A year after Secon left Rochester, Yancich also resigned from the orchestra to accept Hanson's offer to head the school's chamber music program for winds, brass, and percussion.

There were also several important changes in the string department. Gabor Rejto resigned at the end of the 1953–54 school year to accept a position at the University of Southern California. His replacement was Georges Miquelle, born and educated in France. Miquelle came to the United States in 1918, playing for a short while with the Boston Symphony Orchestra before deciding to devote his time to chamber music for several seasons. He then served as principal cellist of the Detroit Symphony Orchestra from 1923 until 1954. Six months after Miquelle came to Eastman, his faculty colleague Andre de Ribaupierre died after a short illness. De Ribaupierre's death occurred in the closing weeks of the first semester, and Hanson appointed Joseph Knitzer as part-time teacher of violin for the remainder of the year. Knitzer joined the faculty full-time in September 1955. Knitzer came to the Eastman School of Music with a very impressive résumé, having studied with Leopold Auer (1845–1930) from 1924 until 1930 and with Louis Persinger (1887–1966) from 1930 to 1936. Knitzer made his Town Hall debut in New York at age twenty-two and later won the prestigious Naumberg Award in 1935 and the Schubert Memorial Prize in 1936. A former concertmaster of the Cleveland Orchestra, he had been head of the violin department at the Cleveland Institute of Music for thirteen years and been appointed head of the string department at Northwestern a year before he joined the Eastman faculty.

Another Naumberg winner joined Knitzer on the Eastman School faculty in 1957. Ronald Leonard became the youngest member of the Eastman string faculty when he came to Rochester to teach at the school and to be principal cellist of the Rochester Philharmonic, replacing Allison MacKown who had resigned. These changes in the string faculty also affected the personnel of the Kilbourn Quartet. Knitzer became first violinist, replacing de Ribaupierre, while John Celentano replaced Paul White as the quartet's second violinist. The violist remained Francis Tursi until 1958, when Francis Bundra took his place, and Georges Miquelle was named cellist. The

Figure 17. The Eastman String Quartet (standing, from left to right, Joseph Knitzer, Francis Bundra, Georges Miquelle, and John Celentano, with Howard Hanson seated at the piano), ca. 1960.

new personnel led to an increase in concert activity, and the group was officially renamed the Eastman String Quartet in honor of the school's founder. In the spring of 1960 the Eastman String Quartet toured southern Europe, the Middle East, and North Africa, playing forty concerts in eight countries under the sponsorship of President Dwight Eisenhower's program of cultural exchange.

It would appear that the process of dealing with faculty appointments was occupying a large portion of Howard Hanson's time as director. These appointments were made long before the advertising of vacancies and the appointment of search committees. Hanson made the decisions himself, after having made discreet inquiries to seek out someone he felt would be the best candidate for the position. The entire process was quite simple, and essentially it worked very well. Nonetheless, Hanson needed all his intuition and skill in dealing with the retirement of Harold Gleason in 1955, a retirement accompanied by the resignation of Gleason's wife, organist Catherine Crozier. The school's director paid tribute to Gleason:

It is with real and profound regret that I receive your decision to retire from active teaching in the Eastman School of Music. Over the years your work has greatly enhanced both the efficiency and the prestige of the Eastman School of Music, first as one of America's most distinguished organ teachers, later in the field of music literature, and finally, as director of graduate studies of the Eastman School of Music. It hardly seems possible that this has embraced a period of 34 years, but the calendar of years confirms your statement and I can hardly blame you for wanting to take a much-deserved vacation from active work. This does not, however, minimize our loss, and your presence will be greatly missed.[8]

The man Hanson selected as the new organ teacher at Eastman was David Craighead. Only thirty-one years old at the time of his appointment, Craighead was already developing a well-deserved reputation as one of the country's preeminent organists. The son of a Presbyterian minister, he had received his first music lessons from his mother. He showed great interest in the organ at an early age, studied privately with Clarence Mader (1904–71), and then became a student of Alexander McCurdy (1905–83) at Curtis. After graduating, he became organist at Pasadena Presbyterian Church in California and served on the faculty of Occidental College in Los Angeles. He now began a teaching career at Eastman that would extend until 1992, and during that period he consistently showed himself to be not only a teacher and artist of the highest rank but also an exemplary faculty colleague and a man of great integrity and impeccable character.

Hired to replace Harold Gleason as head of the music literature department was Eugene Selhorst, who served as acting director of graduate studies during the 1955–56 school year. The following year Wayne Barlow was named director after his return from an exchange professorship at the University of Copenhagen, but the graduate program was soon reorganized with Barlow as associate dean for graduate research studies (involving the master of arts and doctor of philosophy degrees) and Selhorst as associate dean for graduate professional studies (involving the master of music and doctor of musical arts degrees). Separate graduate committees were established for the two divisions, with Verne Thompson serving as secretary of both committees.

Both Thompson and Selhorst were very much involved in the establishment of the school's Collegium Musicum. The origins of the program can be attributed to a letter Howard Hanson wrote to Thompson at the beginning of the 1955 fall semester:

---

[8] Quoted in Harvey Southgate, "Dr. Gleason to Retire from Eastman School," *Democrat and Chronicle* [Rochester], June 4, 1955. SML (news clipping).

There has been one matter which has been on my mind for a good many years and on which I would like your opinion. I have not had a chance to discuss it with anyone except Warren Fox who was enthusiastic about it. The idea, in brief[,] is this. Most of the Music Literature courses throughout the country are, by necessity, taught largely through the use of records as far as listening is concerned. It has always been my ambition some day to have a Music Litera- ture course in which a great deal of music is performed "live" by the various organizations of the School. Certainly there is no institu- tion in the United States which has the facilities to do a better job in the performing of music. The plan would be to try to set aside one night a week, perhaps Monday night, and devote that evening to the performance of music correlated with the Music Literature course as much as possible.[9]

Hanson went on to suggest that the Collegium Musicum might be considered as one of the regular four sessions of the music literature course and that the course's daytime sessions be reduced from four to three. Thompson and Selhorst responded enthusiastically and drew up a list of possible collegium performances, ranging from Gregorian chant to late-nineteenth-century French chamber music. Their list was very comprehensive, but it eventually needed to be modified to provide a series of twenty weekly programs.

To implement the plan, Hanson appointed David Fetler—a member of the conducting staff—to prepare the performances, which took place on Monday evenings from 7:30 to 9:00, followed by a social hour with refreshments. In spite of the enthusiasm for the idea, however, the reality of preparing a weekly program by assembling the necessary performance resources proved very dif- ficult, especially since few of the student performers at the time were trained in historical performance practice. This problem was addressed in 1960 with the formation of an official Collegium Musicum Ensemble, consisting of about twenty-five singers and ten instrumentalists. The ensemble was established as a course for credit at the school and met at regularly scheduled hours for study and rehearsals.

Three years after the proposal that led to the establishment of the Collegium Musicum, Eugene Selhorst suggested a possible curricu- lum for a master of music in church music, presenting at the same time a possible layout for a church music concentration within the doctor of musical arts program. The idea for a church music program had initially been considered following the receipt of a

[9]   Howard Hanson, memo to Verne Thompson, September 8, 1955. SML.

March 7, 1957, letter from Wilburn E. Saunders, president of Colgate-Rochester Divinity School, asking about the possibility of the two institutions cooperating in some manner. In September 1959 a new department of church music under Selhorst's guidance began offering graduate courses, and the graduation ceremonies the following June included the conferral of the master of music degree in church music on the first two Eastman students to complete the curriculum.

Meanwhile, discussions continued concerning who might be selected as permanent head of the church music department. On January 26, 1960, Selhorst wrote to Hanson suggesting M. Alfred Bichsel, a church musician and Lutheran pastor (Missouri Synod) whom he described as a "splendid choral conductor and fine church music scholar."[10] Adding a note of urgency to the matter, he again wrote Hanson a month later asking how the school could accept doctoral students in church music while it was still unable to provide adequate instruction in the field, adding that the workloads of Eastman faculty involved in the church music department were already stretched to the maximum. With Hanson's permission, Selhorst wrote Bichsel on March 9, 1960, asking if he had interest in a position at Eastman combined with a concurrent position at nearby Colgate-Rochester Divinity School, a possibility already explored by Hanson and Saunders. Much of the urgency in Selhorst's mind involved the sudden availability of National Defense Fellowships in Church Music that would greatly assist the Eastman School in launching its doctoral program in the church music field. These fellowships had been made available through the 1958 National Defense Education Act (NDEA). Although originally focused on the sciences, mathematics, and foreign languages, the scope of the NDEA had broadened to include the arts and humanities.

On May 19, 1960, Hanson sent an agreement to Saunders asking his formal approval to a plan whereby the Divinity School would reimburse Eastman for half of Bichsel's salary, moving expenses, and fringe benefits in return for Bichsel's services of seven hours per week. The agreement was quickly signed, and Hanson announced Bichsel's appointment at the faculty meeting held on June 2, 1960. Thus, Bichsel became an associate professor at both institutions beginning in the fall of 1960. The new head of church music at Eastman came from Valparaiso University, where he was professor of music and director of music at the school's Memorial Chapel.

10 Eugene Selhorst, memo to Howard Hanson, January 26, 1960. SML.

Figure 18. M. Alfred Bichsel, teacher of church music, 1960–80.
(Collection of the author.)

A graduate of Concordia Theological Seminary in St. Louis, Bichsel had done graduate work at Juilliard, Eastman, the American Academy in Rome, and the University of Strasbourg, where he had earned his doctorate.

Upon his arrival at Eastman, Bichsel quickly organized the Eastman Polyphonic Choir, an ensemble of about three dozen singers devoted to the performance of sacred choral literature. The group also served as a laboratory choir for graduate students in the church music program. The Eastman Polyphonic Choir gave many public performances, including a significant number in connection with the Collegium Musicum. It also performed a number of times within the context of liturgical settings. One such program occurred on December 19, 1966, during the group's seventh year, when it provided the music for a Lutheran Christmas liturgy as it might have occurred in Leipzig in the year 1740. The liturgical service took place at the Lutheran Church of the Incarnate Word, with David Craighead as organist and the choir singing Bach's Cantata No. 91 *Gelobet seist du, Jesu Christ* and the Kyrie and Gloria from Buxtehude's Missa Brevis. The Gospel for the liturgy was chanted in Latin by the Reverend Marcel Rooney, O.S.B., a Catholic Benedictine monk and an Eastman graduate student who later became the Abbot General of the Benedictine Order.

Bichsel, or "Bix" as he was known to his friends, could be a rather irascible character at times. He felt passionate about music and about life in general. He loved and respected the Christian liturgy, and he was one of the leaders of liturgical renewal within the Lutheran denomination. The subject meant so much to him that he often found more kindred spirits among Roman Catholic clergy, who were in the midst of their own liturgical renewal in the years immediately following the Second Vatican Council than he did among his Lutheran colleagues. Among his close friends were the Reverend Msgr. Francis Schmitt, longtime music director at Boys Town, and the Reverend Robert Skeris, prominent in many Roman Catholic music circles and in later years professor at the Pontifical Institute of Sacred Music in Rome. Bichsel approached everything in life with unbridled enthusiasm and dedication, and he was an inspiration to his students. Sadly, his church music degree programs did not survive at the Eastman School of Music. They were discontinued at the time of his retirement, in spite of the success of a good number of graduates from the programs.

The church music programs and the Collegium Musicum were examples of larger programs initiated during Hanson's later years at the school. Other efforts, however, are also worth noting. In September 1957 the school introduced for the first time double majors at the undergraduate level, called "combination courses of study." The idea was first applied to performance majors who could also complete all requirements for primary and secondary teaching in New York State, thereby combining the performance and music education curricula. In a short while, the double majors also included combining theory or music history with performance.

Then, during the 1959–60 school year, Hanson proposed that the faculty approve a new undergraduate curriculum with a minor in the humanities. Charles Riker, who had joined the faculty in 1930 as an English teacher and now taught a wonderful course in fine arts, was selected to head the new program, which started in September 1960. Students registered for the humanities minor were required to complete all requirements in their major field and also to elect humanities courses that totaled between forty and sixty credit hours. This curriculum was designed for those who wanted more diversification in their studies and a broadening of knowledge in other fields. At the same time, however, the Eastman School moved in the opposite direction by approving a new master of music degree in applied music, which allowed twenty-two credits in applied music and directly related fields and required only eight credit hours in theory and music history.

The new degree program was described as "a permissive major open only to vocalists and instrumentalists of exceptional talent and attainment"[11] and was soon promoted as a terminal degree for students not intending to undertake doctoral study. Its intent, therefore, was somewhat like that of the artist diploma programs now offered by various schools in an effort to attract students of exceptional performing ability. The 1960 Eastman initiative, however, was presented as a genuine academic degree but without much academic content. The new curriculum was vigorously opposed by many of the academic faculty and survived for only a few years before being discontinued. Its brief appearance represented a rather strange departure for an institution that had always prided itself on the comprehensive nature of the education it offered students.

In June 1961 the university purchased the property on the corner of Main and Swan streets, and the building occupying this land was razed the following year. It had increasingly become an eyesore, cutting a wedge into the side of the Eastman Theatre. The original plans for the school and theater had called for the buildings to

---

[11] *Official Bulletin,* Eastman School of Music of the University of Rochester (January 1960): 118.

Figure 19. Main Street before the demolition of the building on the corner of Swan Street, ca. 1960.

occupy a site on the south side of Main Street, bordered by Gibbs Street on the west and Swan Street on the east. However, the owner of the large building on the corner of Main and Swan demanded an exorbitant price for his property, which George Eastman refused to pay, preferring to have his architects alter the plans for the theater. Therefore, the building—with apartments on the upper floors and various retail operations on the ground floor—remained nestled into the side of the auditorium for the next forty years. The structure's deteriorating condition finally convinced the university that it was necessary to remove it. Hanson spoke publicly at the end of 1962 about the need for a new concert hall that would seat about 1,500, and it was obvious that he was thinking about the newly acquired property. But he was nearing the end of his long tenure as director, and such decisions would have to rest with someone else in the future.

One matter, however, urgently needed to be addressed prior to Hanson's retirement: the lack of academic rank and tenure at Eastman. Throughout its history, the school had never conferred any academic rank on its faculty, and there were no formal tenure procedures. People were hired as "teachers" and essentially served at the director's pleasure. A reconsideration of this situation was long overdue, especially since an untenured faculty might be vulnerable to the whims of Hanson's successor. Therefore, a committee on academic rank and tenure was established, and it reported its initial recommendations to the faculty at a meeting on May 29, 1958:

> That tenure and rank be considered independently and that tenure should not depend on rank nor should advancement to a higher rank be a prerequisite for tenure.
> All full time members of the faculty and others as may be appointed to full-time status are to be eligible for the provisions of unlimited tenure.
> Appointment to unlimited tenure shall follow a period of full-time service of ten years at the Eastman School of Music of the University of Rochester.
> Permanent tenure, once granted, can be rescinded only for cause or bona fide financial exigencies of the Eastman School of Music.
> The academic titles to be employed shall be Instructor, Senior Instructor, Assistant Professor, Associate Professor, and Professor.
> Assignment to rank shall be made by the Director of the Eastman School of Music with the approval of the President of the University and the Board of Managers of the Eastman School of Music.
> The Committee on Academic Rank and Tenure shall be a standing committee and shall act in an advisory capacity to the Director of the Eastman School of Music of the University of Rochester.[12]

Of special concern to the Eastman community were two groups among its faculty, those who taught primarily in the school's preparatory department and those who also performed as members of the Rochester Philharmonic Orchestra. The fear was that the particularities of their university employment might exclude them from some, if not all, of the privileges being discussed. The committee had attempted to deal with the preparatory faculty by creating the rank "senior instructor," which would carry a presumption of tenure and its privileges. Issues involving the status of the orchestral musicians were apparently raised by the university, and Hanson attempted to allay fears by suggesting that "the simplest way to handle the titles of the faculty who are also members of the Civic and/or Philharmonic Orchestras is to give them the appropriate title with an asterisk which refers to a note indicating that these appointments are in conjunction with the Rochester Civic Music Association."[13]

---

[12] Faculty meeting minutes, May 29, 1958. SML.
[13] Howard Hanson, memo to Dr. Robert H. McCambridge, November 18, 1958. SML.

The work of the committee on rank and tenure was completed by the opening of the 1961–62 school year. Hanson reported at the first faculty meeting that the committee had submitted its recommendation to McCrea Hazlett, the university provost. On October 17, 1961, Hanson sent this memo to all members of the school's faculty:

> You will shortly receive from me a letter concerning your academic rank in the Eastman School of Music. The committee from the Eastman School of Music, working with Provost Hazlett, has made every effort to deal with the problem fairly and objectively. I hope that the faculty will agree with the committee's recommendations. If any of the recommendations do not seem fair, I want you to feel free to give me your opinions and/or objections.[14]

Attached to the memo was the committee's proposal, as approved by the board of trustees. It established ranks of professor, associate professor, assistant professor, senior instructor, instructor, and lecturer. The senior instructor rank, clearly suggested for the school's preparatory department faculty, was defined as for individuals with ten or more years of full-time service who had shown continuing scholarship and leadership in teaching. Such people would be considered to have presumptive tenure and could be removed only for cause or financial exigencies.

Letters were sent to each faculty member with notification of the rank being conferred. Understandably, several people felt they had not been treated fairly. Among them were two members of the piano faculty who were assigned the rank of senior instructor because of their work with significant numbers of preparatory department students. Both felt they should have been given at least the rank of assistant professor, but Hanson replied that the senior instructor rank carried tenure while that of assistant professor did not. Therefore, their classification would seem to be to their advantage. A more serious objection was raised by Louis Mennini, who had joined the faculty as a teacher of composition and orchestration in 1949. He wrote to Hanson commenting that he had been assistant professor of composition at the University of Texas when he had accepted an appointment to the Eastman School faculty, and he was now being offered the same rank after having served the school for twelve years.[15] Armand Basile, also

---

[14] Howard Hanson, memo to the Eastman School of Music faculty, October 17, 1961. SML.

[15] Louis Mennini, letter to Howard Hanson, October 31, 1961. SML.

dissatisfied with the decision concerning his faculty rank, wrote to Hanson claiming that he felt he was the victim of an injustice.[16]

In spite of the complaining—official and otherwise—the establishment of rank and tenure at the Eastman School of Music had been effectively accomplished. This was a school that had prided itself since its founding in 1921 as being a professional school within the context of a university. That claim was suspect as long as its faculty was not afforded the same privileges and protection as the faculty of the university's other schools and colleges. Eastman faculty members had served essentially at Howard Hanson's pleasure since 1924. Now, in 1961, rules were finally established.

[16]   Armand Basile, memo to Howard Hanson, November 12, 1961. SML.

Chapter 7

1941–64

Broadcasts, Festivals, and Recordings (II)

The Eastman School of Music was fortunate to have become involved in broadcasting serious music at a time when the broadcast industry was still in its infancy. There was a great demand for live music on the radio, and the school was in a position, through its association with Rochester station WHAM, to respond to that demand. The great variety of concerts and recitals broadcast from the school provided the institution with an opportunity to showcase its students and faculty while also giving the Rochester Philharmonic and Rochester Civic orchestras access to a wider audience. During the years immediately preceding World War II, however, Eastman broadcasts began to reflect a more educational focus, of which the "Milestones in the History of Music" series was a prime example. The school was losing its opportunity to simply present live broadcasts of student recitals and concerts, largely because a substantial amount of programming was now broadcast nationally by professional groups.

The New York Philharmonic had started broadcasting its concerts over the radio in 1930, and listening to the Sunday afternoon programs from Carnegie Hall became very popular with radio audiences. The NBC Symphony Orchestra began its broadcasts in 1937 when it was founded and placed under the direction of Arturo Toscanini (1867–1957). In addition, there was the Voice of Firestone, a weekly broadcast of excellent classical music over NBC radio on Monday evenings at 8:30. It was heard weekly from its inception in 1928 until 1956. The Bell Telephone Hour similarly presented radio listeners with live music broadcasting. It went on the air in 1940 and featured the Bell Telephone Orchestra, consisting of fifty-seven musicians directed by Donald Voorhees. In 1942 the program began to feature noted soloists, including opera stars such as Helen Traubel (1889–1972) and Ezio Pinza (1892–1957), pianists such as

Robert Casadesus (1899–1972) and José Iturbi (1895–1980), jazz artists such as Benny Goodman (1909–86), and Broadway stars such as Mary Martin (1913–90).

Faced with the proliferation of classical music broadcasting, it was only natural for the Eastman School's radio programs to move more toward an educational focus. During the 1941–42 school year, Eastman presented a series over the Columbia Broadcasting System (CBS) that was aimed at presenting a comprehensive picture of the development of American music. There were twenty-two programs in the series, and they included works by over seventy composers. A more ambitious broadcast project was planned for the following year, including several concerts of American orchestral music under the direction of Howard Hanson and Paul White, three special Beethoven programs presented by Eastman faculty members Jacques Gordon and Emanuel Balaban, a series of programs devoted to the music of Luigi Boccherini (1743–1805) featuring cellist Luigi Silva, a number of broadcasts of the Eastman School Choir under the direction of Herman Genhart, two performances by the school's opera department, and several programs featuring the Eastman School Little Symphony directed by Frederick Fennell.

This series of radio concerts, however, faced determined opposition from the Musicians' Protective Association of the American Federation of Labor, which insisted that only union members could take part in the broadcasts. The conflict with the musicians' union was covered in *The New York Times*, which reported that "further broadcasting by the Eastman School of Music will not be permitted, because of the policy laid down by James C. Petrillo, president of the American Federation of Musicians."[1] Although Howard Hanson argued that radio audiences wanted to hear both professional and outstanding student performers, the long association between the Eastman School of Music and the broadcast industry was coming to an end. The following year, WHAM began broadcasting a series of concerts on Tuesday evenings by the Rochester Civic Orchestra consisting entirely of professional musicians who were union members. The group was known as the McCurdy Little Symphony for these programs, which originated from Annex I at the Eastman School of Music. These Tuesday evening concerts became a fixture in local radio programming for many years.

---

[1] "Eastman Concerts Off the Air: Musicians Not in Petrillo's Union," *The New York Times*, September 15, 1942: 25. Copyright © The New York Times Co. Reprinted with permission.

Only occasional Eastman School of Music broadcasts occurred over the next twenty years. During the 1944–45 school year, WHAM presented five programs over NBC facilities in connection with the twentieth anniversary of the founding of the American Composers' Concerts. In 1955 Howard Hanson made a series of half-hour films entitled "Music as a Language," which were broadcast by the Educational Television and Radio Center in Ann Arbor, Michigan. The following year he appeared in a series of eleven half-hour live television programs entitled "Paintings in Sound," sponsored by the Rochester Gas and Electric Corporation and broadcast over WHAM-TV in Rochester. In 1958 a series of programs entitled "Evenings at Eastman" were broadcast over WVET in Rochester. This was the most ambitious project from the school since the early 1940s and consisted of about 420 hours of programming. Twenty-one of the programs, bearing the title "History of American Orchestral Music," were chosen by the National Association of Educational Broadcasters for performance over its network the following year. In 1961 five programs featuring student performing groups were broadcast on local television through sponsorship by the Lincoln-Rochester Trust Company.

The changing radio and television broadcast industry had brought an end to the Eastman School's ambitious initiatives that had flourished in the 1920s and 1930s, an end hastened by union rules that made it difficult to feature student groups. But as the school's broadcast opportunities receded, chances to make recordings increased. The initial series of recordings with RCA Victor was interrupted, like so much else, by World War II. Nonetheless, Howard Hanson urged the company to continue to make recordings, even with the understanding that it would take time before they were processed and released to the public. RCA Victor was apparently persuaded by Hanson's argument, and recording sessions were held in Rochester on May 7 and 8, 1942. Included in those sessions were Hanson's Symphony No. 1 ("Nordic") plus music by Burrill Phillips (1907–88), Charles Skilton (1868–1941), Bernard Rogers (1893–1968), William Bergsma (1921–94), and Charles Tomlinson Griffes (1884–1920). RCA had wanted Hanson to record some music by the Hollywood composer Max Steiner (1888–1971), whose movie credits included the score to *Gone with the Wind,* but he artfully dodged the suggestion, which was obviously not to his liking.

Nothing more happened until near the end of 1944, when Hanson wrote to the music director of RCA Manufacturing Company urging the resumption of recordings in Rochester and outlining the history of the relationship between RCA and the Eastman School:

Six years ago Charlie O'Connell and I discussed the comparatively small amount of American music available through recordings. A study of the listing of recordings revealed that comparatively few American works—even among those which were well-known and had been played repeatedly—had ever been recorded. We were both, of course, entirely cognizant of the fact that there would at first be a comparatively small market even for well-known works and I, therefore, agreed to present to the Board of Managers of the Eastman School of Music, a proposal whereby the Eastman School would undertake to supply funds for the payment of an orchestra to record a limited number of American works each year, the orchestra to be an augmented Rochester Civic Orchestra to be known as the Eastman-Rochester Symphony Orchestra. The works to be recorded were selected by Mr. O'Connell and me in the main from compositions which were generally accepted as a part of the American orchestra repertoire. We began recording in 1939 and recorded in that year, in 1940, 1941, and 1942. . . . During those years we recorded 27 compositions by 19 American composers.[2]

Hanson had to wait until March 27, 1945, before receiving word from Morrow that because of continued production difficulties, RCA found it impossible to make recordings with Hanson during the 1945–46 season. He added that he hoped Hanson would be able to arrange to carry over his budgeted funds to another year when the company might be in a position to resume the recordings. Morrow's response upset Hanson, leading him to write to J. W. Murray, the general manager of Victor Records, defending the American music recording project but saying that he found Morrow's letter "to be much too indefinite to constitute even an informal and provisional commitment."[3] The association between RCA Victor and the Eastman School of Music had obviously come to an end.

Over the next several years the recording industry underwent profound changes with the introduction of RCA Victor's "extended play" and Columbia's "long-playing" records. Eventually, Columbia's 33 rpm "LP" became the industry standard, and it was to Columbia Records that Howard Hanson turned for his next series of recordings. Three long-playing records were eventually released on the Columbia label,[4] including the MacDowell Piano Concerto No. 2 in D Minor with Jesús María Sanromá (1902–84) as soloist and

[2] Howard Hanson, letter to Macklin Morrow, October 16, 1944. SML.
[3] Howard Hanson, letter to J. W. Murray, April 17, 1945. SML.
[4] See Appendix 7 for a complete list of the repertoire recorded by RCA and Columbia.

Hanson's Piano Concerto with Rudolf Firkusny (1912–94) as solo-ist. The school's relationship with Columbia was reasonably short, however, principally because a small company called Mercury Records had made a proposal that Hanson could hardly turn down and Columbia could hardly match.

Mercury Records had been founded in Chicago, Illinois, in 1945 by Irving Green, Berle Adams, and Arthur Talmadge. The company soon became a major source of recordings by jazz, classical, rock and roll, and country music artists. In 1951 the company started using a single-microphone monaural recording technique, issuing records under the "Living Presence" name. Four years later it began using three omni-directional microphones to make stereo recordings on three-track tape and later enhanced this technique through the use of 35-mm magnetic tape. The stereo Living Presence records were audio marvels in their day, praised by music lovers and audiophiles throughout the country. Mercury's interest in the Eastman School of Music was something Howard Hanson could not ignore.

When officials at Columbia Records learned of Hanson's pending agreement with Mercury, they felt Hanson had not been entirely can-did in his recent dealings with them. The Eastman School director attempted to address the situation in a personal letter to Goddard Lieberson (BM '35), president of Columbia Records at the time:

> I heard today from a friend . . . that there might be at Columbia Records a feeling that I had not been frank in my dealings with Columbia and that the Eastman School had gone over to Mercury without warning or notice.
>
> If this is true, Goddard, there is a misunderstanding which I would like to clear up. When Dick Gilbert [director of the Masterworks Division at Columbia] was with Columbia I talked with him about our Eastman School recordings and explained to him that we had been approached by several smaller companies and that the proposal from Mercury looked interesting. He asked me how many records Columbia would need to promise us if we were to forgo the Mercury contract. I told him that our desires were modest, that we wished to record only two or three long-playing records a year. He replied that he felt confident that this could be arranged and that he would discuss it with you.
>
> Nothing happened after that for a number of weeks until I got in touch with him again by telephone. He then told me that he [had] spoken with you and contrary to his earlier prediction, you had not agreed but had said that you did not see how Columbia could enter into a recording arrangement with [the] Eastman School which would guarantee even two long-playing records per season. I asked

him if I might then feel free to negotiate with Mercury, to which he replied that he thought this would be entirely proper.

Since the above was a telephone conversation, I then wrote Gilbert a letter forming that conversation.[5]

Lieberson replied ten days later, claiming he had no recollection of any conversation with Dick Gilbert concerning the Eastman School recordings.[6] By this time, Gilbert had left Columbia Records. Whether someone was at fault in the dealings between Hanson and Columbia Records no longer mattered. The Eastman School had a new contract with Mercury Records.

Hanson eventually recorded over forty long-playing records for the Mercury label,[7] a monumental achievement in creating a recorded legacy of the works of American composers. Among the better-selling items was a record containing the *Adagio for Strings, Essay for Orchestra,* and the Overture "School for Scandal" by Samuel Barber (1910–81), coupled with the *Latin-American Symphonette* by Morton Gould (1913–96). Equally popular with the record-buying public was a recording of several works by Charles Tomlinson Griffes and Charles Martin Loeffler (1861–1935). Among these works was Griffes's *Pleasure Dome of Kubla Khan* with Joseph Mariano as flute soloist. The albums each sold about 10,000 copies, a respectable total that must have pleased both Howard Hanson and the management at Mercury Records.

Eastman faculty members were featured soloists in a number of recordings, including pianist Eugene List in both the Concerto in F and *Rhapsody in Blue* by George Gershwin (1898–1937) and cellist Georges Miquelle in *Schelomo* by Ernest Bloch (1880–1959) and the Concerto No. 2 for Violoncello by Victor Herbert (1859–1924). List's rendition of the Gershwin pieces won praise in *High Fidelity* magazine, which stated that the performances "can take a high place among the numerous disc versions of these popular works."[8] Miquelle's performance of *Schelomo* also won a sterling endorsement in *High Fidelity,* with reviewer Alfred Frankenstein stating that "the recording of the Bloch masterpiece is one of the best ever made."[9] These recordings were especially praised because of

---

5 Howard Hanson, letter to Goddard Lieberson, March 9, 1953. SML.
6 Goddard Lieberson, letter to Howard Hanson, March 19, 1953. SML.
7 See Appendix 8 for a list of Hanson's recordings on the Mercury label.
8 Paul Affelder, "Records in Review," *High Fidelity,* Great Barrington, MA (November 1957): 68.
9 Alfred Frankenstein, "Records in Review," *High Fidelity* (August 1962): 80.

Mercury's recording technology, widely considered to be among the best—if not the best—available at the time. Philip Geraci, writing in *High Fidelity,* commented on the high audio standard, stating that "the proper combination and thoughtful mike position and hall selection has resulted in a finely balanced production, and Hanson's performances capture beautifully the carefree idiom of this American music."[10]

Other recordings that proved popular with the buying public included an album that featured performances of Hanson's Symphony No. 4 ("Requiem") and the Symphony No. 3 of Roy Harris (1898–1979) and a recording of the Symphony No. 3 and *Three Places in New England* by Charles Ives (1874–1954). There was great variety to the repertoire Hanson recorded with the Eastman-Rochester Orchestra for Mercury Records, with composers including familiar figures such as Aaron Copland (1900–1980), Alan Hovhaness (1911–2000), Edward MacDowell (1860–1908), Walter Piston (1894–1976), and Roger Sessions (1896–1985) but also less familiar composers such as Richard Donovan (1891–1970), Ronald Lo Presti (1933–85), Ron Nelson (b. 1929), and Johann Peter (1746–1813).

The Mercury recordings, however, were not limited to Howard Hanson and the Eastman-Rochester Orchestra; they also included a much-celebrated series of recordings by Frederick Fennell and the Eastman Wind Ensemble. The first of these was entitled *American Concert Band Masterpieces,* and it included music by Vincent Persichetti (1915–87), Morton Gould, William Schuman (1910–92), Robert Russell Bennett (1894–1981), Walter Piston, and Samuel Barber. Sales figures by the early 1960s indicated that over 12,000 copies of this record had been sold, considerably more than any of Hanson's recordings. Yet, other Eastman Wind Ensemble recordings were even more successful, including a recording of marches entitled *Marching Along,* which sold over 55,000 copies, and a recording of British band classics with sales figures numbering about 24,000. The most surprising best-seller was a record entitled *Ruffles and Flourishes,* which contained excerpts from the official bugle calls of the United States Army plus traditional marches, inspection pieces, and music for rendering honors. This recording had reportedly sold slightly more than 45,000 copies by 1963.

In general, Fennell's recordings of traditional band music sold more copies than his recordings of so-called serious music. Yet, his forays into more serious repertoire were highly appreciated and

---

[10] Philip Geraci, "Records in Review," *High Fidelity* (September 1957): 88.

greatly valued. They included music of twentieth-century composers such as Paul Hindemith (1895–1963), Gustav Holst (1874–1934), Arnold Schoenberg (1874–1951), Igor Stravinsky (1882–1971), and Ralph Vaughan Williams (1872–1958), as well as music by earlier composers such as Giovanni Gabrieli (1557–1612), Wolfgang Amadeus Mozart (1756–91), and Richard Wagner (1813–83). All of the wind ensemble's recordings were received with widespread enthusiasm. R. D. Darrell, writing in *High Fidelity* magazine, praised Fennell's album *Ballet for Band,* saying "if there is any concert band which plays better than Fennell's Eastman ensemble, I have yet to hear it."[11] Fennell's earlier recording of music by Holst and Vaughan Williams brought similar praise in the pages of *High Fidelity* when John M. Conly stated that "the finesse of the band is without precedent in my listening experience."[12] He gave full credit to Fennell, whom he described as being on a crusade to advance the prestige of concert bands—an accurate observation.

The recordings of Frederick Fennell with the Eastman Wind Ensemble and those of Howard Hanson with the Eastman-Rochester Orchestra represented a highly significant achievement for the Eastman School of Music, enhancing the school's reputation and prestige throughout the music world. Hanson deserves much credit for negotiating the contract with Mercury Records. The opportunity to record works by American composers was an important extension of his ongoing commitment to the annual Festivals of American Music. The festivals, combined with the annual symposia, tended to follow a familiar and consistent format, with concerts by the Eastman-Rochester Orchestra, student orchestras, and various other student and faculty groups including chamber ensembles. The Gordon String Quartet performed recitals of American chamber music in 1944, 1945, and 1946. Several student chamber groups played in subsequent festivals, first under the direction of Jacques Gordon and later under the supervision of John Celentano.

One change in the festival format, however, was an end to the annual ballet programs featuring Thelma Biracree and her students. For a time, Biracree shared ballet responsibilities with Olive McCue, who also had a teaching studio in the school's Annex I, but the final ballet program during a Festival of American Music occurred in 1950. Some of the last ballet performances were particularly noteworthy, including Biracree's production of two popular works by

---

11   R. D. Darrell, "Records in Review," *High Fidelity* (September 1960): 86.
12   John M. Conly, "Records in Review," *High Fidelity* (March 1956): 65.

George Gershwin: *Rhapsody in Blue* in 1947 and the Concerto in F in 1948. Biracree's last production for the festival was a choreography based on Hanson's Symphony No. 2 ("Romantic"), a particularly fitting conclusion to their many years of working together.

As the ballet performances at the festivals came to an end, Hanson added evenings of opera productions. The first of these occurred in May 1949 with the production of two operas, *Don't We All* by Burrill Phillips and *In the Name of Culture* by Alberto Bimboni (1882–1960). Music by Phillips had been frequently featured during festivals starting in 1933, but this was the first and only performance of a work by Bimboni. Born in Italy, he had emigrated to the United States in about 1920 and had taught at Curtis for ten years before joining the Juilliard faculty in 1933. In addition, he had been the conductor of summer opera at the Chautauqua Institute since 1936. The 1950 Festival of American Music presented two important chamber operas, *The Telephone* by Gian Carlo Menotti (1911–2007) and *The Devil and Daniel Webster* by Douglas Moore (1893–1969). Other opera productions in subsequent years included Menotti's *Amelia Goes to the Ball* in 1951 and *The Consul* in 1952 and Kurt Weill's (1900–1950) *Street Scene* in 1953.

The 1961 festival, the thirty-first in the annual series, featured a program devoted to inter-American music that included the *Fantasy on a Quiet Theme* by Neil McKay (b. 1924), *Variations for Piano and Orchestra* by Camargo Guarnieri (1907–93), *Cantata for Baritone and Orchestra* "Give Me the Splendid Silent Sun" by Roy Harris, and Symphony No. 14 by Henry Cowell (1897–1965). The soloist in the Guarnieri work was Eastman student David Renner (BM '60, MM '65), while the baritone soloist for the Harris cantata was the distinguished Eastman alumnus William Warfield (BM '42). The program was repeated at the Second International Inter-American Music Festival in Washington, DC, with the American-born Brazilian pianist Yara Bernette (1920–2002) performing the Guarnieri variations.

A rather innovative program was included the following year entitled "The Jazz Idiom," featuring the Modern Jazz Quartet led by John Lewis and the Eastman Wind Ensemble directed by Frederick Fennell. Hanson had shown little sympathy for or understanding of jazz throughout his career, and the inclusion of this program represented a radical departure from the normal fare heard during festival concerts. An even stronger departure occurred during the thirty-fourth festival in the spring of 1964 when an afternoon program was devoted to electronic music with commentary provided by Wayne Barlow of the Eastman School faculty.

The 1964 Festival of American Music was the final festival during Hanson's forty-year tenure as director of the Eastman School of Music, but the festivals lingered on for seven years after his retirement. The 1965 festival, the first during Walter Hendl's tenure as director, featured performances of two piano concertos. Eastman student Robert Silverman (MM '65, DMA. '70) was soloist in a performance of the Piano Concerto by John LaMontaine (b. 1920) on April 27, and Eastman alumnus Alfred Mouledous (BM '49, MM '52) was featured on April 30 in a performance of Hanson's Piano Concerto. The final festival occurred in the spring of 1971, and its concluding program consisted of what was called a "nostalgic review" of first performances that had occurred during the many years of American Composers' Concerts and Festivals of American Music. The program included the *Prelude and Quadruple Fugue* of Alan Hovhaness, *Study in Sonority Op. 7* by Wallingford Riegger (1885–1961), *The Piper at the Fates of Dawn* by Randall Thompson (1899–1984), Symphony No. 1 of Elliott Carter (b. 1908), Concerto for Piano and Orchestra by Henry Cowell, "Mountaineeer Love Song" from the *Folk Song Symphony* of Roy Harris, *Darker America* by William Grant Still (1895–1978), and "Cortège Macabre" from *An Unnamed Ballet* by Aaron Copland.

Many of the programs presented during the later years of the annual festivals could also have been labeled "nostalgic reviews." For example, the concluding program of the thirty-third festival in 1963, with Hanson conducting the Eastman-Rochester Orchestra, included music of Horatio Parker (1863–1919), George Templeton (1856–1948), William Schuman, George Tomlinson Griffes, and Hanson himself. It is worth noting that William Schuman was the only composer represented on the program who had been born in the twentieth century, and he was fifty-three at the time of the festival. In defense of Hanson's programming, the annual concerts were never presented as festivals of contemporary music. They were designed as a celebration of and a tribute to the work of American composers not only of the present but also of the past. The Mercury recordings also reflected this broadness in Hanson's commitment to American music.

The story of the Eastman School's involvement with broadcasting, recording, and performing the works of American composers is perhaps a rather unique accomplishment among American music schools. Although the broadcasting activities began prior to Howard Hanson's arrival as the school's second director, it was Hanson who fully developed the opportunities presented as a result of the school's connection with WHAM. The eventual curtailment of regular broadcasts of music from the Eastman School resulted from developments that were beyond Hanson's control. But his subsequent series of recordings for the Mercury label, following earlier efforts with RCA and Columbia, was perhaps an even more significant contribution to the cause of American music. Yet it was the American Composers' Concerts and the Festivals of American Music that will always remain Howard Hanson's most important achievement. Nearly five hundred American composers had their works performed in Rochester at a time when such opportunities were infrequent at best.

From the time Howard Hanson first arrived in Rochester in 1924, he had firmly believed musical creativity was of primary importance in the musical culture of a nation. He was dedicated, therefore, to creating in Rochester a center of musical composition that would serve the needs of young composers. An important part of this vision was creating an opportunity for the public performance of new works written by these composers, as well as opportunities for repeated hearings of those works deemed among the better compositions already performed. At the same time, he saw the necessity of presenting works of established composers and in doing so offered the public a cross-section of American musical creativity. These thoughts led Howard Hanson to establish the American Composers' Concerts in 1925 and to expand upon the project by presenting a Festival of American Music as an annual event from 1931 until 1971. This was Howard Hanson's most important contribution to musical creativity in America and his unique legacy as an educator.

Interlude

Chapter 8

1955–64

A New Men's Dormitory and Student Life in Rochester

When the Eastman School of Music first opened in 1921, its student population was mainly from the immediate Rochester area, and there was little need for dormitories. However, the new school's facilities and its excellent faculty soon attracted applicants from many other areas of the country. The inability to offer dormitory accommodations became a serious problem, especially with regard to female applicants to the school. Very few parents at that time would have considered sending their daughters to study in Rochester without the assurance of appropriate housing. Therefore, the ability to provide dormitory accommodations for women quickly became not simply desirable but an absolute necessity.

In response to this situation, plans were prepared for the construction of three connecting buildings facing an internal courtyard, two of which were ready for occupancy in time for the opening of the 1925–26 school year, the school's fifth year of operation. They provided accommodations for 123 female students, and the opening of the third building the following September increased available accommodations to 210. Rather than being constructed close to the Eastman School, the dormitories were erected on University Avenue, adjacent to what was then the University of Rochester's main campus on Prince Street. At the suggestion, or perhaps insistence, of Howard Hanson, the three buildings were named for three prominent American musicians: Francis Hopkinson (1737–91), Edward MacDowell (1860–1908), and Stephen Foster (1826–84). In practice, however, they were more commonly called "A House," "B House," and "C House."

The new Eastman School dormitories did nothing to address the problem of providing accommodations for the school's male students. For a while, a limited number of men were housed at 47 Prince Street, in the building that had been the old Institute of

Musical Art. For a number of years, Alpha Nu Chapter of Phi Mu Alpha fraternity was able to offer housing for some of its members. Yet, the vast majority of male students were obliged to seek their own living accommodations, most often from a listing of "approved" rooming houses or at the Central YMCA on Gibbs Street.

The situation was so troubling to Howard Hanson that he conveyed his concerns to the university's board of trustees in his annual report in July 1950:

> The outstanding problem of the Eastman School of Music remains the adequate housing of its men students. This becomes increasingly difficult this year when the registration of men students exceeds that of women. . . . The school greatly needs a men's dormitory which will give to our men student housing which, though not necessarily as elaborate as our splendid dormitories for women, is comfortable, homelike and conveniently located to the Eastman School of Music. I respectfully call this need to the attention of the Board of Trustees.[1]

It was perhaps in response to Hanson's plea that Charles F. Hutchison, a longtime member of the school's board of managers, presented his lovely East Avenue home to the Eastman School of Music in 1951. As will be recalled, Hutchison's wife, Alice Whitney, had been George Eastman's secretary, a position she held for forty-two years. The home she and her husband owned was located next door to the Eastman mansion.

Howard Hanson first reported the possibility of acquiring the Hutchison property to the faculty on October 12, 1950. Hanson was interested because the Hutchison home might be able to provide housing for the school's male students, even though the home was well over a mile from the school. Since there was strong faculty sentiment for a men's dormitory, the Hutchison property was acquired by the Eastman School of Music and quickly began to function as a student union while also providing accommodations for a limited number of male students. Preliminary plans were under discussion concerning the eventual construction of a men's residence hall on the property when larger events at the university intervened.

In 1955 the University of Rochester finally abandoned its downtown Prince Street Campus. The men of the university had relocated many years earlier to a new campus somewhat southeast of downtown Rochester. Their departure had allowed the separate women's

Figure 20. Munro Hall, which became the Men's Residence Hall in 1955.

college to undertake a significant expansion on the old campus by acquiring the buildings now vacated by the men. Rush Rhees, the president of the university from 1900 to 1935, had initially been opposed to the idea of dormitories for women, believing the enrollment of female students should be restricted to local residents. Such a policy proved both unwise and impractical, and students from the College for Women came to be housed in numerous small cooperative dormitories, as well as in the Eastman School's women's residence halls, until their own dormitory was finally opened in 1939.

The new building, which later became the much-needed dormitory for Eastman's male students, was an especially handsome structure that provided very comfortable accommodations for the university women. It was erected on Prince Street, adjacent to the Eastman School residence halls on University Avenue, and it was named Munro Hall in honor of Annette G. Munro, the university's first dean of the College for Women. Enrollment in the women's college expanded at a faster-than-anticipated rate, however, and it was soon discovered that Munro Hall and the smaller cooperative dormitories could not meet the rising demand for student housing. Therefore, the university decided to convert one of its older buildings into yet another dormitory for women. The building was the Carnegie Building on the northeast corner of its campus. Erected in 1911 by means of a gift from Andrew Carnegie, the building had most recently housed the sociology, psychology, and geology departments.

When the policy of separate colleges for men and women was finally abandoned, the women of the university left the buildings on the old Prince Street Campus in 1955 to join the men at the River Campus. As a result, the Eastman School of Music was able to acquire Munro Hall on Prince Street and convert it for use by its male students. Consideration of other alternatives, such as the use of the Hutchison property, was set aside now that the Eastman School had an existing building that could function very well as a dormitory for men. Although it continued to be informally called Munro Hall for many years, the building was now officially known simply as the Men's Residence.

In addition to acquiring the Prince Street dormitory, the Eastman School became the owner of Cutler Union, which had been the center of social life for the College for Women. Its beautiful facilities included an auditorium that seated about 700, various lounges, dining facilities, seminar rooms, and recreation facilities. It was completed in 1933 and was financed by a large bequest from James C. Cutler, a longtime university trustee and prominent Rochester civic and business leader. Eight years later its top floor was converted into additional dormitory accommodations for the College for Women. Eastman's acquisition of Cutler Union coincided with the inauguration of the school's Collegium Musicum, and the connection was hardly coincidental since Hanson immediately sensed that the auditorium was an ideal space for the program he had been envisioning.

The acquisition of Munro Hall and Cutler Union, however, proved an expensive proposition for the Eastman School of Music, since the university insisted on compensation at the combined book value of $931,000 plus an additional $105,000 for furnishings and redecoration. This amount, in excess of $1 million, was transferred from Eastman's reserve to the university's College of Arts and Science building fund. While the school valued the acquisition of a building that could finally provide accommodations for its male students, there was great concern that the costs of maintaining Cutler Union would not justify its rather limited use by the school. Nonetheless, the university's central administration was insistent that the Eastman School acquire both buildings, not simply the dormitory.

There were several reasons why the university wanted to retain Cutler Union by having the Eastman School assume ownership after the women had left the Prince Street Campus. First, the building was only twenty-two years old, and it would have been rather ill-advised to abandon a building that had been such a generous gift only a little more than two decades earlier. Then there was the matter of the university's Memorial Art Gallery, which was adjacent to Cutler Union on the south side of the Prince Street Campus. Retaining ownership of the entire southern portion of the campus protected the immediate vicinity of the art gallery, and the easiest way to accomplish this was to require that the Eastman School take ownership of Cutler Union and its surrounding grounds.

In addition, the university president, Cornelis W. de Kiewiet, apparently felt strongly that the land in question might be necessary for the future development of the Eastman School of Music, reporting to the executive committee of the board of trustees on April 24, 1953, that the school might otherwise "be faced with a confined prospect that would be unattractive."[2] It apparently mattered little that Howard Hanson did not share the president's opinion of the possible future use of either Cutler Union or its surrounding property. Therefore, the Eastman School attained more property than it deemed necessary for its needs, but at least it now had a dormitory for men.

Retrofitting Munro Hall for use by men was a relatively easy task, especially since the dormitory was only sixteen years old and in pristine condition. The building was L-shaped, with a wing on its south end that housed a spacious dining room on the ground floor. Accommodations were on the upper floors as well as on the north side of the ground floor. The fifth floor gave access to two sundecks, presumably designed for discreet sunbathing when the building had served as a women's dormitory. The basement area contained a large recreation room, laundry facilities, the nurse's office, and an infirmary. The school nurse, Elsie Zimmer, was devoted to the Eastman students and generally well liked by everyone. Because the common treatment for most ailments was a supply of APC tablets (a popular analgesic at the time), many students referred to her as "APC Zimmer," and some especially gullible souls actually thought the letters were her real initials.

Of great concern to the school's administration in the 1950s was the fact that the new Men's Residence was connected on all floors (except the fifth) with the adjacent dormitories for women. The

---

[2] Quoted in *University of Rochester 1952–53 Trustee Proceedings* (Rochester, NY, April 24, 1953), 89. RRL.

connection in the basement was maintained as the basic access route between the dormitories but was securely locked every evening. On the first floor the men's dining room connected with the dining hall in C House through a kitchen that served both facilities during mealtimes, but the doors to the dining rooms remained locked except when meals were being served. Locked doors on the upper floors were deemed insufficient, and access between the facilities for men and women was permanently sealed. The era of coeducational dormitories had obviously not yet arrived, but student ingenuity always seems to triumph. A couple of enterprising male students discovered that they could leave the sundeck under the cover of darkness at night and climb over the roof of the building wing above the dining hall, thereby gaining access through a hatch to an attic area that connected with the attic in B House. Their discovery led to an initial coeducational rendezvous in the attic, followed by several other such meetings of which the school authorities were fortunately unaware.

Authority in student matters was handled by the near-legendary dean of students, Flora Burton. Born in the foothills of the Ozarks in Zalma, Missouri, Burton had earned her bachelor of science degree in education from Southern Missouri State College and a master of education degree in guidance and personnel work from the University of Missouri. After additional study at Columbia University, she became director of guidance at Russell Sage College in 1944 and came to Eastman two years later as director of the student residence halls. As previously noted, she became dean of students in 1947, a position she held until her retirement at the end of the 1971–72 school year.

Burton was an unmistakable and unforgettable figure of authority during her twenty-five years as dean at Eastman. She always seemed to be in complete control of any situation that might arise. When the mother of an auditioning student once remarked that it must be difficult to deal with all the students' problems, Burton responded that "we have no problems at the Eastman School of Music." Nothing seemed to shake her self-confidence, and a few well-chosen words or a withering glance was all that was necessary to bring even the most incorrigible student into line. When dealing with a disciplinary or an academic problem, she often began her discussion with a student by saying, "Now, I am going to tell you what you are going to do." If her manner was authoritarian, at least everyone knew where she stood on any given issue. She was honest and direct in dealing with people, and there was little room for misunderstanding or misinterpretation. When necessary, she could show a degree of kindness and compassion, although only rarely did she allow emotion or sentiment to influence her.

Burton's uncanny ability to apparently know everything that was going on at the school and in the dormitories led to much speculation, especially during her earlier years as dean of students, that she maintained some sort of elaborate network of informants. The accusation amused her, and she confided to friends that she really had no need for such a network since there were always sufficient numbers of students who were more than willing to come to her office to volunteer information. (This statement would not have been very comforting to those students who were especially fearful of her authority at the school.) Yet, in spite of the strict discipline she always maintained, she had affection for the students, as well as an unfailing loyalty to the Eastman School and its director, Howard Hanson. In fact, many of the policies for which she was criticized were actually Hanson's directives. She felt it was her responsibility to see that his wishes were fulfilled. To the very end of her long tenure as dean of students, Flora Burton remained a woman of many contradictions, with student opinion of her ranging from genuine admiration to intense dislike.

To everyone, however, she was an unforgettable character. In her later years at the school she seemed to mellow somewhat and to show what many students perceived to be a little more understanding and flexibility. She eventually presided over the transition to coeducational dormitories and did so with her usual thoroughness and efficiency. Upon her retirement in 1972, this tribute by an unidentified student was included in the school's yearbook:

> My first remembrance of Eastman is Dean Burton and one of my last is Dean Burton. It was a comforting thought knowing that her door was always open for you. It was nice to know that you always could get lunch money even on a lean day. It was nice to know that there was an administrator who wouldn't hedge words with you and beat around the bush but would be honest and straightforward to you. It was nice to know that there was someone you could go to with a problem and know that more than likely she'd pick up the phone to solve the problem right then. Dean Burton never agreed with all of Eastman's innovations, but she never did fight progress to the death either. We shall never forget her for all she has done for us and for Eastman. We shall miss you, Dean Burton.[3]

---

[3]   *Eastman School of Music 50th Anniversary Year* (Rochester, NY: Eastman School of Music, 1972), 102.

In the earlier years of separate dormitories for men and women, the dean was responsible for maintaining the many strict rules and regulations governing student behavior. The men and women had separate dormitory councils to deal with various issues and problems in the residence halls. In addition to a dormitory council, the women had a social committee and a judiciary committee, the latter empowered to address infractions of the rules. Women had weekday and weekend curfews with a strict system of signing in and signing out after dinner, and disciplinary matters among female students most often involved students who were late returning to the dormitory.

By contrast, men could come and go as they pleased. Discipline and order were maintained by elected dormitory council officials and also by five resident assistants (then called "proctors"), one living on each floor of the dormitory. One of the few serious issues among the men involved alcohol consumption. Although the drinking age in New York State at the time was eighteen, alcoholic beverages were officially prohibited in all residence halls. Nonetheless, a fair amount of drinking took place, as might be expected among college students, and it was the proctors' unofficial responsibility to ensure that this was done discreetly and in moderation. Proctors also had to deal with occasional problems with noise after "quiet hours" had begun and with a seemingly endless series of college pranks, most of which were rather harmless.

In addition to the student leadership, a "house mother" was assigned to each of the dormitories. These women lived on the ground floor of their assigned dormitory, and they served not only as a social and civilizing influence but also as the on-site administrative official. The most difficult assignment was unquestionably to be house mother for the Men's Residence. One of the early incumbents was especially ill suited for the position and was sometimes seen wandering the upper-floor hallways in her housecoat during the late evening hours. One evening, however, she beat a hasty retreat after being confronted by a handful of naked young men. She was never again seen upstairs in the dorm, and her tenure as house mother was relatively brief.

The living areas in both the Men's Residence and the three women's dormitories were strictly off-limits to members of the opposite sex. However, there were several eagerly awaited open houses each year when guests of the opposite sex were permitted to visit student rooms for a limited amount of time. The rules for such occasions were very strict. Proctors and dormitory officers patrolled the corridors (sometimes referring to this task as "purity patrol"), and

Figure 21. Women's Residence Hall lounge.

doors were expected to be open at all times. There was no presumption of privacy, and a suspiciously closed door could be promptly opened by a proctor using his master key.

Social events at the Eastman School of Music most often took place at Cutler Union or at Hutchison House. The acquisition of Cutler Union greatly diminished the need for the Hutchison residence, although it continued to be used on occasion for recitals, musicales, and social events. The two sororities, Sigma Alpha Iota and Mu Phi Epsilon, and Phi Mu Alpha fraternity were fairly active at the time. The fraternity met for several years in a basement room at Hutchison House, then later held its meetings in Cutler Union. Regular day-to-day social life among students centered around the lounges and recreation rooms in the dormitories, principally in the women's residence halls. For a while the lounge in C House had the only television, and a mixed group of students was always on hand after dinner to watch their favorite television shows. At the time, all the lounges were beautifully furnished. There was an elegance to the public rooms that, unfortunately, was not maintained as the years passed.

The lounges and recreation rooms also provided space for many student groups, including the various religious organizations available to Catholic, Protestant, and Jewish students—organizations that were fairly active at the time. One of the most heavily attended events sometime around 1960 was a joint meeting of Catholic and Protestant students with their respective chaplains. This was considered an especially bold initiative at a time when ecumenism was not much of a priority among either Catholics or Protestants. In 1960 a chapel was dedicated in Howard Hanson's honor on the second floor of Cutler Union. Built with contributions from alumni and friends of the director, the chapel was far too small to provide space for regular worship services. And because of its location in Cutler Union rather than in the residence halls, it failed to become the meditation room envisioned by many of its benefactors.

There was a fairly high level of church attendance among the students. Although the school provided no on-campus chapel services on Sunday, the dormitories were located within easy walking distance of houses of worship of most denominations. Catholics could walk around the block to Main Street to attend Sunday Mass at Corpus Christi Church, although many preferred the longer walk downtown to Franklin Street to attend St. Joseph's, which was destroyed by fire in 1974. First Reformed Church was also on Main Street, and nearby on East Avenue were the First Church of Christ Scientist (Christian Science), Third Presbyterian Church, St. Paul's Episcopal Church, and Asbury First United Methodist Church. Presbyterians were especially well represented in the city. In addition to Third Presbyterian Church on East Avenue, there was First Presbyterian on South Plymouth Avenue, Central (Fourth) Presbyterian on North Plymouth, and Brick (Second) Presbyterian on North Fitzhugh Street. These three downtown Presbyterian congregations merged in 1974 and formed a new church, which they called Downtown United Presbyterian Church.

Baptists and Lutherans had to walk downtown for Sunday morning services, the former group to the Baptist Temple on North Street and the latter group to either Zion Lutheran or the Evangelical Lutheran Church of the Reformation. Both Lutheran congregations were on Grove Street, only about a two- or three-minute walk from the Eastman School. In 1962 Zion Lutheran closed its doors, merged with nearby Concordia Lutheran, and opened a beautiful new church on East Avenue, which was named the Lutheran Church of the Incarnate Word. Another prominent church close to the school was Christ Church on East Avenue, which later served briefly as the local Episcopal cathedral. Temple B'rith Kodesh, located on Gibbs Street across the street from the YMCA and in the same area as the two Lutheran congregations, was also conveniently situated for Eastman students. It was Rochester's oldest synagogue, having been founded in 1843 by German Jewish immigrants. In 1962 B'rith Kodesh moved to a new building on Elmwood Avenue, a considerable distance from the downtown area.

Sunday dinner was served after church rather than in the evening. Dormitory residents were provided with three meals only on Sunday and had to make their own arrangements for lunch Monday through Saturday. While breakfast was served cafeteria style, everyone was seated for dinner and served by a student waiter. There were four dining rooms, three for the women and one for the men. Students were expected to dress appropriately for Sunday dinner, and grace was either said or sung before dinner seven days a week. Some of the men eventually received permission to eat in the women's residence halls, but this concession was only a token gesture and did not lead to genuine coeducational dining.

There were constant complaints about the quality of the food at dinner. The Penguin Restaurant, just around the corner from the dormitories, enjoyed a rather consistent business from Eastman students, particularly on Sunday evenings. However, even when off campus, students were expected to behave in a proper manner. One evening a group of Eastman students, angry because a popular waitress had recently been fired, noisily walked out of the Penguin Restaurant to protest her dismissal. Although the students caused no damage and were not abusive in any way, the owners of the restaurant, Sid and Rosalie Bloom, were understandably upset by the protest and complained to Dean Burton. The offending students were summarily called to the dean's office the following day and told to make amends. The dean "suggested" that an array of cut flowers be sent to Mrs. Bloom as an appropriate gesture of apology. Needless to say, the students complied.

Members of the faculty, including the school's esteemed director and his wife, were occasional guests for dinner at the dormitory. They, too, complained about the meals, but nothing seemed to be done to improve the situation. Students, especially members of the dormitory councils, often registered their displeasure to the school dietician, but with little effect. A small crisis occurred with the publication of the 1960 yearbook, *The Score,* which included an unflattering picture of the dietician with an equally unflattering caption. Some changes were made, but institutional cooking tended to remain institutional cooking.

Finding a suitable place for lunch near the school was a relatively easy matter, since there were a number of inexpensive restaurants and luncheonettes in the downtown area. Students often patronized Turner's Coffee Shop (later Van Dyke Coffee Shop) or the Mid-Way Restaurant just west of the school on Main Street. The Mid-Way later relocated to East Avenue, where it continued to attract business from the Eastman community. Other students ate at the White Swan Restaurant opposite the Eastman Theatre[4] or at the Donut Center just east of the school on Main Street. When truly desperate because of a lack of available cash, students might occasionally have an inexpensive hamburger at the White Tower at the corner of Swan Street and East Avenue. The students' favorite place, however, was the Coffee Time Luncheonette on Gibbs Street, soon renamed the Koffee Break after its purchase by Fred and Helen Klein. For many years the Kleins catered to a highly appreciative student clientele, whether for breakfast, a midmorning cup of coffee, lunch, or a late afternoon piece of apple pie. Fred Klein rewarded his most loyal undergraduate customers each Christmas by pouring them a shot of whiskey in honor of the holidays.

The best meal in downtown Rochester was unquestionably at the YMCA on Gibbs Street. Its second-floor cafeteria was run for many years by a woman simply known to everyone as "Miss Sweeney," and the food was positively marvelous. It did an especially brisk business at dinnertime. Anyone arriving after about 5:45 P.M. would find the cafeteria line extending all the way down the staircase into the main lobby. It was well worth the wait, since the meals were at least as good as anything one could buy in a restaurant for three to four times the amount of money. When Miss Sweeney finally retired, the quality of the food quickly deteriorated, and the long lines of hungry customers disappeared.

For those preferring something other than cafeteria or luncheonette food, downtown Rochester offered a wide array of relatively good restaurants. Lorenzo's on Chestnut Street and Cutalli's on North Street were very popular Italian eating establishments. Eddie's Chop House on Main Street had a long tradition of serving excellent meals, and Chinese food was readily available at Lin Far's on East Avenue. Especially popular with Rochesterians was the Manhattan Restaurant on East Avenue near Main Street, which featured good and relatively inexpensive meals. The Manhattan, which had begun its existence as a cafeteria many years earlier, was

[4] The White Swan was originally located adjacent to the Eastman Theatre on the south side of Main Street, but it later relocated to the north side of Main Street.

a favorite destination for getting something to eat following an evening concert at the Eastman Theatre and was especially noted for its delicious chocolate pie. The Town & Country on Gibbs Street and the East Avenue Restaurant and Bar (commonly known as the "277" because of its address on East Avenue) were also popular post-concert destinations.

Further out Main Street and closer to the dormitories were the Roast Beef Tavern and the East Main Grill (commonly known as the "1076" because of its address). The 1076 was perhaps more popular among students as a location for having a couple of beers than it was for its food. Also popular for weekend partying was the "Gay Nineties Room" at the Treadway Inn on East Avenue at Alexander Street. All these places were within easy walking distance, an important consideration since relatively few undergraduate students had automobiles. Those with cars could go farther afield. Al's Green Tavern on North Goodman Street eventually became a very popular destination on Friday and Saturday evenings, especially with the fraternity crowd. Yet, students at the time were not averse to walking, even during the harshest winter weather. Some hearty souls even made the long trek to Fox's Deli up on Joseph Avenue when seized with an irresistible late-evening urge for a pastrami sandwich.

Students also walked to the various downtown movie theaters. At the time, Rochester could boast of five such theaters. Closest to the dormitories was the appropriately named Little Theatre on East Avenue, and closest to the school was the old Regent Theatre at the corner of East Avenue and Chestnut Street. But the big movie "palaces" were all on Clinton Avenue. The 4,000-seat Loew's Theatre, originally called the Rochester Theatre and by far the largest in the city, was on South Clinton on the site now occupied by the Xerox building. Just north of Main Street was the Paramount Theatre, which had begun its life as the Picadilly and later became the Century. Just up the street from the Paramount was the fabulous RKO Palace, widely considered Rochester's most beautiful and opulent theater (even in comparison with the Eastman Theatre). Its outer lobby—where patrons gathered to purchase tickets—featured mirrored walls, a frescoed ceiling, and a terrazzo floor, while its spacious inner lobby presented ticket holders with lush carpeting, crystal chandeliers, and an ornate arched ceiling. The eventual demolition of the Palace was a terrible loss to the city.[5] The building

---

[5]   Prior to the demolition of the building, the Rochester Theatre Organ Society rescued the theater's Wurlitzer organ, which had cost $75,000 when installed in 1928. Considered one of the finest theater organs ever built by Wurlitzer, it was moved to the Rochester Auditorium Theatre.

should have been preserved as an important downtown landmark. In fact, all these theaters, with the exception of the Little, were ultimately torn down.

The downtown area offered Eastman students much more than eating establishments and movie theaters, providing a wide array of different retailers. The two major department stores were Sibley, Lindsay & Curr and McCurdy & Co., which more or less faced one another in friendly competition on Main Street. A little further west was E. W. Edward's, and around the corner on Clinton Avenue South was the more upscale B. Foreman Company. Smaller clothing stores, such as McFarlin's, National Clothing, and Bond Clothing, were also located on Main Street, as were Neisner's and Woolworth's, which catered to the more budget-conscious buyer. Midtown Plaza opened in 1961, a cooperative endeavor by McCurdy's and Foreman's. It was reported to be the first indoor urban shopping plaza in the United States, and it attracted considerable attention from other cities throughout the country.

At least a half dozen banks were available for student accounts, although most students chose either First Federal Savings & Loan or Genesee Valley Union Trust,[6] which faced one another from opposite sides of Main Street near the intersection of East Avenue. Some students may have been attracted to Rochester Savings Bank at the corner of North and Franklin. Its interior featured a painted wood-coffered ceiling, marble columns, glass mosaics on the walls, and a marble mosaic floor. Rochester Savings Bank was designed by the same architects who had been responsible for the Eastman Theatre, and it remains one of Rochester's most beautiful building interiors.

Scrantom's Book and Stationery Store was next door to First Federal Savings & Loan, and it was an especially popular place for browsing and shopping for books, stationery, office supplies, greeting cards, and sundry other gift and hobby items. In addition, students had easy access to a drug store (Daw Drugs), a grocery store (Pavone's Market), a camera shop (Main Camera), and a dry cleaner (Vogue Cleaners), as well as several barbershops, shoe stores, gift shops, and jewelry stores—all conveniently located within a block or two of the Eastman School.

The purchase of music and scores was facilitated by three downtown music stores, each more anxious than the others for Eastman student business. Levis Music Store, diagonally across from the Eastman Theatre, was perhaps the largest of the three. Mook Music

---

[6] Genesee Valley Union Trust later became Marine Midland Bank and, more recently, HSBC Bank.

Company, opposite the school on Gibbs Street, had a smaller selection, but its stock often included European editions that were otherwise difficult to obtain. Music Lovers' Shoppe served the needs of Eastman students particularly well. Originally on the north side of Main Street, it moved to slightly larger facilities on the south side of the street before eventually abandoning the downtown area for the suburbs. Max Goode, who came to know the music publishing business better than anyone else in town, ably assisted Eastman students in all three locations.

Movie theaters, restaurants, department stores, and many other retailers helped make Rochester a rather pleasant location for Eastman students. Some undoubtedly wished for a more enriching campus life, and some found dormitory living somewhat repressive. But these were the 1950s, and gender-segregated housing and curfews were policies not limited to the Eastman School of Music. Those from large urban areas such as New York or Boston sometimes complained about Rochester's small-town, conservative atmosphere, yet student life was greatly enhanced by the availability of so many downtown businesses, eating establishments, and movie theaters. In addition, the grounds surrounding Cutler Union, including several tennis courts, provided at least the illusion of a "campus." These were probably among the very best years for student living at the Eastman School.

Yet, the years were not without difficulties and serious incidents. Perhaps the most bizarre incident in the school's history occurred during the first month of school in the fall of 1960. Toward the end of September, rumors began to circulate that there had been a plot to blow up the Eastman School of Music. Although most students initially refused to believe the tale because it seemed so implausible, there was quick confirmation that two young women had been arrested by the Rochester police department and charged with possession of explosives, endangering human lives by placing explosives near a building, conspiring to commit a crime, and possession of loaded revolvers. Law enforcement officers had recovered three hundred pounds of dynamite.

Everyone was amazed to learn that one of the conspirators was an Eastman undergraduate student and the other an Eastman alumna and a member of the Rochester Philharmonic Orchestra who had recently dropped out of graduate study at the school. The two young women were sent to the Rochester State Hospital for psychiatric evaluation and were arraigned in early December. Their plan to destroy or at least severely damage the Eastman School of Music had been uncovered when they offered a school employee

$5,000 for his help with placing the dynamite in the building. They later pleaded guilty to a misdemeanor charge of conspiracy, with the older woman also pleading guilty to a misdemeanor charge of possessing two pistols without a permit. Incredibly, the felony charge of possessing dynamite with intent to use it unlawfully was dropped. Each woman received a one-year suspended sentence plus three years' probation, and both agreed to undergo psychiatric treatment. This relatively light punishment led to much conversation and speculation among Eastman students in the weeks following the announcement of the verdict.

During the following school year, a more tragic event stunned the entire school community just at the time when classes had ended and students were preparing for final examinations. Donald Dodge, a junior trombone major from Niles, Michigan, drowned in Lake Ontario. Well-liked by everyone who knew him, Dodge was the U.S. men's single kayak champion in 1961. On May 24 he went to Durand-Eastman Beach to practice the sport in which he excelled to such a high degree. He put his boat into the cold waters of Lake Ontario at about 1:45 P.M. and headed west against the current toward Charlotte Pier, but he never arrived. Four U.S. Coast Guard boats searched for him, as did the Irondequoit police, and Eastman students organized a search later in the evening that covered about twenty miles of shoreline from Durand-Eastman all the way to Pultneyville to the east of Rochester. Unfortunately, these efforts were in vain, and his body was not recovered until June 13. It was a terrible and inexplicable loss that deeply affected the entire Eastman School community, students and faculty alike.

In the fall of 1962 Eastman students joined the rest of the country in enduring the fears and anxieties caused by the Cuban missile crisis. In late August an American spy plane had detected a new series of surface-to-air missiles under construction in Cuba. Then, on October 14, American reconnaissance showed the construction of a site for Soviet medium-range ballistic missiles on Cuban soil. On October 22 President John F. Kennedy faced the nation in a televised address, informing Americans of the seriousness of the issue and announcing a naval quarantine of Cuba. The crisis continued to unfold when an American spy plane was shot down. At the same time Soviet merchant ships, presumably carrying missiles, were approaching Cuban waters. All of these events are commonly thought to have brought the United States and the Soviet Union to the brink of nuclear war. It was a dangerous game of "brinkmanship," and everyone breathed a great sigh of relief when the Soviet merchant ships turned around and avoided a confrontation with the blockading American naval forces. During the crisis, however, there was widespread anxiety and fear. Yet, most students continued to go to the annex to practice, even those who may have wondered if mastering that tortuous passage in Brahms or Prokofiev might be the last thing they accomplished before World War III began.

If the events in October 1962 represented an averted crisis, the summer of 1964 brought a real crisis to Rochester. On July 24, while the Eastman summer session was fully in operation, a serious urban disturbance broke out in the city's seventh ward centering around Joseph Avenue. The ensuing violence and looting continued for about sixty hours, during which time four people lost their lives. In addition, there were more than 350 injuries, 800 arrests, and at least $1 million in property damage. Fueled by serious underlying social and economic conditions, the resulting civic unrest was quelled only when the National Guard was called in to restore order and keep the peace. Rochester's positive self-image, fostered by years of complacency, prosperity, and exemplary labor-management relations, had been dealt a severe blow.

There were few indications of these events in the downtown area or near the Eastman residence halls when students returned for the new school year in September. The rioting had taken place mostly in the city's third and seventh wards, away from the school, the dormitories, and the central retail area. But Rochester would never quite be the same, although the changes were so gradual as to be almost unnoticed at first. Nonetheless, the exodus to the suburbs accelerated, especially among the more affluent city dwellers who could best sustain downtown retailing. Movie theaters and familiar restaurants slowly began to disappear from city streets, as did many of the retailers. The Penguin is the only previously mentioned downtown restaurant still open for business.[7] Al's Green Tavern can still be found on North Goodman Street. Not one of the previously mentioned retailers remains in downtown Rochester, and only one (Music Lovers' Shoppe) remains in business as a suburban store.

Downtown retail business was further damaged by the construction of suburban malls, first relatively small strip malls but then larger retail centers with branches of downtown stores such as Sibley's and McCurdy's. The events of July 1964 were not the cause of these changes, nor were they even particularly a catalyst. Civic unrest was simply a symptom of larger social issues that would affect not only Rochester but countless other cities as well, especially in the northeast.

[7]   A change in ownership in early 2008 has resulted in a new name for this long-standing business.

Student life was changing at Eastman, and not only because of urban unrest. The civil rights movement and anti-war protests would involve students and transform student life on campuses throughout the United States. The earlier Kinsey report, the "pill," and the sexual revolution rapidly changed attitudes concerning student social life and sexual behavior. The Eastman School administration was probably no quicker than the students' parents in either recognizing or approving of what was happening among young people, but they were unable to alter the course of events. Institutions of higher learning soon abandoned the idea that they somehow served "in loco parentis," and coeducational dormitory living became more and more common throughout the country. While the prevalence of the use of alcoholic beverages among students remained a concern, an entirely new meaning would soon be given to the expression "substance abuse." Even the Eastman School of Music, with its conservative history, gradually acceded to the changing times. And even Dean Burton had to adapt.

Twenty years after Munro Hall had been converted into the Men's Residence, it would have been difficult to find anyone among the new generation of undergraduates who would have understood the concept of a judiciary committee that punished students for breaking curfew. Curfews were a thing of the past, along with many of the rules and expectations that had governed earlier student life in the residence halls. Life had changed at the Eastman School of Music. Downtown Rochester had also changed. The healthy interaction between the Eastman student body and the downtown economy was coming to an end.

Chapter 9

1954–72

Summer Session

When Raymond Wilson retired in 1953, he relinquished a number of very important positions at the school. During his long tenure as an administrator and a member of the faculty, Wilson had accumulated many responsibilities, including chair of the piano faculty, director of the summer session, and director of the preparatory department.[1] Following his retirement, Cecile Genhart served with distinction as head of the piano faculty, while Charles Riker, one of Howard Hanson's closest friends, assumed directorship of the preparatory department. Allen Irvine McHose took over the summer session responsibilities.

The differences between McHose and his predecessor could not have been more striking. Raymond Wilson was essentially a facilitator. No one ever served the Eastman School of Music with more dedication and loyalty. As a member of the original Eastman faculty, Wilson had been a central player in the school's development since it first opened its doors to students. Wilson was a dedicated and meticulous teacher and also an administrator with a passion for detail and organization. He had even served as acting director of the school following Alf Klingenberg's resignation in 1923. Somehow, Wilson managed to chair the piano department and to give lessons to ten piano majors each week (technically a half-schedule at the time) while also administering a preparatory department program that had a typical annual enrollment of more than 1,000 children and adults from the Rochester community and its surrounding areas.

His approach to the responsibilities of directing such a large program of instruction was to maintain especially tight control over his faculty, but he earned the respect of those with whom he worked (although to many faculty colleagues he remained "Mr. Wilson"

[1] As previously noted, Wilson was also assistant director of the Eastman School of Music, a position that entailed less specific responsibilities.

Figure 22. Allen Irvine McHose, director of the summer session.

rather than "Raymond"). He accomplished his administrative tasks with a relatively small staff, probably at great personal sacrifice by putting in exceptionally long hours at the school. It has been estimated, for example, that he may have heard as many as 30,000 preparatory and collegiate piano examinations during his career at Eastman. To have accomplished all this while also being responsible for the school's summer sessions was a remarkable achievement.

Allen Irvine McHose had been associated with the Eastman School of Music almost as long as Wilson had, first as a student and then as a member of the faculty. Over the years he had earned Howard Hanson's friendship and respect. When Hanson selected him to head the summer session, McHose had just completed his twenty-fifth year on the faculty. If Wilson could be described as a facilitator, McHose was more of an innovator, and he immediately brought his creativity and energy to bear in providing the summer session with fresh ideas and new programs. He understood that many of the questions and problems facing him in this new position were interrelated. He could not attract students for summer study without the availability of faculty members with whom those students might wish to study. Conversely, he could not maintain a strong faculty for summer teaching without being able to offer his teachers satisfactory employment opportunities and adequate compensation. To achieve his goals, McHose wanted to make the summer session a stimulating educational experience and an exciting place for everyone, students and faculty alike. To a large extent, he succeeded in achieving this goal. Edward Easley, the director of admissions at Eastman for many years, accurately described McHose when he remarked that "he may have been the most creative administrative person at the school."[2]

One important component for the summers was already in place for McHose, although not officially under Eastman School sponsorship. That component was "Opera under the Stars," which presented free opera productions in Rochester's Highland Park. The idea for a series of outdoor opera performances arose from a meeting between Leonard Treash, director of Eastman's opera department, and Thomas McCarthy, president of the Rochester Musicians' Association. Treash and McCarthy developed a plan to present free opera for the benefit of the Rochester community, a plan that also would provide invaluable performance opportunities for young opera students and recent graduates of the Eastman School of Music. Several local precedents for outdoor opera during the summer months may have encouraged Treash and McCarthy. Eighteen years earlier a New York opera company had presented Bizet's *Carmen* and Verdi's *Rigoletto* at the Rochester Red Wing's baseball stadium, and the following year the San Carlo Opera Company had done an entire week of outdoor opera productions at the University of Rochester. Unfortunately, these promising initiatives during the 1930s did not lead to any similar endeavors until Treash and McCarthy developed their plans almost two decades later.

[2] Edward Easley, interview by the author, Rochester, NY, May 24, 2004.

Figure 23. Opera under the Stars rehearsal in Highland Park.

The plan for summer opera in Rochester was initially a cooperative endeavor involving sponsorship by the city and the participation of the Rochester Musicians' Association, which agreed to
provide funds for the opera orchestra through its allotment from
the Music Performance Trust Fund. The trust originated in 1948 to
help address the loss of employment by thousands of musicians
throughout the country as a result of recent technological changes,
particularly the introduction of the long-playing record, which
replaced a great deal of live music in the marketplace. The trust
came into existence as an agreement between the American Federation of Musicians and the recording industry, and it made a provision for the industry to pay a royalty from the sale of recordings to
a newly created fund dedicated to the public interest.

The local Rochester Musicians' Association, therefore, was able to
use its allotment from the trust to pay the salaries of the orchestral
musicians who would play for the summer opera performances.
Leonard Treash and various members of the Eastman School faculty
and staff would donate their services, and local industries and businesses would underwrite the remaining financial costs. The plan
should serve as a model of what can be accomplished when various interested parties are willing to cooperate by pooling resources.
Plans for the inaugural season during the summer of 1953 called for
two opera productions, *La Bohème* by Giacomo Puccini (1858–1924)

and *La Traviata* by Giuseppe Verdi (1813–1901), each of which would have two performances. Audiences estimated at between 10,000 and 15,000 people attended each evening of opera in the park.

The Opera under the Stars series was expanded in 1954 to include two performances each of three different operas: Puccini's *Madama Butterfly, The Marriage of Figaro* by Wolfgang Amadeus Mozart (1756–91), and *Die Fledermaus* by Johann Strauss II (1825–99).[3] (The City of Rochester provided an added service for these performances by liberally spraying the area for mosquitoes prior to each performance.) Opera under the Stars continued to produce three operas each summer until 1960. At that time, however, the orchestral musicians demanded a significant increase in pay, essentially asking for twice as much money as they had previously been paid for accompanying the opera productions. In fairness to the musicians, they were dreadfully underpaid for their services. Since additional funding was not available, the only way to avoid a cancellation of the season was to reduce the number of summer opera productions. The musicians, therefore, could be paid at a higher rate for each rehearsal and each performance, but there would be fewer rehearsals and performances. As a result, Opera under the Stars produced only two operas in 1960 and again in 1961 before, happily, the third opera production was restored in 1962.

With a summer opera season already in place when he assumed leadership of the summer session, McHose decided to also establish a small chamber orchestra to present a series of concerts in Kilbourn Hall under the direction of Frederick Fennell. The establishment of the Eastman Chamber Orchestra helped ensure that McHose would have a complete faculty to teach the summer session, as well as providing an appropriate vehicle for Fennell's talents. (When Fennell left the Eastman faculty a number of years later, several other conductors led the summer orchestra, including Richard Bales, Clyde Roller, Willis Page, and Walter Hendl.) The orchestra personnel involved about thirty players. Several were prominent members of the Eastman School faculty, including John Celentano, Donald Knaub, Eileen Malone, William Osseck, Morris Secon, Millard Taylor, Francis Tursi, and Oscar Zimmerman. Most of these musicians also played with the Rochester Philharmonic Orchestra during the regular season. Other members of the new chamber orchestra included people such as Jon Engberg, who later served for twenty years as associate director of the Eastman School of Music; Raymond

---

[3] A complete listing of the Opera under the Stars productions from 1953 through 1972 is given in Appendix 2.

Gniewek, who was later the concertmaster of the Metropolitan Opera Orchestra for many years; and Walfrid Kujala, who soon became a member of the Chicago Symphony Orchestra and a member of the faculty at Northwestern University's School of Music. The orchestra personnel in subsequent years also included other prominent Eastman teachers such as John Beck, Alan Harris, Ronald Leonard, Joseph Mariano, and John Thomas.

The Eastman Chamber Orchestra featured very interesting programming, including works not customarily heard in Rochester Philharmonic concerts during the regular concert season. For example, the program for the concert on July 2, 1959, included Mozart's Overture to *The Abduction from the Seraglio,* Sinfonia in B-flat Major by Johann Christian Bach (1735–82), Symphony No. 97 by Joseph Haydn (1732–1809), the Suite No. 1 of Ottorino Respighi (1879–1936), *Pavane* Op. 50 by Gabriel Fauré (1845–1924), and the *Rumanian Folk Dances* of Béla Bartók (1881–1945). Summer concerts often featured soloists, principally drawn from the Eastman faculty. During the 1959 summer session, for example, soloists included soprano Josephine Antoine, who sang selected songs of Henri Duparc (1848–1933), and cellist Ronald Leonard, who performed the Concerto for Cello, Op. 129, by Robert Schumann (1810–56). Programming, especially during Fennell's years as conductor of the orchestra, was always imaginative and concerts were well attended, not only by faculty and students but also by members of the Rochester community.

The establishment of the Eastman Chamber Orchestra was also necessary to support the instructional needs of a series of new institutes McHose was designing for music supervisors and conductors. Four such institutes were introduced in 1954: the Band Institute, the Orchestra Institute, the String Institute, and the Choral Institute. Designed to provide practical conducting experience, each institute consisted of a conducting seminar to discuss preparation of a musical score, an instrumental or choral seminar to provide the opportunity for interaction with Eastman teachers and performers, and an institute ensemble for practical application of the principles under discussion. The four institutes for band, orchestra, string, and choral directors were annual summer events for about the next half-dozen years, until McHose sensed that music educators wanted a more intense exploration of materials and performance issues. Therefore, in 1961 he developed a more comprehensive offering of institutes for brass, woodwind, string, vocal, and choral teachers.

Another new initiative in 1954 was the Composers' Workshop, which consisted of lectures, personal conferences with faculty members, and performance sessions for reading student scores followed by comments and suggestions from the faculty performers. Once again, the establishment of the Eastman Chamber Orchestra was a necessary step toward providing faculty performers for the workshop. Subsequent workshops for composers often featured distinguished guest faculty, including Henry Cowell, Alan Hohvaness, Burrill Phillips, and George Rochberg. Members of the nonresident faculty who came to Rochester to teach for McHose often lived in the Eastman residence halls, where they shared dormitory living and food with the summer students.

Other new summer programs introduced by McHose included workshops for piano teachers and church musicians. The Piano Teachers' Workshop was held for nineteen consecutive years beginning in 1957. Harold Weiss, a member of the Eastman School of Music piano department, was involved in all but the last of these annual workshops, serving in the official capacity of workshop coordinator beginning with the ninth workshop in 1965. The piano workshops traditionally drew upon the talent and expertise of the resident Eastman faculty rather than depending on outside guests and clinicians. Nonetheless, there were occasional guest faculty, including Eugene List, who later joined the Eastman faculty in 1964 as professor of piano and chair of the piano department. Other special guests included Eastman alumna and noted educator and composer Merle Montgomery (MM '37, PhD '48), who took part in the 1960 workshop, and Joan Last from the Royal Academy of Music, a guest lecturer in 1964. Willard Palmer, well-known to piano teachers as a clinician and editor of popular teaching editions, lectured at the sixteenth annual Piano Teachers' Workshop in 1972.

Those who registered for the piano workshops were able to enjoy the concerts and recitals scheduled during the workshop week. In 1960, for example, there were three such performances, the first featuring fourteen-year-old pianist Joella Jones,[4] a remarkably talented young woman who was studying with José Echániz at the time. Duo-pianists Joyce and Joanne Weintraub, third-year students at the school studying with Harry Watts, presented a recital two nights later, and Eugene List appeared the next evening as soloist with the Eastman Chamber Orchestra. Workshop registrants also had the opportunity to attend a performance of Gounod's *Faust* at Highland Park two evenings after the orchestra concert. These musical evenings helped support the experience and benefits of attending

---

[4] Joella Jones is currently pianist with the Cleveland Orchestra and a member of the faculty at the Cleveland Institute of Music.

the workshop, as well as enhancing the enjoyment of being a summer student at the Eastman School of Music. McHose hoped this would encourage people to consider returning for future summer study at Eastman.

A Church Music Workshop was introduced in 1957 under the direction of David Craighead. McHose was particularly attuned to the world of church music, since he was a church organist at Brick Presbyterian Church in Rochester. In 1958 separate sections for Catholics and Protestants were offered at the workshop, acknowledging that the musical needs for worship varied considerably between the two Christian groups. Craighead taught the Protestants while the Reverend Benedict Ehmann taught the Catholics. Ehmann was a priest in the Rochester Roman Catholic Diocese, whose knowledge and deep love for music and liturgy had served him well as a pastor and teacher. He had a special affinity for Gregorian chant and was widely known for his early advocacy and support for the liturgical movement in the United States. Father Ehmann's warm, friendly manner was always in evidence during his many years as a priest, and he retained his intellectual curiosity and enthusiasm for learning well into his nineties, much to the delight of his many friends. In 1959 McHose attempted to expand the constituency for the Church Music Workshop by restructuring it as a workshop for "church and synagogue." To provide for the instruction of prospective Jewish students, McHose engaged Dr. Eric Werner, professor of sacred music at Hebrew Union College. In 1962, however, separate workshop sessions for Jewish and Catholic students were discontinued, and within a few years the constituency for the Church Music Workshop appeared to have run its course.

Another interesting and successful initiative was the Music Library Workshop, first offered in 1957 along with the workshops for church musicians and piano teachers. It was the first such workshop offered in the United States, although music librarians were generally members of the Music Library Association and attended its national meetings. However, a forum that would specifically deal with the problems and issues of a music library was a unique and appealing idea. Information concerning the proposed workshop was sent to deans of colleges and universities as well as to directors and curators of various libraries and public institutions, and more than two dozen participants attended the 1957 workshop. They included librarians from Harvard University, the University of Minnesota, the University of California at Berkeley, Ohio State University, Chicago Musical College, Hartt College of Music, the Cleveland Institute of Music, New England Conservatory, and the New York Public Library.

Speakers and discussion moderators at the workshop included Charles Warren Fox, professor of musicology at Eastman and editor of the *Journal of the American Musicological Society;* Pauline Alderman, chair of the department of music literature at the University of Southern California; Elizabeth Smith, reference librarian at Sibley Music Library; Margaret Toth, editor of the University of Rochester Press; Fred G. Tessin from the C. W. Homeyer Company; Lockrem Johnson, director of library service for C. F. Peters Corporation, and Charles Hendry, educational representative for Associated Music Publishers. The highlight of this first workshop for music librarians, however, was a presentation by Harold Spivacke, chief of the music division at the Library of Congress. Spivacke spoke of the various services the Library of Congress offered as well as discussing copyright issues. Encouraged by his initial success, McHose offered the Music Library Workshop in several subsequent summer sessions.

None of Allen Irvine McHose's summer initiatives proved more successful or more popular than the Arrangers' Holiday Concert, which first took place during the 1959 summer session. The concert was a project of the Arrangers' Laboratory Institute, also new in 1959, and featured arrangements by institute participants. The institute faculty was headed by Eastman alumnus Rayburn Wright (BM '43), who later became involved with the development of the jazz degree programs at Eastman. Wright was associated with Radio City Music Hall at the time of the first Arrangers' Holiday Concert, having joined the staff there as an arranger in 1950. He became chief arranger in 1956 and was later appointed co-director of music, a position he held from 1965 until he accepted a full-time appointment at Eastman in 1970. As members of the summer session faculty in 1959, Wright and his colleagues provided instruction in radio and television techniques, scoring for film, and various issues facing school music teachers and professional arrangers. The Arrangers' Holiday Concert was the culmination of these activities, and it was an eagerly awaited event for Rochester audiences each year. These concerts featured some of the country's most renowned jazz artists as guest performers, including the Dave Brubeck Quartet, Duke Ellington, Dizzy Gillespie, Carmen McRae, Marian McPartland, and the Billy Taylor Trio.

Also new in 1959 was the Saxophone Workshop with Sigurd Rascher. Born in Germany, Rascher had taught in Denmark and Sweden before coming to the United States in 1938. In 1939 he appeared with both the Boston Symphony Orchestra and the New York Philharmonic Orchestra, the first saxophonist to perform as a soloist with either organization. He soon achieved a wide reputation

Figure 24. Rayburn Wright (seated) and Donald Hunsberger.

throughout the world, and several important composers such as Paul Hindemith (1895–1963), Jacques Ibert (1890–1962), and Darius Milhaud (1892–1974) dedicated compositions to him. Rascher taught at Eastman for seven consecutive summer sessions and attracted a large number of enthusiastic students. However, he was strictly a classical saxophonist and therefore had no role in Rayburn Wright's Arrangers' Workshop. This was perfectly suitable for the Eastman School of Music at the time. Howard Hanson had no particular fondness for jazz, and the development of a jazz program at the school would not occur until after his retirement.

Another McHose initiative was the Music Executives' Institute. Designed for music executives at universities, colleges, and conservatories, it was first offered during the 1962 summer session. Its presenters included Earl Moore, dean emeritus of the School of Music at the University of Michigan; Howard Anderson, former provost of the University of Rochester; LaRoy Thompson, vice president and treasurer of the University of Rochester; Vincent Duckles, president of the Music Library Association; Henry Steinway, president of Steinway Piano Company; Richard Bosse, president of the National Association of Band Instrument Manufacturers; and Charles Lutton, from Lutton Music Personnel Service. The institute was repeated during several additional summer sessions.

A very special summer session event in 1966 brought national attention to the Eastman School of Music: a two-week workshop-institute in the Suzuki method, attended by string teachers from all fifty states and Canada. The workshop-institute was connected with Project Super (Suzuki in Penfield, Eastman, Rochester), which examined whether the Suzuki approach, which had been so successful in Japan, could be applied to American students. Partially supported by grants from the New York State Council on the Arts and the National Endowment for the Arts and Humanities, it was the first controlled research project outside Japan to involve the direct participation of Shinichi Suzuki. Project Super was coordinated by Donald Shetler and involved one hundred six-year-old students drawn from the Eastman School's preparatory department and the public schools in Rochester and Penfield. Suzuki returned to Rochester three times during the 1966–67 school year to evaluate the students' progress, and Suzuki-method instruction became deeply rooted in the Rochester area, including in the Eastman School's preparatory department. Anastasia Jempelis later served for many years as director of the school's Suzuki program.

All of these programs were designed for teachers, music executives, music librarians, and other music professionals. In addition, the summer session also offered opportunities for continuation of Eastman degree study, including dissertation research, as well as opportunities for those who simply wanted to enroll for lessons. There was a fairly large demand for lessons during the summer, with many students choosing to register for noncredit instruction through the school's preparatory department. However, there was another program that was intended to attract a very different kind of student. The Accelerated Bachelor of Music Program, first offered in 1956, was designed to allow gifted young music students to begin college-level study for the bachelor of music degree after their junior year of high school. Majors were offered in applied music (i.e., performance),[5] composition, theory, history of music, and public school music (i.e., music education). The program entailed attending the two summer sessions following the junior and senior years of high school, then completing the bachelor of music curriculum in three years of collegiate study. Each of the two summers featured a curriculum consisting of lessons (vocal or instrumental) and intensive study of theory and music history, plus participation in an ensemble such as band, orchestra, or chorus.

The new program, perhaps the first of its kind in the country, was highly significant in that it was the first serious attempt to bring

---

[5] Organ was the only instrumental area not available to students in this program.

high school students to Rochester during the summer months to live and study at the Eastman School of Music. In some respects, however, it was based on a rather dubious premise. While it was possible to accelerate the acquisition of theoretical skills and knowledge of music history during two summers, it was very unlikely that a total of twelve weeks of instrumental or vocal lessons could possibly substitute for a full year of collegiate lessons. Many of these "accelerated" students found that they really needed to spend four complete academic years at the school before graduating with the bachelor of music degree. The accelerated program lasted about a dozen years before it was discontinued.

The Eastman School subsequently returned to offering resident programs of study for high school students, but they involved programs specifically designed for the pre-college student rather than an attempt to jump-start the bachelor of music degree. These later programs for high school students, which began in the early 1970s, were coordinated by the Eastman School's preparatory department and did not carry academic credit. They were among the very first programs in the United States that brought pre-collegiate students to a college campus for a summer of intensive music study, and more than thirty years later they remain a very important part of the school's summer session.

Allen Irvine McHose retired at the end of the 1966–67 school year, having made very significant contributions to the school during his thirty-nine years on the faculty. He deserves to be especially remembered for his creative and innovative direction of the summer session for fourteen years. The man chosen to replace McHose as director of the summer session was Daniel Patrylak, McHose's assistant director at the time. Patrylak had earned his bachelor of music and master of music degrees at Eastman, as well as a performer's certificate in trumpet. When offered a summer session job teaching trumpet at a rather nominal hourly rate, his honest response was that he needed more money. Therefore, McHose hired him to call on the public schools throughout the Rochester area in an effort to increase business for the preparatory department. His success in doing so led to his appointment as assistant director. He now became McHose's successor as director.

Patrylak was not fully in charge of the summer session until 1968. By that time there were problems to be addressed and many serious challenges to be faced, not the least of which was the necessity of honestly assessing the viability of the various institutes and workshops being offered by the school. The distinction between an institute and a workshop involved the duration of the program as well as the number of credits earned by registrants. Workshops, such as those for music librarians, piano teachers, and church musicians, tended to be a week in length for one credit hour, while institutes were generally two or three weeks long for three credits. The cost of a credit hour in 1954, McHose's first year, was only twenty-three dollars. Twelve years later it was fifty dollars, and it rose to eighty-eight dollars in 1972. These figures sound unbelievably low in comparison with current educational costs, which can approach $1,000 per credit hour. Yet, the price for studying at the Eastman School was rising at a rather relentless rate, a factor that did little to encourage enrollment.

It was becoming increasingly expensive to run the Eastman School's summer session. Also, the success of its various institutes and workshops had spawned a large number of imitators that were now in direct competition for summer session students. Many Eastman workshops that had originally attracted students from a wide geographic area had become more and more regional in nature and some (such as the Piano Teachers' Workshop) fairly local. It was difficult, for example, to convince piano teachers in St. Louis, Missouri, or Atlanta, Georgia, to attend a workshop at the Eastman School of Music when something similar might be offered much nearer to their homes. Cost and competition were important factors governing decisions about the viability of the workshops and institutes.

At the same time, the school's preparatory department, which provided a significant number of students for the summer session, was beginning to experience serious problems that led to a steady decline in enrollment. Part of this situation might be attributed to the gradual loss of city residents who were slowly abandoning Rochester for its suburbs, but much of the problem was self-inflicted. Neither Walter Hendl, then director of the school, nor the central university administration saw much justification or benefit for supporting and maintaining a large noncredit program that mainly involved the teaching of pre-college students. This resulted in an extended period of relative neglect and lack of support for the department, coupled with unreasonably high yearly tuition increases. As a result, preparatory department enrollment plummeted, affecting not only the regular school year[6] but also the number of students willing to register for summer lessons.[7]

---

[6] For example, there were 1,137 preparatory department students during the regular 1961–62 school year but only 827 ten years later. Enrollment continued to drop in subsequent years, eventually reaching a low of 470 in 1975.
[7] For further discussion of the decline of the school's preparatory department, please refer to Chapter 12.

These were some (but certainly not all) of the issues facing Daniel
Patrylak as he took over responsibilities as summer session director. Of almost immediate concern was the fact that the chamber
orchestra was costing far too much, something the central administration of the University of Rochester had noted with considerable
concern. At the same time, the future of Opera under the Stars was
very much in doubt. To prevent the demise of summer opera, the
Eastman School of Music had to become its official producer. While
city and county funds continued to be allocated for summer opera
productions for a time, the school had to subsidize the endeavor
to keep it afloat. In an effort to consolidate and control expendi-
tures, Patrylak reduced the number of summer chamber orchestra concerts to two programs while hiring the same musicians to
accompany the opera productions. Beginning in 1968, all summer
concerts, including the opera performances and what remained of
the summer orchestra season, were packaged under the umbrella of
"A Summer Music Festival."

The 1968 summer session—Patrylak's first as director—included
a six-week comprehensive String Institute, two three-week institutes
(the Arrangers' Workshop and the Arrangers' Laboratory Institute),
plus a two-week Music Executives' Institute. In addition, there
were nine one-week workshops, eight of which were new summer
session offerings. Included in the new offerings were workshops
in Kodály and Orff techniques for music teachers, a stage band
workshop, an orchestral librarians' laboratory, and a workshop for
concert managers. Kodály and Orff workshops were repeated two
years later, as was the workshop for orchestral librarians. New in
1970 was a Recording Institute attended by seventy students. Patrylak had been instrumental in establishing a new, modern recording studio at Eastman and in placing playback equipment in faculty
studios. The new summer institute was an effort to exploit these
new resources at the school.

Despite attempts to find a steady constituency for the summer
session, however, it was becoming increasingly difficult to market
programs patterned after McHose's successful mix of workshops
and institutes. By 1971 the number of institutes and workshops
offered at the Eastman School summer session had declined to a
mere six. All this is dramatically reflected in summer enrollment
statistics. Summer session enrollment in 1967 was 1,111 students.
In 1971 it was 429. Cost and competition—and increasing opportunities for Eastman faculty to teach elsewhere during the summer months—were taking their toll. In truth, it would be difficult
to build an argument in favor of teaching or studying at Eastman

during the summer rather than at Aspen or Tanglewood, for example. The growth of summer festivals and music camps, in both the United States and Europe, presented a new kind of competition for the Eastman summer session. Moreover, the school's administration began to see the wisdom of having its faculty spread across the country in various programs and at diverse festivals, bringing the Eastman name to a much larger number of potential undergraduate and graduate students than they could possibly do by remaining in town.

Of course, the summer session survived at Eastman, although it eventually became something rather different from what Allen Irvine McHose had envisioned back in 1954. There were always students working on completion of their degrees or on dissertation research and school music teachers taking courses toward their master's degree in music education. And increasing numbers of pre-college students were living in the school's dormitories and taking summer classes and lessons, playing in chamber music groups, or participating in jazz ensembles. Summer at the Eastman School of Music had simply adapted to changing times.

Chapter 10

1961–62

The Eastman Philharmonia's European Tour

The Eastman Philharmonia was founded in the fall of 1958 as an orchestra of about sixty-five players drawn from the very best available talent at the Eastman School of Music. It was not designed to replace either of the two existing orchestras, a senior symphony and a junior symphony, simply known as Orchestra I and Orchestra II. Paul White was the conductor of the former group and Frederick Fennell the conductor of the latter. The new orchestra would have Howard Hanson as its director. The debut performance of the Eastman Philharmonia took place in the Eastman Theatre on October 24, 1958. The program consisted of Rossini's Overture to *Semiramide,* Purcell's *Diocletian Suite,* Stravinsky's *Firebird Suite,* Beethoven's *Leonora Overture No. 3,* Debussy's *Prelude to the Afternoon of a Faun,* and Sibelius's *Finlandia*—repertoire well chosen to highlight the talented young musicians who had been selected as members of the new orchestra.

There is little doubt that Hanson was influenced by the success of the Eastman Wind Ensemble in wanting to form a student orchestra whose members represented the most outstanding talent at the school, selected strictly by audition and with no regard for seniority. Perhaps he even envied Fennell's success with the wind group. But the idea that the school's student population could support a third orchestra proved impractical, and after a short while the situation reverted back to a senior orchestra and a junior orchestra. However, they were now called the Eastman Philharmonia and the Eastman School Symphony Orchestra rather than Orchestra I and Orchestra II. There was powerful psychology behind the new name, and Hanson unquestionably elevated the playing of his senior orchestra by creating the strong suggestion (or reinforcing the notion) that this was indeed an elite group of performing musicians.

In addition to its regular programs in the Eastman Theatre, during its first few seasons the Eastman Philharmonia also gave concerts at several other locations in Rochester, such as the Memorial Art Gallery and the University of Rochester's Strong Auditorium. The orchestra also traveled outside Rochester for several concerts, including performances in Buffalo, Atlantic City, and at Houghton College. The most important out-of-town concert was in Washington, DC, and it came as the result of the invitation mentioned in chapter 7 to participate in the Second Inter-American Festival of Music, held in April 1961 under the sponsorship of the Pan-American Union. The Eastman Philharmonia was the only all-student orchestra invited as a festival participant.

The concert in the nation's capital took place at the end of the orchestra's third season, and a far more exciting opportunity was soon to be announced. In the summer of 1961, the U.S. Department of State selected the Eastman Philharmonia to make a three-month European tour under the auspices of the President's Special International Program for Cultural Presentations. News of this forthcoming tour was communicated in a letter from Howard Hanson to members of the orchestra who would be returning to the school for the fall semester:

We have received word from the American National Theatre and Academy (ANTA), which manages tours for the State Department under the President's Fund, that the State Department is requesting a western European tour of the Eastman Philharmonia for the 1961–1962 season.

The tour is to extend approximately from November 26, 1961, to February 25, 1962, and is to cover France, Germany, the Scandinavian countries, and possibly Italy.

The School will make every effort to arrange studies so that the students involved will not lose academic credits because of the tour. All of the expenses of the students in the orchestra will be paid for by the State Department through the President's Fund.

The Eastman Philharmonia is the first student orchestra to be invited to tour Europe during the concert season and we may all consider the invitation a tribute to you and to the Eastman School. The only previous European appearance of a student symphony under the auspices of the State Department was the summer tour of the Juilliard School Orchestra.

The purpose of this letter is to ascertain whether or not you are interested in making this tour. The principal problem, as I see it, concerns the Rochester Philharmonic Orchestra. I do not see how it will be possible for a student to play with the Rochester Philharmonic Orchestra and also make the European tour because of the obvious conflict of the tour with Philharmonic dates.

This is not to be construed as a suggestion against a student joining the Philharmonic if he or she is invited. This, it seems to me, must be the decision of the individual student.

With best wishes for a pleasant summer and with my congratulations on the honor which has come to your Eastman Philharmonia.[1]

The reference to the conflict with the Rochester Philharmonic Orchestra season reflected the fact that significant numbers of students were members of that professional orchestra. The philharmonic stood to lose about twenty of its players during the proposed three-month tour, and the orchestra management was not sure it could sign enough qualified string players to fill the vacancies. Negotiations between the school and the orchestra continued for some time, and eventually five members of the Eastman artist faculty agreed to play in the Rochester Philharmonic during the period of the tour as a partial solution to the dilemma. An additional problem, involving all members of the Eastman Philharmonia, was their projected three-month absence from school, and the cooperation of the Eastman faculty was elicited to ensure that no one would lose academic credit because of the length of the tour.

Hanson had decided to include Frederick Fennell as his assistant conductor, and the two men spent considerable time discussing orchestra personnel and possible repertoire. Eventually, four programs were projected for the tour:

PROGRAM 1
Franz Schubert (1797–1828) *Symphony No. 5 in B-flat Major*
Samuel Barber (1910–81) *Symphony No. 1*, Op. 9
William Schuman (1910–92) *New England Triptych*
Igor Stravinsky (1882–1971) *Firebird Suite*

PROGRAM 2
Ludwig van Beethoven (1770–1827) Overture: *The Creatures of Prometheus*, Op. 43
Walter Piston (1894–1976) Suite from the Ballet *The Incredible Flutist*
Ottorino Respighi (1879–1936) *The Fountains of Rome*

---

[1] Howard Hanson, letter to members of the Eastman Philharmonia, July 3, 1961. SML.

Edward MacDowell (1860–1908) "Dirge" from *Suite for Orchestra No. 2,*
Op. 48 ("Indian")
Dmitry Shostakovitch (1906–75) *Symphony No. 1 in F Minor,* Op. 10

PROGRAM 3
George Gershwin (1898–1937) *Cuban Overture*
Charles Ives (1874–1954) "The Housatonic at Stockbridge" from *Three
Pieces in New England*
Dmitry Kabalevsky (1904–87) *Colas Breugnon,* Op. 24
Henry Purcell (1659–95) *Dioclesian Suite*
Howard Hanson (1896–1981) *Symphony No. 2* ("Romantic")

PROGRAM 4
Wolfgang Amadeus Mozart (1756–91) Overture: *The Abduction from the
Seraglio*
Wayne Barlow (1912–96) *The Winter's Past* for solo oboe and string
orchestra
Franz Schubert (1797–1828) *Symphony No. 5 in B-flat Major*
Alan Hovhaness (1911–2000) *Prelude and Quadruple Fugue,* Op. 128
Charles Ives (1874–1954) "The Housatonic at Stockbridge" from *Three
Pieces in New England*
Maurice Ravel (1875–1937) *Ma Mère l'Oye*

The actual repertoire performed by the Eastman Philharmonia during the three-month tour was drawn principally from these four projected concert programs. One additional matter concerning repertoire needed to be addressed, however—the acquisition of scores and parts for the national anthems of the various countries to be visited. Such repertoire was not to be found in the Eastman School's orchestral library but was loaned to the school by the Philadelphia Orchestra, courtesy of its esteemed conductor, Eugene Ormandy (1899–1985).

On August 7 another letter went to the students listing the immunizations and inoculations that would be necessary before departure. After the beginning of the school year, a further memo was circulated to orchestra members with a suggested wardrobe for men and women and suggested toilet articles. This memo also admonished the students to ensure that every instrument was in perfect repair prior to departure on the tour. In the meanwhile, the itinerary had become more definite than understood during the summer. The tour would no longer be limited to Western Europe but would also involve travel in the Middle East and Eastern Europe. The projected itinerary now included concerts in Portugal, Spain, Switzerland, France, Luxembourg, Belgium, Sweden,

Cyprus, Syria, Egypt, Lebanon, Turkey, Germany, Poland, the Soviet Union, and the Netherlands. Middle Eastern travel imposed special considerations concerning visas for the four members of the orchestra who were Jewish. This issue had been raised with the Department of State toward the end of September in an effort to avoid any last-minute difficulties. Concerts in the Middle East were undertaken despite constant tension in the area, although anti-Western sentiments were perhaps more frequently directed toward the French and British than toward Americans as a result of the Suez War several years earlier.

The addition of concerts behind the Iron Curtain was an extraordinary development, since the tour was taking place during the height of the Cold War. The members of the Eastman Philharmonia would visit areas of Eastern Europe seldom seen by Americans at that time. Only a year earlier Nikita Khrushchev, the Soviet premier, had appeared at the United Nations General Assembly in New York and responded to a speech by belligerently pounding both fists on the table. A week later Khrushchev erupted into another violent outburst and used his shoe to pound on his desk after listening to a speech that accused the Soviet Union of imperialism in Eastern Europe. It was during this period of heightened tensions that the U.S. State Department was preparing to send these young musicians behind the Iron Curtain.

An official tour photo of the orchestra was taken in the Eastman Theatre on October 2,[2] and two days later students received a list of their personal responsibilities in preparing for the tour departure. Students needed a letter of consent and a medical release signed by a parent or guardian, a medical examination and statement signed by a physician, a dental examination and statement signed by a dentist, passports, and a world health card. In addition, forms were required from local boards of the Selective Service System, permitting the male students who were American citizens to leave the United States. Such permission was necessary because at the time, all young men were required to register at age eighteen for possible military service.

The members of the orchestra left Rochester early in the afternoon on November 24, 1961, departing on two separate flights bound for New York International Airport.[3] After arriving in New York, they

---

[2] See Appendix 3 for a complete list of the orchestra personnel.
[3] New York International Airport, known to most travelers at the time as "Idlewild," was rededicated as John F. Kennedy International Airport following the assassination of President Kennedy in 1963.

were taken to the International Hotel for a briefing session on the Soviet Union. Departure for Europe was scheduled for nine P.M. on Iberian Airlines, but the flight was delayed for more than three hours. It was therefore a group of very weary American students who arrived in Lisbon at around noon the following day. On Sunday, November 26, the orchestra members did some sightseeing around Lisbon and then presented a concert at the Tivoli Theatre. The program consisted of music by Schubert, Hanson, William Schuman, and Stravinsky, and it was played to an enthusiastic full house that demanded and received three encores.

The orchestra traveled from Lisbon to Madrid on Monday, November 27, and presented a concert the following evening at the Palacio de Música. One of the tour's more memorable incidents occurred at this concert when, midway through the first movement of Stravinsky's *Firebird*, the lights in the theater went out. The orchestra kept playing from memory and completed the movement. After the lights had been restored, the concert resumed and concluded with an ovation from a wildly enthusiastic Spanish audience. Additional concerts followed in Seville, Valencia, and Barcelona. Seville was somewhat disappointing because the city was suffering from severe flooding, and the concert had to be transferred to a small, relatively inadequate theater.

Except for Seville, however, the experience of performing in Spain and Portugal was very rewarding for the students, who were greeted everywhere by enthusiastic audiences and standing ovations. The local newspapers were lavish in their praise for the young American performers, with one writer proclaiming that the Eastman Philharmonia was "equal to professional orchestras"[4] and another declaring that "the impression caused by the Eastman Philharmonia could not be improved upon."[5] There were also numerous receptions and opportunities for sightseeing, the latter especially appreciated since few of the student musicians had previously enjoyed the opportunity to travel in Europe.

---

[4] Luis Gomez, *Hoja del Lunes*. Translated and quoted by Charles Riker in *The Eastman School of Music 1947–1962* (Rochester, NY: University of Rochester, 1963), 33.
[5] *Noticiero Universal* of Barcelona. Translated and quoted by Charles Riker in ibid.

Figure 25. The Eastman Philharmonia arriving in Madrid, November 27, 1961.

On Monday, December 4, the orchestra traveled by plane from Barcelona to Geneva, then by bus to Fribourg where the group presented a concert the following evening. The concert was followed by a much-appreciated reception featuring beer, pastry, frankfurters, rolls, and cheese. The following morning it was considerably colder, with fresh snow on the ground, when they proceeded to Rennes, Rochester's "sister city" in France. This was not the easiest voyage of the tour, involving a bus trip back to Geneva, a plane to St. Najaire, then another bus to Rennes. Orchestra members were housed in six hotels, some of rather questionable quality, but everyone was treated to a lavish evening reception at the Hôtel de Ville. Clifford Spohr, a member of the Philharmonia's bass section, recalled the hospitality offered to the orchestra members:

> Rennes . . . gave us a royal dinner reception, complete with marching bagpipers, on the evening of our first day there. After our concert the next day, they offered us a champagne reception. I mention this

because it was the finest treatment given us on our tour, and by a city which is not correspondingly wealthy.[6]

The orchestra next found itself in Paris, prior to continuing on to Luxembourg. The accommodations were at the Hôtel d'Orsay, within view of the Eiffel Tower, and several students were able to attend a performance at Opéra de Garnier, the famous opera house that had provided the inspiration for Gaston Leroux's novel *The Phantom of the Opera*. Weather conditions delayed the orchestra's departure for Luxembourg for a full day, but there was little complaining since the delay allowed for additional, much-appreciated time for sightseeing in the French capital. The departure from Paris was finally scheduled to take place at about seven A.M. on Sunday, but weather conditions not only delayed the flight at the airport for two hours but also diverted it to Brussels. After a five-hour bus ride, the orchestra arrived in Luxembourg only twenty-five minutes prior to the scheduled five P.M. concert at the Palais de la Foire Internationale. Since the members' concert attire was stuck in a truck that had broken down thirty miles away, they had to play the program in their traveling clothes.

Two concerts followed in Brussels, separated by a much-appreciated free day, before the members of the Philharmonia were scheduled to fly to Göteborg. While en route to Sweden, one of the plane's engines stopped, but everyone arrived safely after two very nervous hours in the air. The concert that evening was apparently disappointing, taking place in a large hall without printed programs and attended by a relatively small audience. The orchestra also spent time in Stockholm and performed a concert in Uppsala, again to a small and apparently unenthusiastic audience.

The Philharmonia then traveled from Stockholm to Athens via Milan, Italy, and performed concerts on two successive evenings. The second of the concerts was conducted by Fennell, the first time Hanson had allowed him to conduct since the Eastman Philharmonia had left Rochester. This concert, featuring music by Beethoven, Piston, Respighi, William Schuman, and Stravinsky, was very well received and was followed by a reception given by the American Embassy. Although the weather in Athens was cold and overcast, students were able to visit the city's most important historic sites, including the Parthenon, Erechtheion, and Temple of Athena Nike on the Acropolis.

The orchestra next went to Nicosia, the capital and largest city of Cyprus, where the group experienced balmy and comfortable Mediterranean weather for a change. They performed three concerts

[6]   Clifford Spohr, The European Tour. Unpublished manuscript, April 2, 1962, 6. SML.

in Nicosia, often to audiences of different nationalities, including Greek and Turkish Cypriotes as well as American and British citizens. One of the concerts was attended by the president and vice president of Cyprus and the Greek Orthodox archbishop. The young American students enjoyed a Christmas Eve party that extended into the early hours of the morning, perhaps more like a New Year's Eve party. In the morning some of the students located the only Protestant church in Nicosia, an Anglican congregation, and attended Christmas services.

Prior to leaving Nicosia, the members of the orchestra received information cautioning them that anti-American feeling was running high in Egypt. The American Embassy in Cairo had recently been stoned and the French Embassy burned. With this sobering news, the Eastman Philharmonia departed from Nicosia the day after Christmas, heading for Aleppo in Syria. Upon arrival they were given a police escort from the plane to the terminal and then from the terminal to the bus. The bus ride to the Hotel Rhamses took the young American musicians through areas of great poverty, adding to some of the orchestra members' anxiety. Their concert, however, was very well received by a capacity crowd, although there was a minor disturbance by pro-Egyptian demonstrators during the performance. The concert was followed by a reception, with local cuisine and local entertainers.

On Wednesday, December 27, the orchestra left under very heavy security for Cairo, where the group was to spend four days. However, Egyptian authorities indicated that Carlotta Flatow, associate manager of the orchestra's European representatives, and Eduard Ebner, the person in charge of the Philharmonia's instruments and wardrobe trunks, would not be permitted into the country. Flatow and Ebner were French citizens, and several days earlier the Egyptian government had banned all French nationals from the country because of alleged espionage activities. The crisis was finally resolved, apparently as a result of the personal intervention of Egyptian president Gamal Abdel Nasser.

The orchestra members finally arrived in Cairo, but it was not one of their easier trips. A potentially embarrassing moment was avoided when the orchestra discovered during a morning rehearsal that they were rehearsing the wrong national anthem. The correct anthem was obtained in time for the performance that evening. Two concerts were played, one on Thursday, December 28, and the other the following evening, with Hanson and Fennell sharing conducting responsibilities for the latter program. Hanson had conducted the overwhelming majority of the concerts up to this time and would continue to do so for the remainder of the tour.

Time was set aside for the students to tour Giza and its famous pyramids, as well as to visit the incomparable Egyptian Museum in Cairo. On New Year's Eve they traveled four hours by bus across the desert to Alexandria, where the orchestra performed on New Year's Day to a full house at the Mohamed Aly Theatre. The bus trip back to Cairo was a decidedly unpleasant experience when one of three buses broke down. As a result, everyone had to crowd into the remaining two vehicles for the rest of the journey.

Next on the itinerary was Beirut, which, as Clifford Spohr later noted, was in a state of crisis when the Eastman Philharmonia arrived on January 2.

> Lucky ole us arrived in Beirut, Lebanon, just in time to enjoy the revolution. Tanks, jeeps, soldiers, and roadblocks were everywhere in and around the city while the government was rounding up the last of the insurgents.[7]

Despite the unsettled conditions, the orchestra played three concerts during the next three days—the first in UNESCO Hall, the second at St. Joseph University, and the third at the American University of Beirut. The first concert was broadcast over local radio and also by the Voice of America.

Leaving Lebanon on January 6, the Eastman students flew to Ankara, the Turkish capital, where they enjoyed an embassy reception and several students attended a performance of the *Pearl Fishers* by Georges Bizet (1838–75), sung in Turkish. Concerts were given in Ankara and Izmir before the orchestra moved on to Istanbul. The weather was cold and wet upon arrival, conditions that did not interfere with visits to Hagia Sophia and the Blue Mosque. That evening the orchestra performed a program of music by Beethoven, Piston, William Schuman, and Hanson. The audience included, not for the first or last time during the tour, a number of local music students.

Plans to continue on to Yugoslavia were postponed because of poor weather conditions, and during the two-day delay one student was sent home for medical reasons and another was hospitalized with appendicitis. Projected concerts in Zagreb were canceled because of the delay, and the orchestra then headed for Hanover en route to Berlin. It was a complicated journey, since neither Bulgaria nor Albania permitted planes to encroach on their airspace. Therefore,

---

[7]   Ibid., 13.

the planes carrying the members of the Eastman Philharmonia were required first to fly westward to Italy and then northward to Germany instead of taking a more direct and shorter route. After spending the night in Hanover, the orchestra left for Berlin, where nearly everyone was able to see the famous Berlin Wall. Clifford Spohr later recalled his reactions when viewing this barrier, which separated East Berlin and West Berlin but, more symbolically, separated Communism and the Free World at this critical time in history:

> I saw the wall. The wall is *the* symbol of Communism. It divides Germany into two sections—one [of] which is in a period of immense growth, and one [of] which is still living as if World War Two had just ended. The sight of it was the saddest moment of the tour for ninety silent Americans.[8]

That evening the orchestra played to a capacity crowd, which gave them a standing ovation resulting in three encores. The program consisted of music by Beethoven, Piston, Respighi, William Schuman, and Stravinsky. One local newspaper commented that the concert was "virtually a sensation," adding that "a comparison with the standards of our schools of music is depressing."[9] The following day the group traveled to Münster, first by air to Düsseldorf and then by bus for the remainder of the voyage. There was a morning reception the following day, at which the orchestra was officially greeted by the Lord Mayor and other local dignitaries. The evening concert took place in a modern concert hall and was attended by a small but highly appreciative audience.

Since the group was next going behind the Iron Curtain, all arrangements were now in the hands of the Soviet government. The orchestra left Münster by bus for the long ride back to Düsseldorf and then proceeded by plane to Poznan. Special visa forms and declarations had to be prepared before disembarking, each suitcase was opened, and all passports were thoroughly inspected. It was a new experience for the students, including the orchestra's concertmaster, Richard Kilmer: "My first impression when we landed at Poznan was that they trusted us less than any of the other countries we had visited, for they insisted on a complete customs inspection with opening of suitcases, flight bags and all."[10]

[8]   Ibid., 18.
[9]   *Telegraf.* Translated and quoted by Charles Riker in *The Eastman School of Music,* 33–34.
[10]   Richard Kilmer, Recollections of the 1962 Tour of Poland and the Soviet Union by a Member of the Eastman Philharmonia. Unpublished manuscript, 2–3. SML.

Figure 26. The Eastman Philharmonia in Berlin, January 14, 1962.

Conditions in Poland, compared with Western Europe, also made a deep impression on Kilmer:

> I saw no new construction of buildings in Poznan, or anywhere but Warsaw. There are still ruined buildings and empty lots full of rubble. The buildings left standing are scarred from the war.[11]

Richard Rodean, a Philharmonia bassoonist, also observed the distressed appearance of the new surroundings in Eastern Europe, commenting that "one could not help noticing the lack of lighting in the streets and the scarcity of cars and buses on the streets."[12] This was, of course, about sixteen and a half years after the end of World War II.

The Philharmonia performed in Poznan on the evening of January 18, playing to a full house that demanded and received five encores. Earlier in the day they had held a rehearsal that had been

[11] Ibid., 5–6.
[12] Richard Rodean, Eastman Philharmonia Tour 1961–62. Unpublished manuscript, January 1992, 33. SML.

attended by many local students and local orchestra members. Concerts followed in Krakow, Warsaw, and Lodz, each performance greeted by a wildly enthusiastic audience. Rodean left this vivid description of the orchestra's reception in Krakow:

> Dr. Fennell conducted the first half much to the enjoyment of everyone. As a matter of fact, we played the last movement of the de Falla twice as an encore before intermission. The audience was with us from the start. We played six encores, including the Beethoven overture [Leonora No. 3] to applause that only ceased when the orchestra literally left the stage. It was an unforgettable sight to see old women who were unable to stand during the ovation wave handkerchiefs in the air. Arms were raised high above heads, clapping unceasingly. One old man in the balcony barely got to his feet to applaud. He just stood and slowly applauded as best he could. It's hard to imagine such sincere applause. Hundreds of kids flooded the aisles seeking autographs and hand shakes after the concert.[13]

Travel arrangements in Poland were by bus, and the trip from Poznan to Krakow took almost twelve hours. Many students found this journey one of the biggest ordeals of the entire tour. Richard Kilmer later commented:

> The highways over which we bounced are cobblestone. Imagine riding twelve hours in one day in the back of a bus with a rough engine and very stiff springs over some hundred-plus miles of cobblestones. Many of us did! The countryside appeared very poor and the small villages through which we passed looked near the starvation point. They are true peasant gatherings. The only motive power visible for farming or transportation of produce to the village markets was horses pulling plows or crude wagons.[14]

The journey from Krakow to Warsaw was also very long. One happy event in Warsaw, however, was the arrival of Karen Phillips, the student who had been left behind in Istanbul because of an attack of appendicitis. After four days in the hospital she had recuperated at the home of the American consul general and was now well enough to join her fellow students for the remainder of the tour.

---

[13] Ibid., 35.
[14] Kilmer, Recollections, 9.

On Wednesday, January 24, the orchestra moved on to Moscow. There was heavy press coverage of their arrival in the Soviet Union. The first full day was at leisure, ending with an afternoon reception at the ambassador's residence. A good number of the students attended an evening performance of Prokofiev's *War and Peace* at the Bolshoi Theatre, the most important center for opera and ballet in Moscow. The orchestra's first concert in Moscow, on Friday evening, January 26, was a tremendous success. It took place in the Bolshoi Theatre, and much of it was filmed for NBC-TV. The program featured music of Mozart, Ravel, de Falla, Purcell, and Hanson. Enthusiasm for the young performers was such that the audience refused to leave even after the orchestra had exhausted its encores.

The Bolshoi was the location of another Philharmonia concert the following evening, which was performed to a positively ecstatic full house. Many orchestra members noted that Howard Hanson seemed very tired by the end of the concert, conducting with increasingly slower-than-average tempos. The following evening the orchestra played yet another program, this one broadcast by Soviet television. Hanson seemed exhausted once again, and Fennell conducted the first half of the program. The Eastman Philharmonia had been on the road and performing for slightly more than two months, and everyone, not just the conductor, was tired and frequently irritable. Morale was shaken when it became known that Hanson and his wife were flying to Odessa, the next stop on the tour, while the members of the orchestra had to endure a thirty-hour train ride, traveling in compartments with four beds each. Prior to their final concert in Moscow, the students took a vote to voice their disapproval of the pending transportation arrangements. The incident upset Hanson and his wife, a further strain on the sixty-five-year-old director.

Concerts followed in Odessa, Kishinev, Chernovtski, and Lvov, with the length of the tour continuing to affect student morale. Many focused their frustrations on the seemingly inordinate number of times Hanson's *Romantic Symphony* had been programmed, and they began to hold a lottery to see how long it would take to play the piece each time it had to be performed. While traveling to Chernovtski, several students made up these words to be sung to the tune of "The Battle Hymn of the Republic":

We have heard the slushy strains of the 2nd Symphony,
You have cried and screamed and howled to the Song of Democracy,
You have let the tears fall free in soupy elegy;
His music all sounds the same.

Glory, glory Howard Hanson,
Glory, glory Howard Hanson.
Glory, glory Howard Hanson,
His music all sounds the same.[15]

This may now appear terribly unfair to Howard Hanson, whose vision and leadership were responsible not only for the creation of the Eastman Philharmonia but also for its subsequent invitation to make the historic tour to Europe and the Middle East. The tour schedule had been very demanding on everyone, however, and the school's director was a convenient target for criticism among students who had been traveling and living in hotel rooms—and playing concerts approximately every other day—for nearly three months. While resentment toward Hanson was growing among some of the students, appreciation of Fennell was rising. On the evening of February 8, when the orchestra was in Lvov, Fennell received an enthusiastic ovation at supper, a show of affection and support that must have been very difficult for Hanson to witness. Yet, Fennell had earned sympathy because he had been relegated to such a minor role during the tour. By the end of the tour, the Eastman Philharmonia had played forty-nine concerts. Hanson had conducted thirty-seven of them, while Fennell had conducted only nine. The two men had shared conducting responsibilities for the other three performances.

The Eastman Philharmonia arrived in Kiev on Tuesday morning, February 13. The Leningrad Philharmonic had performed in Kiev the previous day, with the incomparable Mstislav Rostropovitch (1927–2007) as soloist in a performance of Prokofiev's *Concertante for Cello*. The Eastman orchestra had the unenviable task of following the Leningrad players by performing concerts on each of the next two nights, and several students felt the audience reaction was far less enthusiastic than what they had previously experienced on the tour. On Saturday they moved on to Leningrad, where they had ample time for sightseeing, including a visit to the famous State Hermitage Museum. Their concert on Monday evening proved to be the last time they had to play the *Romantic Symphony*. This was followed by two more concerts in Leningrad, the final performances of the tour.

The Philharmonia left Leningrad shortly before midnight on Wednesday, February 22, and arrived in Moscow at about nine A.M. Orchestra members were treated to a buffet reception at the Russian

---

[15]   Rodean, Eastman Philharmonia, 44.

Ministry of Culture, and the following day they visited the Moscow Conservatory. On Saturday they made the three-hour flight to Amsterdam as the first stage of their journey home, and there was widespread relief at being out from behind the Iron Curtain.

On the afternoon of Sunday, February 25, the orchestra members boarded a KLM jet and left Amsterdam, arriving in Montreal at about 5:30 P.M. An hour and a half later they departed from Montreal and arrived in Niagara Falls at about 8:15 P.M., where they were greeted by three busloads of students from Eastman, the mayor of Rochester, officials from the university, and many parents. A bus ride finally brought them back to Rochester, where they arrived after midnight. These musical ambassadors from the Eastman School had visited thirty-four cities in sixteen countries, presenting forty-nine concerts in ninety-three days. They had flown 30,000 miles, covered 2,000 miles by train, and endured 600 miles of bus rides. Exhausted and grateful to be home, the members of the Eastman Philharmonia had made a historic tour as ambassadors of goodwill from the United States of America. Deep and lasting friendships had been forged during the past three months. Experiences had been shared that would remain indelibly imprinted for the rest of their lives.

The Eastman Philharmonia traveled to New York City the following fall to present a concert in Carnegie Hall on November 16, 1962. There had been some personnel changes at the beginning of the new school year, but the level of the orchestra's proficiency and enthusiasm was undiminished. The program chosen by Howard Hanson consisted entirely of American music and included Peter Mennin's (1923–83) *Moby Dick* Concertato; Louis Mennini's (1920–2000) *Arioso for Strings;* John LaMontaine's (b. 1920) Concerto for Piano and Orchestra, Op. 9, with the composer as soloist; Act 1, Scene 2 from Robert Ward's (b. 1917) opera *The Crucible,* with mezzo-soprano Sylvia Friedrich and baritone Kerry McDevitt; and Hanson's *Mosaics for Orchestra.* Mennin, Mennini, LaMontaine, and Ward were all graduates of the Eastman School of Music. This was new repertoire for the orchestra, not having been included during the past season's tour. But the program also included what were listed as "Encores from Russia," which included Camaro Guarnieri's (1907–93) *Dansa Brasileira;* Kent Kennan's (1913–2003) *Night Soliloquy,* with Marjorie Clark Swanson as flute soloist; Wayne Barlow's *The Winter's Past,* with Joseph Turner as oboe soloist; and John Phillip Sousa's (1854–1932) "Stars and Stripes Forever."

Noted New York critic Harold Schonberg was lavish in his praise of the orchestra. Writing in *The New York Times* the following morning, he began his review with "No wonder they made a dent in the Soviet Union!" and ended with these words:

> Somewhere in the publicity these young musicians were mentioned as "fledgling musicians." Nonsense. Most of them could step into any orchestra in the country. It did one's heart good to see their enthusiasm, their skill and, one might add, their fresh young looks. One came out of Carnegie Hall with renewed confidence in Young America.[16]

Not to be outdone, Francis Perkins wrote in *The Herald Tribune* that the orchestra compared favorably with the best professional symphony orchestras in America.[17] All of this praise, not only in New York but also during the tour the preceding season, was well deserved, having been earned by the extraordinary young people who were proud members of the Eastman Philharmonia. Their accomplishment, however, was also a credit to the vision and leadership of Howard Hanson, who was coming to the end of his long career as director of the Eastman School of Music.

---

[16]   Harold Schonberg, "Music: The Eastman Honors Alumni," *The New York Times*, November 17, 1962: 15. Copyright © 1962 by The New York Times Co. Reprinted with permission.
[17]   Quoted in the *Times-Union* [Rochester, NY], November 17, 1962. SML.

Chapter 11

1960–64

The Search for a New Director

Howard Hanson would celebrate his sixty-fifth birthday in October 1961. As inconceivable as the thought might have been to some observers, it was time for the Eastman School of Music to look for new leadership. The process of selecting his successor began in the spring of 1960, initially with the idea that Hanson would retire at the end of the following academic year after having led the school for thirty-seven years. For a variety of reasons, all to be examined here, the search for a new director extended far beyond its original target date, and Hanson eventually completed forty years at the helm before turning over the direction of the school to a successor in 1964.

Many observers thought the time had long since come for new leadership at Eastman. These people felt strongly that Howard Hanson had provided less real leadership as the years slipped by. Yet any fair assessment would have to give him great credit for his immeasurable accomplishments and his widespread influence in American music education. Hanson may not have been a great composer, but he was a great educational leader. That leadership role came not only from his directorship of one of America's finest music schools but also through his various positions of leadership in the National Association of Schools of Music (NASM). The content and philosophy of the bachelor of music curriculum, as well as the development of the master's degree in music and the doctor of musical arts degree, all owed much to his vision and leadership. He had been a tireless spokesperson—and most often a very inspiring one as well—for the education of musicians.

Hanson was also the single most important advocate of his generation for the cause of American music. His American Composers' Concerts, which had started during the 1925–26 school year, and the Festival of American Music, which had been an annual event since its inception in the spring of 1931, had given countless numbers of American composers an opportunity to hear their works in

Figure 27. Howard Hanson, director of the Eastman School of Music, 1924–64.

public performance. Hanson was doing all this for American music and American musicians long before anyone else showed similar initiative, and he furthered these efforts through his many recordings of works by American composers. This passionate advocacy of American music alone should qualify Howard Hanson for consideration as the dominant figure in twentieth-century American music education.

But even great men have great faults, and justifiable criticism of his leadership was intermingled with praise for his accomplishments. Hanson had always charted a very independent course for the Eastman School of Music. Students during his years as director felt only nominally part of a larger university. The physical separation of the two campuses made this perhaps inevitable, but Hanson's style of leadership and his priorities were important factors in determining that the school would be almost an autonomous part of the university. Rush Rhees and his successor, Alan Valentine, had been content with this arrangement, but Cornelis de Kiewiet, the current University of Rochester president, had a decidedly different concept of leadership. He was an advocate of strong centralization of authority, and de Kiewiet and Hanson were able to work together only with difficulty. Hanson later complained about de Kiewiet's leadership:

> The new president's policy . . . called for a strong centralization of authority in the university administration, the final authority resting with the president and filtering down to the deans through a series of vice-presidents, provosts, and other university officers. Coupled with this was his insistence that the central core of the university should be the College of Arts and Sciences. Under this policy the College of Arts and Sciences became, itself, the university, the rest of us being adjuncts of the main body. Fortunately for us, the Eastman School was located in downtown Rochester, four miles from the River Campus, and our physical separation kept us from being entirely drowned in the Genesee.[1]

For years, Eastman's generous endowment and ample cash reserves allowed its director to pursue an independent course for the school. Yet there was a price for this independence, and that price was paid by the school's faculty. Faculty salaries were pitifully low, and many found it necessary to supplement their annual salaries by teaching overtime, for which they received much-needed extra compensation.

[1]   Hanson, Autobiography, 338–39.

Typical workloads, therefore, were heavy. The most exploited members of the faculty were those who also played in the Rochester Philharmonic Orchestra. Their salaries were among the lowest at the Eastman School, a situation excused on the grounds that they were also employed by the orchestra. In truth, neither the orchestra nor the school compensated these men and women adequately. They were forced to do two jobs to make an adequate living.

Low salaries led to a serious problem for many retirees, since retirement benefits were tied to salary levels. This often caused deep resentment among individuals who had loyally served the school for decades and then found themselves with a pension that barely met their needs. Nevertheless, most people, even those most critical of the situation, remained at Eastman in spite of many opportunities to seek positions elsewhere. Part of Hanson's administrative talent was his ability to convince people that the opportunity to teach at Eastman was, in essence, its own reward. Salaries might be better elsewhere, but "elsewhere" was not the Eastman School of Music.

Except for allowing his faculty to play in the philharmonic, Hanson seems to have had little or no interest in allowing or encouraging his performance faculty to pursue careers in any manner other than by teaching in their studios. Very few Eastman faculty members maintained a performing career, nor was such a career encouraged. Accepting concert dates was fine, but only when doing so did not interfere with teaching. Orazio Frugoni, one of the few members of the faculty who regularly performed and recorded, was on tour in South America during the summer one year when an opportunity arose to extend his tour for several weeks into September. He sent Hanson a telegram requesting permission to return to Eastman a week or so after instruction had officially started, but he was told in no uncertain terms to return in time for the first lessons of the semester.[2]

In all matters, Hanson ran the school with the help and advice of just a few people in whom he had confidence—primarily Flora Burton, Allen Irvine McHose, and Charles Riker. He did not feel comfortable delegating much responsibility. The department structure at Eastman was loose and, in many areas, basically nonfunctioning. Members of the faculty were generally not even involved in auditioning prospective students. There were few functioning faculty committees, other than those that governed graduate degree study.

[2]   Orazio Frugoni related this story to the author on several occasions.

There is little evidence that Hanson's efforts in 1948 to organize departmental committees led to any real faculty involvement in the leadership of the school. The committees were supposed to meet at the beginning of each quarter, with matters of general interest referred to the entire faculty after appropriate action had been taken by the individual department. The entire faculty, however, met only two or three times during the academic year. Attendance was taken at these meetings to guarantee faculty members' presence, but most meetings consisted of little more than official business such as voting on degrees. More than one faculty member stayed long enough only to have his or her attendance noted before slipping out the back door. Little of substance or importance was ever discussed.

In addition, the school's director had become more and more isolated. His daily schedule was carefully guarded by his secretary, Mary Louise Creegan, and it was often extremely difficult, if not impossible, for a faculty member (or anyone else, for that matter) to get an appointment to see him. When faculty complaints concerning his inaccessibility reached Hanson, he responded that barriers had been set up "with the intention of protecting his time."[3] His solution was to suggest that any requests for an appointment be submitted in writing. Such a policy did little, if anything, to encourage or assist faculty members in their efforts to meet with the director. The result was not only a marginalized faculty but, even worse, a director increasingly isolated from the advice and opinions of his Eastman colleagues.

None of this went unnoticed by the University of Rochester administration. Several years earlier university president de Kiewiet had observed in a report to his board of trustees that "there was a lack of the discussion and debate amongst faculty [at the Eastman School] which so often results in intellectual vitality."[4] In the same report the president spoke of other problems at Eastman, including financial, personal, and geographic issues. The last of these was a reflection of his concern over the separation of the campuses, an issue that would resurface many times well into the future. At the same time, however, there was recognition and appreciation of the Eastman School's prominence among American music schools and acknowledgment that it had achieved this prominence under Hanson's leadership. Nonetheless, some aspects of the school's present administration called into question Hanson's continued effectiveness as director.

[3]   Faculty meeting minutes, June 6, 1955. SML.
[4]   Quoted in *University of Rochester 1952–53 Trustees Proceedings*, 72. RRL.

Even his advocacy of American music had become somewhat tarnished by a growing conservatism that threatened to isolate the school from the real world. When he had first arrived at Eastman, Hanson had spoken of the need for "a spirit of toleration and sympathy for every honest creative effort of the present,"[5] but by his last years as director he had become intolerant of and unsympathetic toward many newer compositional ideas and techniques. In particular, he had an absolute disdain for atonality, especially for Arnold Schoenberg and twelve-tone music. These were not simply matters of personal taste but an attitude that affected his teaching and his concert programming. As a composer, Hanson had become something of an anachronism. Once considered a shining light among the younger generation of composers, he now seemed during his mature years to represent only the past, not the present and certainly not the future. Although he remained an excellent craftsman and a superb orchestrator, many observers judged him as having little to say that was really new.

Therefore, while Howard Hanson's pending retirement may have been dreaded by those who feared change, it was also anticipated with some degree of optimism and hope for the future by those who felt the Eastman School needed fresh leadership if it was to maintain a leadership role in the education of American musicians. Only the most callous observer would deny Howard Hanson credit for developing the Eastman School of Music into the world-renowned institution it had become by 1960. But times were changing, and there was a feeling that the school was becoming more and more insular, isolated from the real professional world. It was time for a change.

On March 25, 1960, Hanson sent a memo to President de Kiewiet identifying possible candidates for the Eastman position. Four were from the Eastman School—Allen Irvine McHose, Wayne Barlow, Eugene Selhorst, and Frederick Fennell. Hanson mentioned that Barlow had recently been runner-up for the position of dean of the School of Music at Northwestern University and that Fennell had been a candidate for president of the New England Conservatory in Boston. These comments may have been intended to impress the university president with the excellent qualifications of internal candidates in general, not just Barlow and Fennell. The memo also mentioned six additional people who might be candidates for the director's position. Each of the six was an Eastman alumnus—Peter

[5] Howard Hanson, quoted in *Democrat & Chronicle* [Rochester, NY], January 10, 1926. SML (news clipping).

Mennin (director of the Peabody Conservatory of Music), Donald Pearson (chair of the music department at Vassar College in Pough-keepsie, New York), Donald Engle (executive director of the Martha Baird Rockefeller Foundation and former manager of the Philadelphia Orchestra), William Bergsma (newly appointed to the Juilliard faculty and runner-up to Mennin for the Peabody position), Thomas Gorton (president of NASM and dean of the School of Fine Arts at the University of Kansas), and LaVahn Maesch (president of the Music Teachers National Association and director of the Conservatory of Music at Lawrence University). It is very significant that the first ten people mentioned as possible successors to Howard Hanson had all earned degrees from the Eastman School of Music. And it is even more significant that Howard Hanson obviously insisted on being very much involved in the search for his own successor.

A committee, or "administrative group," consisting of Flora Burton, Wayne Barlow, Eugene Selhorst, Allen Irvine McHose, and Frederick Fennell, had been formed by the beginning of the 1960–61 school year to assist Hanson in matters concerning the selection of a new director. Burton was the only member of the committee never mentioned as a possible candidate for the position.[6] On September 12, 1960, Hanson addressed a memo to university provost Howard Anderson, outlining the basic qualifications for the new director. He argued that the person should be a distinguished musician, an able and experienced administrator, an artist, and a man of proven abilities.

> He should have national status. He should be a man with powers of communication which would enable him to be a distinguished spokesman for the institution. The appointee should, if possible, be a man in his forties so that he would have the possibility of twenty or more years of service. He should be a man with a genuine love for, and interest in, young people.[7]

During early 1961 Hanson sent letters to various people asking for recommendations of additional candidates. On May 5, 1961, he sent Provost Anderson a list of forty names, assisted once again by his five-person "administrative group." Of particular interest in this communication to the provost was the justification for seeking an

---

6 It would be safe to assume that no woman was considered for the directorship of the school at the time.
7 Howard Hanson, memo to Provost Howard Anderson, September 12, 1960. SML.

Eastman alumnus as his successor: "[I]t would seem only natural that the new director be an alumnus of the Eastman School of Music since the Eastman School has furnished so many deans, directors and chairmen of departments to the music schools of the United States."[8] On May 19 letters were sent to William Bergsma, Thomas Gorton, Peter Mennin, and Edward Stein asking about their possible interest in the Eastman position. The first three had been on Hanson's initial list of potential candidates a year earlier. Stein, new to the list, was dean of the School of Fine Arts at Boston University. Gorton and Mennin subsequently agreed to come to Rochester for discussion.

A new player in the drama emerged on May 31, 1961—Sol Linowitz, chairman of the board at Xerox and a member of the University of Rochester's board of trustees.[9] On May 31 Linowitz, who would prove to be a major influence in the search for Hanson's successor, sent a letter addressed to Provost Anderson, with copies to fellow trustees Marion Folsom and Joseph C. Wilson. Folsom, a former cabinet member in the Eisenhower administration, had a long history of leadership at the Eastman Kodak Company, Rochester's leading employer. Wilson was the founder of Xerox, where he worked closely with Linowitz. He was also chairman of the board of trustees of the University of Rochester. Linowitz's letter suggested that Isaac Stern (1920–2001), Erich Leinsdorf (1912–93), and Leonard Bernstein (1918–90) be consulted for suggestions. At the time, Stern was one of the most prominent artists appearing before the public, while Bernstein and Leinsdorf were music directors of two of America's most esteemed orchestras. Thus, Linowitz was sensibly advocating reaching out beyond Hanson and his inner circle of advisers and seeking recommendations from prominent people in the professional world of music. Significantly, Linowitz did not send Hanson a copy of this letter, but Anderson wisely chose to show it to the Eastman School director. Hanson graciously accepted Linowitz's suggestion, and letters were sent to the three distinguished American musicians on June 5, 1961.

Any thoughts of having a new director in place for the 1961–62 school year had long since vanished, and an important development at the University of Rochester ensured that Hanson's retirement

8   Howard Hanson, memo to Provost Howard Anderson, May 5, 1961. SML.
9   Linowitz subsequently had a brilliant career in Washington, serving as ambassador to the Organization of American States during the Johnson administration. He later helped negotiate the transfer of the Panama Canal and represented President Jimmy Carter in the 1978 Middle East peace negotiations.

would come no earlier than the end of the 1962–63 school year. This development was the resignation of Provost Anderson in June. For some time, de Kiewiet had wanted to relinquish his responsibilities as president, and Anderson had been appointed provost to keep de Kiewiet at the helm. With Anderson now leaving, little could be done to retain de Kiewiet. Negotiations with de Kiewiet quickly led to his appointment as president emeritus, while the provost's position was taken by McCrea Hazlett, dean of the College of Arts and Science. All of this meant the University of Rochester had no president, and the selection of Hanson's replacement at the Eastman School of Music would have to wait until a new president was appointed. And so the search went on, but at a somewhat leisurely pace.

On November 3, 1961, Linowitz wrote Hanson suggesting Lukas Foss as a possible candidate. His letter was followed, perhaps not coincidentally, on November 13 by a letter from Leonard Bernstein also strongly promoting Foss's candidacy, adding that he regretted that Hanson was retiring after so many years as director at Eastman. Although Foss enjoyed a well-deserved reputation as an educator, composer, conductor, and pianist, Hanson was decidedly unenthusiastic, as he indicated in writing to Linowitz on November 15, 1961. In truth, he probably could not imagine that anyone other than an Eastman School graduate could succeed him. This, if nothing else, effectively eliminated Foss from consideration.

The Eastman Philharmonia European tour occupied much of Hanson's attention during the 1961–62 school year, but he returned to the question of his successor with a detailed memo on April 20, 1962, addressed to Provost Hazlett and Joseph C. Wilson, in which he outlined a very comprehensive plan for proceeding with the search. Much of this memo deserves to be quoted:

1. That we begin an intensive search for the new director not later than September, 1962, and that the decision be reached not later than June of 1963.
2. That in June of 1962 we announce four new appointments: Dr. McHose as Associate Director; a new Director of Summer Session; Associate Dean Barlow as Chairman of the Composition Department; and Donald O. White as Chairman of the Theory Department.
3. That in 1962–63 Dr. McHose work closely with me in the administration of the School and be readily available for consultation by the central administration of the University.
4. That in 1963–64 the files which have accumulated during my administration be moved to an office in Cutler Union. . . .

5. That during the year 1963–64 the new director have the opportunity of consulting with Dr. McHose, Dean Burton, and me as much as he wishes, and that he be consulted in matters of appointments, educational policy, and the like. *Note:* This would also give the new director a year in which to conclude his own affairs—particularly important if the new director is the administrator of another institution.

6. That I announce at an appropriate time my retirement at the end of forty years of service as director. *Note:* This should go far to dispel any ideas, which may still exist, that I am retiring involuntarily. Forty years is a nice round number and anyone might be expected to seek retirement after four decades of service.

7. That at the time of the above announcement my appointment as director of the Institute of American Music be announced, together with the appointment of Frederick Fennell as associate director of the Institute.

8. That in 1962–63 and, if necessary, in 1963–64 every effort be made to secure additional funding for the underwriting of the institute.

9. That in 1964 the new director . . . take over the administration of the Eastman School of Music. . . .

10. That I remain a member of the Board of Managers of the Eastman School of Music as the only living member of the Board who was appointed by George Eastman.

11. That in the year 1963–64 . . . I make a further study of the relationship of the University of Rochester to the Rochester Civic Music Association. . . .

12. That a preliminary budget for the American Institute be drawn up and discussed.[10]

This is an extraordinary document, the details of which deserve some commentary. Hanson had been at the center of efforts to select his own successor from the very beginning of the process back in 1960. His April 20, 1962, memo makes it abundantly clear that he continued to see himself as the primary instrument in the search for the new director. He had already secured the university's acquiescence to the proposal that he become the director of a new Institute of American Music, which would carry on and expand upon the goals of promoting American music. He saw this new institute, which would be housed in Cutler Union and funded by the university, as a more thorough vehicle for the promotion of American music than what had already been accomplished during his years as director of the school. The institute would advance the cause of

---

[10] Howard Hanson, memo to Provost Hazlett and Joseph C. Wilson, April 20, 1962. SML.

American music through scholarship, performance, publication, and recordings. And he would guarantee his continuing guidance over the destiny of the Eastman School by remaining on the school's board of managers. To prepare for the transition in leadership, Hanson had decided to appoint Allen Irvine McHose associate director and to allow Wayne Barlow to become chair of the composition department. In later years, it was suggested that McHose's appointment may have been made without Hanson's knowledge or approval. The April 20, 1962, memo clearly indicates otherwise.

Everything being done at the time was still clearly under Hanson's influence and control. Even the timetable for the new director allowed Hanson to retain a controlling influence for a year after the new director had been selected. The next director of the Eastman School of Music would be chosen no later than June 1963, but he would not assume his responsibilities until the 1964–65 school year. During the intervening year, the new director would have the opportunity to consult with Hanson on matters of faculty appointments and policy, but Hanson would basically remain in charge.

Of special importance in this document is the sixth paragraph. It has been repeatedly suggested ever since Hanson's retirement that his departure from the directorship of the Eastman School of Music was not voluntary. This paragraph certainly suggests otherwise. It is possible that forthcoming changes in the selection process and the eventual appointment of Walter Hendl as the school's third director may have led Hanson to have second thoughts about the wisdom of his retirement. But in 1962 at least, there appeared to be no doubt in his mind that his pending retirement was entirely his own decision.

Hanson did not have to wait long for an answer to his April 20 memo. Provost Hazlett responded only three days later, indicating that he and Wilson were in complete agreement and would follow through in accordance with Hanson's suggestions. News of Hanson's forthcoming retirement was released on May 2, including the announcement that he would now involve himself with the affairs of a new Institute of American Music. The official announcement of the retirement came on May 12, 1962, indicating June 1, 1964, as the effective retirement date. It had taken two years simply to arrive at a specific date for Hanson's departure.

Everything proceeded during the first semester of the 1962–63 school year much as it had during the previous two years. Hanson wrote another comprehensive memo on December 17, 1962, in which he discussed the challenges for the future, including budget deficits that were becoming a major concern for the first time in the school's history. He also reviewed suggested nominees for the director's position, including several who had recently accepted other positions. The latter group included Peter Mennin, who had been chosen to head the Juilliard School of Music, and Frederick Fennell, who had left Eastman to accept a position as associate conductor of the Minneapolis Symphony. As previously noted, Fennell's departure was a serious loss for the Eastman School of Music. He had contributed so much during his many years at the institution that it was almost inconceivable that he would leave. Some blamed Hanson for Fennell's decision, although this was probably an unfair accusation. Fennell's own aspirations as a conductor surely contributed heavily to his decision to accept the offer from Minneapolis.

Hanson's memo also noted that seven of the suggested nominees would be sixty or older by 1964, a factor that would probably exclude them from further consideration. That group included Allen Irvine McHose, who had been on Hanson's initial list of ten possible candidates for the director's position. However, the thirty remaining names among the suggested nominees presented a wide array of possible choices, including a few such as Wayne Barlow, William Bergsma, Thomas Gorton, and Eugene Selhorst who had also been on the initial list back in March 1960. But the list of possible candidates now included such names as Victor Allesandro (music director of the San Antonio Symphony), Wilfred Bain (dean of the School of Music at Indiana University), Leonard Bernstein (music director of the New York Philharmonic), William Doty (professor of composition at Northwestern University), Frank Hughes (dean of the College of Fine Arts at the University of Texas), Raymond Kendall (dean of the School of Music at the University of Southern California), Luther Noss (dean of the School of Music at Yale University), and Sol Schoenbach (director of the Settlement Music School in Philadelphia).

One name notably absent from the list was Walter Hendl, associate conductor of the Chicago Symphony Orchestra and the man who eventually succeeded Hanson at the Eastman School. Hendl's name was apparently first mentioned by Norman Dello Joio, the noted American composer, in the spring of 1963, but there is no indication that the suggestion received any serious consideration. All of this changed with the appointment of W. Allen Wallis as the new president of the University of Rochester. Had Hanson and his "committee" acted more expeditiously, his obvious preference to be succeeded by an Eastman alumnus might have been realized.

Wallis's arrival as the university's new president totally altered the situation. On October 2, 1963, he appeared at an Eastman faculty meeting, asking that a president's advisory committee be selected to assist him in choosing a new director for Eastman. The faculty eventually chose Wayne Barlow, Bernard Rogers, Eugene Selhorst, Cecile Genhart, Millard Taylor, and M. Alfred Bichsel. Except for Bichsel, the committee consisted of people who had enjoyed a very long association with Eastman. The formation of the committee was a clear indication to everyone that W. Allen Wallis, not Howard Hanson, was now in charge of the search.

While the committee proceeded with its task of sorting through the qualifications of potential candidates, Wallis met privately with Walter Hendl in Chicago to discuss the possibility of the conductor applying for the Eastman position. Hendl later recalled his reaction to Wallis's suggestion: "I could not believe what he was saying. I thought it was pretty crazy."[11] Hendl was later invited to a meeting with Wallis and several others, including Sol Linowitz, at the University Club in New York City. That meeting led to a decision by the university president that Walter Hendl would succeed Howard Hanson as the next director of the Eastman School of Music. Unbeknown to any member of the president's advisory committee, Hendl was invited to Rochester. The committee was asked to attend a luncheon at the university's faculty club, and Wallis arrived with Hendl. The significance of Hendl's appearance was immediately apparent to everyone.[12]

In reporting to the university trustees, Wallis made it clear that the principal qualification he sought in the person chosen to head the Eastman School was musical talent:

> A primary criterion as the search for the successor to Dr. Hanson had been pursued had been musical talent. Because it would make readily possible the attraction of other musical talent, this was felt to be of greater importance than administrative ability. This criterion, the President emphasized, Mr. Hendl had met in high degree.[13]

From the advice he received from various sources outside the Eastman School of Music, the university president was confident that he had found his man. The chair of the university's board of trustees, Joseph C. Wilson, later wrote that Hendl had been recommended "by some of the greatest names in music."[14] Nonetheless,

---

[11] Walter Hendl, interview by the author, Erie, PA, July 16, 2004.
[12] M. Alfred Bichsel, a member of the president's advisory committee, related the circumstances surrounding the luncheon meeting with Wallis and Hendl to the author on several occasions.
[13] Quoted in *University of Rochester 1963–64 Trustees Proceedings,* 41. RRL.
[14] Quoted in W. Allen Wallis, notes on the appointment of Walter Hendl. SML.

many within the Eastman community later accused Wallis of making a rather capricious decision. Yet, he had actually acted very deliberately. Those people to whom he had looked for advice had convinced him that the Eastman School of Music needed a professional musician of stature as its new director, someone well-known in international music circles, preferably a performer. Once Wallis was convinced of this course of action, the only remaining question was the choice of that professional musician, and the suggestions he obtained from people whose judgment he trusted led him to Walter Hendl.

News of the pending appointment spread quickly through the halls of the Eastman School of Music. The general reaction among the faculty was one of great surprise, intermingled with disappointment and disapproval. While everyone considered Walter Hendl a musician of superb ability and talent, they also knew he had little experience in academia and no real experience as an administrator. Even more unsettling to some members of the faculty was their knowledge that Hendl had a history of personal problems that had seriously jeopardized his career in the past. A letter addressed to the university president was quickly drawn up and signed by a number of the school's tenured and senior faculty, asking Wallis to reconsider his decision. There was, of course, a special irony in the fact that the Eastman faculty had been seeking their new leader mainly from within the world of academia, while the university president had ultimately chosen a symphony orchestra conductor from the professional world of music.

Word spread quickly throughout the United States and beyond concerning Hendl's pending appointment. Peter Mennin, still a candidate for the Eastman position, formally withdrew from consideration. Various Eastman alumni, who had shown a particularly active interest in the selection of Hanson's successor, banded together in a last-minute effort to promote and support the appointment of Frederick Fennell. Others simply protested the apparent choice of Hendl. But the decision had been made, and such protests were in vain. Howard Hanson was to be succeeded as director by Walter Hendl, and the president officially communicated the news to the faculty in a memo dated June 8, 1964, which included these words:

> Finding a successor to Howard Hanson has been the most difficult and at the same time the most important task in my presidency. I have had generous assistance from many people—in professional music and music education, in Rochester and throughout the country, Eastman graduates and graduates of other schools. I am indebted to all these people, but above all to the Faculty Advisory committee,

for shaping my understanding of Eastman's problems and opportunities. I selected Walter Hendl in the light of his capacities and our needs as I appraise them.[15]

Many members of the Eastman faculty remained unconvinced, not only by the choice of Hendl but especially by the manner in which the appointment had been made. But not all reaction was negative, especially outside the school. For example, President Wallis received a telegram from the English conductor Sir John Barbirolli (1899–1970), strongly approving of Hendl's appointment, and a letter from Louis Lane (b. 1923), the associate director of the Cleveland Orchestra, who wrote that Hendl was an excellent choice for the position. Letters indicating strong approval of the choice were also received from several other distinguished musicians, including Gregor Piatigorsky (1903–76) and Isaac Stern.

Hendl received many personal messages of congratulations, including a letter dated June 12 from Sol Linowitz, who mentioned that Isaac Stern had been one of the first to recommend him as especially well qualified for the Eastman position. Perhaps the first to write to the school's new director was Rochester-born composer David Diamond (1915–2005), who was delighted to hear of Hendl's appointment: "I have just heard the good news about Rochester! and am so very happy for you; and for the school. I must say!! I know that you will bring it to the artistic heights it has long deserved."[16] Diamond's congratulatory words betrayed his long-standing dislike of Howard Hanson. The letter was written from Florence, Italy, a little more than a week before Hendl's appointment was officially announced.

An interesting congratulatory letter was sent about a week after the announcement by William Schuman (1910–92), president of the Lincoln Center for the Performing Arts:

> Music at Eastman is now safe. I was very worried. For a long time, they were flirting with the Music Education boys. You will give it the expert professional stamp a fine school must have. . . . At the time of my appointment to Juilliard, way back in the dark ages of 1945, I received a telegram from Howard Hanson which said, "Welcome to the Aspirin Club." You will find your new post exciting and rewarding. I send you my affectionate greetings for a long, happy and constructive tenure. Let's meet in the fall of the year.[17]

[15] W. Allen Wallis, memo to the Eastman faculty, June 8, 1964. SML.
[16] David Diamond, letter to Walter Hendl, May 31, 1964. Private papers of Walter Hendl.
[17] William Schuman, letter to Walter Hendl, June 11, 1964. Private papers of Walter Hendl.

Schuman's letter is very indicative of an attitude that existed primarily outside Rochester—namely, that the school needed a professional musician rather than an "educator" or "academician" to lead it into the post-Hanson era. This was the attitude W. Allen Wallis had embraced.

Hanson addressed his faculty on June 4, 1964, one of his last functions as director. He emphasized that the decision to retire had been his own, saying he could have stayed longer had he wished to do so. Many in the room wondered if this was merely wishful thinking, perhaps possible under the previous university administration but not likely under the present one. Hanson also spoke of the necessity that the new director be an appointee of the president and that he should enjoy the president's complete confidence and support. He reminded the faculty that he had experienced the unqualified loyalty of both Rush Rhees and George Eastman when appointed to the Eastman position forty years earlier. The institution Hanson had essentially built during his forty-year tenure was now to be in the hands of someone else. The Hanson era was over. The Hendl years were about to begin.

Part Two

The Post-Hanson Years

Chapter 12

1964–66

The New Director:
The First Two Years

Walter Hendl, the Eastman School's third director, was born in West New York, New Jersey, on January 12, 1917, the only child of working-class, German-speaking immigrants. His father, William Hendl, had been born near Vienna and had come to the United States when he was only three years old. His mother, Ella Kittel, came to America from Bergedorf, a small town near Hamburg, when she was ten. Neither of his parents had attended high school, and his father was essentially an unskilled laborer. They were perhaps typical of many immigrant families at the time. Three years after Walter's birth they moved to Union Hill (soon renamed Union City), a town of about 25,000 people, many of them German immigrants or first-generation Americans of German descent.

When Walter was twelve, his mother sent him to study with a local piano teacher, but he did not become serious about music until he was in high school. Something of a turning point in his life occurred when he and a friend went to Carnegie Hall in November 1933 to hear Josef Hofmann (1876–1957), considered by many at the time the greatest pianist of his generation. Hendl later recalled that "for the first time in my life I experienced music. I began to imagine how wonderful it would be to have people applaud you for something that you do, and I decided then and there that I wanted to become a great pianist."[1] The friend with whom he had attended Hofmann's recital studied piano with Clarence Adler (1886–1969), a former student of the famous virtuoso Leopold Godowsky (1870–1938). Hendl eagerly auditioned for Adler at his apartment on Central Park West in Manhattan, and he was accepted as a student for

---

[1] Donald McQuaid, *Walter Hendl: The Early Years* (Erie, PA: Ruth S. Jageman, 2003), 26.

Figure 28. Howard Hanson with Walter Hendl. (Collection of the author.)

a fee of $2.50 a week. Under Adler's guidance he plunged into a serious effort to become a professional pianist, an aspiration apparently supported by his mother, who purchased a baby grand piano to replace the player piano that had stood in the family parlor since Walter's birth.

His passion for the piano included more than practicing for his lessons with Adler; Hendl was also a regular member of the audience at piano recitals at New York's Carnegie Hall and Town Hall. He was assisted in this endeavor by a former grade school teacher who worked in the Carnegie Hall box office and sympathetically arranged for Hendl to be admitted without charge to both concert venues. Hendl's thirst for music was such that he sometimes heard three or four piano recitals a week. Such exposure to music making was probably as important in his musical development as were his lessons with Clarence Adler.

Graduating second in his class from Union City High School in 1934, Walter Hendl faced an uncertain future. The Great Depression made it unlikely that he could attend college, and so he obtained a position at Sarah Lawrence College in Bronxville, New York, where he accompanied voice students four days a week for a salary of sixty dollars a month. All the while, he continued his piano lessons with Adler. Three years later he was accepted as a student at the Curtis Institute of Music in Philadelphia, where he initially studied with Josef Hofmann and then with David Saperton (1889–1970) after Hofmann left Curtis in the middle of Hendl's first year. His admission to Curtis was nothing short of miraculous, considering his late start as a serious student of the piano.

During his second year at Curtis, Hendl began to experience pain and partial paralysis in his neck and shoulders, brought on by compulsive over-practicing that sometimes involved as many as ten hours a day. At the suggestion of Randall Thompson (1899–1984), who had succeeded Josef Hofmann as director at Curtis, he decided to redirect his energies toward becoming a conductor and auditioned for Fritz Reiner (1888–1963), with whom he studied for two years. Reiner had been teaching at Curtis since 1931 and also became conductor of the Pittsburgh Symphony Orchestra in 1938. Hendl later described Reiner as demanding and even brutal at times and said that all the students were frightened by his presence. Those students, Hendl's classmates at Curtis, included Lukas Foss (1922–2009) and Leonard Bernstein (1918–90).

While still a student at Curtis, Hendl was given an opportunity in the fall of 1939 to teach at Sarah Lawrence College. The American composer William Schuman (1910–92), who was on the faculty, received a Guggenheim Fellowship and asked Hendl to teach his classes while he was away in Salzburg for the year. This was Hendl's first experience with teaching, and his responsibilities included a music appreciation course for non–music majors as well as several piano students. His new employment at Sarah Lawrence necessitated commuting between Bronxville and Philadelphia, a four-hour journey by train, which gave Hendl time to study the scores he was preparing for Reiner. His studies with Reiner at Curtis were followed by summer study with Serge Koussevitzky (1874–1951) at Tanglewood in Massachusetts. Koussevitzky, who directed the Boston Symphony Orchestra from 1924 to 1949, had been appointed director of the Berkshire Music Center at Tanglewood when it opened in 1940. Studying with the famous maestro was a wonderful opportunity for a young conductor, although Hendl later admitted that Koussevitzky had shown little confidence in his potential. The favorite student that summer had been his Curtis classmate Leonard Bernstein.

Hendl served in the U.S. Army for three years during World War II, somehow becoming a competent jazz pianist in the process. Following his discharge from the army he became assistant conductor of the New York Philharmonic under Artur Rodzinski (1892–1958) from 1945 to 1949. He also composed incidental music for *The Dark of the Moon,* a musical that subsequently had a successful New York run and national tour in 1945. In 1949 he accepted an appointment as music director of the Dallas Symphony Orchestra, becoming the youngest permanent conductor of a major U.S. orchestra. Upon arriving in Dallas, he put on a cowboy hat, accepted an appointment as an honorary deputy sheriff, judged a beauty contest, went to a fashion show, played jazz piano for a local school, and lunched with the Rotarians. In his view, this was all part of his job now that he was a Texan. Hendl remained in Dallas until 1958, and his departure from the music director position there was perhaps the first indication that his personal struggles and inner conflicts had the capacity to undermine efforts to realize the full potential of his considerable musical talent.

His career, however, was rescued by his old mentor Fritz Reiner, who was then the music director of the Chicago Symphony Orchestra. Reiner invited Hendl to be the associate conductor in Chicago, where he also became musical director of the Ravinia Music Festival. In addition, he was music director of the Caramoor Festival in 1962 and 1963 and continued his summer position as music director of the Chautauqua Symphony Orchestra, a post he had held since 1953. In all these endeavors he was building a solid reputation as one of America's most promising young conductors, a reputation greatly enhanced by stellar recordings on the RCA Victor label, with Hendl brilliantly conducting concerto accompaniments for artists such as Jascha Heifetz (1899–1987), Gary Graffman (b. 1928), Van Cliburn (b. 1934), and Erick Friedman (b. 1939). All of this was preparing him to fulfill his apparent aspiration to succeed Reiner as music director in Chicago, and it was likely devastating to him when Jean Martinon (1910–76) was chosen as the orchestra's new leader in 1963.

In all probability, Hendl viewed the choice of a Frenchman to lead Reiner's orchestra as indefensible and almost unexplainable. Even worse was the thought that perhaps he had no future as a conductor. Bernstein had been appointed conductor in New York in 1958, Leinsdorf in Boston in 1962. Lukas Foss had his own orchestra, the Buffalo Philharmonic, but Hendl remained associate conductor in Chicago. It looked like a professional dead end. And so, he seized the opportunity to become director of the Eastman School of Music. It was not the first time Walter Hendl had struck out in an entirely new direction.

Accordingly, Hendl accepted the offer to succeed Howard Hanson at the helm of the Eastman School. W. Allen Wallis quickly responded to his acceptance, sending a letter that outlined the terms of his appointment while also confirming that Hendl was additionally being offered a full professorship with indefinite tenure. The terms stipulated that the new director and his wife were required to reside in Hutchison House, which was proving to be of limited use to the school in view of the acquisition of Cutler Union. The university president added these personal comments:

> I was delighted to have your telegram and phone call accepting my invitation that you head the Eastman School of Music. The few people who know of this share my enthusiasm. It is going to be a big job and a tough one to restore the school to the position it should occupy. I am confident that you will do it, and that you will gain lasting satisfaction from it that will outweigh both the things you are giving up in your present career and the burdens of the Eastman job.[2]

Wallis also confided to his new music school director that he wanted to adopt the title of "dean" within the next two or three years, but in fact the change from "director" to "dean" of the Eastman School of Music took almost forty years to become a reality.

Hendl came to Rochester and met with the faculty on June 16, 1964, holding three meetings to discuss issues and needs for the future. The faculty, which had rarely been asked for opinions on such matters, quickly let the director know of various problems at the school, including scheduling of classes, heavy teaching loads, and lack of an adequate system for academic advising of undergraduate students. Many also expressed a desire to do more chamber music coaching and argued for closer cooperation and collaboration with the Rochester Philharmonic Orchestra. In addition, there was strong support for the use of professional accompanists and for developing a program to teach pianists how to be effective collaborative artists.

These meetings with the new director also produced a number of suggestions for projects that might require foundation support. These included a "composer-in-residence chair" to be held each academic year by a different important composer and a similar suggestion for a yearly "string quartet in residence." Other ideas included (1) a research project to study a group of children from kindergarten

---

[2]   W. Allen Wallis, memo to Walter Hendl, June 4, 1964. SML.

through high school, with the aim of better incorporation of music into school curricula; (2) the construction of a mid-sized auditorium at the school; (3) the development of a complete music theater program in which opera, musical comedy, and musical plays could be studied and produced; (4) replacement of the Austin organ in the Eastman Theatre and the Skinner organ in Kilbourn Hall; and (5) the development of an electronic music studio. All of these ideas gave Walter Hendl much to contemplate concerning his new responsibilities as director at Eastman. The larger benefit of these meetings, however, was the message sent to the Eastman faculty that their ideas were not only welcome but very much needed as the school charted its course for the future. This was a faculty that had rarely been a part of the decision-making process in the past.

  In early September, the school's new director was interviewed by Peter Jacobi of *The New York Times*. It was his first real opportunity to project a vision for the school he was now to lead. Jacobi reported some of his comments:

> I believe firmly in the necessity of producing in the musician an integrated human being. But during formative college years the young musician's most important task is to concentrate on his music.
>
> We'll make forays into new fields of research and take cognizance of advanced techniques in composition and education.
>
> We'll teach reality. The music profession is rough for performer and composer. We do not want to encourage pipe dreams. Also we'll encourage molding not merely the traveling virtuoso but the man of music who can identify with a geographic area and dominate that area.
>
> We must find projects and concepts that encourage what I consider vital—narrowing the gap between funds and grants available for scientific education and monies available for music and the arts.[3]

Hendl described the task he was confronting as having to "make haste slowly," the customary translation of *"festina lente,"* a Latin phrase perhaps first attributed to Augustus Caesar (63 B.C.–A.D. 14). But the new Eastman director would quickly learn that many problems in his new position would not wait for slow solutions.

  Among the personnel difficulties immediately confronting him was the resignation of violinist Joseph Knitzer, who was going to

---

[3] Peter Jacobi, "The Hendl Method," *The New York Times*, September 6, 1964: X7. Copyright © 1964 by The New York Times Co. Reprinted with permission.

Ann Arbor to teach at the University of Michigan. Richard Posner, a student of Knitzer's at the time of his resignation, later described him as "a great psychologist," "tough as nails," and having a "wonderful feel for what a student needed for the real world,"[4] adding that he truly regretted not being able to study with him for more than two years. Knitzer's tenure in Ann Arbor was tragically short. He died on July 1, 1967, at age fifty-four, succumbing to the cancer with which he had courageously struggled for a number of years. Also leaving the faculty in 1964 was the cellist Georges Miquelle, who retired at the end of the 1963–64 school year. Knitzer and Miquelle were very visible and important members of the string faculty at Eastman, and their departure momentarily left the school at a disadvantage in attracting and recruiting qualified violin and cello applicants. Other retirements were pending, and timely decisions needed to be made.

The school held its annual opening convocation in Kilbourn Hall on September 15. W. Allen Wallis was in attendance to formally introduce Walter Hendl to the Eastman community. His remarks included these comments:

> As soon as I came to the University two years ago, this problem of director of the school was at the top of the agenda, and within the first month I started doing something about acquainting myself with the problem and the possibilities. Now that's not as hard to do from the base of the Eastman School as it would be from practically any other base, because we have a large number of alumni among the most outstanding musicians in the world, and so you have a point where you can go for help to start. To talk about the problem, about the musical world, and what it is likely to be in the next thirty years, what the role of music education ought to be, what the role of the Eastman School should be.
>
> And one of the things that both made me feel good, but made me feel overburdened too, was that time and time again, whether the person had any connection with the Eastman School or not, as I left them they would look at me very solemnly and seriously, no matter how cheerful the meeting had been, or how many cocktails we might have consumed in the course of it, and they would say that what happens to Eastman is of the greatest importance to the future of American music.[5]

---

4   Richard Posner, telephone interview by the author, July 10, 2006.
5   W. Allen Wallis, Notes for Convocation Address, September 15, 1964. SML.

Figure 29. Eugene List, teacher of piano, 1964–75.

The new school year was an occasion not only to greet the school's third director but also to welcome two distinguished additions to the faculty: Eugene List and his wife, Carroll Glenn, both of whom brought impressive performing credentials to the school. List had been a pianistic prodigy, making his debut at age ten by playing the Beethoven Concerto No. 3 in C Minor with the Los Angeles Philharmonic under the direction of Artur Rodzinski. He went on to study with Olga Samaroff (1882–1948) and won the 1934 Philadelphia Orchestra Youth Contest, which led to a performance of the Shostakovitch Piano Concerto No. 1, the American premiere of the work. The following year he made his debut with the New York Philharmonic, again performing the Shostakovitch. After graduating from Juilliard, List entered the Special Services Division of the U.S. Army in 1942 and concertized extensively during the war. His most notable performance was a concert for Churchill, Truman, and Stalin at the Potsdam Conference in July 1945. Following the war, he and his wife toured the occupied countries in Europe under the auspices of the U.S. Army. By the time he celebrated the twenty-fifth anniversary of his New York debut, he estimated that he had given almost 2,000 concerts to audiences totaling almost a million people, excluding his radio broadcasts and recordings.

Carroll Glenn had the distinction of being the youngest student ever accepted for Juilliard's regular course when she entered the school at age eleven. Her New York debut took place in 1939 following her receipt of the Naumburg Foundation Award. Within a relatively short period, Glenn won all four major music awards then offered in open competition in the United States: the Naumburg, the Town Hall, the National Federation of Music Clubs, and the Schubert Memorial. She concertized extensively in the United States, Europe, South America, and the Far East and brought this wealth of experience to her teaching at Eastman, much to the benefit of her many students during her twelve years of teaching at the school.

List and Glenn were only the first of a considerable number of musicians who joined the Eastman faculty during Hendl's years as director. The faculty had shown remarkable stability over the years, with many members serving the school for thirty years or more before retirement. Hendl arrived at the beginning of the school's forty-fourth year of operation, yet the original trombone teacher (Emory Remington) and percussion teacher (William Street) were still teaching full-time. They were not alone among those who had served the school since the 1920s. Elvira Wonderlich and Herman Genhart had been among Howard Hanson's first appointments to the faculty back in 1925, and Paul White and

Cecile Genhart had been appointed in 1926. More than a dozen other members of the 1964–65 faculty had been teaching at Eastman since the 1930s. Among the more prominent and visible members of the teaching staff, there was an impression of stability and continuity, with comparatively few resignations to accept appointments elsewhere. All this was about to change for a variety of reasons, however, not the least of which was the increasing numbers of excellent music schools and departments throughout the country that were competing in the recruitment of faculty—often with highly competitive salary offers that placed the Eastman School of Music at a decided disadvantage.

Unfortunately for Walter Hendl, he also had to deal with a number of unexpected deaths among Eastman faculty. The first of these was Verne Thompson, who passed away on November 24, 1964. Thompson, whose impressive credentials have been previously noted, contributed a great deal to the school's music literature curriculum and to the establishment and development of the Collegium Musicum. His friend and colleague, Eugene Selhorst, paid tribute to him in these words:

> His thirst for music was literally insatiable, and it was his constant involvement with real music-making that gave his courses in music literature such unique richness and authority. As advisor and administrator it is difficult to imagine anyone more ideally fitted than Dr. Thompson, anyone more firm in his insistence on the highest of standards, and at the same time so infinitely helpful and sympathetic to the students under his wing.[6]

Thompson's untimely death led to the midyear appointment to the music literature department of Hendrik VanderWerf in February 1965.

The departure of four longtime faculty members was announced on June 3, 1965, at the final faculty meeting of Hendl's first year as director. Retiring from the music education faculty were Howard Hinga and Karl Van Hoesen, and the school was also losing conductors Herman Genhart and Paul White. This was a time when a mandatory retirement age was in place, although a limited number of faculty members were somehow exempted from the requirement—a policy that caused obvious resentment among those for whom no such exception was made. A number of resignations were also announced at the faculty meeting, including that of composer

6 Quoted in *The Score 1965* (Rochester, NY: Eastman School of Music, 1965), 18.

Louis Mennini, who had accepted an offer to become dean of the School of Music at the North Carolina School of the Arts. Hendl, however, was also able to announce several important faculty appointments, including two visiting professors: Burrill Phillips, who was coming to Eastman as visiting professor of composition, and Laszlo Halasz, who was joining the teaching staff as visiting professor of conducting. Other additions to the faculty included Richard Pittman, who had a relatively brief but productive career as a conductor at Eastman, and cellist Alan Harris, who taught at the school until 1975, then left to teach at the Cleveland Institute of Music before returning to Eastman about twenty years later.

Hendl also announced a very significant new appointment when he informed the Eastman faculty that Brooks Smith would join the full-time faculty in the fall of 1966 to teach accompanying and piano. Smith was well-known throughout the world as a collaborative pianist, especially with regard to his work for twenty years with the great violinist Jascha Heifetz. As a young and very promising piano student, he had been awarded a full scholarship for study at the Juilliard School, where his teachers were Rosina Lhevinne (1880–1976) and Josef Lhevinne (1874–1944). After graduating from Juilliard in 1939, he accompanied such singers as Risë Stevens (b. 1913) and Mack Harrell (1909–60) and later became director of the newly organized Aspen Music School and Festival. He had worked with many of the leading artists of his day, and he was coming to Eastman at Hendl's invitation to open a new department of accompanying.

New to the faculty for the 1965–66 school year would be Donald Shetler and Katherine Crews. Shetler was coming to Eastman from Case Western Reserve as a professor of music education. Crews, who was teaching at Ohio University, would be an associate professor of music education at Eastman. The hiring of Shetler and Crews coincided with the selection of Everett Gates as the new chair of the music education department. Gates had an interesting and somewhat unusual background, having studied engineering during his first two years of college before coming to the Eastman School of Music, where he earned his bachelor of music degree in 1939. He remained at the school for graduate study, as well as for the opportunity to take more engineering courses at the University of Rochester. Because of the advent of World War II, however, he did not complete his master's degree until 1948.

During the war, Gates worked for Taylor Instruments in Rochester, a company that provided control equipment for the Oak Ridge Laboratories and for the Manhattan Project, which developed the atomic bomb. Following the war he did private teaching and professional studio work, then returned to Eastman to work on his doctorate. Gates joined the Eastman faculty in 1958 and became chair of the music education department when William Larson retired. Gates was not supportive of the long-standing policy of hiring a large number of part-time faculty members in music education and felt strongly that the department needed full-time people, of whom Shetler and Crews were the first to be appointed. He was not especially unhappy to see Larson retire, a man he described as "very aloof" and with "his own psychological problems,"[7] the latter a reference to the fact that Larson had originally come to Eastman as the school's psychologist. On the other hand, Gates greatly admired Karl Van Hoesen, whom he described as a superb musician, adding that he "learned more from him than [from] anyone else at Eastman."[8]

Hendl's second year as director began with the announcement that a new department of conducting and ensembles was being established, with Donald Hunsberger as chair and Lazslo Halasz as head of the conducting curriculum. The school year continued with a number of special events, something of a trademark of the Hendl administration. First there was a celebration of the Polish Millennium on October 26, 1965, with a chamber music concert in Kilbourn Hall under the direction of John Celentano. The program included music of Jan Kleczynski (1756–1828), Jan Maklakiewicz (1899–1954), Feliks Nowowiejski (1877–1946), Witold Lutosawski (1913–94), Karol Szymanowski (1882–1937), Tadeusz Paciorkiewicz (1916–98), and Kazimierz Serocki (1922–81). Very little, if any, of this music had previously been heard in Rochester. Two months later Hendl held a special convocation in Kilbourn Hall in honor of the seventieth anniversary of the birth of Paul Hindemith (1895–1963). The convocation opened with remarks by the director, followed by personal recollections by Eastman faculty members William Cerny and Robert Sutton. Several musical selections concluded the convocation.

On December 16, 1965, the Eastman Philharmonia was joined by the Eastman School Chorus and the Children's Chorus from the Rochester City School District in the Western Hemisphere premiere of the Requiem, Op. 27, by Dmitry Kabalevsky (1904–87), which the composer dedicated "to the memory of those who were killed in the struggle against fascism." Kabalevsky used words by Robert Rozhdestvenski (1932–94) as his text, and the English translation was provided by Ronald V. Harrington. The Children's Chorus,

---

[7]   Everett Gates, telephone interview by the author, May 23, 2005.
[8]   Ibid.

prepared by Milford Fargo, attracted much favorable comment for the excellence and beauty of its singing, and the performance provided Fargo with the idea for a permanent children's chorus, which he inaugurated the following September.

The major event of the 1965–66 school year, however, was not connected with either Hindemith or Kabalevsky but involved Igor Stravinsky (1882–1971) and Robert Craft (b. 1923), who were distinguished visitors at the Eastman School for five days in March. Craft, a noted conductor and writer, had become Stravinsky's closest associate over the years. Hendl later commented on Stravinsky's visit to Eastman:

> Igor Stravinsky did not come to Eastman to teach, but the impact of his week with us was immeasurable. And how could it have been otherwise? Exposure to the actuality of Stravinsky provided an immediate and unforgettable demonstration of the mystique of creativity itself, and of the self-renewing vitality of the creative life, a vitality quite beyond mere energy.[9]

"Stravinsky Week," as it was officially called, commenced on Monday, March 7, with a program of Stravinsky's chamber and vocal works, including the Sonata for Two Pianos (1944), *Three Shakespeare Songs* (1953), *Three Pieces for String Quartet* (1914), *Concertino* (1920), *Three Japanese Lyrics* (1913), the anthem *The Dove Descending Breaks the Air* (1962), *Elegy for John F. Kennedy* (1964), and the *Duo Concertant* (1932). A convocation for students and faculty took place on Tuesday, with Stravinsky and his wife joining Hendl on the Kilbourn Hall stage.

Provision was made on Wednesday for college and secondary school visitations to Eastman, with the Eastman Wind Ensemble performing the *Symphonies of Wind Instruments* (1920, revised 1947) and the Eastman School Symphony Orchestra performing two excerpts from the ballet *Petrushka* (1911, revised 1947). The day's events also included an open rehearsal of sections from *The Flood* (1962), with Robert Craft conducting the Eastman Philharmonia. A seminar entitled "The Performer and Contemporary Compositional Techniques," including discussion of Stravinsky's Septet, took place on Thursday, March 10; it involved Stravinsky, Craft, and Hendl along with Eastman faculty members Bernard Rogers and John Celentano.

---

[9] Quoted in "Stravinsky Week," *Notes from Eastman* (Rochester, NY: Eastman School of Music, September 1966), 3.

Figure 30. Igor Stravinsky with the Eastman Philharmonia, March 1966.

The week ended with a gala concert performed by the Eastman Philharmonia in the Eastman Theatre on Friday. Stravinsky
opened the program by conducting *Fireworks,* Op. 4 (1908), followed by Robert Craft conducting the "Largo" from the Symphony
in E-flat, Op. 1 (1905–7), *Four Etudes* (1929), *Variations: In Memoriam
Aldous Huxley* (1965), and excerpts from the television drama *The
Flood.* The program concluded with the composer conducting the
suite from the ballet *The Firebird* (1945 version), after which he was
awarded the honorary degree doctor of humane letters. Stravinsky
was delighted with the Eastman Philharmonia and later spoke very
highly of his experiences at Eastman.

It is hardly possible to describe the pleasure this great composer
gave to the orchestra and to the students and faculty at the Eastman
School of Music. It had been a glorious week for everyone, but the
chief beneficiary was probably Walter Hendl. Even his severest critics, including those most strongly opposed to his selection as the
school's third director, had to concede that "Stravinsky Week"—and
all the extraordinary benefits it had brought to the Eastman School
community—was an event that could never have taken place during Howard Hanson's years as director. As Hendl concluded his
second year at Eastman, he had every reason to feel a genuine sense
of accomplishment. He had made some very significant additions

to the faculty and had brought a new sense of professionalism and excitement to the institution. W. Allen Wallis must have felt a growing confidence that his selection of Walter Hendl had been a wise choice. Yet there were problems to be solved, not the least of which was the simple fact that the operating reserve for the Eastman School of Music was nearly depleted. University Provost McCrea Hazlett had cautioned Hendl the previous August that "we need to take bold and imaginative steps in securing funds not merely for inauguration of new programs, but for the continuance of old ones."[10] An added factor, of which Hazlett may not have been completely aware, was that the Eastman School of Music faculty was becoming increasingly unwilling to continue working at the current salary levels. The immediate future would witness a level of activism never before seen among Eastman faculty members.

[10] McCrea Hazlett, memo to Walter Hendl, August 23, 1965. SML.

Chapter 13

1966–68

The Faculty Association

During Howard Hanson's lengthy tenure as director of the Eastman School of Music, the faculty never mounted a concerted effort
to secure better compensation. Individual faculty members occasionally attempted to gain improvement for themselves, but usually with minimal or no success. The situation affected everyone,
but some more than others. As previously noted, members of the
Rochester Philharmonic Orchestra who taught at Eastman were
especially ill treated because of their double employment. The policy of paying them lower salaries for their work at the school was
somehow justified by the salaries they were making as members of
the orchestra. The two income sources perhaps combined to constitute an adequate living, but to earn that adequate living, these
faculty members had to play the full philharmonic season—including the "pops" and educational concerts—as well as maintaining a
full teaching schedule at the school. Some of the most distinguished
members of the faculty found themselves in this situation, and it is
a tribute to their loyalty to the school and to their students that they
did not seek jobs elsewhere.

Another group of faculty members who were paid rather low
salaries were those with significant teaching responsibilities in the
school's preparatory department. Historically, there had been no
clear distinction between the collegiate and preparatory faculties,
since many faculty members had taught both collegiate and preparatory students. The exact ratio of preparatory-to-collegiate responsibilities varied greatly from one individual to another, but the
faculty members with the lowest salaries were generally those who
taught mainly in the preparatory department. As already recounted,
these people with dual responsibilities had posed something of a
dilemma when academic rank was introduced at the school. The
issue for most of them, however, was not rank but money. At the
time of Walter Hendl's appointment as the school's third director, a
new junior faculty member with considerable preparatory depart-

ment teaching responsibilities could have been making as little as $5,000 per year before taxes. While senior members of the faculty were better compensated, the general salary levels at Eastman, as they had developed during Hanson's long tenure as director, could only be described as rather abysmal.

Eastman School salaries had been quite generous when the school first opened in 1921. The lowest salary was $2,500 and the highest was $10,000, but the range for everyone else was between $3,000 and $8,000. (Forty years later, three dozen full-time members of the Eastman faculty were making less than that $8,000 figure.) Alf Klingenberg, the school's first director, earned $7,500 per year, and the Eastman School offered Jan Sibelius a $20,000 salary in an unsuccessful effort to recruit him as the school's principal teacher of composition and theory. While the offer to Sibelius was positively extravagant, the salaries earned by Eastman faculty were generous by the standards of the day. As a matter of fact, they may have been more generous than the salaries then earned by their faculty colleagues at the University of Rochester. However, as the years passed, Eastman School salaries had gradually fallen further and further behind, and there was no support from Howard Hanson or anyone else in the administration to do much about it. In addition, teaching loads were heavy at Eastman, with some studio teachers required to teach as many as twenty-five hours per week. Moreover, because base salaries were so low, many faculty members taught an overload to earn extra money. It was not uncommon, therefore, for someone to be teaching as many as thirty or more hours per week.[1]

If the members of the Eastman faculty were somehow content to quietly bear with their situation during the Hanson years, they began to show increasing willingness to confront the problem once Walter Hendl arrived on the scene. The first step in addressing the issue was the formation of a committee of professors and associate professors who studied the 1965–66 faculty salaries at the Eastman School of Music. The committee submitted its report at a faculty meeting on November 23, 1966. The findings were based on five sources. The first was a survey of nine other music schools of high quality, carried out by Associate Director Allen Irvine McHose at the request of the university's central administration. The second source was a broader survey instituted by the committee and carried out by Charles A. Lutton, director of Lutton Music Personnel Service, at the time the largest and most prominent placement

---

[1] The author's teaching load during his first years at Eastman was as high as thirty-two hours per week.

service in America for professional musicians. Lutton's survey provided detailed information on more than a thousand faculty members in thirty-three diverse music schools. The third source for the committee's report was the current "Economic Status of the Profession" report from the American Association of University Professors (AAUP), covering 161,921 faculty members in all disciplines at 905 institutions. The AAUP findings were supplemented by the "Salaries in Higher Education" report from the National Education Association, which covered an even greater number of faculty members at 995 colleges and universities. The final source for the committee's report consisted of salary information reported by the University of Rochester to the AAUP.

The committee's report presented some sobering observations. In the first place, not one of the nine schools polled by McHose had an average or a minimum salary in any rank as low as those at the Eastman School of Music. Simply stated, the Eastman School was compensating its faculty at a lower rate than any of its competitors. Charles Lutton provided support for this conclusion by showing that average salaries at Eastman were lower than the average salaries in his broader sampling of thirty-three schools, almost four times the number of institutions McHose had studied. These reports provided solid statistical evidence to support what each member of the Eastman faculty already understood: they were inadequately compensated for their work at the school.

This situation was deemed even more serious when it was reported by the committee that average salaries at the university's River Campus colleges were 48 percent higher than those at the Eastman School of Music. No member of the faculty could find any reasonable explanation for the fact that University of Rochester faculty members in other disciplines were earning so much more than the Eastman faculty. Therefore, in concluding its report, the committee made three basic recommendations: the institution of salary parity between the Eastman School of Music and the other colleges of the university, the establishment of stated maximum teaching loads, and the formation of a faculty advisory committee. These recommendations, along with the committee report, were adopted unanimously by those attending the faculty meeting and were then submitted to Walter Hendl and to the University of Rochester administration.

The surveys that led to these recommendations simply confirmed what virtually everyone at Eastman intuitively knew about the salary situation at the school. Statistics for the 1966–67 school year show that salaries among full-time members of the faculty ranged from $4,700 to $15,000, with the average salary only a little more than $9,000. Only eleven members of the performance faculty earned more than $10,000 per year, while twenty-eight members of the performance faculty were among those earning the lowest salaries. Among those earning less than $7,500 were several of the school's most widely known and distinguished teachers. Especially disturbing were the salaries of those members of the full-time faculty who also played in the Rochester Philharmonic Orchestra, among whom the salary range was between $5,800 and $8,300 per year, well below the median.

As a result of the action taken at the November 23 faculty meeting, an Eastman Senators Committee was formed to pursue these issues, the committee consisting of Eastman faculty members who were either present or former members of the University of Rochester Faculty Senate. The committee members were composer Wayne Barlow, M. Alfred Bichsel from the church music department, musicologist Charles Warren Fox, Eugene Selhorst from music literature, theorist Robert Sutton, Millard Taylor and Francis Tursi from the string department, and music librarian Ruth Watanabe. The group met with Walter Hendl and Associate Provost Robert France on December 20, 1966, at which time France informed them that the University of Rochester preferred not to make comparisons between salary levels at Eastman and those at the River Campus colleges. Furthermore, he told the committee that the university's policy was that the only permissible method of salary negotiation would be on an individual basis. There was to be no collective bargaining.

Dependence on individual negotiations, however, was not the path Eastman faculty members were choosing to follow. Therefore, the committee communicated with President Wallis immediately following the winter recess.[2] The committee asked for an acknowledgment of the serious inequity existing at Eastman, an inequity that threatened the school's position of leadership in music education, and asked the university president to recommend to the trustees that the forthcoming 1967–68 budget should correct the inequity. There was little expectation that the university administration would simply comply with these requests, but the communication with the president presented the faculty's position on salaries with unmistakable clarity.

To create a stronger bargaining position, the Eastman School of Music faculty decided to formally organize by creating a Faculty Association. The group came into existence at a meeting held on

---

[2] Eastman Senators Committee, memo to W. Allen Wallis, January 6, 1967. SML.

Thursday, January 19, 1967, with Robert Sutton, associate professor of theory and composition, chosen to be its president. Wayne Barlow, professor of composition and associate dean for graduate research studies, was selected as the group's vice president and treasurer, and Anastasia Jempelis, a senior instructor in violin and viola, was elected secretary. Dues were established at ten dollars per year. A policy board was formed consisting of Phyllis Clark from the piano department, Everett Gates from the music education department, Gilbert Kilpack from the humanities department, and Ronald Leonard from the string department. The association met on January 31, 1967, at which time Robert Sutton announced that President Wallis had not accepted the findings or recommendations of the salary report. Sutton also reported that the board of directors of the Eastman School Alumni Association had sent a letter to the university president, with copies to Joseph Wilson, chair of the board of trustees, expressing concern over the low level of Eastman faculty salaries. An official faculty meeting was held later the same day, with President Wallis presiding, but by his request the secretary recorded no minutes of the meeting.

Meetings of the Faculty Association continued throughout the spring semester, with concerns broadening beyond salary levels to include a study of teaching loads, especially among those whose responsibilities included both studio and classroom teaching. Reports of the tension between the faculty and administration became public in April, with newspaper articles commenting on the situation at the school. When the Faculty Association met in early May, the school's associate director, Allen Irvine McHose, reported that the coming salary offers for the 1967–68 school year would include the largest increases in the history of the Eastman School, an announcement taken as evidence that the pressure being exerted by the association was having a positive effect. At the same meeting the association voted to retain the firm of Branch, Jefferson, Friedman, Van Voorhis, and Wise as legal counsel, with John Branch to serve as its lawyer.

Branch met with the association on May 19, 1967, and recommended continuation of gathering and maintaining up-to-date information on faculty salaries. He also suggested revising the association's negotiating position to include demands for attaining salary parity with the River Campus through adjusted increases over a period of not more than two years. Furthermore, Branch recommended that the university's board of trustees be asked to establish an evaluation committee to study conditions and long-range goals at the Eastman School of Music. Branch also suggested that the association's policy board be authorized to carry out an information and public relations program.

The Faculty Association resumed its activities in September, first by introducing a resolution at a general faculty meeting that included this affirmation:

> We, the faculty of the Eastman School of Music, affirm our endorsement of the Eastman School of Music Faculty Association, and call upon the Director of the Eastman School of Music and the President of the University of Rochester to recognize the Association as a legitimate organization of faculty members of the School, and to give serious consideration to its requests and recommendations and prompt, direct responses to its communications.[3]

The resolution was passed by faculty vote, with a request that it be transmitted in writing to Director Hendl and President Wallis, asking for an early reply. The association met on October 26, at which time it elected officers for the new school year. Sutton and Barlow were reelected to their posts, and Vincent Lenti was elected association secretary. Everett Gates, Gilbert Kilpack, and Ronald Leonard would remain as policy board members, and Gladys Leventon from the piano department would replace Phyllis Clark.

The association's struggle for better salaries at Eastman was greatly assisted by cooperation from the Rochester Chapter of the AAUP. One of the larger issues the salary negotiations had uncovered was that the University of Rochester had been submitting its salary statistics to the AAUP without including the Eastman figures. This information, published annually by the AAUP, presented a very favorable picture of faculty compensation at the university, but it did so only by excluding over eighty members of its faculty who worked at the Eastman School of Music and earned far less than their colleagues in other colleges and schools of the University of Rochester. Including the Eastman salaries would obviously diminish the university's ranking and reputation with regard to faculty compensation.

The unfairness of this situation was at least partially acknowledged in December 1967, when the university submitted its salary figures to the AAUP while also submitting—for the first time ever—separate figures for the Eastman School of Music. To explain the lower salary levels at Eastman, the university added a footnote

---

3 Resolution, faculty meeting minutes, September 19, 1967. SML.

to indicate that the Eastman figures included persons whose primary teaching responsibilities were in the pre-college division as well as persons who had full-time appointments with the Rochester Philharmonic Orchestra. While this observation was accurate, it avoided acknowledging the simple fact that these thirty-six people were nonetheless full-time teachers at the Eastman School and were still being paid very low salaries for their work. Who they taught and whatever other professional work they might be doing were not pertinent considerations.

It was during this period that Joseph Mariano, principal flute in the orchestra, approached the school's administration indicating that he wished to leave the Rochester Philharmonic and wondering if the administration would be willing to do anything financially to offset the loss of income he would incur if he resigned from the orchestra. Walter Hendl was not especially supportive of the historic ties between Eastman and the Rochester Philharmonic and was therefore inclined to help Mariano leave the orchestra so he could devote all his time and energy to his Eastman teaching. The university administration therefore granted permission to Eastman's administration to negotiate with Mariano and any other members of the Eastman faculty who wanted to discontinue their employment with the Rochester Philharmonic. A sizable number of faculty members were potentially involved in such negotiations:

John Beck, instructor of percussion
Abram Boone, senior instructor of violin
Alan Harris, assistant professor of cello
Stanley Hasty, associate professor of clarinet
Anastasia Jempelis, senior instructor of violin
Donald Knaub, associate professor of tuba
Eileen Malone, professor of harp
Joseph Mariano, professor of flute
Sidney Mear, professor of trumpet
George Osborn, instructor of trombone
William Osseck, associate professor of clarinet
Verne Reynolds, associate professor of horn
Robert Sprenkle, professor of oboe
John Thomas, assistant professor of flute
K. David Van Hoesen, associate professor of bassoon
Milan Yancich, assistant professor of horn and ensembles
Oscar Zimmerman, professor of double bass

Nine of the faculty members were principals in the orchestra, and the ensuing negotiations led to a significant number of resignations at the end of the 1967–68 season. The Rochester public was made fully aware of this development through the daily newspapers, which announced on March 28, 1968, that five principal players and seven others were leaving the orchestra at the end of the season. To many readers this was disturbing news, since members of the school's faculty had been performing with the Rochester Philharmonic Orchestra (often as principals) for forty-five years. Moreover, this factor added to the continuing problems facing the philharmonic's future.

Several days later, Howard Hanson commented on the situation in an article appearing in the Rochester evening newspaper, the *Times-Union:*

> [I]t is becoming increasingly difficult to combine teaching and orchestral playing. This problem is certainly not limited to Rochester. It is familiar to every symphonic city where the artists of the symphonic orchestra are also members of music school faculties. Yet, in spite of all of the logistic and financial difficulties involved, I am convinced that . . . the problems can be solved. The orchestras need artists of the calibre of a Mariano or Sprenkle. The students also need the instruction of men with such experience and dedication.[4]

Hanson continued by suggesting the use of associates to replace the first-desk players at some of the services, adding that "the question is not what is best for the school, nor what is best for the orchestra, but what is best for the community."[5] The suggestion to not require the more important first-desk players to participate in all of the orchestra's concerts reflected the fact that the responsibilities of members of the orchestra—as well as those of members of the school's faculty—had been increasing over the years. The orchestra performed fifteen symphonic programs per season, but it was also involved in a significant number of "pops" and educational concerts. Hanson was essentially recommending that first-desk players should perform only the symphonic concerts, perhaps a reasonable suggestion but one that found few sympathetic ears at the time.

Hanson returned to the topic once again on April 14, obviously frustrated and perhaps somewhat angered by the failure of the school administration and the Civic Music Association, which managed the orchestra, to reach any agreement.

---

[4] Quoted in *Times-Union* [Rochester, NY], April 2, 1968. SML (news clipping).
[5] Ibid.

The exodus represented the final break-down of a cooperative arrangement between the Eastman School and the C.M.A. which had existed for over 40 years. Perhaps this break-down was inevitable. Perhaps, with better communication, it could have been avoided.[6]

Communication, however, was not particularly good. Neither the school nor the Civic Music Association management made any real effort to accommodate the continued participation of Eastman faculty as members of the orchestra. The lack of commitment to preserving an arrangement that had somehow served both organizations for forty years doomed any prospects for agreement.

Hanson's regret over the breakdown of cooperation between the school and the orchestra was somewhat disingenuous. He had long recognized that the combination of full-time orchestral playing and full-time teaching was simply too much to ask of anyone. Yet during his many years as the school's director, he had never negotiated any change in the arrangement that had kept so many of his faculty members overextended by holding both full-time positions. Historically, the Eastman School of Music had subsidized the orchestra essentially to guarantee the availability of teachers of orchestral instruments on its faculty. But the growth of the orchestral department at the school in combination with the increasingly heavy performance schedules of the Rochester Philharmonic and Rochester Civic Orchestra was creating too heavy a demand on those musicians who were doubly employed by the orchestra and the school. Hanson had acknowledged this problem nine years before these events in the spring of 1959, when he wrote a memo to the university president, Cornelis W. de Kiewiet, complaining that the situation was resulting in lower standards of teaching.[7]

In view of this recognition that a problem existed, it is surprising that nothing was done at the time to address the issue. Instead, Hanson's attention was quickly redirected toward his opinion that the Civic Music Association was taking unfair financial advantage of the school. The financial situation was outlined in a memo dated March 27, 1959, from Hanson to de Kiewiet:

> [T]he payment by the Eastman School of Music to members of the orchestra for teaching services will amount this year to $76,849.81. If to this is added the $50,000 contribution [to the Civic Music Association] the total amounts to $126,849.81. Adding to this $53,775, the salaries

---

[6] Quoted in *Times-Union* [Rochester, NY], April 14, 1968. SML (news clipping).
[7] Howard Hanson, memo to Cornelis W. de Kiewiet, March 20, 1959. SML.

paid to orchestral faculty members who are *not* in the orchestra, the total salary budget for the entire orchestral department amounts to $180,624.81, which would be sufficiently large to engage full-time members for our orchestral faculty.[8]

Hanson's interpretation of these figures led him to conclude that there was no longer any advantage for the school to subsidize the orchestra. The funds could be redirected to faculty salaries. At the same time, Hanson raised questions concerning the fees paid by the orchestra for use of the Eastman Theatre, fees he felt were unreasonably low. His conclusion, which he outlined in a report to the school's board of managers, was that for the school to continue to operate without a deficit, it had to be relieved of financial pressures from the Civic Music Association and it had to make the Eastman Theatre at least partially self-sustaining.[9]

These considerations led to difficult negotiations with the Civic Music Association and eventually to a new agreement in the spring of 1960, setting revised fees for the use of the theater. Yet these issues were debated once again the following spring, when the school suggested that the fees paid by the Civic Music Association still remained far below the actual costs to the school. At a meeting on March 17, 1961, Hanson went so far as to state that what he interpreted as an inflexible attitude on the part of the orchestral management led him to the conclusion that it would be better if his faculty members "did not have two responsibilities."[10] The ongoing difficulties between the Eastman School of Music and the Civic Music Association were simply a reflection that both institutions had important budgetary problems and that neither side could afford to be generous.

Now, four years after he had retired as the director of the Eastman School of Music, Howard Hanson was somehow attempting to salvage the relationship between the school and the Rochester Philharmonic. The suggestion that the orchestra should hire associates to replace the important first-desk players at the educational and "pop" concerts may have seemed entirely reasonable to him

[8]   Howard Hanson, memo to Cornelis W. de Kiewiet, March 27, 1959. SML (original emphasis).
[9]   Howard Hanson, Report to the Board of Managers, spring 1959 [undated]. SML.
[10]   Minutes of the Study Committee Examining the Proper Relationship of the Eastman School of Music, University of Rochester, to the Civic Music Association, March 17, 1961. SML.

at the time. The orchestra would retain the services of these valued players only for the important symphonic concerts, thereby allowing them to devote more of their time, energy, and talent to teaching. Unfortunately, Hanson failed to persuade anyone, and the exodus of significant numbers of Eastman faculty members from the orchestra became inevitable.

The issue had become a crisis largely because these faculty members felt they were unfairly compensated by the Eastman School of Music and resolved to do something to remedy the situation. Therefore, most of them seized the opportunity to earn more money for their Eastman teaching, even if it entailed leaving the orchestra. By the 1969–70 season, the only Eastman faculty members remaining in the Rochester Philharmonic Orchestra were John Beck, Abram Boone, Eileen Malone, George Osborn, Milan Yancich, and Oscar Zimmerman.[11] The orchestra had lost its principal flute, principal clarinet, principal bassoon, principal French horn, principal trumpet, and several other key players who were now just faculty members at the school and no longer performing with the philharmonic. As a result of these resignations, many instrumental students at the school no longer had the opportunity to see and hear their teachers performing in the orchestra on a weekly basis. In addition, over the years many students had played second stand in the orchestra, sitting next to their Eastman professors and learning by sharing an invaluable professional experience. This, too, was lost as a result of the resignations. The Rochester Philharmonic Orchestra and the Eastman School of Music would increasingly chart separate paths in the future, notwithstanding periodic efforts to cooperate more fully in personnel matters.

Nonetheless, the issues addressed at the time were essentially financial and not professional. As a group, members of the Eastman School faculty who had played with the Rochester Philharmonic Orchestra had been among the most poorly compensated for their teaching, and this situation was now substantially changed for the better. As faculty salaries at the school continued to rise to more acceptable levels, the activities of the Faculty Association gradually lessened. As a group, senior instructors who mainly taught in the preparatory department may have derived the least benefit from the association's efforts. They were in the least favorable negotiating position, and, as the associate provost had pointed out at the end of 1966, salary negotiations could only be pursued on an individual basis.

---

[11]   Three other members of the orchestra had begun teaching at Eastman: Richard Jones (instructor of trumpet), Jonathan Parkes (instructor of oboe), and William Cahn (associate in percussion).

For most members of the faculty, however, the Faculty Association had provided an invaluable service by focusing attention on salary inequities, attention that undoubtedly led to an overall improvement in the compensation offered to Eastman teachers. The association's president, Robert Sutton, to whom his faculty colleagues owed so very much, may have paid a heavy price for his leadership, however. Despite the fact that he was recommended to be the next chair of the theory department, he left the Eastman School of Music in 1974 after having been passed over for that post.

In truth, faculty salaries at the Eastman School would probably have improved in the coming years with or without the activism of its faculty and its willingness to confront the administration about the basic unfairness in levels of compensation. The increasingly competitive nature of music education in the United States would have made it impossible for the school to either attract or retain top-rated faculty in the years to come without a change in salary policies. Howard Hanson may have had the unique ability to convince his faculty that the Eastman School of Music was the only place to teach irrespective of the salary he was offering, but that line of reasoning found less and less acceptance in the years following his retirement.

Chapter 14

1966–71

The Hendl Years Continue

Although the most difficult issue confronting Walter Hendl during his third year as director of the Eastman School was the faculty campaign for better salaries, he was by no means inactive in his responsibility to other matters of importance at the school. Prominent among these matters was the ongoing necessity of making important faculty appointments. The 1966–67 school year began with welcoming the return of Josephine Antoine to the school's voice department. Antoine, who had taught at Eastman from 1957 to 1959, was back in Rochester to resume a very successful teaching career at the school. New to the voice department in the fall of 1966 was a young tenor named John Maloy, who would distinguish himself in the years to come not only through his exceptional teaching but also by means of a long, successful tenure as chair of the voice department. A graduate of Indiana University, where he studied with Anna Kaskas, Maloy was the recipient of a Fulbright grant for study at the Hochschule für Musik in Hamburg, Germany, during the 1957–58 school year. For the next seven years he was a leading tenor in various German and Swiss opera houses. He returned to the United States for graduate study at the University of Southern California and at the Eastman School, where he now found himself on the faculty.

This was also the year the Eastman School of Music welcomed Brooks Smith to its faculty. Hendl had announced his appointment the previous year, and Smith now arrived to develop new courses in accompanying for Eastman piano students. Also new to the piano department was Maria Luisa Faini, who arrived in September following a serious automobile accident earlier in the summer. She came to Eastman as a visiting professor of piano to teach for Orazio Frugoni, who had been granted a sabbatical leave for the academic year. Faini was an Italian who had studied with Carlo Angelelli (1872–1936) and Alfredo Casella (1883–1947), eventually becoming Casella's assistant at the Academia Chighiana in Siena. She

Figure 31. John Maloy, teacher of voice, 1966–2006.

earned an artist diploma from the Academia de Santa Cecilia in
Rome and won both the Muzio Clementi and Camerata Napole-
tana competitions. As with most European musicians of her generation, her career was interrupted by World War II, but she eventually
resettled in the United States in 1949, teaching in Hartford, Connecticut, until her appointment as visiting professor at Eastman.
She had been a frequent recitalist not only in Connecticut but also in
New York City and Washington, DC. An appearance in Washington
on December 15, 1958, drew rave comments from Paul Hume, the
noted music critic of *The Washington Post*, whose review included
these remarks:

> Last night she played one of those engaging, wholly satisfying recit-
> als you long to hear every time you enter a concert hall, but seldom
> do. . . .
>   Among the many qualities that enhance her playing remarkably
> in these days of strong pianists is this personable artist's unusual
> deftness of touch, her fleet but always secure scales even in the most
> rapid passages, and her unceasingly light and shadow, nuance and
> balance, wrought with fingers and pedals, all of which she masters
> with a command that is concealed in the light of her musicianship.[1]

Although she had anticipated spending only a year in Rochester,
Faini accepted a full-time appointment to the faculty as an associate
professor in the fall of 1967, following Frugoni's decision to remain
in Italy after his leave of absence. Unfortunately, Frugoni was expe-
riencing many difficulties in sustaining what had once been considered a very promising performing career, being seriously affected
by the combination of pressure from full-time teaching and steadily
increasing performance anxieties. He soon stopped performing, but
he enjoyed a fruitful career in Italy as a teacher, as well as being a
frequent judge at major international piano competitions.

   Among the other new faculty members in 1966 was Mary Aver-
sano, who came to teach Italian at the school and brought her love
of the language and the culture of Italy to her many students during
a tenure at Eastman that extended from 1966 until her retirement
in 1986. Alice Benston from the University of Chicago also joined
the faculty in 1966 as chair of the humanities department, replacing
Charles Riker in that position. Riker, who had been a close friend

---

[1] Paul Hume, "Maria Faini in Engaging Recital," *The Washington Post*, December
16, 1958. Author's collection.

and associate of Howard Hanson's, did not enjoy a similar relation-ship with Walter Hendl. He learned that he had been replaced as chair of the department by reading about Benston's appointment in the morning newspaper. Other new faculty appointees included Adrienne Auvil and Bernard Flores in theory and Peter Stone in music literature. Perhaps the most important faculty appointment of the new school year, however, was that of Samuel Adler. Bernard Rogers had initiated the process that led to Adler's appointment by asking Walter Hendl to select representative scores from about fifteen composers who were in their mid-thirties. Rogers examined and compared the works of these young composers, who included Samuel Adler, which led to his recommendation that Adler be offered a teaching position at Eastman.

Samuel Adler taught at Eastman for twenty-nine years and was chair of the composition department from 1974 until his retirement in 1995. Born in Germany, he came to the United States in 1939 and was educated at Boston University and Harvard University. His composition teachers were Herbert Fromm (1905–95), Walter Piston (1894–1976), Randall Thompson (1899–1984), Paul Hindemith (1895–1963), and Aaron Copland (1900–1980). He studied conduct-ing with Serge Koussevitzky (1874–1951), and he founded and con-ducted the Seventh Army Symphony Orchestra while serving in the United States Army from 1950 to 1952. Adler had received teach-ing grants from both the Rockefeller and Ford foundations and had been the recipient of the University of Houston's Charles Ives Memorial Award in 1963. Although he was only thirty-eight years old at the time of his appointment to the Eastman faculty, Adler became a major and influential factor in his department's sub-sequent ability to recruit large numbers of highly talented young composition students who came to Eastman for undergraduate and graduate study.

Warren Benson joined Adler on the composition faculty in Sep-tember 1967, hired to replace Bernard Rogers who retired at the end of the 1966–67 school year. Born in 1924, Benson was an excellent percussionist who had played timpani in the Detroit Symphony while an undergraduate at the University of Michigan. A com-poser of many orchestral, band, choral, chamber, and solo works, he had won seven ASCAP[2] Awards for Serious Music. Benson had also received two successive Fulbright teaching grants to establish a five-year bilingual music course at Anatolia College in Salonika,

---

[2] American Society of Composers, Authors, and Publishers.

Greece. He had been a consultant to Voice of America and a resident composer at the MacDowell Colony in 1955 and 1963. Prior to accepting his appointment at Eastman, he was composer in residence and professor of music at Ithaca College, where he had been on the faculty for thirteen years. Benson served the Eastman School with great distinction until his retirement in 1993.

One prominent composer who was not invited to join the Eastman faculty was David Diamond. Recall that Diamond had been among the first to congratulate Walter Hendl when he was appointed the school's third director. In his letter to Hendl at the time, he had inquired about the possibility of being engaged by the school when Bernard Rogers retired.[3] He candidly admitted that Hanson had never been particularly fond of him, and he perhaps felt the many years of estrangement from his alma mater might now come to an end. But Hendl did not respond to Diamond's overture, nor is there any record that he responded three years later when Diamond approached him once again at the time of Rogers's retirement in 1967.

Other new faculty members in September 1967 included Willis Page, Zvi Zeitlin, and Russell Saunders. Page was appointed professor of conducting and head of the orchestral conducting program. A native of Rochester, he had graduated from the Eastman School of Music in 1939 with a bachelor of music degree and with performer's certificates in both double bass and tuba. Following his graduation he became a member of the Boston Symphony Orchestra, playing double bass under Serge Koussevitzky. While in Boston he studied conducting with Arthur Fiedler (1894–1979), Charles Munch (1891–1968), and Pierre Monteux (1875–1964), then became associate conductor of the Buffalo Philharmonic under Josef Krips (1902–74). In 1959 he accepted an appointment as conductor of the Nashville Symphony and remained there until coming to the Eastman School of Music eight years later.

The violinist Zvi Zeitlin was forty-four years old when he joined the faculty in 1967, and he has enjoyed an exceptional teaching career at Eastman well into the twenty-first century. Born in Dubrovna, Belarus, Zeitlin was raised in Israel. He came to the United States to study at the Juilliard School of Music, from which he received a diploma and a post-graduate diploma. His teachers included Sascha Jacobsen (1895–1971), Louis Persinger (1887–1966),

---

[3]   David Diamond, letter to Walter Hendl, May 31, 1964. Private papers of Walter Hendl.

Figure 32. Zvi Zeitlin, teacher of violin 1967–.

and Ivan Galamian (1903–81). Zeitlin's career as a concert artist has taken him to Europe, Australia, New Zealand, Central and South America, and to all regions of the United States, where he has presented recitals and appeared as soloist with numerous symphony orchestras. However, it is as a teacher that he will certainly be best remembered, consistently one of the most sought-after violin teachers in the country.

Figure 33. Russell Saunders, teacher of organ 1967–92.

When Russell Saunders joined David Craighead in the organ department in 1967, few could have predicted the extraordinary record these two men would compile over the next twenty years in establishing the Eastman School of Music as the preeminent educational institution in the United States for the study of organ. It would be difficult to imagine two more different men, yet they complemented one another to a remarkable degree. During their many years of working together, they demonstrated an exemplary spirit of collegiality and a genuine friendship that benefited their students immeasurably. The Eastman School of Music's dominance in major organ competitions in the coming years was a fitting tribute to their ability to attract and develop talented students. A good number of these students had the opportunity to study with both of these extraordinary men.

Saunders was not only a great teacher but also a great personality at Eastman. His charm, wit, and uninhibited personality made him an unforgettable character at the school. Saunders came to Eastman from Drake University, where he had taught since 1947. He had received his bachelor of music education and master of music degrees in organ from Drake. Saunders spent the 1953–54 school year at the Hochschule für Musik in Frankfurt, where he studied organ with Helmut Walcha (1907–91), harpsichord with

Maria Jäger, and choral conducting with Kurt Thomas (1904–73), the noted German choral conductor who later became director of the famous Thomaskantoren and Thomasschule in Leipzig.

Another new faculty member at this time was the pianist Frank Glazer. He had initially joined the teaching staff in 1965 as a visiting professor, then accepted a full-time appointment as professor of piano in the fall of 1968. Glazer, born in Wisconsin, had gone to Berlin at age seventeen to study piano with Artur Schnabel (1882–1951). It was from Schnabel that Glazer developed his appreciation for the Viennese classics, especially Beethoven and Schubert. Glazer made his Town Hall debut in New York at age twenty-one and his orchestral debut three years later when he played the Brahms Second Piano Concerto with the Boston Symphony under the direction of Serge Koussevitzky. During subsequent years he concertized extensively, including recitals in the United States, Europe, South America, and the Near East. When he appeared in Town Hall on the twenty-fifth anniversary of his New York debut, Raymond Ericson of *The New York Times* commented that "time apparently has made no inroads on the pianist's technical skills; it has only deepened his perceptions about the music he plays, and this recital was, on the whole, a beautiful one."[4]

Also joining the faculty in 1968 was Edwin McArthur, appointed professor of opera and musical director of the opera department. McArthur, who had been music director of the St. Louis Municipal Opera for twenty-three seasons, had just completed his eighteenth season as music director of the Harrisburg Symphony Orchestra. He had enjoyed a rich and varied career as a conductor, opera director, and accompanist, but he was best known for his twenty-eight-year collaboration with the great Norwegian soprano Kirsten Flagstad (1895–1962). Born in Denver, Colorado, McArthur had studied with the Lhevinnes at the Juilliard School and had spent a five-month residency at Bayreuth for special study with Karl Kittel (1874–1971). In addition to accompanying Flagstad, he had worked with other great singers such as Ezio Pinza (1892–1957), Frances Alda (1883–1952), Freida Hempl (1885–1955), and Dusolina Giannini (1902–86).

One of Hendl's new appointees, Willis Page, remained at Eastman for only two years, leaving in 1969 to accept an appointment as conductor of the Des Moines Symphony Orchestra as well as a position on the faculty at Drake University. Page had replaced

---

[4] Raymond Ericson, "Recital Offered by Frank Glazer," *The New York Times*, November 18, 1961, 14. Copyright © 1961 by The New York Times. Reprinted with permission.

Laszlo Halasz, who had been visiting professor for two years, and now Jonathan Sternberg would accept a visiting professorship in September 1969 to replace Page. Sternberg had been educated at the Juilliard School and the Manhattan School of Music, after which he pursued studies in musicology at New York University and Harvard. Apart from a few lessons with Leon Barzin (1900–1999) and two summers with Pierre Monteux, he was largely self-taught as a conductor. After moving to Vienna, where he made his conducting debut, Sternberg became associated with the noted Haydn scholar H. C. Robbins Landon (b. 1926) and made a series of important recordings for Landon's recently established Haydn Society. He then conducted the Halifax Symphony for a year before accepting the post of principal conductor of the Royal Flemish Opera in Antwerp for five years. Returning to the United States in 1966, he became the principal conductor of the Harkeness Ballet York in 1966 and was appointed music director and conductor of the Atlanta Municipal Theater in 1968. From Atlanta, this much-traveled conductor came to the Eastman School of Music for two years. He accepted an appointment in 1971 at Temple University, where he taught and conducted for the next twenty years.

The number of important new appointments during Walter Hendl's first few years as the school's third director was somewhat bewildering to an Eastman faculty that had been accustomed to lengthy tenures and faculty stability in the past. Part of the necessity for new appointees arose from the fact that a significant number of people were reaching retirement age. A number of these teachers, such as Karl Van Hoesen, Paul White, and Herman Genhart, have been previously mentioned as having retired at the end of the 1964–65 school year. Elivra Wonderlich retired from the theory department the following year, having taught at Eastman since 1925. Anne Theodora Cummins, another unique and wonderful personality, retired the same year after having been at the school since 1924. The 1966–67 school year not only marked the end of Bernard Roger's long tenure at the school but also saw the retirement of William Street and Allen Irvine McHose. Street had taught percussion at Eastman since 1927, and John Beck, who had been his student, now became the principal percussion teacher at the school.

McHose, whose long service to Eastman included being the school's associate director as well as director of the summer session, will principally be remembered as the chair of the theory department for many decades and the author of textbooks for freshman and sophomore theory courses. Use of McHose's texts was soon a thing of the past, not only at Eastman but elsewhere, since the approach to teaching undergraduate theory was rapidly changing. Those who treated McHose with a certain condescension or even disdain at the time of his retirement might have been well advised to remember that he had been one of the very first to develop an approach to the study of harmony based on actual musical practice. Admittedly, the basis for his methodology was rather narrow, confined to the Bach chorales, but it was an enormous and positive step forward from the purely academic and mechanical approach to part writing characterized by his predecessors and many of his contemporaries. Donald White had assumed leadership of the theory department when McHose had been appointed the school's associate director, although he was somewhat of a caretaker rather than an innovative leader during his rather brief tenure prior to retiring in 1970. To no one's surprise, Daniel Patrylak was given McHose's general administrative tasks by being appointed assistant director at Eastman.

Another retirement that should be noted was that of Charles Warren Fox, who stepped down as chair of the musicology department at the end of the 1970–71 school year, although he continued to teach at least part-time for a while longer. Fox was one of the most unforgettable characters in the entire history of the Eastman School of Music, and anecdotes about this brilliant yet somewhat eccentric man could provide material for an entire book. He lived in a simple, sparsely furnished apartment above Tuzz's Pinnacle Grill on Monroe Avenue, had little need for material possessions, and never owned a car (nor was he able to drive). Fox had given away his scores to the Beethoven string quartets because he had committed all of the quartets to memory and had no further use for the scores. He also had no use for attending concerts. During his long career at Eastman, the school had conferred doctorates in musicology on more than forty of his students, and almost everyone who had contact with him stood in awe of his brilliant mind. His lectures on the second movement of the Beethoven Seventh Symphony and the finale of Mozart's "Jupiter" Symphony were legendary. He was one of those few individuals who were truly irreplaceable. After he left, there was never anyone quite like him.

Another unique and special person who left the faculty at about the same time was Cecile Genhart, who had begun teaching at Eastman in 1926 and had served as chair of the piano faculty since Raymond Wilson's retirement in 1953. Genhart announced that she was resigning from the faculty to return to her native Switzerland. Especially during the past twenty years or so, she had been a rather dominating force in the piano department, and many of her students had gone on to occupy important teaching positions throughout the United States. The idyllic retirement in the country of her birth, however, did not provide the satisfaction she was anticipating, and she subsequently returned to Rochester and taught for about another ten years.

Genhart's decision to leave Eastman in 1971 left the school without any of the major teachers who had been the cornerstone of the piano department in the 1950s and 1960s. Armand Basile had resigned in 1965 and Orazio Frugoni in 1967. The fourth member of group, José Echániz, died of cancer in his Pittsford home on December 30, 1969. Faculty concern for his health was initially stirred when Echániz was giving a New York recital—his first New York recital in eleven years—but was able to perform only the first half of the program. Later appearances, including a Kilbourn Hall recital in honor of the twenty-fifth anniversary of his appointment to the Eastman faculty, were also canceled. His death shortly after Christmas in 1969 saddened the entire Eastman community. Echániz was a warm and generous man who earned the respect, affection, and admiration of everyone who knew him. He had been not only a gifted and highly appreciated teacher at the school but also a most beloved colleague and friend.

Echániz's death created the necessity of hiring a new piano teacher, and Walter Hendl selected Barry Snyder, a former student of Cecile Genhart who had been a triple prize winner at the 1966 Van Cliburn Competition, including capturing the silver medal. Snyder, who had earned his bachelor of music and master of music degrees at Eastman, as well as his performer's certificate and artist's diploma, had been teaching for only two years following an appointment to the faculty at Georgia State University. While some were concerned that such a young and relatively inexperienced teacher had been selected to join the artist faculty, his subsequent contributions to the school as a teacher, recitalist, and collaborative pianist have more than justified the confidence placed in him at the time of his appointment to the faculty in 1970.

Eighteen months following the death of José Echániz, the school community lost another beloved figure when Julius Huehn died on June 8, 1971. Huehn was chair of the voice department and had been a member of the Eastman faculty since 1952. A big man, standing about six feet four inches tall, with an especially deep and resonant speaking voice, Huehn was a formidable presence at the school. He enjoyed matching low notes with pianist Maria Luisa Faini who, although a foot shorter than Huehn, had an equally low voice (probably as a result of years and years of cigarette smoking). An avid baseball fan, Huehn never missed a World Series game and was often found in the student lounge during the World Series, watching a game on a television set provided to the school by the nearby Music Lovers' Shoppe. Occasionally, he even stayed home to watch a game, and one year he posted a note on his studio door saying he was not teaching because his grandmother had died. John Maloy, his young faculty colleague, assumed the note was genuine and called to offer his sympathy, much to Huehn's amusement.

In addition to faculty appointments made in response to retirements, resignations, and the untimely deaths of several members of the teaching staff, Hendl made an important appointment to the administration by hiring Richard D. Freed as the school's first public relations director. Freed, who was also named assistant to the director at the Eastman School and an associate director of university relations, had been a contributor to *Saturday Review* as well as a staff critic for *The New York Times*. One of the first outcomes of his appointment to the Eastman post was the creation of a new publication entitled *Notes from Eastman,* which Freed was to edit. The school had been without an alumni publication for over a decade, and this initiative was greatly appreciated by the alumni who had been kept unduly uninformed for many years.

Another new member of the school administration was Ruth Glazer, who accepted an appointment as concert manager in 1968, the same year in which her husband, Frank Glazer, joined the full-time piano faculty. Ruth Glazer, a graduate of Wheaton College, had attended the New England Conservatory of Music and been a member of the Boston Light Opera Company. After teaching voice at Vassar College, she became choral director and instructor in voice at Bennett College before accepting a position there as director of programs and concerts. Her appointment to the Eastman School administrative staff followed the death of Robert Sattler, who had served as concert manager and director of the placement bureau for a number of years.

Ruth Glazer brought an incredible amount of creativity, enthusiasm, and energy to her new position. The first project on her agenda was to revitalize and expand the annual series of recitals in Kilbourn Hall, and the result was the inauguration of the "Great Performers Series" in the fall of 1968. Programs over the next several years featured important guest artists, as well as recitals by members of the Eastman School faculty. Performers during the inaugural 1968–69 season included the Juilliard Quartet and the Fine Arts Quartet, the

Figure 34. The Eastman Quartet (from left to right, Frank Glazer, Francis Tursi, Ronald Leonard, and Millard Taylor.)

noted Austrian organist Anton Heiler (1923–79),[5] the famous mezzo-soprano Jennie Tourel (1900–1973), the Eastman Brass Quintet, faculty artist Zvi Zeitlin accompanied by Brooks Smith, pianist Frank Glazer, and the Eastman Quartet. The latter group represented a strong departure from the past at the Eastman School, since it was not a string quartet but a piano quartet. Its members were violinist Millard Taylor, violist Francis Tursi, cellist Ronald Leonard, and pianist Frank Glazer. In addition to the Kilbourn Hall recitals during the year, the Great Performers Series included a gala Eastman Theatre concert featuring tenor Jan Peerce (1904–84) with Walter Hendl conducting the Eastman Philharmonia.

During the next two seasons the Great Performers Series included programs presented by the Contemporary Chamber Ensemble, the Amadeus Quartet, the Borodin Quartet, English mezzo-soprano Dame Janet Baker (b. 1933), Swiss tenor Ernst Haefliger (1919–2007), baritone Hermann Prey (1929–1998), and Julian Bream (b. 1933) performing on lute and guitar. Eastman faculty members who participated included flutist Joseph Mariano, pianists Eugene List and

---

[5]   Heiler's recital took place at the Lutheran Church of the Incarnate Word rather than in Kilbourn Hall.

Maria Luisa Faini, violinist Millard Taylor, cellist Ronald Leonard, and organist David Craighead. The importance of the Great Performers Series to the Rochester community was heightened with the announcement in December 1969 that the Civic Music Association, which managed the Rochester Philharmonic Orchestra, would henceforth concentrate entirely on sponsorship and support of the orchestra and divest itself of its impresario activities. Those activities had been a prominent feature of musical life in Rochester, but they were coming to an end. The only consistent presentation of recitalists in the future would be from the Eastman School.

In addition to the Great Performers Series, Ruth Glazer also organized an imaginative and popular series of Sunday afternoon concerts at the University of Rochester's Memorial Art Gallery. These programs took place every other week and featured Eastman students and faculty members performing together. But her most creative, yet somewhat controversial, initiative was the "Musical Picnic" that took place on the evening of November 13, 1970. This gala event provided ticket holders with box suppers served to them in their Eastman Theatre seats at 6:30 P.M. Various events took place as a prologue to supper, including entertainment on the balcony level provided by blues singer Esther Satterfield and jazz organist Joe Galante. Meanwhile, accordionist Robert Neusatz was providing similar entertainment on the mezzanine.

A short film on children and music entitled "The Great Concert Hall Caper" was shown following supper, then the Eastman Philharmonia performed the "Rakoczy March" from the *Damnation of Faust* by Hector Berlioz (1803–69) and *Carnival of the Animals* by Camille Saint-Saëns (1835–1921), with Mayor Stephen May of Rochester providing the narration. While all this was happening, a local artist was on stage sketching the animals, later distributing his drawings to the children in the audience. Children were then asked to spin a large music wheel set on the stage to select various pieces that were performed by Eastman students located throughout the theater. Finally, the Eastman Wind Ensemble concluded the official program at 8:30 by playing *Remembrance* by Warren Benson, Copland's *The Red Pony,* and the "On the Mall March" of John Phillip Sousa (1854–1932). The fun-filled evening also included student hostesses costumed as various opera characters, wandering minstrels, folk groups, balloons, souvenirs, and rather gaudy decorations in the main hall and second-floor corridor.

There was something of a circus atmosphere to the Musical Picnic, an event that involved perhaps as much as one-third of the entire Eastman School student population. The event was also somewhat disruptive to the day's usual activities. Ruth Glazer attempted to shut the school late in the afternoon and prevent anyone from entering who did not have a ticket. That decision, if carried out, would have prevented preparatory department students from attending their regularly scheduled classes and lessons, and it took intervention from the highest levels of the school administration to persuade her to allow those students to enter the building and meet their teachers. Although the Musical Picnic was highly successful in attracting an extremely large and enthusiastic audience, especially people who did not regularly attend concerts, the event was never repeated.

The many new faculty and administrators at Eastman brought new ideas and perspectives to an institution that had grown perhaps a little too comfortable with itself under four decades of leadership by Howard Hanson. Those ideas and perspectives led to important new initiatives. Perhaps the first of these was the formation of Musica Nova under the direction of Richard Pittman, newly appointed to the conducting and ensembles faculty. Musica Nova was the first performing group at the Eastman School of Music exclusively concerned with contemporary music, and it presented its first performance on November 18, 1966, featuring music by Niccolo Castiglioni (b. 1932), Luciano Berio (b. 1925), Arnold Schoenberg (1874–1951), and Anton Webern (1883–1945).

The Musica Nova concert was a defining moment in establishing a new image for the school following the retirement two years earlier of Howard Hanson, a man who had come to represent a conservative and traditional approach to new music. It was therefore almost ironic that the Eastman School of Music chose to honor its second director only ten days later with an entire week devoted to his music. "Howard Hanson Week" began on November 28, 1966, with a program of his sacred music. The week's events included a convocation at which Hanson spoke on "The Arts in an Age of Science," a special concert for area college and high school students, a composition seminar, and a concluding gala concert on December 2 that involved the Eastman Philharmonia, the Eastman Wind Ensemble, and the Eastman Chorus, all performing works by Hanson.

Hendl eventually scheduled two other composer "weeks," one in honor of Peter Mennin (1923–83) in December 1967 and the other in honor of Aram Khachaturian (1903–78) in March 1968. His problem, however, was that he had first brought the "superstar" (Igor Stravinsky) to Eastman; and Hanson, Mennin, and Khachaturian generally failed to arouse sufficient enthusiasm to merit continuation of these kinds of activities in the future. None-theless, other visitors did come to Eastman with some regularity, certainly much more so than during the many years when Han-son was director of the school. The distinguished writer and critic Irving Kolodin (1908–88) was a guest at Eastman on April 10, 1967, followed eight days later by the composer Herbert Fromm. Paul Henry Lang (1901–91), one of the country's most respected crit-ics and musicologists, was at Eastman on February 23, 1968, for two sessions with faculty and students, and noted Haydn scholar H. C. Robbins Landon gave two lectures at the school on May 15, 1969. Oboist Robert Bloom (1908–94), who had taught at Eastman during the 1936–37 school year, returned on November 20, 1969, for a two-day visit to give a master class for oboe students and to present a lecture on the use of ornamentation in baroque per-formance practice. Bloom additionally conducted members of the Eastman Wind Ensemble in a performance of Mozart's *Serenade in C Minor* and Richard Strauss's *Serenade in E-flat Major.*

Yet another distinguished guest of the school was Eastman alumnus Vladimir Ussachevsky (1911–90), the director of the Columbia-Princeton Electronic Music Center. He came to Eastman in December 1969 for three days of lecture-demonstrations in con-nection with the school's new electronic music studio, which had opened two years earlier under the direction of Wayne Barlow. Barlow, who counted Ussachevsky as a personal friend, had pre-pared for the opening of Eastman's studio by visiting the labora-tory at the University of Toronto and participating in its 1963–64 seminar in electronic music. He was then given a leave of absence for the 1964–65 school year to take advantage of a Fulbright research grant to visit several outstanding European studios. East-man's new electronic music studio, when it opened in 1967, was once again a bold statement concerning new directions the school was charting for itself.

Another new venture for the Eastman School was the creation of the Jazz Laboratory in the spring of 1967 under the supervision of Donald Hunsberger, who had been named chair of the recently cre-ated department of conducting and ensembles. The Jazz Laboratory was an outgrowth of the annual summer Arrangers' Workshop and Arrangers' Laboratory Institute. Hunsberger provided much of the basic instruction, while Jack End worked with the newly formed Eastman Jazz Ensemble. End was an Eastman graduate who had taught at the school following his graduation. He was subsequently an arranger for various bands and a producer-director for a local television station, and he did a great deal to promote interest in jazz throughout the Rochester area. He was now deputy director of university relations for the University of Rochester and was involved with the Eastman Jazz Ensemble until Chuck Mangione was appointed to the faculty in 1968.

Jazz had led very much of an "unofficial" life at the Eastman School of Music for many years, with the exception of the summer session. Nonetheless, many students had demonstrated a keen interest in jazz while attending the school, including Mangione, who studied at Eastman from 1958 to 1963. Born and raised in Rochester, he and his brother Gap had a group called the Jazz Brothers, which recorded a number of albums for Riverside Records. His later collaboration with saxophonist Gerry Niewood produced one of the most popular jazz groups in the United States during the early 1970s, and he achieved international recognition through his 1977 jazz-pop recording *Feels So Good*. Mangione left the Eastman School faculty in 1972, two years after Rayburn Wright came to Eastman as the school's first full-time teacher of jazz and chair of the newly formed department of jazz studies and contemporary media. The addition of jazz to the school's curricula did not initially meet with unanimous approval from the faculty, and Wright deserves much credit for allaying their concerns and suspicions. He was, in so many respects, the perfect choice to lead the new department, and he came to be widely admired throughout the school.

In spite of all the new faculty appointments and the development of new courses and programs, there were several areas of concern at the school. There was, for example, no real continuity within the orchestral program. Clyde Roller had resigned at the end of the 1964–65 school year, and he was replaced by Lazslo Halasz, who came to Eastman as a visiting professor for just two years. Willis Page followed Halasz but resigned two years later, followed by Jonathan Sternberg who also remained at the school for only two years. Perhaps Walter Hendl felt that he himself provided the necessary continuity for the orchestra program, but in fact the constant changing of orchestral conductors had a decidedly negative impact.

A similar situation arose in the choral program. George Corwin became choral director when Herman Genhart retired after conducting the Eastman School Chorus for almost forty years. But Corwin was choral director for only two years, as was his successor, Milford Fargo. Fargo deserves much credit for establishing the Eastman Chorale as a new performing ensemble separate from the larger Eastman School Chorus, as well as for establishing the Eastman Children's Chorus, which had a short yet brilliant existence at the school. John Dexter succeeded Fargo as choral director but remained in charge of the program for only five semesters. Stability in the orchestral and choral programs was desperately needed, but solutions to the problem seemed to elude the school's administration.

Many of the new initiatives at the school had arisen because of Walter Hendl's desire to delegate responsibility to the faculty. As early as 1966, he had formed various committees to study important issues, and the faculty found itself more and more involved in the decision-making process at the school. The most important of these new faculty groups was the committee on academic policy, to which was entrusted decisions concerning undergraduate curricula. Committee members included representatives from the different departments, plus elected student representatives and ex officio members of the administration. One problem that came to their attention and occupied considerable time and effort was the long-standing requirement for two years of physical education within the bachelor of music curriculum. Concerns over several injuries to students in recent years led many to question the wisdom of maintaining this requirement. The committee on academic policy addressed the issue and presented its recommendations to the faculty at a meeting on December 19, 1968. Essentially, it recommended that the two-year required program be discontinued after September 1969 and that proper physical education facilities under appropriate supervision be made accessible to Eastman students who might be interested in such activities.

The recommendations created such heated discussion that further discussion was postponed until the next faculty meeting. Following the winter recess, the committee on academic policy issued a new statement concerning physical education requirements that attempted to refute some of the arguments made in favor of retaining the current two-year requirement for undergraduates. The matter was addressed once again at a faculty meeting on January 21, 1969, at which Eastman's two physical education teachers, Joan Mars and David Clark, presented a proposal for invigorating the four-semester program. Reinvigorating the program was not what the Eastman faculty wanted, however, and they overwhelmingly approved a motion that the physical education requirement be discontinued after September 1969.

Among the weightier issues at the Eastman School during these years was the school's involvement in the Contemporary Music Project (CMP) for Creativity in Music Education. This comprehensive project had received $1.38 million in funding from the Ford Foundation in 1963, and a grant of $70,000 from Music Educators

National Conference (MENC) three years later allowed the Eastman School to become one of six regional administrative centers for
the project. Various activities at the school eventually led to a workshop on the teaching of comprehensive musicianship at the college
level in June 1969. The objectives of the workshop were "to review
and summarize the pedagogy of comprehensive musicianship that
had evolved from the activities of the last several years" and "to
explore a variety of techniques, conditions and attitudes towards
music which can be used for a more effective teaching of musicianship, with emphasis on fresh approaches to the basic subject matter
which can lead to a more penetrating comprehension and critical
evaluation of the art of music."[6]

The CMP project ended in 1973, with its supporters declaring
that its purposes had been fulfilled. The project had many critics
who claimed that an enormous amount of money had been spent
to little purpose, with many of its conclusions and concepts widely
ignored or rejected. In truth, the project may have contributed significantly to the ongoing reassessment of theory and musicianship
teaching that was leading to significant changes in the undergraduate curriculum at Eastman and other institutions.

The flurry of activity at the Eastman School of Music during the
second half of the 1960s must have kept Walter Hendl very busy.
For a man with practically no experience as an administrator, he
was constantly faced with decisions concerning faculty, staff, and
programs of study. It also might be accurate to suggest that, as a
conductor, he was not necessarily disposed toward being a team
player. Nonetheless, he delegated authority in many matters, not
only to Daniel Patrylak but also to the Eastman faculty. His dealings
with the central administration were probably reasonably cordial
because he enjoyed the confidence of President Wallis. Yet issues
arose that pointed to occasional tension between the Eastman director and his superiors at the university.

In 1967, for example, Hendl learned that an "Eastman School of
Music Committee" had been formed on the River Campus to study
the possibility of relocating the school from its present site in downtown Rochester. He immediately sent a memo to Robert France, the
university's associate provost, remarking that "it doesn't seem quite
right that an Eastman School of Music Committee can conceivably
be formed and meetings scheduled without my ever having heard
about it in advance—does it?" He added this postscript:

6 "CMP Workshop at Eastman in June," *Notes from Eastman* (Rochester, NY: Eastman School of Music, June 1969), 6.

Don't you also marvel that students will come to our school and be willing to live in the Cadillac Hotel[7] for the privilege of studying with our teachers and performing in our ensembles? How many years will it take before the University will move in the direction of residence space for our students?[8]

All this arose because of the condition of the school's facilities after more than forty years of continuous use. Questions concerning either renovating those facilities or relocating the school to a site on or near the university's main campus had already been raised when Hendl arrived as the new director in 1964. The same questions were still being heatedly debated when he left the school eight years later. The issue was at first discussed only at the administrative level, but it eventually came to involve the entire Eastman community, with the fundamental choice of renovation or relocation becoming a highly charged and emotional topic. Increasing numbers of people at Eastman came to view efforts to relocate the Eastman School of Music as a threat to the school's identity and mission. It was not simply a discussion of buildings and facilities but, at a more fundamental level, a discussion involving the relationship of the Eastman School of Music with its parent institution, the University of Rochester.

---

[7] The Cadillac Hotel, in spite of its name, was not one of Rochester's more luxurious hotels.
[8] Walter Hendl, memo to Robert France, January 10, 1967. SML.

Chapter 15

1964–72

Renovate or Relocate?

The Eastman School of Music's main building was forty-three years old at the time of Howard Hanson's retirement, and very little had been done to the building other than basic maintenance during its existence. The adjacent Eastman Theatre was forty-two years old and was showing unmistakable signs of its age. The school's two annex buildings on Swan Street also dated from the 1920s, as did the women's residence halls on University Avenue. Clearly, there were reasons to be concerned about the age and condition of the school's facilities, especially considering the increasing numbers of students enrolled each year for degree study. The school's collegiate enroll-ment had been 467 students in 1932, but that number had grown to 529 by 1940 and to 593 in 1950—almost a 30 percent increase in less than twenty years. The 1960s produced further increases in enroll-ment, with totals ranging from a low of 632 in 1964 to a high of 731 in 1968. The school's facilities had not been originally designed for that many full-time collegiate students. Howard Hanson had long held the opinion that an enrollment of 550 was ideal, but the growth of the graduate department and other educational developments were producing increasingly higher numbers. Could the school's present facilities accommodate projected future enrollment?

Determined to examine the status and future of the Eastman School's facilities, university officials met to discuss these issues on June 26, 1964. It is perhaps significant that this meeting occurred just at the time Howard Hanson was vacating the director's office but prior to Walter Hendl's arrival on the scene. During the discus-sion it was noted that Cutler Union and the Eastman dormitories were located too far away from the school, as well as being situated in neighborhoods that were unmistakably deteriorating, raising serious concerns for student safety in the coming years. In addition, there was concern over the lack of a good campus atmosphere and of recreation and athletic space for Eastman students, although such issues may not have been much of a priority with many Eastman students at the time. Finally, it was acknowledged that the East-man School facilities were in reasonably good condition but would require major renovation in the near future. Conversation ensued about the possibility of moving the school to the River Campus by constructing an entirely new facility, but the university president, W. Allen Wallis, expressed the opinion that the costs of doing this would probably be prohibitive.

As a result of these and other conversations concerning the East-man School facilities, the university engaged Ellerbe Architects from Minnesota to do a study on a possible renovation and expansion of the school at its present downtown location. The request to Ellerbe outlined facilities requirements that assumed an enrollment of 600 collegiate students, including teaching facilities, administrative offices, classrooms, practice rooms, auditoriums, the library, a recording studio, a ballet studio, ensemble rooms, and practically anything else necessary for the future needs of the Eastman School of Music.

Thomas Ellerbe submitted his evaluation study to the University of Rochester in November 1964, outlining an ambitious plan for renovating, air-conditioning, and expanding the Eastman School's physical plant. His recommendations were based in part on the fact that the original building plans for the school had made provision for as many as eight additional stories on the main building. There-fore, he proposed adding six floors to the existing five, effectively doubling the amount of space the building could provide for the school's future. The new sixth floor would feature a classroom and twenty-one teaching studios, while the new seventh floor would house the music education department, which would have seven offices and an audio-visual room. The seventh floor would also pro-vide space for an instrument repair room, a storage room, a large ensemble room, and six more teaching studios. The new eighth floor was planned to include five offices for the theory department, two ensemble rooms, and five more studios.

The new ninth floor was envisioned as the location for student and faculty dining facilities and lounges. Relocating the lounges to the ninth floor created usable space off the main corridor on the east side of the building, and Ellerbe suggested that the location of the former student and faculty lounges be used for four new first-floor classrooms. The Ellerbe plan recommended relocating the school's administrative offices to the new tenth floor, with space for the direc-tor, associate director, dean of students, associate dean, director of admissions, registrar, placement director, concert manager, director of publicity, and alumni secretary. The tenth floor would also house the student medical facility, a bookstore, and three more teaching studios. Space on the ground floor previously used for administrative offices would be given over to the school's preparatory department administration, while the offices on the mezzanine would be allocated to the graduate department. Space on the school's second floor that had formerly housed the preparatory department administration, as well as the medical office on the third floor, would be renovated as teaching studios.

The top floor in Ellerbe's plan was reserved for a new gymnasium, with lockers and showers, plus a large swimming pool. The space formerly occupied by the gymnasium on the ninth floor of Annex II would become a new opera studio, including an office and three coaching rooms, and the eighth floor of the annex would be remodeled to provide for a ballet studio, with showers and dressing rooms. Ellerbe recommended that Annex I and the existing library building be demolished and that a larger three-story library be built on the site of the two former buildings. Musicology offices and seminar rooms would be located on the third floor of the library, and Ellerbe recommended providing for the possibility of several additional stories if increased library capacity became necessary at some point in the future. Ellerbe's recommendations for the Eastman Theatre were rather modest, basically involving air-conditioning and new seats. However, he also recommended construction of a new fully air-conditioned auditorium on the corner of Main and Swan streets that would seat 1,200 people.

Estimated cost for all the new construction and renovation was $10,491,000. If the recommendations had been implemented, the Eastman School of Music might have had facilities that would have been second to none anywhere in the world. It is doubtful, however, that anything as ambitious and extensive as these proposals was ever seriously contemplated. The value of the Ellerbe report was that it supported the notion that the school could remain in its present location and still be provided with the facilities needed not only to maintain its present programs but also to allow expansion during the foreseeable future. Ellerbe suggested that the school's instructional program could be temporarily moved into the six new floors of the main building once they were completed, thereby allowing for the renovation of the lower stories without interrupting the instructional program. He also envisioned temporarily relocating the resources of the Sibley Music Library when space became available in Annex II. Theoretically, all of this was possible, but it failed to address the question of how instructional programs could really be maintained amid the confusion and noise of construction and renovation. This was, after all, a music school.

In spite of this concern, Walter Hendl reported to the members of the university's faculty senate in January 1965 that the decision had been made for the school to remain in its present downtown location rather than moving to a new location closer to the rest of the university. Renovation had been deemed preferable to relocation. He cited five principal reasons for this decision. The first was the school's large preparatory department, for which a central location with access to public transportation and parking facilities was thought to be an absolute necessity. He also spoke of the faculty members who had dual and triple functions involving preparatory department teaching, collegiate teaching, and performing as members of the Rochester Philharmonic Orchestra—all of which seemed to require a common downtown location. The Sibley Music Library, which served many organizations and individuals in the downtown area, was another factor supporting the school's present location, as was the perception that the Eastman Theatre had a sentimental or nostalgic value, especially among the school's many alumni. Finally, all these considerations were related to ongoing discussion among city officials about an urban renewal program in the area of the school and theater. Eastman, therefore, would remain in its present location, a decision supported in part by the expectation of improvements to the downtown area.

Two years later, however, the question was reopened when President Wallis established his Eastman School of Music Committee, the move that had so upset Walter Hendl. Once brought into the discussion, the Eastman School director appointed his own committee to study the question of the school's location. Members of the committee included composer Samuel Adler, humanities professor Alice Benston, and public relations director Richard Freed, plus Donald Shetler from the music education department and Hendrik VanderWerf from musicology. It is interesting that no one from the performance faculty was included on the committee and that its members were all relatively new appointees to the faculty or staff. The group reported back to Hendl on December 21, 1967, and the general assessment was as follows: "Many of us feel that before another penny is expended on renovation of our present plant (let alone major investments in remodeling or expansion at the site), we must consider, seriously and immediately, the advantages of moving the School to the River Campus."[1]

1   Faculty Committee, report to Walter Hendl, December 21, 1967. SML.

President Wallis asked the university's office of planning and institutional studies and the office of university plant to reexamine the issues concerning the Eastman School's location and physical plant. Preliminary discussions were held with Walter Hendl and Daniel Patrylak, and a report was circulated among university officials by the end of 1968. While the report concluded that there were no absolute reasons for integrating the Eastman School of Music with the other campuses of the university, it also concluded that there were no compelling academic or programmatic reasons for the school to remain in its present downtown location. These conclusions were apparently endorsed by the Eastman School's administration. Therefore, assessment of the situation had changed dramatically between January 1965, when Hendl had announced to the faculty senate that the Eastman School would not move from its present location, and December 1968, when the consensus had apparently shifted greatly in favor of moving the school.

The report commented on several emerging factors, the first being new efforts to reduce the size and scope of the school's preparatory department. Three or four years earlier, the preparatory department had been considered one of the main reasons for the Eastman School to remain centrally located in the city. But Howard Hanson had retired, and his successor had no particular interest in the preparatory department and no real appreciation of the reasons that had led to its creation. From the earliest days of the school, it had been considered an integral part of the school's educational mission, playing a very important role in fulfilling George Eastman's vision for "building musical capacity on a large scale from childhood."[2] Hanson, who had demonstrated little personal interest in the school's preparatory program, had nonetheless respected its importance and allowed the department's administration to maintain a large and active presence at the school. All this was conveniently set aside by a decision to dramatically reduce the school's commitment to its preparatory department. Hendl preferred to envision a preparatory program that would concentrate mainly on providing pre-collegiate training for more gifted students.

The unexpected death in 1968 of the preparatory department's director, Charles Riker, provided an opportunity to reassess the department's mission and role within the school and the university. Therefore, no successor director was appointed, and the department

[2] Quoted in William L. Chenery, "Philanthropy under a Bushel," *The New York Times,* March 21, 1920: XXX8. Copyright © 1920 by The New York Times Co. Reprinted with permission.

was allowed to function for more than two years under the supervision of its registrar,[3] but without anyone really being in charge. In addition, the administration noted the opportunity presented by the pending retirement within the next half dozen years or so of several faculty members who had dual teaching responsibilities in the preparatory and collegiate areas. A policy of not replacing these people was a very convenient way to shrink enrollment. Equally convenient was a series of rather substantial tuition increases over the next several years. The rising cost of preparatory department study would do its part in curtailing enrollment and would help lead to an eventual reduction in the department's size. Under these negative pressures—as well as demographic factors then at work in Rochester—it is not surprising that enrollment fell precipitously, and there is little reason to doubt that it would have declined from its normal level of about 1,100 students to a target level of 300 by 1975 if current policies had prevailed. There was even discussion of a possible enrollment level as low as 50 to 100 students. This policy, while conveniently eliminating one of the reasons for retaining the school's present location, could hardly be reconciled with George Eastman's vision for the school, but that was apparently not a consideration among those in charge of planning for the school's future.

In addition to attitudes that now discounted the importance of the preparatory department in discussion of the school's future location, it was acknowledged that recent developments in the relationship between the school and the Rochester Philharmonic Orchestra would significantly diminish the number of full-time Eastman faculty performing as members of the orchestra.[4] Moreover, the university administration had grown understandably impatient with the lack of definite plans for urban renewal in the areas around the school, theater, and dormitories and could see little prospect that anything substantial would be done in this regard in the foreseeable future. Urban unrest in the summer of 1964 and the slow exodus to the suburbs left city authorities with many serious problems, of which renewal of the Gibbs Street area around the Eastman School of Music was only one. Finally, there was a realistic acknowledgment that adding floors to the Eastman building would not only be expensive but would also be complicated by the difficulties of

[3] Virginia Cooper, the preparatory department registrar, retired in November 1970. The author was then selected to lead the department, although it was several months before he was allowed to use the title "director" and several years before the department's downward spiral was finally reversed.
[4] As detailed in Chapter 13.

maintaining instruction during construction. Perhaps it was simply preferable to relocate the school and its facilities to a location on or near the River Campus, preferably in Genesee Valley Park or, less likely, on the university's South Campus.

This line of reasoning fit very comfortably with a university administration that had become increasingly uncomfortable with the fact that its music school was so isolated from the rest of the university. Perhaps that isolation had been less acutely felt while the Women's College had remained on the Prince Street Campus, but the merging of the colleges for men and women in 1955 had left the Eastman School of Music as the only important part of the University of Rochester in the downtown area. Although this fact may have been of little concern to the Eastman community at the time, it quickly grew in importance within the university's central administration, especially in the mind of W. Allen Wallis.

With the central administration increasingly committed to relocating the Eastman School, a report was requested from Mark Meredith, acting administrator of the university's office of planning and institutional studies. Meredith's report, issued on April 18, 1969, referred to the conclusions reached the previous year and presented two alternatives. Alternative I was to renovate and add new buildings to the existing site at an estimated cost of $16.4 million, noting, however, that this would involve serious problems during the renovation process and might not produce the most satisfactory results. Alternative II was to build an entirely new plant for the school on the Park Campus at a cost of $18.3 million, noting that this appeared to offer the greatest total benefits to the school as well as avoiding disruption of ongoing instructional programs. Meredith added that he assumed the Eastman Theatre would remain in its present location as a civic auditorium.

The question of the future of the Eastman Theatre was an important one, and the subsequent renovation of the theater—including its scope—must be seen against the background of the evolving plan to relocate the school away from the downtown area. Initial discussions concerning the possible renovation of the theater had taken place in the spring of 1968, precisely at the same time the central administration had reopened the question of the school's location. At that time the decision was made to hire the Ellerbe firm as the principal architects to study the physical aspects of the Eastman Theatre, with George C. Izenour Associates as theater consultants and Bolt, Beranek and Newman as acoustical consultants.

Ellerbe received a preliminary report from the acoustical consultants on November 8 that made several important recommendations, including provision of a new stage shell, enlargement of the orchestra pit by extending it several rows into the existing audience area, and elimination of the mezzanine to provide for raking the main floor up to the mezzanine level. The report also recommended possible replacement of the existing wall material with a more sound-reflective material and the installation of horizontal sound-reflecting surfaces immediately in front of the proscenium. In addition, the consultants presented two alternatives if the decision was made to retain the theater's massive Austin pipe organ. The question of the organ's future in the theater was a difficult one. It had been the largest theater organ in the world when it was installed, but it was now badly in need of repair and rebuilding, and obvious questions existed concerning the appropriateness or the necessity of having an immense theater organ in a modern concert hall.

Ellerbe Architects produced a report on February 25, 1969, that outlined several alternative plans or "priorities" for the renovation of the theater. A full program of renovation, including maintenance-oriented items, fully upgrading the stage and auditorium facilities, and making various structural changes, would cost the university $4,455,000. The cost for the same program without new stage facilities would be $2,902,000. Eliminating the recommendations of the acoustical consultants would further reduce the cost to $1,882,800, and limiting the renovation to maintenance-oriented items could be accomplished for $913,000.

While the university was thus involved in plans for the renovation of the theater, it was also proceeding with plans intended to eventually relocate the Eastman School to the River Campus. Provost Robert Sproull received a report from Mark Meredith on August 22, 1969, outlining a possible general schedule for the proposed renovation or relocation of the Eastman School, suggesting that the entire process would take about five years, from the selection of an architect to the actual occupancy of the facilities. In addition, the report outlined new housing requirements for 400 Eastman undergraduate students, facilities that would need to be near the new Eastman academic buildings. It was also suggested that dormitory capacity might be increased to 600, thereby providing additional dormitory space for 200 River Campus students.

It was not until the following month that the Eastman School administration became truly involved in the matter of the school's future location. At the request of the president, Walter Hendl submitted a report to the university administration in which he stated that "all of [the] faculty, including the old-timers who had held out in the past, now recognize the desirability—and, indeed, the need—

for the move."[5] Hendl's summary of faculty opinion was certainly overstated and obviously not based on any real dialogue with his faculty, as subsequent events would show. While there might have been considerable enthusiasm at the time over prospects for new buildings, it would not have been difficult to find others who hesitated to support such a move. Hendl also commented on the difficulties surrounding the school's present location, stating that the building was in a "grubby neighborhood and one which has proved actually dangerous to our students who commute between our dormitories and the School."[6] Notwithstanding the fact that plans for renovation of the Eastman Theatre were already in progress, he added a few rather unkind comments about the theater, observing that it was not a particularly distinguished hall for live concerts and was too large for the school's basic needs.

The president's response gave Walter Hendl his first indication of how far plans had progressed toward providing a new home for the school. The president wrote:

> You will be glad to know that for fully a year I have had a very small task force studying the details of what would be involved in moving the Eastman School to the River Campus. I have felt for sometime [sic] that it would be a tragedy not only to fail to move the School out here, but even worse to make investments that would fix it downtown for at least another forty years. The overwhelming obstacle to moving the Eastman School to the River Campus is, of course, financial. I expect to have within a matter of days a preliminary report on the magnitude of the financing that would be required, but preliminary indications are that the difference in cost between moving out here and doing what would have to be done down there is not nearly as great as earlier estimates indicated.
>
> Until we know something more definite about this subject, I think there is little to be gained by discussing it. If the move appears to be a real possibility, that will be the time to get discussions going—and, like you, I have no doubt that the sentiment will be overwhelmingly in favor of this move.[7]

The Eastman School faculty, which was only peripherally aware of what was happening, was finally apprised of these developments when President Wallis attended a faculty meeting on November

5   Walter Hendl, memo to W. Allen Wallis, September 2, 1969. SML.
6   Ibid.
7   W. Allen Wallis, memo to Walter Hendl, October 13, 1969. SML.

11, 1969. A committee was to be appointed, with Hendl as chair, to study the question of the school's location and gather opinions from the faculty. Members of the committee, in addition to Hendl, were Alice Benston from the humanities department, Dean Flora Burton, Edward Evans from musicology, and John Maloy and Verne Reynolds representing the performance faculty. The committee issued a report in January 1970 stating that about fifty faculty members *conditionally* favored relocation, around thirty preferred to remain at the present downtown location, and eight expressed ambivalence on the issue.

Many of those who favored relocation were somewhat cautious in offering their support, troubled by concerns over the exact location of a new site for the school and the manner of planning for the new buildings. The committee shared these concerns by expressing the opinion that the actual decisions regarding the school's physical plant and facilities should be made by those best acquainted with the problems of musical education—namely, the Eastman School faculty and administration. Among those who opposed a move were some who feared the school might lose its distinctive identity or its professionalism. Some also worried about the preparatory department (unaware of plans to reduce its size in any case) or about how a move from downtown might further damage relations and opportunities for cooperation with the Rochester Philharmonic Orchestra.

Faculty opinion, therefore, was quite divided in the early months of 1970, as well as beset with many questions. Among those supporting a move to the River Campus was pianist Eugene List, who wrote to Walter Hendl:

> I feel the Eastman School should move to the River Campus if this move is possible. We need a new building, and it would give us a more dynamic thrust for the future. It would give us a more competitive "new" look in relation to other music schools. It would eliminate one of the undesirable features of present student life: the fact that the students must walk through a rough, unsafe neighborhood to and from school. It would provide a more diversified student social life for our students, in my opinion. Would be good for U. of R. students as well. I feel this would in no way compromise the basic strength of the Eastman School. It would retain its autonomy and unique character.[8]

[8] Eugene List (also signed by Carroll Glenn), memo to Walter Hendl, January 25, 1970. SML.

Letters and memos supporting the move were also submitted by composers Samuel Adler and Warren Benson. Others, however, were more conditional in their support, such as violinist Zvi Zeitlin who wrote in favor of new facilities for the school with the important reservation that "any move to the River Campus must keep in mind the necessity to protect . . . standards from negative outside influence."[9] Zeitlin's colleague in the string department, Ronald Leonard, wrote in a similar vein. Leonard commented that the more important question was the attitude of the university administration toward the Eastman School, worrying that "it would be all too easy to let Eastman gently fall into what could eventually become a minor department of the university."[10]

Several members of the faculty, including conductor Donald Hunsberger and Donald White, chair of the theory department, wrote memos in opposition to moving the school. One of the most thoughtful memos was written by Eugene Selhorst, the associate dean for graduate professional studies:

> I have no strong feelings *pro* or *con* either location—downtown or in the campus area. But I do have strong feelings and a profound hope that we will have in Rochester in the near future a Center for Musical Art, incorporating the U of R's Eastman School of Music, the Rochester Philharmonic Orchestra, the Artist's Series, and the Sibley Music Library, all housed in handsome well-equipped buildings, easily accessible by public transportation and with ample parking facilities. Whether this is downtown or near the present U of R campus, I hope it will be done with vision, daring, and imagination.[11]

Perhaps the most volatile and angry response came from M. Alfred Bichsel, head of the school's church music department. Bichsel had been a member of the director's search committee in 1964 and had never forgiven the university president for appointing Walter Hendl as director of the school. His memo reflected his distrust of the entire process:

> Why should we waste our time and effort giving our views and opinions when, in all probability and likelihood, the president will decide the future of the Eastman School of Music with complete disregard

9   Zvi Zeitlin, memo to Walter Hendl, February 6, 1970. SML.
10   Ronald Leonard, memo to the faculty committee, January 26, 1970. SML.
11   Eugene Selhorst, memo to Walter Hendl, January 26, 1970. SML (original emphasis).

for faculty opinion? I love the Eastman School of Music; I love my
work; I love my students; I love and respect most of my colleagues;
my job is teaching and I'll continue to do this to the best of my ability, but I cannot see being led down the primrose path again. I am
just a little too old to fall for this kind of line.[12]

While the faculty was involved in these obviously emotional reactions to plans for the school's future, Ellerbe Architects submitted a
new "priority" for the theater renovation that provided for all the
maintenance work, including air-conditioning and a new electrical
service, but without redecorating offices and classrooms or replacing the theater's two elevators. It was only at this time that officials
at Eastman were finally informed of the specific details for the theater renovation. To that date, no one at Eastman had apparently seen
any of the Ellerbe "priorities," nor did they even know the identity
of the project's consultants. Failure to keep the school's administration and faculty "in the loop" was unfortunate and probably inex-
cusable. Concerns were immediately expressed over deficiencies in
the plans that would need to be addressed if the planned renovation of the theater's facilities were to be successful. Of a more serious nature, however, was the fact that Hendl and several important
members of his faculty had growing reservations about the choice
of acoustical consultants.

On June 24, 1970, the university's office of public information
finally issued an official announcement of the theater's renovation,
including news that the Eastman Kodak Company was providing
a grant of $1.7 million in support of the project. The press release
announced that new seats, air-conditioning, and new carpeting
would be installed, along with new electrical wiring and other
technical equipment. Lobbies, restrooms, stairways, lockers, and
other areas in the theater would be redecorated, and improvements
would be provided for the stage and the backstage dressing rooms.
Exterior work would include remodeling the main marquee and
sandblasting the facade facing Main and Gibbs streets.

Throughout the summer months, increased concerns were
expressed at the school. Some questioned the lack of plans to address
major deficiencies in the stage lighting system or to provide an up-
to-date sound system or recording studio. Others emphasized that
the architects and consultants should have been discussing their
plans with those who actually utilized the theater, not simply with

---

[12] M. Alfred Bichsel, memo to Walter Hendl, February 21, 1970. SML.

university administrators. The main pressure, however, was applied for a change in acoustical consultants, even though the university worried that such a change would inevitably delay the renovation and make it almost impossible to meet a November 1971 completion date. That date was especially important, since the 1971–72 school year was scheduled to be a festive celebration of the school's fiftieth anniversary. Any delay in reopening the theater would upset plans for the opening events of that important celebration.

Nonetheless, Eastman views prevailed concerning the acoustical consultants. Paul S. Veneklasen and Associates was appointed the new chief acoustician, with O. I. Angevine Jr. as associate consultant. Communication between the school and the university, however, was still far from ideal. An important meeting was scheduled with the Ellerbe architectural firm in St. Paul, Minnesota, in early September, to which no one from Eastman had been invited. At Hendl's insistence, Daniel Patrylak was sent to represent the Eastman School, and he successfully argued that appropriate people from Eastman should meet as soon as possible with Veneklasen, Angevine, and a representative from Ellerbe. This led to a series of meetings with Eastman faculty and staff during the fall.

Problems persisted, however, at least in part because of concerns for keeping the project within the limitations of the agreed budget. Renovating the theater while simultaneously making plans to relocate the school put budgetary constraints on the amount the university would be willing to spend on the theater facilities. Certainly, no one was prepared to authorize the full renovation program Ellerbe had recommended at a cost of almost $4.5 million. Something more limited would have to suffice, although this meant eliminating several aspects of the renovation that had been recommended by the architects and consultants. Veneklasen, for example, was concerned that the plans seemed to omit corrections of major faults involving balance, echoes, and reverberation. Ellerbe Architects voiced concern that the planned work might prove inadequate, to the detriment of the firm's reputation. None of this quickened the renovation process, and some began to understand that the best they could hope for would be to reopen the theater in January 1972.

One additional issue remained to be addressed: the fate of the gigantic Austin theater organ. As the senior member of the organ department, David Craighead had expressed his negative opinion of the instrument the previous year when he had written Patrylak on April 22, 1969, stating that it would be a grave error to relocate the organ to another position in the theater (if this was ever even a remote possibility) or even to replace it with a new instrument in the same location. An overture to the American Association of Theater Organ Enthusiasts was made in October the following year in an attempt to find someone who might be interested in removing the organ for possible use elsewhere. Two months later the final decision to remove the organ was made, and advertisements were placed in *Diapson* (the official journal of the American Guild of Organists) and *The Theater Organ* (the official journal of the American Theater Organ Society).

No one stepped forward to preserve the organ, and the administrative costs of disposing of it through a private sale were considered too substantial to justify any attempt to sell it. Therefore, the general contractor for the renovation project was charged with the responsibility of dismantling and disposing of the instrument. Except for several ranks of pipes that were acquired by local churches, the mighty Austin organ—the world's largest theater organ in 1922—was simply to be discarded, a decision the university was forced to defend vigorously amid considerable criticism for many months thereafter. A news release from the university dated February 23, 1971, announced that the Eastman Theatre renovation costs had risen to $2.13 million, and the final figure by the time the project was completed was $2.3 million. Fortunately, the generosity of the Eastman Kodak Company relieved the university of any major financial burden.

Eight days prior to the university's February 23 announcement about the theater renovation, Walter Hendl submitted a new report to W. Allen Wallis concerning the future location of the Eastman School of Music. His report outlined the decision made in 1964 that the school remain at the Gibbs Street location and mentioned a 1966 proposal (never enacted) to construct a center for the performing arts, of which Eastman would be the central feature. He mentioned the 1967 Eastman faculty committee that had recommended relocation of the school, as well as referring to his own letter of September 1969 that had supported moving the school from the downtown area. He reiterated the arguments in favor of a move, as well as those in favor of renovation at the school's present location. Then, he unexpectedly concluded his report by stating that "given the option to make a recommendation, it would be to remain at our present location."[13] Between September 1969 and February 1971, Hendl had changed his mind.

---

[13] Walter Hendl, Report to the Chancellor on the Future Location of the Eastman School of Music, February 15, 1971. SML.

Increasing faculty concerns over the prospect of moving the school to the River Campus may have been partly responsible for Hendl's apparently abrupt reversal on the issue. He was astute enough to know that opposition to relocating the school was firm, while support for the move was generally tempered by various conditions and anxieties. He also knew, perhaps better than anyone, that the theater renovation had initially proceeded with little attention to opinions at the Eastman School of Music. Therefore, it might be detrimental to the school's future if a new physical plant was constructed without the full involvement of the school's administration and faculty. Planning for a music school requires special considerations that are particular to the nature of such an institution. Based on some of the decisions and priorities of the theater renovation, Hendl may have wondered if these considerations would receive appropriate attention. Perhaps it would be better to deal with a known quantity in downtown Rochester, even with its limitations and problems, rather than trust the future to an unknown quantity somewhere else.

At the root of the problem were the very significant distinctions at all levels between the Eastman School of Music and its parent institution, the University of Rochester. Eastman students, especially at the undergraduate level, generally had a significantly different outlook regarding the educational process and a different expectation of the purposes and outcome of that education than their university counterparts. They spent week after week at the school pursuing activities, such as practicing four or five hours a day, for which there was nothing comparable throughout the rest of the university. It was not that they necessarily worked harder than their River Campus counterparts but simply that the requirements of their study were entirely different. This was, after all, a professional music school. Members of the Eastman faculty had widely different backgrounds, most without terminal degrees and a few at the time with no academic degree. Many of the faculty pursued professional careers that had little, if anything, in common with the academic careers of their counterparts at the River Campus. These faculty members were just getting accustomed to the idea of academic rank and in all probability had not completely thought through the issues of tenure and promotion. Students and faculty alike often wondered if the rest of the university understood them or really cared about what they were doing.

In situations like this, perceptions are often more important than realities. There was a long-standing perception that Eastman essentially benefited from its independence and autonomy and that there were reasons to be suspicious of the central university administration and its motives. Even Warren Benson, who favored moving the school, cautioned that "it is of paramount importance that our position of preeminence among American schools of music be maintained both for our own good and for the good of the University as a whole."[14] Norman Peterson, for many years a member of the organ department, asked if moving the school to the River Campus would "herald the end of the Conservatory type of training for which Eastman is globally famous."[15] Questions such as these expressed a reluctance to place the school's future in someone else's hands. They were emotional responses to the situation and perhaps at times quite irrational. But they reflected an undercurrent of feeling at the Eastman School of Music that would make questions of the school's location inevitably difficult.

Whatever the obstacles, the university's president was apparently determined to relocate the Eastman School and believed it was in the best long-term interests of the school to move into a new physical plant near the rest of the university. In spite of the fact that the matter was still under discussion at various levels, the university administration was already studying the relative merits of several possible locations for the new Eastman School buildings. Sasaki Dawson DeMay Associates did an initial study that evaluated nine sites on or near the River Campus. The university then narrowed the choices to three locations. The first of these was identified as the Park Campus Site, consisting of about ten acres of land in the area of Genesee Valley Park. The second was the Lattimore Site, an open field space north of the graduate living center, including the southern part of the Lattimore parking lot. The third and final possible location for the new Eastman School of Music buildings was the River Boulevard Site, consisting of land between River Boulevard and Mount Hope Cemetery. Sasaki Dawson DeMay was asked to do a comprehensive study of these three sites, and the firm complied with a detailed report in May 1971.

W. Allen Wallis was undoubtedly acting in good faith in his desire to relocate the Eastman School of Music, based on his assessment of

---

14 Warren Benson, memo to Walter Hendl, March 10, 1970. SML.
15 Norman Peterson, memo to Flora Burton, January 23, 1970. SML.

what was the best course of action not only for the school but also for the university. The circumstances that ultimately led to abandoning the dream of a new physical plant for the music school and choosing instead to renovate the downtown facilities—which eventually included new construction as well—all occurred after Walter Hendl's successor had arrived in Rochester to become the fourth director of the Eastman School of Music. Those circumstances fall outside the parameters of this volume and will need to be related at some point in the future.

Chapter 16

1971–72

Fiftieth Anniversary Year: The Celebration

The Eastman School of Music had welcomed its first students in September 1921, and now the school was planning to celebrate that event with a lavish year-long celebration of its fiftieth anniversary. Almost two dozen new works of music were commissioned for the occasion, each to receive a premiere performance during the anniversary year. The school applied for grants from various organizations, such as the New York State Council on the Arts and the National Endowment for the Arts, to support this ambitious commissioning plan. All of the school's performing ensembles would take part in the festivities, and the annual Great Performers Series would feature several important guest artists, as well as recitals by distinguished members of the faculty. Especially noteworthy were plans for four special Festival Concerts in the Eastman Theatre, each presenting a recitalist of major international renown. In addition, four symposia were scheduled throughout the school year that would bring many important scholars to Rochester as participants. Many of the most important events would also include lavish post-concert receptions at Hutchison House, the home of the school's director, Walter Hendl. The project director for this year-long anniversary celebration was Donald Shetler, who had been appointed the Eastman School's first director of development in 1968.

In retrospect, it is curious that the celebration was very much about the present rather than the past. No plans were made to publish a history of the institution or even an updated version of the history Charles Riker wrote at the time of the school's twenty-fifth anniversary.[1] There was no school historian at the time, and archival activities were practically nonexistent. The school's fiftieth

---

[1] Riker, *The Eastman School of Music*. A supplement to this volume was published at the time of the school's fortieth anniversary.

anniversary simply did not concern itself with the institution's history. No important event was scheduled that would bring together those who had been present for the opening of the school in 1921 or those with personal recollections of George Eastman. The celebration during 1971–72 was event-filled, but apparently without curiosity or nostalgia for the past.

The opening event of the anniversary year was a performance on October 1 by the Eastman Philharmonia with Walter Hendl directing. Because the Eastman Theatre renovations were yet to be completed, the concert was held in Strong Auditorium at the university's River Campus, not an ideal location. The concert had been preceded by changes in the assignments of the orchestra personnel, with several first and second chair players eliminated or demoted—a situation understandably greeted with frustration and resentment by some of the student players. The evening's program consisted of Beethoven's *Leonora Overture No. 3*, Piano Concerto No. 1 by Serge Prokofiev (1891–1953), and the Symphony in D Minor by César Franck (1822–90). Soloist for the concerto was Katherine Collier (BM '70, MM '73), a candidate for the master of music degree and performer's certificate at the Eastman School of Music. At the time, she was a student of Barry Snyder, but she had previously studied with Cecile Genhart. In spite of the less-than-ideal location for the concert and the personnel issues, the evening was deemed an impressive and successful start to the fiftieth anniversary year celebration.

Several other events during October also needed alternate venues because of the ongoing theater renovation. The first of these was a concert on October 15 by the Eastman Jazz Ensemble led by Chuck Mangione, which was performed in the Palestra on the River Campus, and the second was the annual concert presented in honor of United Nations Week in Rochester. The latter concert, which was not officially part of the fiftieth anniversary celebration, featured the Eastman Wind Ensemble conducted by Donald Hunsberger, and it took place in the Nazareth Arts Center at nearby Nazareth College on October 22. Transferring concerts to the River Campus and Nazareth College was definitely an inconvenience, but it did present an opportunity to bring Eastman School performers to audiences who otherwise might not have heard the school's performing groups during the anniversary year.

The opening events of the Great Performers Series all took place in Kilbourn Hall, starting with a vocal recital on October 5 by the famous English mezzo-soprano Dame Janet Baker (b. 1933), accompanied by Martin Isepp. Her program consisted of music by Mozart, Monteverdi, Rossini, Schubert, Fauré, and several early

English composers. Especially gratifying was the generous selection from infrequently heard works of Claudio Monteverdi (1567–1643). Ten days later, Nikolaus Harnoncourt (b. 1929) and the Concentus Musicus of Vienna appeared in Kilbourn with a program of music by Tomaso Albioni (1671–1751), William Lawes (1602–45), Jean-Philippe Rameau (1683–1764), Giovanni Legrenzi (1626–90), and Johann Sebastian Bach (1685–1750). The Great Performers Series continued on October 26 with a recital by Eastman faculty member Carroll Glenn, assisted by her husband, Eugene List, and faculty colleagues Brooks Smith and John Beck.

Kilbourn Hall was also the site for a Musica Nova concert on October 19, with Walter Hendl conducting. The program included a performance of *Consortium*, by Joseph Schwantner, a twenty-six year-old assistant professor at Eastman.[2] Schwantner's work was dedicated to Richard Pittman, who had originated the Eastman School's Musica Nova series in 1966. Pittman was now the conductor of the Boston Musica Viva and had premiered *Consortium* on September 23 at Harvard University's Busch-Resinger Museum. The featured work on the Musica Nova concert, however, was not Schwantner's piece but the newly commissioned *Facets* by Ulysses Kay (b. 1917), the first of the compositions commissioned in honor of the school's anniversary. Kay was a professor at Herbert H. Lehman College at City University of New York (CUNY). He had earned a master's degree from the Eastman School after graduating from the University of Arizona and had been awarded the Prix de Rome and a Fulbright grant for further study in Italy. Among his many honors was having been chosen as a member of the first group of American composers sent to the USSR on a cultural exchange sponsored by the U.S. State Department. His commissioned work for Eastman, scored for woodwind quintet and piano, was performed by faculty members Joseph Mariano, Stanley Hasty, Robert Sprenkle, K. David Van Hoesen, Verne Reynolds, and Frank Glazer, with Hendl conducting.

The month of October ended on a sad note with the sudden death of Josephine Antoine on October 30, the day after her daughter's wedding in Jamestown, New York. This delightful and talented woman was greatly mourned by her many friends and admirers at Eastman. The sense of loss was perhaps more deeply felt because her death came less than five months after that of her colleague Julius Huehn. Both Antoine and Huehn were sixty-three at the time of their passing.

---

[2] Eight years later, Schwantner earned the prestigious Pulitzer Prize in Music for his composition *Aftertones of Infinity*.

Two newly commissioned works written by Eastman faculty members were given premieres during November. Warren Benson's *Capriccio for Violin, Viola, Violoncello, and Piano* was presented by members of the Eastman Quartet in a Kilbourn Hall Great Performers Series concert on November 9, and Samuel Adler's Concerto for Organ and Orchestra received its first performance in an Eastman Philharmonia concert at Lake Avenue Baptist Church on November 12. Soloist for the concerto was David Craighead, who also performed the *Prelude and Allegro for Organ and Orchestra* by Walter Piston (1894–1976) and Symphony No. 3 for Organ and Orchestra by Camille Saint-Saëns (1835–1921). Craighead was deeply impressed with Adler's work, declaring it an important landmark among compositions for organ and orchestra and expressing hope that it would receive many more performances in the future.

The month of November ended with a recital in Kilbourn Hall by the noted harpsichordist Rafael Puyana (b. 1931). Opportunities to hear a fine harpsichord recital in Rochester were limited. Fernando Valenti (1926–90) had performed twice in Kilbourn during the 1950s, and Puyana had previously appeared at Eastman on February 14, 1961. Both men were former students of Wanda Landowska (1879–1959), the leading figure in the modern revival of interest in the harpsichord. Puyana's program opened with the Suite in F Minor by Jean Nicolas Geoffroy (d. 1694), followed by two sonatas of Domenico Scarlatti (1685–1757). The first half of the recital ended with the Bach Concerto in D Major (after Vivaldi), and the second half was devoted entirely to Bach's monumental Fourth Partita.

December began with the first of the four special Festival Concerts scheduled in celebration of the anniversary year. World-renowned violinist Henryk Szeryng (1918–88) appeared in a December 7 recital with pianist Charles Reiner, presenting an outstanding program of music by Beethoven, Bach, Schumann, Ponce, and Ravel. The work by Manuel Ponce (1882–1948), which was probably receiving its first Rochester performance, had been written for and dedicated to Szeryng. Among those attending both Szeryng's recital and his master class at Eastman was senior violinist Marcus Lehmann, who described the experience in these words:

It was so inspiring to watch and play for one of the greatest artists. I had gotten so used to recordings it was refreshing to actually see the mind and energy behind a performer like Szeryng. This type of experience cannot even be put into words, to see one who has overcome so much and seeks only the joy in performing. It was an invaluable and essential moment in my musical experience, and many felt the same.[3]

It was unfortunate that Szeryng's outstanding recital had to take place at the Nazareth Arts Center rather than the Eastman Theatre, but the venue was changed once again because of the theater's unavailability as a result of ongoing renovations. Happily, this would be the last time a concert had to be relocated, since the theater was finally scheduled to reopen in January.

The month of December also featured the first of the symposia scheduled in celebration of the anniversary year. This was a gathering of music critics for five days beginning December 8, and participants included Alfred Frankenstein from *The San Francisco Chronicle*, Henry Pleasants from *The International Herald Tribune*, Harold Schonberg from *The New York Times*, Alan Rich from *New York Magazine*, Irving Lowens from *The Washington Evening Star*, Thomas Willis from *The Chicago Tribune*, Michael Steinberg from *The Boston Globe*, Paul Hume from *The Washington Post*, William Mann from *The London Times*, Martin Bernheimer from *The Los Angeles Times*, James Goodfriend from *Stereo Review*, and Hans H. Stuckenschmidt, a writer and critic from Berlin. Much to the chagrin of the Eastman School, Alan Rich later wrote a particularly unflattering account of the school in *New York Magazine*. This was hardly the kind of national publicity the school had anticipated from the symposium.

On the evening of the symposium's second day, an event occurred that positively stunned the school community: the unexpected death of Emory Remington. Less than two weeks shy of his eightieth birthday, Remington (or "the Chief" as he was known to so many) had spent his day teaching at the school—an activity he had pursued for about the last half century—before going to a nearby restaurant, the Italian Village, for dinner. He collapsed and died at the restaurant. When the news was conveyed to the school, the Wind Ensemble concert scheduled for 8:15 P.M. was immediately canceled. No one in the group could possibly have performed under the circumstances that evening. Few people, if any, were as beloved at the school as the Chief, and many students openly wept when they were told what had occurred. A memorial service was later held at Christ Church on East Avenue, and Howard Hanson eulogized Remington as perhaps only Howard Hanson could:

---

[3] Quoted in *Eastman School of Music 50th Anniversary Year*, 27.

Figure 35. Walter Hendl with Emory Remington. (Collection of the author.)

> He loved music. He loved that most noble instrument, the trombone. But most important of all, he loved people, and above all he loved his students. We today must not mourn for him, but only for his loved ones and for ourselves. He died as he wanted to die, as he had so frequently said, doing what he loved to do—teaching his beloved instrument to his beloved students![4]

Remington's success as a teacher was legendary. His influence on brass playing in general, and on the trombone in particular, was revolutionary and far-reaching. Yet his ideas and methods were uniquely his own. He was not a representative of any particular "school" of playing other than the one he devised himself:

> In those days no one asked fundamental questions, so no one had any answers. No one even thought about questions of tongue place-ment, breath control, and so on. . . . I just played as it seemed right

---

[4] Howard Hanson quoted in ibid., 39.

to me. There was very little material then that treated the vocal line. The old school was to "spit it out." I was strong on articulation in the mouth like a singer. I didn't blow into the horn, I sang into it with as little resistance as possible. From the very beginning, I have always treated the instrument as just another voice.[5]

Meanwhile, the Music Critics Symposium continued. While the critics were debating the finer points of their profession, a chamber orchestra concert took place on December 11 in Kilbourn Hall with Walter Hendl conducting. The concert featured three newly commissioned works, all sponsored in part by grants from the National Endowment for the Arts and the Charles E. Merrill Trust. The first of these was entitled *Music for Chamber Orchestra* and had been written by Rochester native David Diamond (1915–2005). Diamond had studied at both the Cleveland Institute of Music and the Eastman School of Music, as well as with Roger Sessions (1896–1985) in New York City and Nadia Boulanger (1887–1979) in Paris. A composer of numerous symphonies and string quartets, as well as many other works, he was teaching at the Manhattan School of Music.

The relationship between Diamond and Hanson had never been especially cordial, and, as a result, the former had always had a very estranged relationship with the Eastman School. Therefore, it may have been a particularly appropriate gesture to include Diamond among the composers of commissioned works. Regrettably, he was unable to attend the performance, but he reacted strongly to reports that suggested his work had been given a rather inadequate performance. In response, he wrote to Donald Shetler to complain about the concert:

> Since the performance of my work on 11 December, more and more information has been coming to me from individuals, students, friends, and some of the critics who know me personally giving me their rather distressing reactions to the quality of the performance and the breaking down in my work so that Walter had to repeat the first part. From Alec [Wilder] I heard that all three works suffered from lack of preparation.[6]

Alec Wilder (1902–80), who had communicated with Diamond about the performance, had a commissioned work on the same

5   Emory Remington quoted in ibid., 40.
6   David Diamond, letter to Donald Shetler, January 23, 1972. SML.

chamber orchestra concert. His work was entitled *Entertainment #4 for French Horn and Chamber Orchestra,* and the December 11 premiere featured Verne Reynolds as French horn soloist. Wilder, who was slightly older than Diamond, was also a native Rochesterian and had likewise studied at the Eastman School of Music. A man of great wit and diverse talents, he was well-known in popular music circles for his arrangements for Frank Sinatra, as well as for being a highly skilled and successful song writer. An especially original and creative talent, Wilder was also the composer of many serious compositions and the author of a masterful book on the American popular song.[7]

The third composer of a commissioned work on the December 11 program was the only one of the trio who was not a Rochester native. Juan Orrego-Salas (b. 1919) was born and educated in Santiago, Chile, and he later came to the United States to study composition with Aaron Copland (1900–1980) and musicology with Paul Henry Lang (1901–91). He had recently been appointed professor of composition and director of the Latin American Music Center at Indiana University. His commissioned work for the Eastman School celebration was entitled *Volte* and was scored for piano, fifteen wind instruments, harp, and percussion.

Four days following the December 11 program, yet another commissioned work was premiered in Kilbourn Hall, the commission once again supported in part by grants from the National Endowment for the Arts and the Charles E. Merrill Trust. The occasion for the premiere was a Great Performers Series recital by violinist Zvi Zeitlin, and the work in question was the Sonata for Violin and Piano by Eastman composer and French horn professor Verne Reynolds. Zeitlin performed the sonata with his faculty colleague Barry Snyder. He later commented on the work's complexity and difficulty by saying he had probably never played a sonata with more notes, but he added that "the more we got to know it, the greater our involvement and excitement in playing it."[8]

Several major events of the fiftieth anniversary celebration took place immediately after the school's winter break. The first of these was the long-anticipated and long-overdue reopening of the Eastman Theatre with a gala concert on January 7, 1972. The program featured the Eastman Philharmonia with the school's director once again on the podium, and it opened with the world premiere of

---

[7]   Alec Wilder, *American Popular Song: The Great Innovators 1900–1950* (New York: Oxford, 1972).

[8]   Zeitlin quoted in *Eastman School of Music 50th Anniversary Year,* 46.

Festival Fanfare by Eastman alumnus Charles Strouse (b. 1928). Strouse's stirring fanfare was followed by performances of the Overture to *William Tell* by Gioachino Rossini (1792–1868), the Tchaikovsky Piano Concerto No. 1 in B-flat Minor with Eugene List as soloist, and Symphony No. 1 by Gustav Mahler (1860–1911). As will be related, the significance of this gala concert extended far beyond the evening itself.

Four days after the Philharmonia concert, the Eastman Brass Quintet presented a program in Kilbourn Hall that featured yet another work commissioned for the anniversary year, Robert Gauldin's *Variations on a Rock Tune*. A member of the school's theory and composition faculties since 1963, Gauldin had earned his master's degree and doctorate from Eastman and had taught at William Carey College in Mississippi for a half dozen years before returning to Eastman as a faculty member. Members of the Eastman Brass Quintet at the time were Daniel Patrylak and Alan Vizzutti, trumpets; Verne Reynolds, French horn; Donald Knaub, trombone; and Cherry Beauregard, tuba.

On January 14 the Eastman Theatre was the scene of the second special Festival Concert, this one featuring the Russian piano virtuoso Vladimir Ashkenazy (b. 1937). His recital opened with a Haydn Sonata in G Minor and continued with music of Robert Schumann (1810–56) and Sergei Rachmaninoff (1873–1943), the latter composer represented by his *Variations on a Theme of Corelli,* which was given a truly outstanding performance. Ashkenazy may have been at the height of his pianistic powers in 1972. He had first come to the attention of the piano world by actually losing a competition, placing second in the 1955 Chopin Competition in Warsaw. The jury decision was controversial at the time, and Ashkenazy subsequently went on to a highly successful and extensive career, certainly more so than that of the competition's gold medal winner, Adam Haraciewicz (b. 1932).

A piano event in a somewhat lighter vein took place in Kilbourn Hall on January 17. Eugene List's interest in music for multiple pianos had led to the presentation of several programs over the years that featured music requiring the collaborative efforts of several pianists. The January 17 program was entitled "Monster Concert," and the title was more than appropriate. Some of the music was serious, or at least attempted to be serious, while some of it was definitely of a less weighty nature. The program opened with the Sonata for Three Hands by Johann Wilhelm Hässler (1747–1822), followed by the Sonata for Five Hands by Johann Dalberg (1760–1812), Rachmaninoff's Romance for Six Hands (at one piano), and the Sonata for

Figure 36. Vladimir Ashkenazy with Eastman student Cathy Callis and Eastman faculty member Eugene List, January, 1972.

Eight Hands by Bedrich Smetana (1824–84)—all performed by East-man faculty members Maria Luisa Faini, Frank Glazer, List, and Brooks Smith. Also of particular interest was a performance of *Hexa-méron*, a set of six variations written by six composers on a theme by Vincenzo Bellini (1801–35). The composers involved in this collabora-tive endeavor were Franz Liszt (1811–86), Sigismund Thalberg (1812–71), Johann Peter Pixis (1788–1874), Henri Herz (1803–88), Carl Czerny (1791–1857), and Frédéric Chopin (1810–49). A touch of humor was noted when William Cerny of the Eastman faculty was chosen to per-form Variation V, which had been written by Carl Czerny.

The Monster Concert continued on a more serious note with the *Paris Suite* for four pianos by Darius Milhaud (1892–1974), once again performed by Faini, Glazer, List, and Smith. Something ter-ribly amiss happened at the end of the work, with the three gentle-men pianists all concluding together while Faini continued playing for an additional bar of music. When asked after the concert what had happened at the end of the Milhaud, Faini responded with apparent seriousness, "I don't know. *They* must have gotten mixed up."[9] Her response may have been an example of her customary

---

[9]   The author posed the question to her.

Figure 37. The Monster Concert, January 17, 1972. Shown in the photograph (from left to right) are pianists Edward Easley, Wallace Gray, Maria Luisa Faini, and Brooks Smith.

self-confidence or, more likely, an even better example of her sense of humor. Eugene List then performed *Two Cuban Dances* by Louis Moreau Gottschalk (1829–69), a composer for whom he had a special affinity. The concert ended with a rousing rendition of the Overture to *Semiramide* by Rossini, arranged for eight pianos, sixteen pianists, and thirty-two hands, performed by various members of the Eastman faculty and staff.

The following week featured two performances on successive evenings of *A Midsummer Night's Dream* by Benjamin Britten (1913–76). Directed by Leonard Treash and designed by Thomas Struthers, the productions were conducted by Edwin McArthur. As often happens with opera productions, several mishaps added to the evening's entertainment, including "Puck" left dangling in midair when his flying harness snagged and the fog machine emitting so much fog at such an unbelievable rate that the entire stage area was practically obscured from view.

February provided the occasion for the second symposium of the anniversary year, this one devoted to music, teaching, and learning. Participants included Paul Willems of the International Federation of Musical Youth in Belgium, Sir Keith Falkner of the Royal College of Music in London, Charles Gary from the Music Educators

National Conference, James Nielson representing the LeBlanc Corporation, Harris Danziger from the Third Street Music School Settlement in New York City, Elizabeth Szonyi from the Franz Liszt Academy in Budapest, Robert Petzold from the University of Wisconsin, Louis Wersen from the Philadelphia public school system, Rudolfo Zubrisky from the Sociedad Argentina de Educación Musical, and Henning Bro Rasmussen, secretary-general of the International Society for Music Education in Denmark. Connected with the symposium was a special convocation on February 12 at which an honorary doctor of music degree was conferred on Shinichi Suzuki (1898–1998), the educator and violin teacher who had created the Suzuki method that had met with such outstanding success not only in Japan but also in the United States.

A week earlier the school had suffered the sudden death of yet another member of its faculty when Eugene Selhorst died on February 6 at age fifty-seven. Selhorst, who had ably helped fill the void left when Harold Gleason retired in 1955, had contributed heavily to the development of graduate professional studies at the school and had been perhaps more instrumental than anyone in establishing the school's church music program. A memorial Mass was held at Corpus Christi Church in Rochester on February 10. Howard Hanson served as eulogist, while M. Alfred Bichsel was the homilist. William Cerny and Walter Hendl were the lectors, and music was provided by the Eastman Polyphonic Choir, which sang works of Hässler and Bach. It was certainly an ecumenical gathering at a Roman Catholic funeral Mass, with the homily preached by a Lutheran pastor and the eulogy delivered by a former elder of the Presbyterian Church.

The service for Selhorst was attended by many from the Eastman community who came to mourn the death of yet another friend, colleague, teacher, and scholar. Within less than a year, the Eastman School had lost four of its most respected and distinguished faculty members: Eugene Selhorst, Julius Huehn, Josephine Antoine, and Emory Remington. Moreover, three other retired members of the voice faculty—Arthur Kraft, LeRoy Morelock, and Nicholas Konraty—had also died during 1971 and 1972. It was a particularly painful period for the Eastman community.

Meanwhile, on February 11 the Eastman Philharmonia performed once again in the Eastman Theatre under the direction of Walter Hendl. The highlight of the concert was the premiere of one of the most important of the anniversary year's commissioned works, *Partita for Harpsichord and Orchestra* by Krysztof Penderecki (b. 1933). Penderecki, who had been born and educated in Poland, was teaching at the Folkwang Hochschule für Musik in Essen,

Figure 38. Kryzstof Penderecki (left) with Warren Benson and Samuel Adler, February 1972.

Figure 39. Eastman Philharmonia at Carnegie Hall, February 15, 1972.

Germany, after having served for about a dozen years on the faculty at the University of Cracow in Poland. He had earned much recognition throughout the world for his compositions, and he was a very important composer for the Eastman School to have commissioned for its anniversary year. The entire concert program, consisting of Aaron Copland's *El Salón México* and the Mahler Symphony No. 1 in addition to the Penderecki work, was repeated four nights later in New York City at Carnegie Hall.

Penderecki had written his *Partita* for Felicja Blumental (1908–91), the noted Polish-born pianist who appeared as soloist at the Eastman premiere. Blumental had impressive credentials, having studied at the National Conservatory in Warsaw with Zbigniew Drzewiecki (1890–1971), Poland's most distinguished and successful piano teacher. She later continued her studies in Switzerland with Jozef Turczynski (1884–1953), another exceptional Polish teacher and the noted editor of Chopin's piano works. Blumental had an exceptionally large repertoire and was known as a champion of many long-neglected works as well as an advocate for the music of Brazil, especially that of Heitor Villa-Lobos (1887–1959). Her performance of the Penderecki *Partita* was a gratifying opportunity to collaborate with her native country's most distinguished composer. The following year she performed Penderecki's *Partita* once again, this time in Warsaw for the Polish premiere. It was her first visit to the country of her birth in thirty-five years.

While the Penderecki premiere and other celebratory events of the anniversary year were taking place, there were increasing concerns within the Eastman community over a growing crisis between the Rochester Philharmonic players and the orchestra's management. The orchestra's conductor, Samuel Jones, had dismissed four players and placed a fifth on probation in January. As a result, he was charged with violating several union rules. Adding to the orchestra's woes was the March 3 resignation of Walter Hendl as music adviser. In submitting his resignation, the school's director complained that the orchestra's management seldom consulted him on important matters involving guest conductors, soloists, and programming. Hendl also urged the management to rescind the dismissals, although there is evidence that he had initially supported at least some of the decisions that led to those dismissals. The management's best offer at the time was to allow the dismissed players to re-audition for their positions, but, understandably, that offer was rejected by the orchestra committee. The orchestra's crisis was not resolved until October when a new board was elected that reinstated the musicians. It was a difficult time for the Rochester Philharmonic, and there was much sympathy at the Eastman School for the plight of the musicians, as well as concern for the orchestra's future.

As these events were unfolding, the school's fiftieth anniversary celebration continued. The third and fourth symposia took place in April and May, respectively. The first of these was a gathering of distinguished musicologists, the presiding chairman being Edward Evans from the Eastman School. Papers were presented by Imogene Horsley from Stanford University, Robert D. Donington from the University of Iowa, Barry S. Brook from CUNY, Denis Stevens from Columbia University, Ruth Steiner from Catholic University, Kurt von Fischer from the University of Zurich in Switzerland, and Drits Noske and Frank Harrison from the University of Amsterdam in the Netherlands. The featured speaker was the eminent musicologist Gustave Reese, whose topic was "The Place of Musicology in a School of Music." The fourth and final symposium, devoted to the issue of support for the arts, opened on May 4, 1972. Eastman alumna Merle Montgomery, who was president of the National Federation of Music Clubs, spoke on "The Responsibility of the Community." Participants included representatives from the National Endowment for the Arts, the Kennedy Center for the Performing Arts, and several other important organizations and institutions.

Concerts and recitals during the final months of the fiftieth anniversary celebration included faculty recitals by Frank Glazer and Eileen Malone and an appearance by the Guarneri String Quartet playing an all-Beethoven program on March 9. All three events were part of the Great Performers Series. Glazer presented an especially interesting program of piano music, playing the final sonatas written by Haydn, Schubert, Mozart, and Beethoven. The special Festival Concerts concluded with a piano recital by Rudolf Serkin (1903–91) on March 15 and a violin recital by Isaac Stern (1920–2001) on May 3. Serkin presented an all-Beethoven program featuring four of the composer's sonatas, and he was awarded an honorary degree at the concert's conclusion. Stern's recital included music of Brahms, Mozart, Schumann, Bartók, Dvorak, and Paganini. He was also the recipient of an honorary degree, conferred at a separate ceremony in Kilbourn Hall the following afternoon.

The performance of commissioned works continued at a rather frenzied pace throughout the spring semester. *Piece for Studio Orchestra and Soloist* by Oliver Nelson (1932–75) received its premiere on March 3 in a performance featuring Rayburn Wright and the Eastman Studio Orchestra, with Nelson as soloist on soprano saxophone. The composer, who had performed with and arranged for Duke Ellington, Count Basie, Bill Evans, and many others, had been named "Best Arranger 1967–68" by *Downbeat Magazine* and "Best Arranger 1968" by *Record World Magazine.* Nelson spent the entire week at Eastman visiting classes, teaching, and rehearsing. Shortly after the concert in the Eastman Theatre, the Studio Orchestra went on tour to Atlanta, Cincinnati, and Nashville, and Nelson joined them for those concerts as well.

Two entirely different commissioned works received their first performances the following week in an Eastman Theatre concert featuring the Eastman School Symphony Orchestra. *Soundscapes for Orchestra and Electronic Tape* by Eastman School of Music composer Wayne Barlow (1912–96) and *Circle for Orchestra* by Alavaro Cassuto (b. 1938) were featured on the program. Cassuto, assistant to Leopold Stokowski (1882–1977) with the American Symphony Orchestra, was Portuguese and had studied with György Ligeti (b. 1923) and Karlheinz Stockhausen (b. 1928).

On April 7 the Eastman Wind Ensemble gave the premiere performance of *A Nostalgic Jazz Odyssey* by John Williams (b. 1932). The popular Williams, who had won a 1969 Emmy Award for his musical score for the television production of *Heidi,* had trained at Juilliard and apprenticed as an orchestrator with Mario Castelnuovo-Tedesco (1895–1968) in Los Angeles. The concert on April 7 also featured the premiere of Howard Hanson's *Dies Natalis II.* Hanson's score had originally been written for orchestra on the occasion of the Nebraska centennial. The new version for wind ensemble, given its first performance at this concert, was dedicated to Donald Hunsberger and the Eastman Wind Ensemble.

The following week the Eastman Jazz Ensemble gave the first performance of a work entitled *Piece for Soloist and Jazz Ensemble,* for which Jack End (1918–86) had received a commission. A native Rochesterian, End was a graduate of the Eastman School where he had taught for ten years starting in 1940, the year of his graduation. He had been an arranger for various bands and orchestras and a producer-director for WROC-TV in Rochester before becoming associate director of radio and television for the University of Rochester and, more recently, deputy director of university relations. As has been related, many considered End to have been especially influential in the development of an appreciation for jazz in the Rochester area. He had played an important role in establishing the jazz program at the Eastman School several years earlier.

The fast pace of performances of works commissioned for the anniversary year continued with *Biograma* by Bruno Maderna (1920–73), which received its first performance by the Eastman Philharmonia on April 16. A noted composer and conductor, Maderna was co-director with Luciano Berio (b. 1925) of the Studio di Fonologia Musicale in Milan, Italy, and had recently been named composer-conductor at the Berkshire Music Festival. The commission for *Biograma* was sponsored in part by a grant from the Charles E. Merrill Trust and the Eastman School of Music Class of 1947. Maderna conducted the entire program, which included Debussy's *Iberia* and the Schumann Symphony No. 1, in addition to his own piece.

Finally, two more commissioned works were premiered on April 24. The first of these, *Concerto da Camera*, was written by Gunther Schuller (b. 1925), director of the New England Conservatory, who was noted for writing in a "third-stream" idiom that was an amalgam of contemporary classical concepts and avant-garde jazz. The commission was sponsored in part by the National Endowment for the Arts and the Charles E. Merrill Trust. *Concerto da Camera* was performed by Zeitgeist in Musik under the direction of the composer. On the same evening in Kilbourn Hall, Frederic Rzewski played the first performance of the Sonata for Piano by Edgar Valcácel (b. 1932), a premiere sponsored by a grant from the American Aeolian Corporation. The composer had done post-graduate study with Alberto Ginastera (1916–83) and Aaron Copland and had received a Guggenheim Fellowship to study electronic music at Columbia University with Vladimir Ussachevsky (1911–90) and Alcides Lanza (b. 1929). Rzewski was one of the foremost interpreters of new music for piano, as well as a composer with a growing reputation of his own. In addition to the works by Valcácel and Schuller, Zeitgeist in Musik also played the world premiere of Joseph Schwantner's *Modus Caelestes*, which he had written for the group.

The unfortunate story of one final commissioned work needs to be related, although the work in question and the concert that was to be the occasion for its first performance never materialized. The Eastman School of Music had approached the noted Soviet composer Rodion Shchedrin (b. 1932) in December 1969 with a formal offer to have him write and perform a new piano concerto. Shchedrin, an outstanding pianist, accepted the proposal four months later, and both parties planned for the premiere of the concerto to take place at a December 17, 1971, concert in the Eastman Theatre. As has been related, however, the theater renovation was not completed by that date. Therefore, the first performance of Shchedrin's concerto was rescheduled for a May 11 concert by the Eastman Philharmonia in Washington, D.C.'s John F. Kennedy Center for the Performing Arts. However, the composer communicated with Walter Hendl in March indicating that he had suffered some form of hand injury and suggesting the substitution of an orchestral work.

Hendl initially indicated that the substitution was acceptable to the school, adding that the performance dates would now be May 9 and 11, with rehearsals beginning April 28. The first of these performances would be in the Eastman Theatre and the second in the nation's capital.

On April 3, however, a decision was reached to cancel the Kennedy Center concert, and on April 6 Shchedrin was advised of the postponement with the hope that he might have more time to complete the originally commissioned piano concerto. Four days later Hendl spoke by telephone with the composer and firmly insisted that the piano concerto was the commission and that no substitute would be acceptable. The performance of a work originally intended to be featured in the gala reopening of the Eastman Theatre in December (a reopening that had been postponed) and then intended to be featured in the gala conclusion of the festival year at the Kennedy Center in May (an event now canceled) was simply not going to happen.

The Fiftieth Anniversary Festival was coming to an end, but not in the manner envisioned by its planners. A growing leadership crisis at the Eastman School of Music, which had been more or less successfully kept from public scrutiny for months, was now very much in the news. All attention was diverted from a spirit of celebration to the turmoil swirling around the school's beleaguered director.

Chapter 17

1971–72

Fiftieth Anniversary Year: The Crisis

During the festive celebration of the Eastman School of Music's fiftieth anniversary a leadership crisis, which had been slowly and quietly developing for a number of years, erupted and enmeshed the entire school community in a drama that led to Walter Hendl's resignation only eleven days before the 1972 commencement ceremonies. Ten years after this event, Hendl spoke candidly of a problem with alcohol abuse, which he blamed for the circumstances leading to his resignation.[1] Finding himself in a position as an administrator for which he had little or no background and beset with numerous questions and doubts about his career, he returned to a problem that had plagued him in the past and that would prove the instrument of his undoing at the Eastman School.

Hendl had never gained the full sympathy and support of the Eastman faculty, many of whom had been opposed to his initial appointment in 1964. That opposition made it all the more difficult for a man who was unfamiliar with and uncomfortable in his new role as director of the Eastman School of Music. His reappointment to the directorship in 1969 for another five-year term again lacked strong faculty endorsement. W. Allen Wallis retained a high level of confidence in the man he had chosen to lead the Eastman School of Music, perhaps attributing any faculty opposition to lingering questions over the manner in which the director had been selected five years earlier. Therefore, he was determined to give Walter Hendl a second five-year term as director.

Hendl undoubtedly understood that his leadership position at the school was in trouble. He was a performing musician, a superbly qualified conductor, but he was not an academician, a music educator,

---

[1] Stephen Wigler, "The Return of Conductor Walter Hendl," *Democrat and Chronicle* [Rochester, NY], October 25, 1982: 4C.

or an administrator. Worried that his contract would not be renewed in 1969, he had written to his good friend Peter Mennin at the Juilliard School asking for an opportunity to spend time with him and expressing fear that he would not be given a second term as director.[2] Even after his reappointment for a second term, Hendl had personal misgivings about his situation. In late 1970 he wrote his friend Henry Pleasants, who was living in London while working as the music critic for *The International Herald Tribune.* In his letter to Pleasants, Hendl expressed dissatisfaction with his present position, complaining that he was not only unhappy with his specific situation at Eastman but also generally unhappy working in America. He was prompted to write Pleasants to see if there were possibilities of employment in England.[3] He even added a postscript to the letter underscoring the fact that he was totally serious.

Hendl's letter to Pleasants also mentioned his forthcoming marriage to an old family friend whom he had known for eighteen years. The marriage, Hendl's third, took place on December 22, 1970. His new wife, once a baby-sitter for his daughter Susan, was Barbara Heisley of Williamsport, Pennsylvania. He later confided that he had asked her to marry him years earlier, but she refused. Now they were finally married, and Hendl could not have found a more supportive spouse for the troubled times ahead.

Very shortly after his marriage Hendl met with Louis Mennini, dean of music at the North Carolina School of the Arts and the older brother of Peter Mennin. Central to their conversation was discussion of an idea that Mennini might come to Eastman as a new assistant or associate director during Hendl's second term as director. Hendl explained that this would be a new position that would not affect the responsibilities then held by Daniel Patrylak but nonetheless providing him with much-needed administrative and academic expertise and assistance. As a college administrator who was an Eastman alumnus and a former member of the faculty, Mennini was an obvious choice for consideration for this kind of position.

On January 7, 1971, Mennini responded with a letter thanking Hendl for the opportunity to meet with him and outlining some thoughts he felt might be helpful if Hendl decided to approach the University of Rochester administration with a formal request for the addition of a new administrative position at Eastman. Mennini concurred that such a position should not interfere with the

---

[2]   Walter Hendl, memo to Peter Mennin, January 2, 1969. SML.
[3]   Walter Hendl, letter to Henry Pleasants, December 8, 1970. Private papers of Walter Hendl.

responsibilities currently performed at Eastman by Daniel Patrylak but that the person who held the position would assist the director in other administrative matters, including serving as Hendl's personal representative. Mennini suggested that this might especially involve working as the liaison between the school and the university. His letter outlined some of his qualifications as an administrator and ended with an assurance that Hendl would enjoy his complete trust and loyalty if he were selected for the position.[4] In view of what would transpire over the next eighteen months, it is to be regretted that some arrangement of this kind did not take place, for it might have avoided the crisis that would engulf Hendl and the entire school during the second semester of the following year.

There was rather widespread concern at the Eastman School of Music that certain areas of leadership were being neglected. Yet no effective movement had yet emerged to recommend any changes that might lead to the kind of leadership so many people felt was lacking. The catalyst for change eventually came not from the faculty but from the students, specifically the undergraduate Student Association and its president, Arthur Stidfole, a senior bassoonist and composition major. During the fall the association had communicated a number of its concerns to the director's office. Issues included dissatisfaction with the policy of academic advising, concern over increasing enrollment and its effect on the school's facilities and resources, questions of space utilization, and complaints that many students were not being given sufficient opportunities to perform in the school's large ensembles. As president of the Student Association, Stidfole referred these matters to Hendl's office but generally failed to receive any constructive response.

Hendl had perhaps always enjoyed a larger measure of support and sympathy from the students than from his faculty, even though the students generally understood that he had a serious problem. The previous spring a group of orchestral students had presented him with a request that he conduct the Eastman Philharmonia the following year, following a stirring performance under his direction of Respighi's *Festa Romana*. Therefore, the news that Hendl would indeed conduct the orchestra throughout the 1971–72 season was greeted with widespread enthusiasm and approval. From the very first concert in October, however, it was obvious to at least some observers that the year would not provide the kind of experience anticipated by many orchestra members. Student doubts

---

[4]   Louis Mennini, letter to Walter Hendl, January 7, 1971. Private papers of Walter Hendl.

concerning Hendl's ability to deal with the ongoing responsibilities of serving as their conductor reached a crisis on the evening of January 7, 1972, the gala concert that marked the reopening of the Eastman Theatre. Rehearsals for that event had been problematic, and Hendl's behavior at the concert itself was very erratic, with serious consequences that affected the performance. Students began to complain to one another and ultimately to the Student Association leadership.

Reacting to increased student concern, Stidfole decided to confer with Frank J. Dowd Jr., associate provost for student affairs at the University of Rochester, with whom he had become acquainted while serving on a university-wide committee the year before. He contacted Dowd for an appointment and decided that Richard Decker, vice president of the Student Association, should accompany him to the meeting. Decker was a horn player and a senior, like Stidfole, and both young men were candidates for the school's performer's certificate. Prior to their meeting with Dowd, the two students met privately with a number of Eastman professors whom they knew were unhappy with Hendl's handling of some of the school's problems. Several of these faculty members endeavored to cast more light on how administrative inaction might be damaging the school. Everyone spoke confidentially, however. At the time, no member of the faculty wanted to become directly involved.

Stidfole and Decker traveled to the university's River Campus on a Saturday morning and met with Dowd in the administration building on River Boulevard. Dowd led them to the office of the university's president, Robert Sproull,[5] where they presented the Eastman student body's concerns. They were assured that the administration would take the matter under advisement. A lengthy meeting of the Student Association soon followed, as did continued discussions—mainly off-campus—with members of the Eastman faculty. Weeks passed, and nothing further happened. Nonetheless, the fact that the student leadership was taking a position against the school's director became rather widely known throughout the school. Several faculty members who were friends and supporters of Hendl approached Stidfole to defend the director and to caution that serious consequences might result from continuing the course of action the Student Association was pursuing.

In the meanwhile, the university administration was not inactive. Hendl had sent W. Allen Wallis a warning in early February that a group of "dissident students" would likely contact him. Hendl

---

[5]   W. Allen Wallis had recently been given the new title of chancellor of the University of Rochester, and Sproull was elevated from provost to president.

had been apprised of growing student unrest by Flora Burton, the dean of students, and he quickly communicated with the university chancellor to defend himself, remarking that this was the first time in a quarter-century of conducting that members of an orchestra had criticized his work. In response to the student allegations that had been brought to his attention, Wallis asked President Sproull for a confidential report on the situation at the school. Sproull discussed the matter at length with the university's vice president for planning, Robert France, and sought input from Eastman professors Samuel Adler, Warren Benson, and Everett Gates. He reported to the chancellor that faculty concerns were probably reasonably accurate but were likely motivated by respect and affection for Walter Hendl.[6] He also spoke with admiration for Stidfole and Decker, mentioning their outstanding achievements as Eastman students.

Sproull's report outlined major areas he felt required attention at Eastman, with the largest problem that of faculty development. This included a lack of progress in finding replacements in the voice department for Julius Huehn and Josephine Antoine, questions in the piano area concerning decisions following the retirement of Cecile Genhart and the death of José Echaniz, the lack of progress in seeking a conductor to replace Jonathan Sternberg, lingering bitterness over the failure to replace Emory Remington with one of his own students, ongoing difficulties in the choral program with no apparent effort to find an interim conductor, and several important tenure questions on which the administration had failed to obtain any initiative from the Eastman director.

The reference to Eastman's choral program pertained to Hendl's decision to cancel the chorus and chorale for the spring semester, a decision he reached in reaction to widespread student dissatisfaction with the direction of choral activities at the school. This decision was made in the absence of prior consultation with appropriate members of the faculty, for which Hendl received harsh criticism not only from the Student Association but also from the faculty. By mid-semester he had backtracked, perhaps under pressure from the central administration, and formed a chorus for the remainder of the school year that would be under the capable direction of John Balme, an exchange student from the Royal College of Music in London.

The lack of progress on tenure matters was an even more serious situation and one with a longer history. Hendl's frequent lack of attention to such areas undoubtedly reflected his lack of prior

---

[6]   R. L. Sproull, memo to W. Allen Wallis, February 25, 1972. RRL.

experience with issues of faculty development such as promotion and tenure. Sproull's memo to Wallis was also critical of budgetary decisions and control, mentioning that library and student services were habitually overspent. He expressed concern over the lack of analysis and planning for the preparatory department and questioned the expenses incurred in establishing a jazz program that had hitherto not added any additional students to the school's enrollment. Some of these issues had been the subject of discussion in the past. He concluded his reported by stating that he was convinced the Eastman School of Music was "drifting." Although he did not accuse the Hendl administration of misfeasance, he did see much evidence of what he called "nonfeasance," by which he meant inaction on crucial issues.

The student leadership was unaware of Sproull's report. Frustrated at what it incorrectly interpreted to be inaction at the highest administrative levels, the executive committee of the Student Association called a general student meeting—to which faculty members were invited—on the evening of Monday, March 13. The meeting would be held in the dining hall of the Men's Residence at 6:00 P.M., and its purpose would be to start "a meaningful dialogue toward the solution of the numerous problems facing the Eastman School at this time."[7]

The result of this meeting was the adoption of a "Resolution Concerning the Directorship," which was approved by a vote of 358 to 9. In addition, the students prepared a petition addressed to Chancellor Wallis urging him to consider the resolution's provisions. The petition was signed by 374 students. The resolution was rather lengthy, but it deserves to be quoted in its entirety:

Whereas, The Director of the Eastman School of Music is charged with fulfilling certain responsibilities:

Whereas, In the past two years, faculty vacancies have not been promptly and carefully filled;

Whereas, In recent years, the general physical conditions under which faculty and students have worked have deteriorated to the extent that our educational experience has been severely hindered even though the Director was made aware of such conditions by the Student Association;

[7] Executive committee of the Student Association, memo, March 13, 1972. Personal papers of Richard Decker.

Whereas, An adequate overall orchestral experience has not been provided for the students;

Whereas, Most students have been denied any choral experience for a significant part of this 1971–72 school year;

Whereas, No response has been made to numerous student and faculty inquiries into possible improvements in the advisor system of the Eastman School of Music including a detailed recommendation submitted by the Student Association Council at the request of the Director;

Whereas, The treatment of many of the internationally known guests of the Eastman School of Music by the Director has been such as to reflect poorly on this school's image in the international music community;

Whereas, No philosophy of choral experience has been established thereby prohibiting proper appointment of a choral director;

Whereas, The Director has severely damaged relations between the Eastman School of Music and the Local Musicians' Union #66;

Whereas, The Director has ignored the advice of Division Heads concerning ensemble placement to the extent that it has contributed to the steady deterioration of orchestral morale especially in the Philharmonia from the beginning of this year;

Whereas, The deportment of the Director has been such as to steadily lose the respect of the school; and,

Whereas, The failure of the Director to fulfill numerous other obligations to the Eastman School of Music has caused growing discontent among both faculty and students; therefore,

Resolved, That the Director should be relieved of his present position.

Resolved, That the next Director of the Eastman School of Music be chosen by the Eastman School faculty with student consultation subject to the approval of the University of Rochester Administration.

Resolved, That no Director should be appointed without the approval of the Eastman School of Music.

Resolved, That an Interim Board of Eastman School of Music faculty members be appointed by the Eastman School of Music faculty subject to the approval of the University of Rochester Administration to assume the powers and responsibilities of the Director's Office until such time that a new Director can be appointed.

Resolved, That this Interim Board will form the core of a search committee to find a new Director which will submit its findings to the general faculty and to the University of Rochester Administration.

Resolved, That this Interim Board be ready to assume responsibilities of the Directorship upon its vacancy.[8]

This resolution was a rather thorough condemnation of Hendl's administration, but it is perhaps best understood in light of the fact that this was the 1970s, a time of widespread student activism on campuses throughout the United States. Therefore, what was transpiring at Eastman might be explained as a sign of the times. Yet the reasons behind the student uprising at Eastman and the methods the students chose in pursuing their goals represent a unique story. For example, over forty members of the Eastman faculty were present at the meeting when the resolution was presented and approved. Students were not acting in a vacuum or without the quiet encouragement and support of prominent members of the faculty. And while a number of students later had reservations about the action taken on March 13, the attendance at the meeting represented 80 percent or more of the entire undergraduate student body, and the resolution received only nine dissenting votes.

The student meeting took place on a Monday, as mentioned, and the resolution was forwarded to Chancellor Wallis the following morning with a request for a reply by Thursday, only forty-eight hours later. The university administration was all too familiar with student demands, having dealt with a group of student activists who had occupied part of a building on the River Campus three years earlier. The growing crisis at the Eastman School must have been very troubling to them, especially since there appeared to be such widespread support for the student resolution. The administration, however, tried to keep one step ahead of the students, and Wallis sent this memo to the Eastman faculty the same day he received the student resolution:

[8]   Quoted from a copy supplied by William Decker. The resolution was also printed in its entirety in the 1971–72 Eastman School yearbook, *Eastman School of Music 50th Anniversary Year,* but with an error in the eleventh paragraph through the use of the word "department" instead of "deportment."

Over a year ago, Walter Hendl and I concluded that the School required an additional appointment at the top administrative level. An appropriate title for the position we have in mind is Dean of Faculty, since the incumbent will have broad responsibility for the development of faculty and curriculum. Mr. Hendl and I expect that the relation between him and the Dean will follow closely the model of Chancellor and President which has proved very helpful to me in the University Administration.

The heavy burden of the Fiftieth Anniversary Festival has slowed recruitment efforts, and Mr. Hendl and I agree that a concentrated search must begin promptly to bring an outstanding musical leader to the School as Dean. To help in the recruitment I have appointed the following faculty committee: Samuel Adler, Edward G. Evans, Jr., Robert Gauldin, Eugene List, Verne Reynolds, Zvi Zeitlin.

Mr. Sproull, Mr. France, and I will devote our best energies to the search for a Dean. Both the Committee and we will be happy to have suggestions of possible candidates for this important appointment from other members of the faculty.[9]

Two days later the Eastman Faculty Association held a meeting attended by seventy-four faculty members. With only one abstention, they voted to commend the students for their "dignified, restrained and responsible conduct during the trying circumstances of the current crisis of administration."[10] They expressed regret over the procedure used to form the new search committee but expressed confidence in the committee membership. Nonetheless, they called upon their colleagues to ensure that no one would be appointed dean of faculty without a majority vote of the committee and a full report to the faculty concerning the search. The following Monday the student leadership adopted a similar resolution, although they went a step further than the faculty in insisting that no one be appointed dean of faculty without the *unanimous* vote of the search committee.

What had been an internal matter within the school and university became very public with an article on April 12, 1972, by *Democrat and Chronicle* columnist Theodore Price. Entitled "Students Ask Hendl's Ouster," Price's article finally made the Rochester public aware of the struggles taking place at the Eastman School of Music.

[9]   W. Allen Wallis, memo to the faculty of the Eastman School of Music, March 14, 1972. SML.
[10]   Resolutions passed by the faculty at the Faculty Association meeting held Thursday, March 16, 1972. SML.

It is remarkable that the story had been so well confined since the Student Association meeting thirty days earlier that had produced the resolution calling for the director's removal. The resolution, of course, had made no reference to Hendl's personal struggles, and the April 12 article—as well as subsequent public comments in the coming weeks—similarly avoided the topic. Everyone close to the situation, however, privately acknowledged that those struggles were the root cause of the current difficulties and the call for Hendl's resignation.

On the same day Price's article appeared, the University of Rochester Student Senate at the River Campus passed a motion in support of the Eastman School students. Two days later the university's student newspaper, *Campus Times,* published an editorial with the headline "Why Walter Hendl," which reviewed much of the history behind the Hendl administration from his appointment in 1964 up to the present crisis. The editorial applauded the proposal to seek a dean of faculty at Eastman but asked the pointed question of why they should not "closely examine the possibility of appointing a new Director of Music."[11] That same day the Student Association met with the Eastman School Alumni Council to discuss the ongoing crisis, although neither party issued any public statement. The *Campus Times* reentered the fray on April 17, 1972, with an editorial entitled "Silence Condemned," stating that it was time for the university to be held accountable and urging all students and faculty to pressure the central administration to discuss and define its role in the matter.

All these developments put pressure on the student leadership to succeed in the goal of securing Hendl's resignation as director of the school while also pressuring the Eastman faculty to finally make its opinions known and to show a little leadership of its own. It also created enormous pressure on W. Allen Wallis's administration, which found itself subjected to criticism from all sides. But most of all, it put pressure on the one person probably least able to deal with a crisis—Walter Hendl. Perhaps too few of the involved parties paused to think of the personal toll this controversy was taking on the school's director. Many years later Richard Decker, who had been vice president of the Student Association during the tumultuous 1971–72 school year, reflected on this very point:

---

[11] Larry Hirsch, "Why Walter Hendl," *Campus Times* [Rochester, NY], April 14, 1972: 4.

> I have mixed feelings about my role as a student political leader at
> the time of Hendl's departure. Part of my activities could certainly
> be viewed as legitimate in terms of spearheading an issue that was
> of great importance to the Eastman community and certainly had
> widespread support from both faculty and students at the time. On
> the flip side, in my zeal to highlight the leadership crisis at Eastman
> at the time, at times I showed an extreme youthful insensitivity to
> Mr. Hendl and his personal struggles. I attribute the crisis in part to
> the University of Rochester's "ostrich-head-in-the-sand" mentality
> about ignoring what were probably years of criticisms by Eastman
> faculty and others.[12]

The crisis in the spring of 1972 left little time for such sentiments.
Nonetheless, the personal price Hendl paid for the drama in which
he was enmeshed was enormous. When Isaac Stern appeared for a
May 3 recital in the Eastman Theatre, he remarked to the Student
Association president that he hardly recognized his old friend.[13] He
asked W. Allen Wallis about the situation and offered his help, and
he reinforced the offer with a personal note to the university chancellor two days later. Stern, of course, had been a strong supporter
of Hendl's candidacy for the Eastman position in 1964.

An information meeting for students had been held in Cutler
Union on April 21, 1972, a few weeks prior to Stern's recital. It was
attended by approximately one hundred students to hear a report
from Robert Gauldin, a member of the five-person search committee. Gauldin appeared unofficially rather than as a designated representative of the committee. He reported that the committee had
assembled a list of more than sixty possible candidates for the dean
of faculty position and had selected ten highly qualified people for
serious consideration. The committee intended to speak with each
of the ten, who would also be interviewed by Wallis, Sproull, and
France at the River Campus. When a student asked pointedly if the
candidates were being considered for the No. 1 or No. 2 position at
Eastman, Gauldin was enthusiastically applauded when he replied
that the committee's strength lay in the fact that it was considering
strong candidates who would not be willing to come to Eastman
as the No. 2 person.[14] Gauldin's unusually candid response to the
student's question was the first public acknowledgment that the
search committee was indeed looking for Hendl's replacement, not

12   Richard Decker, e-mail to the author, May 19, 2005.
13   Arthur Stidfole, telephone interview by the author, May 17, 2005.
14   Theodore Price, "Two Reports on Eastman," *Democrat and Chronicle* [Rochester,
NY], April 22, 1972. SML (news clipping).

for a No. 2 person. The committee had apparently understood this from the very start of its work, but the university was not prepared to announce it in public for the obvious reason that Walter Hendl still remained director of the school. Gauldin's remark at the April 21 meeting was therefore somewhat of an indiscretion on his part, for which he received a rather strong rebuke from the university's central administration.[15]

The next escalation of the crisis occurred on April 28, when members of the faculty assembled at a Faculty Association meeting and unanimously declared themselves in agreement with a new petition signed by almost four hundred Eastman students. The petition read:

> We, the undersigned, restate the conviction expressed in the RESOLUTION CONCERNING THE DIRECTORSHIP dated March 13, 1972, that Walter Hendl is not now and will not be nearly adequate in any administrative capacity involving the Eastman School of Music. We charge the University of Rochester Administration with full responsibility for the continuing confusion regarding the present musical and administrative crisis. The administrative situation has existed long enough over the continuing protests of significant portions of the Eastman School of Music constituency. We therefore deserve the right to expect a solution agreeable to the faculty and students of the Eastman School of Music to be made by September, 1972.

What had started with a meeting between two Eastman undergraduate students and high-level university officials about two months earlier had reached a point where the solution to the crisis was a foregone conclusion. Succumbing to the constant pressures of the past several months, Hendl was admitted to a hospital in Jamestown, New York. On May 23, 1972, Chancellor Wallis announced to the faculty that Walter Hendl had resigned as director of the Eastman School of Music for reasons of health.

While this might have signaled the end of the drama, several scenes were yet to be played. Hendl had not only been director at Eastman, a position from which he had now resigned, but he was also a tenured member of the faculty, a position from which he was now technically on leave of absence. Although his health was too precarious to permit him to conduct the forthcoming season at the Chautauqua Institute, Hendl wrote to Wallis later in the summer to

---

[15]   Robert Gauldin, interview by the author, Rochester, NY, October 25, 2006.

assure him that he would be back at Eastman to conduct the orchestra after his leave of absence.[16] News of this proclamation must have spread because the Eastman Alumni Council reacted strongly to the prospect by sending this communication to the university chancellor:

> While the members of the Council harbor no ill will for Walter Hendl, we are unanimously opposed to his return to the Eastman faculty. We respect and share the University's desire to be supportive to the man in light of his illness; however, we cannot countenance that support in the form of continued faculty involvement.[17]

Alumni Council intervention was probably unnecessary, and Hendl's eventual return to the Eastman School of Music was as a guest ten years later, not as a member of the faculty.

The news of Walter Hendl's resignation was generally greeted with relief by a large number of faculty members and students, most feeling that a change in leadership was absolutely necessary for the future of the school. The hiring in 1964 of a professional musician with little or no experience in academia was viewed as having been a profound mistake. This mistake was immeasurably greater in view of Hendl's apparent inability to gain control over his personal struggles with alcohol abuse. Much of this was surely connected with the man's self-doubts about his once promising conducting career, which seemed to have come to a dead end. Walter Hendl was a conductor, not an administrator, and his significant talent as a conductor should have led him to the kind of professional success enjoyed by people such as Leonard Bernstein and Erich Leinsdorf. Instead, he was trapped in academia, ultimately surrounded by a hostile student body and an unsympathetic faculty who could only see the steady accumulation of problems and difficulties judged to be a result of his lack of leadership ability.

As emotions subsided, however, many began to see that Hendl's eight years as director at Eastman had not been totally unproductive. Although he was the subject of criticism concerning faculty development, there was also much to admire in terms of faculty appointments during his administration. The hiring of Samuel Adler in 1967, followed by Warren Benson in 1968, did much to establish a department that would arguably become the finest compostion

---

[16]   Walter Hendl, memo to W. Allen Wallis, August 6, 1972. RRL.
[17]   Kenneth Wendrich (chair, Eastman School of Music Alumni Council), letter to W. Allen Wallis, October 25, 1972. SML.

faculty in the country. Performance areas of the faculty were also greatly strengthened by the hiring of Eugene List and Carroll Glenn in 1964, Frank Glazer in 1965, and Zvi Zeitlin in 1967. They were all musicians with excellent performing credentials, and they did a great deal to address the criticism that the school under Howard Hanson was not interested in anyone who had a performing career. Other notable appointments to the performance faculty included Alan Harris, Barry Snyder, Maria Luisa Faini, John Maloy, and Russell Saunders—all of whom contributed to enhancing Eastman's reputation as a school for training performing musicians.

It was also during the Hendl administration that the issue of providing adequate faculty salaries was finally addressed. Moreover, members of faculty found themselves increasingly involved in decisions affecting students and curriculum through the formation of a number of new faculty committees in 1966. Not the least of these was the committee on academic policy,[18] which governed the undergraduate curricula. Hanson had limited faculty involvement in such matters, a decision for which he surely deserves criticism, but the era of a faculty seen solely as classroom and studio teachers had come to an end. Ideas and criticism were expressed, sometimes officially and other times unofficially through the Faculty Association, and because of this the school was a healthier institution. Faculty opinion, creativity, and leadership were no longer inhibited by an administration that afforded them little value or credibility.

Other developments of importance during the Hendl years included the establishment of the department of conducting and ensembles in 1965, the equipping of an electronic music studio in 1967, and the creation of a new department of jazz and contemporary media in 1970. The school also introduced several new, very important performing organizations such as Musica Nova, the Jazz Ensemble, the Jazz Lab Band, and the Eastman Chorale—all of which contributed greatly to the enrichment of the educational experience provided to Eastman's undergraduate and graduate students. These initiatives also signaled changes in the school's self-image concerning its mission and the challenges its graduates would face in the future. They were a sign that the insularity for which the Eastman School of Music had often been criticized was perhaps coming to an end. The many distinguished visitors to the school, including those such as Igor Stravinsky who came prior to the festivities of the fiftieth anniversary year, also clearly signaled that Eastman was changing.

---

[18]   Now called the undergraduate curriculum committee.

Cynics might complain that Walter Hendl deserves little personal credit for any of the positive developments during his years as director of the Eastman School of Music, but such an observation would be terribly unfair. Those who welcomed his appointment in 1964 did so because they felt the institution would profit from having a prominent professional musician—a respected conductor—at its helm. Many of the positive decisions that followed his arrival at Eastman were seen by his supporters as evidence of the kind of change he could bring to the school. He was seen as belonging to the real professional world that existed outside the confines of an institution led for so many years by Howard Hanson, and he brought to the director's position a professional outlook that had significant influence on the school and its subsequent development. While his administrative failings and personal struggles cannot be denied, the accomplishments of his eight years as director of the Eastman School of Music should not be ignored.

Epilogue

A young musicologist on the faculty at M.I.T. was visiting his parents in Stockbridge one day when he happened to see a recent issue of the Rochester daily newspaper, the *Democrat and Chronicle*. His family had many ties to Rochester. Both his parents were graduates of the Eastman School of Music, and his paternal grandfather had been the first trumpet teacher at the school. The newspaper had been brought to Stockbridge by his aunt, who lived in the Rochester area where she was a kindergarten teacher.

The young man glanced at the newspaper and noticed an article discussing Walter Hendl's resignation and the fact that the University of Rochester was searching for a new director for the Eastman School of Music. He read the article with considerable interest, set down the newspaper, and said to himself, "I could do that job." Until that moment he had never entertained any thought of becoming an administrator.[1]

The story of Robert Freeman's twenty-four years as the Eastman School's fourth director remains to be related.

[1] Robert Freeman, interview by the author, March 5, 2005.

Appendix 1

1932–72

Members of the Eastman School of Music Faculty

This is a list of individuals who taught at the Eastman School of Music during the period September 1932 through June 1972. The dates of their faculty service are indicated, although this information is at times difficult to ascertain with absolute certainty. Especially in the earliest days of the school, individuals may have started providing instruction prior to being listed in any of the school's official publications. Conversely, individuals might have been included in those publications without actually teaching any students that particular year. Termination dates are also difficult to determine accurately, since a number of faculty members continued to teach part-time after their official retirement. Since academic rank was not instituted until the 1962–63 school year, it is difficult to determine full-time versus part-time status or those who might have taught only in the school's preparatory department. A further complication arises from the fact that graduate students, who were later considered teaching assistants rather than faculty members, were sometimes included in faculty listings without indication of their student status. Therefore, for the sake of at least attempting to be complete, the list includes all individuals identified in various school publications as providing instruction during the regular academic year. Special summer session faculty members are not included.

Adler, Samuel	Composition	1966–94
Albright, Philip	Double Bass	1965–66
Alexander, Florence (see Schoenegge, Florence Alexander)		
Ames, William Thayer	Theory/Composition	1928–38
Andal, Dennis	Piano	1949–86
Antoine, Josephine	Voice	1957–59, 1966–71

Arey, Rufus	Clarinet	1927–54
Armstrong, William Edwin	Piano	1949–58
Austin-Ball, Thomas	Voice	1923–43
Auvil, Adrianne	Theory	1966–72
Auzin, Norma	Violin	1966–74
Aversano, Mary	Humanities (Italian)	1966–86
Babcock, William	Humanities (German)	1966–67
Baer, Michael	Psychology	1968–69
Baker, Charles	Violoncello	1963–66
Baker, Martha Jordan	Piano	1963–66
Balaban, Emanuel	Opera	1925–44
Barlow, Wayne	Composition	1937–78
Barnett, Alan	Humanities (English)	1957–62
Basile, Armand	Piano	1952–65
Baustian, Robert	Piano	1947–49
Beach, Edwin Vance	Violoncello	1941–43
Beck, John	Percussion	1959–2008
Beckwith, Ellen Hatch	Music Education	1931–61
Bellingham, Bruce	Music Literature	1969–74
Belov, Samuel	Viola/Violin	1921–49
Benson, Warren	Composition	1967–93
Benston, Alice	Humanities	1966–75
Berman, Barbara	Humanities (Psychology)	1969–86
Berry, Charles Raymond	Organ	1946–47
Betts, Edwin	Trumpet	1944–62
Bichsel, M. Alfred	Church Music	1960–80
Bickal, Janet Regottaz	Humanities (English)	1955–57
Bickal, Robert	Humanities (English)	1954–57
Billings, Lillian	Piano	1949–71
Binford, Haven Anchea	Piano	1943–46
Bloom, Robert	Oboe	1936–37
Bockstruck, Else	Physical Education	1936–45
Bogardus, Jared	Piano	1959–76
Boone, Abram	Violin/Viola	1947–73
Bour, Jean-Antoine	Humanities (French)	1960–62
Bradley, Frederick	French Horn	1944–57
Briddell, M. Phyllis (see Hayden, M. Phyllis Briddell)		
Broel, Gladys Rossdeutscher	Piano	1939–76
Bruno, Anthony	Clarinet	1944–80
Bundra, Francis	Viola (Eastman Quartet)	1960–61
Burnes, Trudy	Piano	1962–63
Bussell, Margaret Rose	Piano	1946–49
Cahn, Ruth	Percussion	1968–

Cahn, William	Percussion	1968–70
Call, Lucy Lee	Voice	1921–55
Canning, Thomas	Theory	1947–63
Cantor, Arnold	Clarinet	1960–64
Castle, Joyce	Voice	1965–66
Celentano, John	Chamber Music/Violin	1946–80
Cerny, William	Piano/History	1959–72
Chadwick, Elizabeth Watson	Piano	1941–51
Chadwick-Cullen, Charlene	Voice	1962–65
Cheswell, William Tegg	Humanities (French)	1964–81
Clark, Dale	Trombone	1953–58
Clark, David	Physical Education	1958–71
Clark, Edwin de Forest	Organ	1945–47
Clark, Marvin Dale	Trombone	1948–62
Clark, Phyllis	Piano	1959–90
Clute, Sherman	Music Education	1924–49
Coit, Lottie Ellsworth	Introduction to Music	1935–56
Coleman, Walter Barton	Flute	1956–59
Collins, Michael	Musicology	1965–68
Cooper, Mabel	Piano	1921–41
Cooper, Philip	Humanities (English)	1957–63
Corwin, George	Ensembles/Choral	1963–67
Cosman, Blair	Piano	1945–82
Craighead, David	Organ	1955–92
Crews, E. Katherine	Music Education	1965–72
Croxford, Lyndon	Piano	1924–47
Crozier, Catherine (see Gleason, Catherine Crozier)		
Cummins, Anne	Humanities (French)	1924–66
Dake, Emeline	Music Education	1945–57
Davis, Emily (see Vanderpool, Emily Davis)		
Davis, Ralph	Physical Education	1931–58
Decaux, Abel	Organ	1923–36
Dechario, Rachel	Violin	1977–92
DeLorenzo, Leonardo	Flute	1924–35
Denker, Fred	Piano	1944–45
Dexter, John	Choral Ensembles	1969–74
Diamond, Jerome	Piano	1926–66
Diercks, Thelma Chock	Piano	1957–59
Dolan, Mary	Music Education	1961–67
Droege, John	Fine Arts	1969–70
Dumm, Thomas	Viola	1969–70

Duncan, Hazel Sampson	Piano	1929–41
Duncan, James Lloyd	Piano	1955–57
Dunford, Benjamin	Theory	1953–54
Dunkel, Wilbur Dwight	Humanities (English)	1933–34
Dunlap, Jack	Education	1937–39
Dunning, Anthony	Humanities (French)	1952–59
Eccleston, Marion (see Sauer, Marion Eccleston)		
Echániz, José	Piano	1944–69
Echániz, Judith Borling	Piano	1962–63
Ellis, Jean Marion	Piano	1943–44
End, Jack	Clarinet/Theory/Ensemble	1940–75
Engleman, John	Percussion	1968–69
Erhart, Marie	Piano	1923–71
Evans, Edward	Musicology	1968–73
Evenson, Pattee Edward	Trumpet	1935–49
Fabricant, Sylvia	Physical Education	1944–60
Fagan, Arthur	Conducting/Ensembles	??
Faini, Maria Luisa	Piano	1966–82
Fairbanks, Gar	Music Education	1957–59
Fargo, Milford	Music Education/Chorus	1957–86
Farrell, Peter Snow	Violoncello	1949–54
Faulkner, Monica	Humanities (Sociology)	1969–71
Fennell, Frederick	Conducting/Ensembles	1940–62
Fermin, Adelin	Voice	1921–35
Fernandez, Carmen	Voice	1965–66
Ferrer, Gloria Consuelo	Piano	1950–54
Fetler, David	Theory/Ensembles	1956–64
Field, Lorene Carpenter	Violin	1942–44
Finckel, George	Violoncello	1928–37
Finley, Wilbur Reed	Clarinet	1941–44
Fish, Gloria	Piano	1949–54
Flores, Bernal	Theory	1966–70
Foreman, Arthur	Oboe	1926–36
Fortuna, Joseph	Violin	1936–42
Fox, Charles Warren	Musicology	1932–70
Frick, Charlotte	Piano	1941–43
Friedman, Peter	Humanities (Sociology)	1971–73
Frugoni, Orazio	Piano	1952–67
Fuerstner, Carl	Opera/Piano	1945–50
Garlick, Donald	Violoncello	1944–49
Garlick, Glennes Jones	Violin/Viola	1944–49
Garner, Reuben	Humanities (History)	1970–72
Gates, W. Everett	Education	1958–80
Gauldin, Robert	Theory	1963–96

Gemmalo, Zena Baranowski	Clarinet	1944–49
Genhart, Cecile Staub	Piano	1926–82
Genhart, Herman	Opera/Chorus/Conducting	1925–65
George, Patricia	Flute	1964–66
Geppert, David	Theory	1955–70
Gerig, Reginald	Piano	1950–53
Gibson, Gordon	Music Literature (Visiting)	1966–69
Gilbert, Margaret	Piano	1952–68
Gillette, Dorothy (see Scott, Dorothy Gillette)		
Giuffrida, Robert	Humanities (Italian)	1961–62
Glazer, Frank	Piano	1965–80
Gleason, Catharine Crozier	Organ	1938–55
Gleason, Harold	Organ/Music Literature	1921–55
Gleaves, Charles	Trumpet	1950–58
Glenn, Carroll	Violin	1964–75
Goldthorpe, J. Harold	Music Education	1932–38
Gordon, Jacques	Violin	1942–48
Graue, Jerald	Musicology	1971–82
Gray, Ralph	Humanities (Science)	1962–72
Gray, Wallace	Piano	1941–76
Green, Douglass	Theory	1970–76
Green, Mary Kathryn	Piano	1952–56
Greene, Carlotta Ward	Music Education	1930–45
Grocock, Robert	Trumpet	1948–49
Gulick, Sidney Lewis	Humanities (English)	1932–33
Gunther, Virginia	Physical Education	1943–44
Haave, Ethel-Mae	Humanities (English)	1945–52
Hagenah, Elizabeth Artman	Piano	1953–54
Halasz, Laszlo	Conducting/Ensembles (Visiting)	1965–67
Hall, Clarence	Opera/Scenic Design	1929–58
Halliley, Richard	Voice	1924–35
Halstead, Zilah	Piano	1932–56
Hambrecht, George	Flute	1949–50
Hanson, Howard	Composition	1924–64
Hanson, John	Theory	1970–76
Hargrave, Mary Ann Wix	Piano	1957–60
Harris, Alan	Violoncello	1965–76, 1995–
Harris, Raymond	Music Education	1952–53
Harrison, Guy Fraser	Conducting/Ensembles	1944–45

Harrison, Lucile Bigelow	Harp	1921–38
Hasty, Stanley	Clarinet	1955–85
Hayden, Donald	Music Education	1960–64
Hayden, M. Phyllis Briddell	Piano	1948–51
Haywood, Frederick	Voice/Choral	1924–54
Hendl, Walter	Conducting/Ensembles	1964–72
Herr, Dori Paoletti	Humanities (Italian)	1957–61
Heschke, Richard	Church Music	1967–69
Hill, Barbara Ferrell	Piano	1950–53
Hinga, Howard	Music Education	1938–65
Hoirup, Marlene Jensen	Piano	1968–70
Holloway, Phyllis Jane	Piano	1944–46
Holly, Grant	Humanities	1969–71
Holmes, Norma	Piano	1946–50
Honda, Yuko	Music Education	1968–70
Hoskam, Jessie (see Kneisel, Jessie Hoskam)		
Houseknecht, Bruce	Music Education	1969–74
Hoyle, James	Humanities (English)	1966–68
Hudgins, Mary Nan	Piano	1956–59
Huehn, Julius	Voice	1952–71
Hunsberger, Donald	Ensembles/Conducting	1962–2002
Hunsberger, Marjorie (Polly)	Violoncello	1962–2002
Hurst, Dorothy	Piano	1957–58
Husband, Anna Stucki	Piano	1941–44
Ingram, Madeline	Piano	1956–66
Ireland, Dwight	Music Education	1939–42
Jedele, Mary	Piano	1957–59
Jefferson, Alice	Piano	1943–50
Jempelis, Anastasia	Violin	1949–94
Johnson, Jane Meriwether	Piano	1958–60
Johnson, Louise	Flute	1943–45
Johnson, Lucile Bigelow (see Harrison, Lucile Bigelow)		
Jones, Richard	Trumpet	1967–78
Jordan, Elsa	Physical Education	1944–52
Jordan, Irene	Voice	1969–70
Kaaskoek, Ruth	Piano	1949–52
Karier, Clarence	Physical Education	1960–62
Kaskas, Anna	Voice	1959–74
Keenan, Gertrude	Piano	1927–36
Kéfer, Paul	Violoncello	1924–41
Kellinger, Cesi	Humanities (Italian)	1956–??

Kilpack, Gilbert	Humanities (English)	1962–76
Kilpack, Joanne Mott	Humanities (French)	1962–67
Kimball, Marian	Physical Education	1929–36
Kirk, Edgar	Bassoon	1954–57
Klein, Charlotte	Piano	1963–65
Klingensmith, Maree	Humanities (Science)	1968–75
Klinzing, Ernestine	Piano	1921–57
Knaub, Donald	Trombone/Tuba	1951–77
Knauss, Effie	Violin	1921–54
Kneisel, Jessie Hoskam	Humanities (German)	1932–76
Knitzer, Joseph	Violin	1955–64
Kompanek, Rudolph	Theory	1970–71
Konraty, Nicholas	Voice	1929–57
Kostka, Stefan	Theory	1969–74
Krachmalnick, Morris	String Ensemble	1945–47
Kraft, Arthur	Voice	1936–60
Krick, Charlotte (see Shear, Charlotte Krick)		
Kujala, Walfrid	Flute	1952–??
Laird, Sharon	Violin	1966–70
LaMontaine, John	Composition (Visiting)	1961–62
Landow, Max	Piano	1922–49
Lanigan, Elizabeth	Music Education	1938–60
Larson, William	Music Education/Psychology	1929–54
LeBlanc, Normand	Clarinet	1954–61
Lehman, Paul	Music Education	1970–75
Lenti, Vincent	Piano	1963–
Leonard, Ronald	Violoncello	1957–75
Lessen, Elizabeth Sher	Piano	1966
Leventon, Gladys Metcalf	Piano	1928–74
Lewis, Robert Hall	Composition	1953–55
Liddell, Donald	Piano	1923–56
Lischner, Rose	Opera/Accompanist	1932–33
List, Eugene	Piano	1964–75
Livingstone, Ernest	Musicology	1949–53, 1962–87
Lockhart, Frederick	Horn Ensembles	1950–53
Luvas, Helen	Piano	1947–48
MacDonald, Donald	Flute	1940–??
MacKenzie, Hugh	History	1932–36
MacKown, Allison	Violoncello	1937–57
MacKown, Marjorie Truelove	Piano	1921–57
MacLeod, Elinor	Piano	1947–50
MacNabb, George	Piano	1922–60
MacRury, Norma	French	1938–39

Mahrt, William	Musicology	1971–73
Maki, Daniel	Flute	1966–??
Malone, Eileen	Harp	1931–89
Maloy, John	Voice	1966–2006
Mangione, Chuck	Jazz	1968–72
Manning, Clinton	Tuba, Double Bass	1942–49
Mariano, Joseph	Flute	1935–74
Marjarum, Edward	Humanities (English)	1933–45
Mars, Joan	Physical Education	1960–71
Martin, Ellen (see Rosevear, Ellen Martin)		
Maurey, Elaine	Piano	1965–66
Mauser, Susanna	Piano	1960–62
McArthur, Edwin	Opera	1968–73
McCann, Evelyn (see Prior, Evelyn McCann)		
McConnell, Albert	Trumpet	1941–45
McCrory, Martha	Violoncello	1945–46
McGowan, William	Humanities (Philosophy)	1960–67
McHose, Allen Irvine	Theory	1929–67
Mear, Sidney	Trumpet	1949–80
Meigs, Carol	Elementary Theory	1965–89
Mellon, Edward Knox	Trumpet	1929–41
Mennini, Louis	Theory/Composition	1949–65
Messineo, Joseph	Humanities	1969–70
Metcalf, Gladys (see Leventon, Gladys Metcalf)		
Meyer, Harold	Violoncello	1957–??
Miller, Charles	Music Education	1924–38
Miquelle, Georges	Violoncello	1954–64
Mitchell, Lyndol	Theory	1952–63
Montean, John	Humanities (Education)	1959–61
Montgomery, Merle	Piano/Music Education	1943–45
Moore, Clarence	Humanities (Italian)	1935–36
Morese, Louise Crafts	Physical Education	1932–35
Morlock, W. LeRoy	Voice	1929–67
Morris, Frank	Acoustics	1946–48
Morrow, Ann	Music Education	1937–53
Mueller, Harold	Flute	1955–57
Murray, Robert	Opera	1965–75
Nathanson, Irving	Double Bass	1946–47
Nelson, John	Humanities	1953–56

Newbury, Constance	Physical Education	1936–43
Northrup, Ruth (see Tibbs, Ruth Northrup)		
Oliver, Karl	Piano	1948–49
Olson, Carolyn Schoenegge	Piano	1954–63
Osborn, George	Trombone	1962–??
Osborn, Robert	Music Education	1969–70
Osseck, William	Clarinet/Saxophone	1946–87
Page, Willis	Conducting/Ensembles	1967–70
Parkes, Jonathan	Oboe	1967–99
Patrylak, Daniel	Trumpet	1958–75
Paul, Thomas	Voice	1971–97
Payne, Dorothy	Theory	1968–78
Penn, William	Theory	1971–78
Peterson, Norman	Organ	1947–70
Pezzi, Vincent	Bassoon	1932–54
Philips, Paul	Bassoon	1934–54
Phillips, Burrill	Composition	1933–49, 1965–66
Phillips, Helen	Piano	1944–46
Pieffer, Phyllis	Piano	1967–68
Pittman, Richard	Conducting/Ensembles	1965–69
Prior, Evelyn McCann	Piano	1935–74
Proctor, George	Music Literature	1965–67
Propst, Patricia	Piano	1956–57
Provenzano, Aldo	Composition/Theory	1964–70
Quillen, Kathleen	Humanities (English)	1969–76
Rauch, Henry	Piano	1952–66
Rehfuss, Heinz	Voice	1969–73
Rejto, Gabor	Violoncello	1949–54
Remington, Emory	Trombone	1922–71
Remington, Frederick	Trumpet	1930–35
Reynolds, Verne	French Horn	1959–95
Ribaupierre, Andre de	Violin	1948–55
Riker, Charles	Humanities (Fine Arts)	1930–68
Rogers, Bernard	Composition	1929–67
Roller, A. Clyde	Conducting/Ensembles	1962–65
Rosen, Lynn	Humanities (Literature)	1968–73
Rosevear, Ellen Martin	Piano	1957–65
Rossdeutscher, Gladys (see Broel, Gladys Rossdeutscher)		
Royce, Edward	Theory	1923–47

Rubadeau, Duane	Humanities (Psychology)	1967–68
Rubin, David	Humanities (English)	1952–54
Russell, Armand	Composition	1959–61
Santuccio, Mary Jo Cook	Piano	1966–69
Sauer, Marion Eccleston	Violin	1926–36
Saunders, Russell	Organ	1967–92
Schatz, Harry	Violin	195?–??
Schempf, William	Humanities	1942–43
Schmidt, Paul	Tuba	1925–42
Schneeberg, Nan	Humanities	1963–65
Schoenegge, Florence Alexander	Piano	1924–29, 1932–38
Schwandt, Erich	Musicology	1968–75
Schwantner, Joseph	Composition	1970–2000
Scott, Darrell	Theory	1963–77
Scott, Dorothy Gillette	Piano	1921–35
Scoutten, Eldon	Music Education	1945–46
Secon, Morris	French Horn	1952–59
See, Genvieve	Humanities (French)	195?–??
Selhorst, Eugene	Music Literature	1955–72
Sempowski, John	Humanities (Psychology)	1968–73
Shear, Charlotte Krick	Piano	1941–43
Shelton, Sonja	Piano	1967–68
Shenk, Mary	Piano	1953–??
Shetler, Donald	Music Education	1965–88
Silva, Luigi	Violoncello	1941–49
Smith, Barbara Barnard	Piano	1943–49
Smith, Brooks	Piano/Accompanying	1966–74
Smith, Harold Osborn	Organ/English/Opera	1924–54
Smith, Marlowe	Voice/Music Education	1938–67
Snyder, Barry	Piano	1970–
Soderlund, Gustave	Theory/Counterpoint	1928–52
Spouse, Alfred	Music Education	1938–55
Sprenkle, Robert	Oboe	1937–82
Springer, Virginia	Music Education	1960–67
Stalker, Mildred	Piano	1937–52, 1966–77
Stark, Mary	Music Education	1942–44
Starke, Charles	Trumpet/Music Education	1941–76
Sternberg, Jonathan	Conducting/Ensembles	1969–71
Stevens, Betsy Fincke	Piano	1956–59
Stone, Peter	Musicology	1966–73
Stonequist, Martha	Piano	1960–63
Strait, Joan Stewart	Piano	1950–55
Street, Stanley	Percussion	1950–55
Street, William	Percussion	1927–67

Struthers, Thomas	Opera (Scenic Design)	1967–75
Sutton, Robert	Theory	1955–74
Swanson, Marjorie	Piano	1964–65
Swift, Robert	Music Education	1971–76
Swingley, Richard	Oboe/English Horn	1947–60
Sze, Yi-Kwei	Voice	1971–80
Taylor, Millard	Violin	1944–79
Taylor, Sharlyn Clark	Pre-School Music	1954–70
Terepka, Donna	Piano	1947–53
Thayer, Bernadine	Trumpet	1945–47
Thomas, Deborah	Humanities (English)	1969–73
Thomas, John	Flute	1946–49, 1954–95
Thompson, Verne	Music Literature	1948–64
Thorpe, Christina	Music Education	1935–36
Thyhsen, John	Trumpet	1962–66
Tibbs, Ruth Northrup	Theory	1924–52
Tinlot, Gustave	Violin	1925–42
Tomasick, Paul	Clarinet	1963–75
Toribara, Masako	Voice	1965–99
Treash, Leonard	Opera	1947–76
Truitt, Austin	Music Education	1953–70
Turney, Mildred	Piano	1965–76
Tursi, Francis	Viola	1949–88
Van Arsdall, Susan	Physical Education	1957–60
Van Hoesen, K. David	Bassoon	1954–91
Van Hoesen, Karl D.	Violin/Music Education	1926–65
Vanderpool, Emily Davis	Piano	1951–90
VanderWerf, Hendrik	Musicology	1965–86
Vas, Sandor	Piano	1923–54
Versteeg, Willem Hendrik	Violoncello	1936–41
Virkhaus, Taavo	Conducting	1966–76
Wadsworth, Charles	Physical Education	1954–56
Walsh, Pierrette	Humanities	1961–63
Warner, Richard	Theory	1949–55
Watanabe, Ruth	Musicology	1946–84
Watson, Elizabeth (see Chadwick, Elizabeth Watson)		
Watson, Nelson	Double Bass	1924–45
Watts, Harry	Piano	1921–24, 1926–61
Weed, Marion	Voice	1921–37
Weiss, Harold	Piano	1947–74
Wentworth, Ruth (see Yost, Ruth Wentworth)		

Wetherald, Houghton	Humanities (Art)	1970–95
White, Donald	Theory	1932–70
White, Paul	Violin/Conducting/Ensembles	1928–65
Whybrew, William	Music Education	1949–??
Wieber, Alexander	Humanities (German/Russian)	1967–94
Wilbraham, Hazel	Physical Education	1931–36
Wilkins, Hannah	Music Education	1962–64
Williams, Bryon	Music Education	1946–52
Williams, Clarence	Music Education	1959–60
Williams, David Russell	Theory	1965–80
Wilson, Raymond	Piano	1921–53
Wilt, Thomas Jefferson	Flute	1945–46
Winkler, Ralph	Music Education	1965–67
Wonderlich, Elvira	Theory	1925–66
Woodbury, Ward	Opera Department	1949–54
Woolcock, C. W.	Music Education	1944–46
Woolford, Jeanne	Voice	1922–48
Wright, Rayburn	Jazz	1970–90
Yancich, Milan	French Horn	1957–92
Yegudkin, Arkaty	French Horn	1926–53
Yost, Robert	Piano	1938–41
Yost, Ruth Wentworth	Elementary Music/Piano	1936–41
Zecchino, Ralph	Music Education	1963–66, 1977–80
Zeitlin, Zvi	Violin	1967–
Zimmerman, Oscar	Double Bass	1945–76

Appendix 2

1953–72

Opera under the Stars Productions: The First Twenty Years

This is a list of the operas produced at Highland Park during the first twenty seasons of the Opera under the Stars program. All productions were done in English.

First Season (1953)
La Bohème — Giacomo Puccini (1858–1924)
La Traviata — Giuseppe Verdi (1813–1901)

Second Season (1954)
Madama Butterfly — Giacomo Puccini (1858–1924)
The Marriage of Figaro — Wolfgang Amadeus Mozart (1756–91)
Die Fledermaus — Johann Strauss II (1825–99)

Third Season (1955)
Tosca — Giacomo Puccini (1858–1924)
The Barber of Seville — Gioacchino Rossini (1792–1868)
Carmen — Georges Bizet (1838–75)

Fourth Season (1956)
Rigoletto — Giuseppe Verdi (1813–1901)
Così fan tutte — Wolfgang Amadeus Mozart (1756–91)
Faust — Charles Gounod (1818–93)

Fifth Season (1957)
Hansel and Gretel — Engelbert Humperdinck (1854–1921)
Die Fledermaus — Johann Strauss II (1825–99)
Martha — Friedrich Flotow (1812–83)

Sixth Season (1958)
Don Giovanni — Wolfgang Amadeus Mozart (1756–91)
The Consul — Gian Carlo Menotti (1911–2007)
The Bartered Bride — Bedrich Smetana (1824–84)

Seventh Season (1959)

I Pagliacci	Ruggiero Leoncavallo (1857–1919)
Gianni Schicchi	Giacomo Puccini (1858–1924)
Falstaff	Giuseppe Verdi (1813–1901)
La Bohème	Giacomo Puccini (1858–1924)

Eighth Season (1960)

The Magic Flute	Wolfgang Amadeus Mozart (1756–91)
Faust	Charles Gounod (1818–93)

Ninth Season (1961)

The Abduction from the Seraglio	Wolfgang Amadeus Mozart (1756–91)
Carmen	Georges Bizet (1838–75)

Tenth Season (1962)

Susannah	Carlyle Floyd (1926–)
Così fan tutte	Wolfgang Amadeus Mozart (1756–91)
La Traviata	Giuseppe Verdi (1813–1901)

Eleventh Season (1963)

Tosca	Giacomo Puccini (1858–1924)
The Marriage of Figaro	Wolfgang Amadeus Mozart (1756–91)
Aida	Giuseppe Verdi (1813–1901)

Twelfth Season (1964)

The Barber of Seville	Gioacchino Rossini (1792–1868)
The Taming of the Shrew	Vittorio Giannini (1903–66)
Cavaleria Rusticana	Pietro Mascagni (1864–1945)
I Pagliacci	Ruggiero Leoncavallo (1857–1919)

Thirteenth Season (1965)

Hansel and Gretel	Engelbert Humperdinck (1854–1921)
Madama Butterfly	Giacomo Puccini (1858–1924)
Street Scene	Kurt Weill (1900–1950)

Fourteenth Season (1966)

Rigoletto	Giuseppe Verdi (1813–1901)
Don Giovanni	Wolfgang Amadeus Mozart (1756–91)
The Bartered Bride	Bedrich Smetana (1824–84)

Fifteenth Season (1967)

Don Pasquale	Gaetano Donizetti (1797–1848)
The Crucible	Robert Ward (1917–)
The Merry Wives of Windsor	Carl Otto Nicolai (1810–48)

Sixteenth Season (1968)
La Traviata — Giuseppe Verdi (1813–1901)
The Marriage of Figaro — Wolfgang Amadeus Mozart (1756–91)
La Bohème — Giacomo Puccini (1858–1924)

Seventeenth Season (1969)
Madama Butterfly — Giacomo Puccini (1858–1924)
The Barber of Seville — Gioacchino Rossini (1792–1868)
Il Trovatore — Giuseppe Verdi (1813–1901)

Eighteenth Season (1970)
Tosca — Giacomo Puccini (1858–1924)
The Tales of Hoffmann — Jacques Offenbach (1819–80)

Nineteenth Season (1971)
Die Fledermaus — Johann Strauss II (1825–99)
Romeo and Juliet — Charles Gounod (1818–93)

Twentieth Season (1972)
The Magic Flute — Wolfgang Amadeus Mozart (1756–91)
Brigadoon — Alan Lerner (1918–86) & Frederick Loewe (1901–88)
Hansel and Gretel — Engelbert Humperdinck (1854–1921)

1961–62

Eastman Philharmonia Personnel

Apple, Darwin	Violin I	Halfmann,	
Barlow, Robert	Harp	Virginia	Violin II
Baty, Janice	Violin I	Hall, Barbara	Cello
Bell, Glen	Trumpet	Hall, John	Trumpet
Bianchi, Carl Jeff	French Horn	Hamilton, John	Viola
Bishop, Elizabeth	Bassoon	Harnish, Margaret	Violin II
Blahovec, Melinda	Violin II	Harris, Jane	Oboe
Bussenschutt, Joan	Violin II	Hoffman, Monte	Cello
Campbell, Larry	Trombone	Hood, Boyd	Trumpet
Campbell,		Hoyle, Wilson	Cello
Richard	Bassoon	Johnston, Daniel	Bass Clarinet
Carlson, Marlan	Viola	Junkunc, Laddie	Violin II
Chenevey, Paul	Viola	Kennedy, Dennisse	Violin I
Clark, Marjorie	Flute	Kilmer, Richard	Violin I
Cocuzzi, Frank	Percussion	Kirkpatrick, Gary	Piano
Cowley, David	Cello	Landis, John	Trumpet
Dechario, Tony	Trombone	Lang, Mary Jane	Clarinet
Dengler, Patricia	Flute	Larason, Dayna	Oboe
D'Onofrio, Joseph	Violin I	Larrison, Spencer	Violin II
Emerson, Janet	Viola	Levitin, Susan	Flute
Enyeart, Carter	Cello	Lillya, Ann	Viola
Fickett, Norman	Timpani	Loomis, Ralph	Clarinet
Filosa, Albert	Viola	Ludwig, Sylvia	Violin I
Frattle, Rosemary	Double Bass	Macisak, Janice	Violin II
Frizelle, Dorothy	Horn	Masters, Jacqueline	Violin II
Gibson, Gerald	Contra Bassoon	Monardo,	
Gibson, Lawrence	Violin II	Dominick	Trombone
Gilbert, Donald	Percussion	Moore, Thomas	Violin II
Gordon, Betty		Narmour, Gene	Trombone
Carol	Violin II	Nice, Carter	Violin I
Gorton, Judith	Violin II	Oncavage, Carole	Horn
Greer, Mary	Viola	Panke, Gayel	Harp
Haffner, Barbara	Cello	Parkes, Jonathan	Oboe
Hagreen, Robert		Patterson,	
Bruce	Horn	Elizabeth	Double Bass

Perantoni, Daniel	Tuba	Swanson, Philip	Piccolo
Phillips, Karen	Viola	Taylor, Lawrence	Violin I
Preiss, James	Percussion	Tlucek, Hyacinthe	Violin I
Premezzi, Lance	Violin II	Triantafillou,	
Rodean, Richard	Bassoon	Helene	Cello
Salaff, Peter	Violin I	Van Sickle, Linda	Horn
Sandidge, Dan	Clarinet	Van Steenkist, Jane	Cello
Slobodzian,		Webster, Albert	Double Bass
Stephanie	Violin II	Webster, Richard	Double Bass
Smith, Colin	English Horn	Willis, Linda	Violin I
Snedden, Linda	Violin I	Wyre, John	Percussion
Spencer, Herbert	Horn	Zimmerman,	
Spohr, Clifford	Double Bass	Robert	Double Bass

Appendix 4

1932–72

Conductors Who Appeared with the Rochester Philharmonic Orchestra

This list identifies conductors who appeared with the Rochester Philharmonic Orchestra in its regular subscription concerts during the period 1932 through 1972, indicating the concert season(s) of their appearance with the orchestra.

Kazuyoshi Akiyama	1968–69, 1969–70, 1970–71
Victor Allesandro	1956–57
Howard Barlow	1944–45
John Barnett	1957–58
Sir Thomas Beecham	1943–44, 1944–45, 1945–46
Leonard Bernstein	1945–46, 1946–47
Theodore Bloomfield[a]	1958–59, 1959–60, 1960–61, 1961–62, 1962–63
Arturo Bodansky	1932–33
Charles Bruck	1967–68
Carlos Chávez	1969–70
Aaron Copland	1964–65, 1969–70
Walter Damrosch	1932–33
David Diamond	1965–66
Issay Dobrowen	1933–34
Antal Dorati	1966–67
Georges Enesco	1946–47, 1947–48
Peter Erös	1967–68
Arthur Fiedler	1962–63
Lucas Foss	1965–66
Vladimir Golschmann	1933–34, 1935–36, 1946–47
Eugene Goossens[b]	1932–33
Howard Hanson	1955–56, 1957–58, 1963–64

Guy Fraser Harrison	1932–33, 1933–34, 1934–35, 1935–36, 1936–37, 1937–38, 1938–39, 1939–40, 1940–41, 1941–42, 1943–44, 1944–45, 1945–46, 1946–47, 1947–48, 1948–49, 1949–50, 1950–51, 1951–52, 1955–56, 1956–57, 1957–58, 1958–59
Sir Hamilton Harty	1932–33, 1933–34, 1934–35, 1935–36
Walter Hendl	1964–65, 1965–66, 1969–70, 1970–71, 1971–72
Theodore Hollenbach	1958–59, 1969–70
Jose Iturbi[c]	1934–35, 1935–36, 1936–37, 1937–38, 1938–39, 1939–40, 1940–41, 1941–42, 1942–43, 1943–44, 1956–57, 1957–58, 1970–71
Werner Janssen	1934–35
Donald Johanos	1963–64
Thor Johnson	1952–53
Samuel Jones	1966–67, 1968–69, 1969–70, 1970–71, 1971–72
Milton Katims	1957–58, 1962–63
Howard Kitchell	1958–59
Andre Kostelanetz	1944–45, 1955–56
Josef Krips	1958–59, 1962–63
Erich Leinsdorf[d]	1946–47, 1947–48, 1948–49, 1949–50, 1950–51, 1951–52, 1952–53, 1953–54, 1954–55, 1955–56, 1956–57, 1957–58, 1958–59
Richard Lert	1971–72
Henry Lewis	1971–72
Jean Martinon	1958–59
Dimitri Mitropoulos	1944–45, 1945–46, 1949–50
Pierre Monteux	1956–57, 1957–58, 1958–59
Charles Munch	1948–49
Fernando Previtali	1955–56, 1956–57, 1957–58
Fritz Reiner	1932–33, 1933–34, 1935–36, 1944–45
Artur Rodzinski	1945–46
Max Rudolf	1956–57, 1957–58, 1971–72
Gerard Samuel	1957–58
Kenneth Schermerhorn	1971–72
Thomas Schippers	1956–57
Gunther Schuller	1966–67, 1969–70
Jacques Singer	1957–58
Nikolai Sokoloff	1933–34
Georg Solti	1958–59
Laszlo Somogyi[e]	1962–63, 1963–64, 1964–65, 1965–66, 1966–67, 1967–68, 1968–69, 1969–70
Henry Sopkin	1957–58
Leopold Stokowski	1958–59, 1963–64, 1964–65
Igor Stravinsky	1935–36, 1944–45
William Strickland	1956–57

Walter Suskind	1961–62, 1965–66
Michael Tilson Thomas	1970–71
Werner Torkanoswky	1962–63
Georges Tzipine	1963–64
Eduard Van Beinum	1955–56
William Van Otterloo	1967–68
Paul White	1957–58
Haig Yaghjian	1963–64
David Zinman[f]	1970–71, 1971–72

[a] Theodore Bloomfield, conductor of the Rochester Philharmonic Orchestra (1959–63).

[b] Eugene Goossens, conductor of the Rochester Philharmonic Orchestra (1925–31).

[c] Jose Iturbi, conductor of the Rochester Philharmonic Orchestra (1936–44).

[d] Erich Leinsdorf, conductor of the Rochester Philharmonic Orchestra (1947–56).

[e] Laszlo Somogyi, conductor of the Rochester Philharmonic Orchestra (1963–69).

[f] David Zinman, conductor of the Rochester Philharmonic Orchestra (1973–85).

1932–72

Artists Who Performed in Eastman Theatre Concerts

Alicia Markova and Anton Dolin Ballet: 27 February 1948

American Ballet Theater: 25 February 1958, 10 April 1962, 28 October 1963, 25 November 1966, 31 January 1968, 10 March 1969

Ana Maria's Spanish Ballet: 6 December 1950, 5 December 1952

Anderson, Marian (contralto): 8 January 1937, 27 January 1939, 10 January 1941, 23 January 1942, 7 January 1944, 30 November 1945, 27 November 1948, 2 February 1951

Arrau, Claudio (piano): 3 January 1958

Ashkenazy, Vladimir (piano): 14 January 1972

Azumi Kabuki Dancers: 20 January 1956

Babin, Victor (piano duo with Vita Vronsky): 21 March 1947

Ballet Russe: 12 January 1934, 23 November 1934, 22 November 1935, 26 November 1937, 9 March 1939, 13 March 1941, 13 March 1942, 7 March 1947, 3 and 4 March 1950, 26 October 1955, 17 October 1959

Ballet Theater: 19 November 1943, 17 November 1944, 8 March 1946, 9 March 1951, 17 October 1952, 2 January 1954, 24 March 1956

Bjorling, Jussi (tenor): 24 March 1950

Bori, Lucrezia (soprano): 11 November 1932

Boston Symphony Orchestra: 14 December 1935, 7 December 1936, 6 December 1937, 5 December 1938, 11 December 1939, 9 December 1940, 8 December 1941, 11 December 1945, 11 December 1946, 10 October 1947, 8 December 1948, 20 October 1949, 19 October 1950, 24 October 1953, 15 October 1957, 14 October 1958, 21 October 1959, 24 October 1960, 16 October 1961

Brailowsky, Alexander (piano): 24 January 1947, 29 October 1948, 22 February 1952

Casadesus, Gaby (piano): 18 December 1962

Casadesus, Robert (piano): 22 January 1943, 26 January 1945, 27 January 1955, 18 December 1962

Charles Weidman Dance Company: 21 January 1949

Chicago Opera Ballet: 30 January 1960
Cleveland Orchestra: 10 February 1960, 16 March 1970
Cliburn, Van (piano): 4 December 1961, 31 March 1967
Concertgebouw Orchestra: 16 October 1954, 3 May 1967
Curzon, Clifford (piano): 1 February 1952
Dance Theatre of Berlin: 18 December 1955
Danish National Orchestra: 20 November 1952
DePaur Infantry Chorus: 14 October 1949, 7 December 1951, 24 October 1952
DePaur's Opera Gala: 18 April 1958
Dichter, Mischa (piano): 13 November 1967
Don Cossack Choir: 20 November 1942, 5 January 1945, 7 December 1945, 12 December 1949
Eddy, Nelson (baritone): 29 March 1938
Elman, Mischa (violin): 31 October 1941, 23 October 1947
Enesco, Georges (violin): 18 February 1938, 23 February 1940
First Piano Quartet: 23 October 1945, 17 October 1947, 11 October 1948, 12 October 1951, 16 October 1953
Flagstad, Kirsten (soprano): 26 January 1940
Florence Festival Symphony Orchestra: 3 October 1957
Francescatti, Zino (violin): 8 January 1943, 23 February 1945, 16 January 1948, 9 January 1953, 9 March 1961
Gieseking, Walter (piano): 12 May 1956
Gilels, Emil (piano): 26 October 1964
Goldovsky, Boris (piano): 13 February 1956
Gorin, Igor (baritone): 14 November 1947
Gould, Glenn (piano): 9 April 1960, 16 April 1963
Greco, José (dance): 17 January 1962, 18 March 1968
Hall Johnson Negro Choir: 6 January 1933, 9 February 1934
Hayes, Roland (tenor): 11 January 1935
Heifetz, Jascha (violin): 10 November 1933, 12 February 1937, 25 November 1938, 19 February 1943, 9 November 1951
Hess, Myra (piano): 17 November 1939, 28 November 1947
Hofmann, Josef (piano): 19 January 1934, 17 January 1936, 8 March 1940
Horowitz, Vladimir (piano): 13 January 1933, 9 January 1942, 25 February 1944, 22 February 1946, 6 February 1948, 20 January 1950, 16 March 1953
Iturbi, José (piano): 9 March 1934, 28 February 1936, 25 February 1938, 24 January 1941
Janis, Byron (piano): 9 February 1965
Jean Leon Destine and Co.: 22 January 1954
Joos European Ballet: 30 October 1936, 5 January 1940, 22 November 1946
Kapell, William (piano): 24 February 1950

Kitchell, Eva (dance satirist): 2 February 1950
Korjus, Miliza (soprano): 8 February 1946
Kreisler, Fritz (violin): 19 November 1932, 7 December 1934, 11 December 1936, 21 October 1938, 18 October 1940, 27 October 1944, 25 October 1946
Kryssa, Oleh (violin): 17 November 1970
Lehmann, Lotte (soprano): 20 March 1936, 21 March 1941
Leningrad-Kirov Ballet: 23 November 1964
Leningrad Philharmonic: 15 November 1962
Little Singers of Paris: 29 November 1955
London Festival Ballet: 16 February 1955
London, George (bass-baritone): 19 March 1955
London Symphony Orchestra: 30 September 1964
Luboshutz, Pierre (piano duo with Genia Nemenoff): 13 February 1956
Maier, Guy (piano duo with Lee Pattison): 25 January 1935
Martha Graham Dancers: 29 January 1945
Martinelli, Giovanni (tenor): 23 February 1934
Martini, Nino (tenor): 1 November 1935
Maynor, Dororthy (soprano): 30 January 1953
McCormack, John (tenor): 20 January 1933
Mdivani, Marina (piano): 17 November 1970
Menuhin, Yehudi (violin): 10 February 1933, 7 January 1938, 8 December 1939, 20 February 1942, 25 January 1946, 11 November 1957, 16 December 1968
Metropolitan Opera Company: 12 April 1934, 10 April 1935, 30 March 1936, 19 April 1937, 11 April 1938, 3 April 1939, 24 March 1940, 5 May 1941, 6 and 7 February 1942, 12 April 1943, 8 May 1944, 7 May 1945, 20 April 1946, 19 May 1947, 17 May 1948, 11 April 1949, 14 May 1950, 14 May 1951, 21 May 1953, 24 May 1959, 28 May 1960
Metropolitan Opera National Company: 29 and 30 October 1965, 14 and 15 November 1966, 28 September 1967
Milstein, Nathan (violin): 17 March 1944, 7 February 1947, 4 February 1949, 30 November 1959
Moffo, Anna (soprano): 7 January 1963, 6 January 1965
Moiseiwitsch, Benno (piano): 31 January 1957
Montoya, Carlos (guitar): 21 January 1967
Moscow Philharmonic: 4 February 1970
Moscow State Symphony: 17 March 1969
National Ballet of Canada: 24 January 1959
National Ballet of Washington: 12 November 1971
NBC Opera Company: 3 December 1956, 16 November 1964
Nemenoff, Genia (piano duo with Pierre Luboshutz): 13 February 1956
New Philharmonia Orchestra: 17 November 1971
New York City Opera Company: 21 March 1960, 24 and 25 November 1961, 26 and 27 November 1965

New York Civic Center Orchestra: 13 October 1944
New York Philharmonic: 14 April 1957
Nikolaidi, Elena (contralto): 12 October 1950, 20 November 1953
Nilsson, Brigit (soprano): 17 November 1969, 7 December 1970
Niveu, Ginette (violin): 11 November 1949
Oberkirchen Children's Choir: 11 December 1970
Oistrakh, David (violin): 9 December 1963, 23 February 1970
Pattison, Lee (piano duo with Guy Maier): 25 January 1935
Peerce, Jan (tenor): 25 February 1949, 20 February 1953
Philadelphia Opera Company: 22 October 1943
Philadelphia Orchestra: 23 October 1958, 27 April 1961, 29 September
      1962, 17 May 1965, 15 June 1967
Philharmonic Piano Quartet: 10 November 1950
Piano Quartet: 29 November 1960
Pinza, Ezio (bass-baritone): 19 March 1943
Pittsburgh Symphony Orchestra: 8 November 1965
Pons, Lili (soprano): 16 December 1932, 27 March 1943, 8 December
      1944
Ponselle, Rosa (soprano): 27 October 1933
Powers, Marie (actress/singer): 10 October 1955
Poznan Choir: 5 November 1965
Prague Symphony Orchestra: 25 February 1972
Rachmaninoff, Sergei (piano): 3 March 1933, 2 November 1934, 30
      November 1936, 6 January 1939, 30 November 1942
Ricci, Ruggiero (violin): 2 February 1934
Robert Shaw Chorale: 1 April 1959, 9 March 1964
Robeson, Paul (bass-baritone): 8 October 1942
Roger Wagner Chorale: 4 March 1957
Romanian Folk Dance Troupe: 22 October 1968
Royal Ballet: 4 January 1961
Royal Philharmonic Orchestra: 12 October 1963, 4 January 1968
Rubinstein, Artur (piano): 23 March 1939, 21 November 1941, 16 March
      1945, 18 October 1946, 18 March 1949, 29 March 1951, 19 March
      1954, 23 February 1959, 15 December 1960, 8 January 1962, 30 January 1964, 18 January 1965, 19 February 1969
Sadler's Wells Theatre Ballet: 24 October 1951
San Francisco Ballet: 22 February 1964
Sayao, Bidu (soprano): 25 November 1949
Schnabel, Artur (piano): 6 March 1937
Schoop, Trudi (comic ballet): 21 January 1938
Segovia, Andres (guitar): 9 February 1962
Serkin, Rudolf (piano): 2 December 1954, 16 December 1963, 13 March
      1972
Shankar, Ravi (sitar): 9 December 1967
Singher, Martial (baritone): 3 January 1947

Spalding, Albert (violin): 21 February 1941
Spivakovsky, Tossi (violin): 23 February 1951
Steber, Eleanor (soprano): 19 March 1948
Stern, Isaac (violin): 9 December 1949, 17 November 1958, 18 April 1966
Stern-Istomin-Rose Trio: 9 May 1968
Stevens, Rise (soprano): 21 March 1952, 3 May 1972
Szigeti, Joseph (violin): 29 March 1946, 24 November 1950, 14 November 1955
Theatre Royal Windsor: 29 November 1968
Thomas, John Charles (baritone): 1 December 1933, 27 November 1936, 27 October 1939
Tibbett, Lawrence (baritone): 28 October 1932, 22 March 1935, 24 February 1939, 20 March 1942
Tokyo Classical Ballet: 25 February 1963
Traubel, Helen (soprano): 21 February 1947
Vienna Boys Choir: 17 November 1933, 22 October 1948, 3 March 1969, 18 March 1972
Vienna Philharmonic: 27 November 1956
Vienna Symphony Orchestra: 2 March 1964
Vronsky, Vita (piano duo with Victor Babin): 21 March 1947
Wagnerian Festival Singers: 29 October 1937
Warfield, William (baritone): 19 February 1954
Watts, Andre (piano): 8 February 1962, 16 April 1970
Wigman, Mary (dance): 17 February 1933
Yugoslav Folk Ensemble: 28 November 1969

Appendix 6

1932–72

Eastman Faculty and Guest Artists in Kilbourn Hall Recitals

This list is derived principally from the annual series of Kilbourn Hall recitals and concerts scheduled during the regular academic year. It does not presume to be a complete listing of programs that took place during this forty-year period.

Aguilar Lute Quartet: 6 December 1932
Amadeus Quartet: 6 April 1970
American Ballad Singers: 11 November 1941, 30 November 1943
American Society of Ancient Instruments: 28 November 1945
American Troubadours: 12 November 1946
Antoine, Josephine (soprano): 15 April 1958
Appleton, Vera (piano duo with Michael Field): 2 April 1963
Arey, Rufus (clarinet): 30 November 1937, 16 December 1944, 26 December 1952
Ars Antigua of Paris: 21 March 1971
Baker, Janet (mezzo-soprano): 17 January 1970, 5 October 1971
Barrere, Georges (flute): 13 December 1938
Basile, Armand (piano): 11 November 1952, 6 April 1954, 19 March 1957, 4 February 1958, 6 December 1960
Bauer, Harold (piano): 26 March 1935
Beardslee, Bethany (soprano): 9 November 1954
Belgian Piano Quartet: 14 January 1941, 26 February 1943
Bernac, Pierre (baritone): 10 January 1950
Bloch, Suzanne (lute): 26 March 1946, 22 February 1955
Borodin Quartet: 13 April 1971
Braggiotto, Mario (piano duo with Jacques Fray): 17 March 1942
Brancato, Rosemarie (soprano): 17 March 1936
Bream, Julian (lute): 17 November 1959, 2 December 1963, 8 October 1970
Britt Trio: 14 March 1944

Budapest String Quartet: 13 March 1933, 26 February 1934, 22 March 1938, 13 January 1942

Cadek Quartet: 1 November 1966

Celentano, John (violin): 1 March 1966, 2 February 1972

Chabay, Leslie (tenor): 4 December 1951

Collegium Musicum of the University of Illinois: 28 October 1958

Concentus Musicus of Vienna: 15 October 1971

Contemporary Chamber Ensemble: 11 November 1969

Coolidge String Quartet: 11 January 1944

Copinsky Trio: 23 January 1934

Costa, Sequiera (piano): 17 January 1967

Craighead, David (organ): 28 February 1956, 4 December 1962

Crozier, Catherine (organ): 23 March 1948, 16 January 1953, 15 December 1953

Dance Trio: 15 February 1938

Deller, Alfred (countertenor): 23 October 1962

Die Weiner Solisten: 17 March 1964

Doktor, Paul (violin): 9 January 1962, 1 December 1964

Dougherty, Celius (piano duo with Vincenz Ruzicka): 13 November 1945

Eastman Brass Quintet: 30 March 1965, 5 April 1966, 10 December 1968, 23 February 1971, 11 January 1972

Eastman Quartet: 11 October 1966, 8 January 1969, 6 October 1969, 9 November 1971

Eastman String Quartet: 30 October 1951, 18 December 1951, 25 February 1952, 25 March 1952, 28 October 1952, 16 December 1952, 3 February 1953, 31 March 1953, 25 October 1955, 13 December 1955, 14 February 1956, 24 April 1956, 23 October 1956, 5 December 1956, 29 January 1957, 5 March 1957, 8 October 1957, 4 February 1958, 1 April 1958, 11 November 1958, 16 December 1958, 20 January 1959, 17 February 1959, 13 October 1959, 8 December 1959, 29 March 1960, 1 November 1960, 6 December 1960, 14 March 1961, 26 September 1961, 5 December 1961, 16 January 1962, 3 April 1962, 2 October 1962, 4 December 1962, 5 February 1963, 5 March 1963, 22 October 1963, 10 December 1963, 3 March 1964

Eastman Woodwind Quintet: 18 November 1956, 23 February 1965

Echániz, José (piano): 26 February 1946, 28 October 1947, 28 March 1950, 27 October 1953, 16 December 1958, 22 October 1963, 14 January 1964, 7 December 1965, 25 October 1966

English Duo Singers: 8 March 1949

English Singers: 11 December 1933

Enters, Anga (dance): 24 October 1932, 18 February 1936, 17 December 1940, 2 November 1943, 5 February 1946, 5 December 1950

Eto, Kimio (koto): 8 December 1964
Faini, Maria Luisa (piano): 20 May 1967, 16 March 1968, 7 January
     1971
Field, Michael (piano duo with Vera Appleton): 2 April 1963
Fine Arts Quartet: 27 March 1969
Fortuna, Joseph (violin): 22 March 1937, 14 March 1939, 25 February
     1941
Fray, Jacques (piano duo with Mario Braggiotto): 17 March 1942
Frugoni, Orazio (piano): 24 February 1953, 23 November 1954, 24 April
     1956, 10 March 1959, 7 November 1961, 19 October 1965
Fuerstner, Carl (piano): 19 October 1948
Garbousova, Raya (cello): 13 November 1962
Genhart, Cecile Staub (piano): 12 April 1938, 4 February 1941, 6 April
     1943, 23 January 1945, 10 February 1948, 14 November 1950, 18
     December 1951
Gieseking, Walter (piano): 9 November 1937
Glazer, Frank (piano): 19 November 1968, 29 February 1972
Glenn, Carroll (violin): 26 October 1971
Gordon, Jacques (violin): 24 November 1942
Gordon String Quartet: 19 February 1935, 28 March 1939, 16 March
     1943, 31 October 1944, 16 December 1944, 9 January 1945, 23 Janu-
     ary 1945, 30 October 1945, 18 December 1945, 15 January 1946, 26
     February 1946, 29 October 1946, 26 November 1946, 17 December
     1946, 25 February 1947
Grandjany, Marcel (harp): 8 March 1960
Griller String Quartet: 25 November 1947
Guarneri Quartet: 9 March 1972
Haefliger, Ernst (tenor) 24 November 1969
Hambourg Trio: 10 May 1935
Hasty, Stanley (clarinet): 20 January 1959, 5 December 1961, 6 October
     1969
Hendl, Walter (piano duo with Muriel Kilby): 11 January 1966
Hess, Myra (piano): 31 January 1933
Huehn, Julius (baritone): 16 March 1954
Humphrey, Doris (dance): 15 January 1935
Humphery-Weidman Dancers: 10 January 1939
Hungarian String Quartet: 28 February 1950
Hutcheson, Ernest (piano): 23 October 1933
Instrumental Ensemble: 15 January 1952
Instrumental Ensemble (Vas, Celentano, Tursi, MacKown): 2 March
     1954
Instrumental Trio (Taylor, MacKown, and MacKown): 13 November
     1951
Jempelis, Anastasia (violin): 22 March 1966
Juilliard String Quartet: 3 October 1968

Kaplow, Maurice (violin): 14 February 1956
Karr, Gary (double bass): 17 November 1964
Kaskas, Anna (contralto): 10 January 1961
Kilbourn Quartet: 3 January 1933, 1 December 1936, 6 April 1937, 30 November 1937, 12 April 1938, 29 November 1938, 31 January 1939, 9 January 1940, 24 October 1950, 17 January 1951, 6 March 1951, 13 March 1951
Kilby, Muriel (piano duo with Walter Hendl): 11 January 1966
Knitzer, Joseph (violin): 5 November 1963
Kolisch Quartet: 19 January 1937
Komitas String Quartet: 19 February 1963
Konraty, Nicholas (baritone): 22 March 1937, 14 March 1939, 1 April 1941, 5 January 1943
Kountz, Emma (piano): 5 February 1963
Kraft, Arthur (tenor): 3 November 1936, 30 January 1940, 3 February 1942, 22 February 1944
Kroll Sextet: 13 November 1934, 26 November 1935
Kroll String Quartet: 9 November 1948
Landow, Max (piano): 1 December 1936, 14 February 1939, 31 March 1942, 4 April 1944
Laretei, Labi (piano): 14 March 1967
LaSalle Quartet: 2 February 1965
Leinsdorf, Erich (piano): 16 March 1954
Leonard, Ronald (cello): 25 March 1958, 11 November 1958, 24 September 1963, 7 April 1964, 13 December 1966, 16 November 1970
List, Eugene (piano): 17 March 1967, 24 February 1970
Loesser, Arthur (piano): 26 September 1961, 2 October 1962
Loewenguth Quartet: 7 November 1961
Luboshutz, Pierre (piano duo with Genia Nemenoff): 12 March 1940
MacKown, Allison (cello): 21 November 1939, 24 February 1942, 1 February 1944, 29 March 1949, 31 March 1953
MacNabb, George (piano): 1 April 1941
Malone, Eileen (harp): 25 February 1941, 3 February 1953, 8 March 1955, 12 April 1972
Mann, Bloch, Mann Ensemble: 12 November 1940
Mariano, Joseph (flute): 29 November 1938, 15 January 1946, 13 December 1955, 16 January 1962, 9 December 1969
Matthews, Edward (baritone): 1 November 1932
Miquelle, Georges (cello): 22 February 1955
Modern String Quartet: 19 October 1948
Morgan, Mac (baritone): 2 December 1952
Mozart Vocal Trio: 26 February 1952
Nemenoff, Genia (piano duo with Pierre Luboshutz): 12 March 1940
New Art Wind Quintet: 7 February 1961
New Music String Quartet: 14 December 1954

New York Brass Quintet: 20 February 1962
New York Pro Musica: 18 February 1958, 7 April 1959
Niles, John Jacob (American folk music): 14 November 1944
Paganini String Quartet: 2 March 1948
Pascal String Quartet: 27 January 1948
Pasquier Trio: 25 January 1938, 20 February 1940, 21 January 1947, 18
     January 1949
Philharmonic Instrumental Quintet: 7 December 1943
Philharmonic Woodwind Quintet: 26 November 1940, 14 December
     1948, 17 November 1953
Poulenc, Francis (piano): 10 January 1950
Pressl, Yella (harpsichord): 28 November 1944, 3 February 1947
Prey, Hermann (baritone): 29 October 1970
Pro Musica Antigua Ensemble of Brussels: 25 October 1949
Pro Musica Antiqua Society of New York: 12 February 1957
Puyana, Rafael (harpsichord): 14 February 1961, 30 November 1971
Rejto, Gabor (cello): 19 December 1949, 5 January 1954
Reynolds, Verne (French horn): 10 December 1963
Ribaupierre, Andre de (violin): 6 December 1949, 9 February 1954
Riker, Charles (piano): 14 December 1948
Rococo Ensemble: 5 April 1960
Roth Quartet: 16 February 1937
Ruzicka, Vincenz (piano duo with Celius Dougherty): 13 November
     1945
Salzedo Concert Ensemble: 13 February 1945
Salzedo Trio: 15 December 1936
Schmitz, E. Robert (piano): 16 February 1937, 8 November 1938
Schumann, Henrietta (piano): 17 March 1936
Scott, Tom (folk song singer): 30 November 1948
Secon, Morris (French horn): 8 October 1957
Segovia, Andres (guitar): 28 January 1936, 18 March 1947, 20 February
     1951
Shankar, Ravi (sitar): 17 October 1961
Shapiro, Eudice (violin): 11 January 1965
Silva, Luigi (cello): 25 November 1941, 5 January 1943, 6 January 1948
Society of Ancient Instruments: 23 January 1933
Sprenkle, Robert (oboe): 9 January 1945, 13 March 1951, 1 April 1958
Stanley String Quartet: 19 January 1960
Stradivarius Quartet: 14 December 1937
Taylor, Millard (violin): 8 February 1949, 6 February 1951, 9 April 1957,
     1 March 1960, 7 April 1964, 17 March 1970
Tinayre, Yves (baritone): 11 March 1941, 10 April 1945
Tinlot, Gustave (violin): 1 March 1938
Torre, Rey de la (guitar): 25 November 1958
Tourel, Jeanie (mezzo-soprano): 13 February 1969

Trapp Choir: 7 November 1939
Trapp Family Singers: 10 November 1942
Treash, Leonard (bass): 16 December 1947
Trio Concertante: 15 November 1960
Trio of New York: 12 January 1943
Tursi, Francis (viola): 15 February 1950, 6 February 1951, 4 January
     1955, 16 October 1962, 17 April 1964
Valenti, Fernando (harpsichord): 19 April 1955, 19 November 1957
Vas, Sandor (piano): 9 March 1937, 1 March 1938, 2 April 1940, 2 Febru-
     ary 1943, 18 December 1945, 26 November 1946, 17 January 1951,
     25 March 1952
Wasantha Wana Singh and His Group: 15 November 1949
Weidman, Charles (dance): 15 January 1935
Weiss-Mann, Edith (harpsichord): 26 March 1946
Wilson, Raymond (piano): 20 February 1933, 6 April 1937, 31 January
     1939, 3 February 1942
Winslow Dancers: 5 December 1939
Winslow-Fitzsimmons Dancers: 16 December 1941
Zeitlin, Zvi (violin): 22 January 1969, 15 December 1971
Zimmerman, Oscar (double bass): 26 November 1946, 3 April 1962

Repertoire Recorded by Howard Hanson and the Eastman-Rochester Orchestra for RCA Victor and Columbia

RCA Recordings

Barlow, Wayne	*The Winter's Passed*
Bergsma, William	"Introduction and Finale" from *Gold and the Señor Commandante*
Braine, Robert	Habañera *Lazy Cigarette*
Pavanne	*El Greco*
Chadwick, George	*Jubilee*
Copland, Aaron	*Music for the Theatre*
Griffes, Charles	*Poem* for flute and orchestra
	The White Peacock
Hanson, Howard	*Lament for Beowulf*
	Suite from the opera *Merry Mount*
	Symphony No. 1 ("Nordic")
	Symphony No. 2 ("Romantic")
Keller, Homer	*Serenade* for clarinet and strings
Kennan, Kent	*Night Soliloquy* for flute, piano, and strings
Loeffler, Charles	*Pagan Poem*
MacDowell, Edward	"Dirge" from *Indian Suite*
Paine, John Knowles	*Oedipus Tyrannus*
Phillips, Burrill	*Concert Piece* for bassoon and strings
	Selections from McGuffey's Readers
Rogers, Bernard	*Soliloquy* for flute and strings
	Suite of Fairy Tales
Skilton, Charles	*War Dance*
	Sunrise Song
Spencer, Norman	*Dance Suite*
Still, William Grant	"Scherzo" from *Afro-American Symphony*
Vardell, Charles	*Joe Clark Steps Out*

Columbia Recordings

Grieg, Edvard	*Holberg Suite*
Hanson, Howard	Concerto for Piano and Orchestra (Rudolf Firkusny, piano)
	Symphony No. 2 ("Romantic")
MacDowell, Edward	Concerto No. 2 in D Minor (Jesus Maria Sanroma, piano)
Mennin, Peter	Symphony No. 3
Riegger, Wallingford	Symphony No. 3

The Mercury Recordings

Howard Hanson and the Eastman-Rochester Orchestra

Record Number	Composer	Titles
MG50049/SR90049	Ferde Grofé	*Grand Canyon Suite* *Mississippi Suite*
MG50053/SR90053	John Pozdro	Symphony No. 2
	William Pursell	*Christ Looking over Jerusalem*
	Ron Nelson	*For Katharine in April*
	Martin Mailman	*Autumn Landscape*
	Robert Stern	*In Memoriam Abraham*
	Neil McKay	Larghetto
	James Sutcliffe	*Gymnopedie*
	Robert Gauldin	*Diverse Dances*
	Joseph Scianni	Adagio Cantabile
	Paul Earls	*And on the 7th Day*
MG40000/MG50073	Howard Hanson	Songs from "Drum Taps"
	Randall Thompson	*Testament of Freedom*
MG40001/MG50074	Thomas Canning	Fantasy on a Hymn by Justin Morgan
	Arthur Foote	Suite in E Major for string orchestra
	Louis Mennini	*Arioso*

Record Number	Composer	Titles
MG40002/MG50075	Samuel Barber	*Adagio for Strings* *Essay for Orchestra* Overture to the *School for Scandal*
	Morton Gould	Latin-American Symphonette
MG40003/MG50076	Wayne Barlow	*The Winter's Passed*
	Aaron Copland	*Quiet City*
	Howard Hanson	Serenade for flute, strings, and harp Pastorale for oboe, strings, and harp
MG40003/MG50076	Homer Keller	Serenade for clarinet and strings
	Kent Kennan	*Night Soliloquy* for flute, piano, and strings
	Bernard Rogers	*Soliloquy* for flute and strings
MG40004/MG50077	Howard Hanson	Symphony No. 4 ("Requiem")
	Roy Harris	Symphony No. 3
MG40005/MG50078	Henry Cowell	Symphony No. 4
	Alan Hovhaness	*Arevakal*, Concerto No. 1
	Wallingford Riegger	*New Dance*
MG40008/MG50081	Deems Taylor	*Through the Looking Glass*
MG40009/MG50082	Edward MacDowell	*Second Indian Suite*
		Suite for Orchestra No. 2
MG40010/MG50083	Walter Piston	Symphony No. 3
MG40012/MG50085	Charles Tomlinson Griffes	Pleasure Dome of Kubla Khan "The White Peacock" "Clouds" "Bacchanale"
	Charles Martin Loeffler	*Memories of My Childhood* Poem

(continued)

Record Number	Composer	Titles
MG40013/MG50086	Richard Donovan	*New England Chronicle*
	Wells Hivley	*Tres Himnos*
	Quincy Porter	Poem and Dance
40014/50087	Samuel Barber	Symphony No. 1
	Howard Hanson	Symphony No. 5 ("Sinfonia Sacra") *Cherubic Hymn*
MG50103/SR90103	Elliott Carter	*The Minotaur*
	Colin McPhee	*Tabuh-Tabuhan*
MG50104/SR90018	George Chadwick	Symphonic Sketches
MG50106	Alan Hovhaness	Prelude and Quadruple Fugue
	Ronald LoPresti	"The Masks"
	Roger Sessions	Suite from *The Black Maskers*
MG50114	Howard Hanson	Fantasy Variations on a Theme of Youth
	Bernard Rogers	*Leaves from the Tale of Pinocchio*
	Harold Triggs	*The Bright Land*
MG50134/SR90134	Lyndol Mitchell	*Kentucky Mountain Portraits*
	Robert McBride	*Mexican Rhapsody*
	Ron Nelson	*Savannah River Holiday*
	Charles Vardell	*Joe Clark Steps Out*
MG50136/SR90136	John Alden Carpenter	*Adventures in a Perambulator*
	Burrill Phillips	Selections from *McGuffey's Readers*
MG50138/SR90002	George Gershwin	Concerto in F *Rhapsody in Blue*
MG50147/SR90147	William Bergsma	*Gold and the Señor Commandante*
	Bernard Rogers	*Once upon a Time*
	Kent Kennan	Three Pieces for Orchestra

Record Number	Composer	Titles
MG50148/SR90148	Samuel Barber	Symphony No. 1 *Adagio for Strings* Essay No. 1 for Orchestra Overture to the *School for Scandal*
MG50149/SR90149	Charles Ives	Symphony No. 3 *Three Places in New England*
MG50150	Howard Hanson	*Elegy in Memory of Serge Koussevitsky* *Song of Democracy*
	Richard Lane	Four Songs for mezzo-soprano and orchestra
MG50163/SR90163	Victor Herbert	Concerto No. 2 in E for violoncello and orchestra
	Johann F. Peter	Sinfonia for string orchestra
MG50165/SR90165	Howard Hanson	Symphony No. 1 ("Nordic") Fantasie-Variations on a Theme of Youth
MF50166	George Gershwin	*Cuban Overture*
	Robert McBride	*Mexican Rhapsody*
	Morton Gould	Latin-American Symphonette
MG50175/SR90175	Howard Hanson	Suite from *Merry Mount*
	George Gershwin	*Cuban Overture*
MG50192/SR90192	Howard Hanson	Symphony No. 2 ("Romantic") *Lament for Bewoulf*
MG50206/SR90206	Douglas Moore	*Pageant of P. T. Barnum*
	Walter Piston	Ballet Suite from the *Incredible Flutist*

(continued)

Record Number	Composer	Titles
MG50223/SR0–223	Ernest Bloch	Concerto Grosso No. 1 Concerto Grosso No. 2
MG50224/SR90224	Samuel Barber	Capricorn Concerto Music from the ballet *Medea*
MG50257/SR90257	Alberto Ginastera	Overture from *The Creole Faust*
	Camargo Guarnieri	Three Dances
	William Grant Still	Ballet Suite "Sahdji"
MG50263/SR90263	Morton Gould	*Fall River Legend;* Spirituals
MG50267/SR90267	Howard Hanson	*Mosaics*
MG50277/SR90277	William McCauley	Five Miniatures for Flute and Strings
	Wayne Barlow	*Night Song*
	Charles Martin Loeffler	Deux Rhapsodies
MG50286/SR90286	Ernest Bloch	*Schelomo*
	Victor Herbert	Concerto for Violoncello No. 2
MG50299/SR90299[a]	Anatole Liadov	*Baba Yaga* *Enchanted Lake* *Kikimora*
	Camargo Guarnieri	*Dansa Brasileria*
	Wayne Barlow	*The Winter's Passed*
	Kent Kennan	*Night Soliloquy*
	Edvard Grieg	*The Last Spring*
	John Philip Sousa	"The Stars and Stripes Forever"
MG50326/SR50326	Morton Gould	*Fall River Legend*
	Charles Vardell	*Joe Clark Steps Out*
MG50337/SR90337	George Chadwick	Symphonic Sketches
	Martin Mailman	*Autumn Landscape*
	Ron Nelson	*For Katharine in April*

Record Number	Composer	Titles
MG50361/SR90361	Ron Nelson	*Savannah River Holiday*
MG50379/SR90379	William Schuman	*New England Triptych*
	Charles Tomlinson Griffes	Poem for flute and orchestra
	Peter Mennin	Symphony No. 5
MG50394/SR50394	Morton Gould	Latin American Symphonette
MG50421/SR90421	Roy Harris	Symphony No. 3
MG50422/SR90422	Charles Tomlinson Griffes	*Pleasure Dome of Kubla Khan* *Poem* "The White Peacock"
MG50423/SR90423	Howard Hanson	Suite from *Merry Mount*
	Alan Hovhaness	Prelude and Quadruple Fugue
	Walter Piston	*The Incredible Flutist*
	Roger Sessions	*The Black Maskers*
MG50429/SR90429	Howard Hanson	Four Psalms
	Virgil Thompson	*The Feast of Love* Symphony on a Hymn Tune
MG50430/SR90430	Howard Hanson	Piano Concerto *Mosaics*
	John LaMontaine	*Birds of Paradise*
MG50449/SR90449	Howard Hanson	Symphony No. 3
SR90524	Howard Hanson	Excerpts from *Merry Mount*
	George Templeton Strong	Chorale on a Theme of Hassler
	Horatio Parker	Prelude to the opera *Mona*

[a] Recorded with the Eastman Philharmonia.

Appendix 9

The Mercury Recordings

Frederick Fennell and the
Eastman Wind Ensemble

Record Number	Composer	Titles
MG40006/50079		*American Concert Band Masterpieces*
	Vincent Persichetti	Divertimento
	Morton Gould	Ballad
	William Schuman	"George Washington Bridge"
	Robert Russell Bennett	"Suite of Old American Dances"
	Walter Piston	"Tunbridge Fair"
	Samuel Barber	"Commando March"
MG40007/50080		*Marches by Sousa and Others*
	John Philip Sousa	"Fairest of the Fair" "Manhattan Beach" "Black Horse Troop" "Daughters of Texas" "Rifle Regiment" "Corcoran Cadets" "Hands across the Sea" "Semper Fidelis"
	Jenkins-Neff	"Pieces of Eight"
	Howard Hanson	"March Carillon"
	Edwin Franko Goldman	"Cheerio"

Record Number	Composer	Titles
MG40007/50080	Henry Fillmore	"His Honor"
	Frederick E. Bigelow	"Our Director"
	Harry Alford	"Glory of the Gridiron"
	Karl L. King	"Pride of the Illinois"
	Edwin E. Bagley	"National Emblem"
MG40011/50084		*La Fiesta Mexicana*
	Owen Reed	"La Fiesta Mexicana"
	Peter Mennin	"Canzona"
	Vincent Persichetti	"Psalm"
	Virgil Thompson	"A Solemn Music"
	Howard Hanson	"Chorale and Alleluia"
MG40015/50088		*British Band Classics*
	Gustav Holst	Suite No. 2 in F
	Vaughan Williams	Folk Song Suite Toccata
	Gustav Holst	Suite in E-flat
MG50105/SR90105		*Marching Along*
	John Philip Sousa	"The U.S. Field Artillery March" "Washington Post" "The Stars and Stripes Forever"
	Frederick W. Meacham	"American Patrol"
	Edwin Franko Goldman	"On the Mall"
	Earl F. McCoy	"Lights Out"
	Karl I. King	"Barnum and Bailey's Favorite"
	Kenneth J. Alford	"Colonel Bogey"
	John N. Klohr	"The Billboard"
MG50111/SR90111		*The Spirit of '76*[a]

(continued)

Record Number	Composer	Titles
MG50112/SR90112		*Ruffles and Flourishes*[b]
MG50113		*Marches for Twirling*[c]
MG50143/SR90143		*Hindemith-Schoenberg-Stravinsky*
	Paul Hindemith	Symphony in B-flat Major
	Arnold Schoenberg	Theme and Variations, Op. 43A
	Igor Stravinsky	*Symphonies of Wind Instruments*
MG50170/SR90170		*March Time (Goldman and Others)*
	Edwin Franko Goldman	"Illinois" "Boy Scouts of America" "Onward-Upward" "Children's March" "Interlochen Bowl" "Bugles and Drums"
	Roland F. Seitz	"Grandioso"
	Richard Rodgers	"Guadalcanal"
	Daniel W. Reeves	"Second Regiment of Connecticut"
	Kenneth J. Alford	"Mad Major"
	Ronald B. Hall	"Officer of the Day"
	Henry Fillmore	"Americans We"
MG50173/SR90173		*Winds in Hi-Fi*
	Percy Grainger	A Lincolnshire Posy
	Darius Milhaud	Suite Francaise
	Richard Strauss	Serenade in C-flat Major, Op. 7
	Bernard Rogers	Three Japanese Dances
MG50176/SR90176		*Mozart Serenade No. 10 in B-flat, K. 361*
	Wolfgang Amadeus Mozart	Serenade No. 10 in B-flat Major

Record Number	Composer	Titles
MG50197/SR90197	Wolfgang Amadeus Mozart	*British Band Classics Volume II*
	Gordon Jacob	Suite "William Byrd"
	Gustav Holst	Hammersmith: Prelude and Scherzo Op. 52
	William Walton	"Crown Imperial— A Coronation March"
MG50207/SR90207		*Hands across the Sea*
	John Philip Sousa	"Hands across the Sea"
	Gustav Ganne	"Father of Victory"
	Mariano San Minguel	"The Golden Bar"
	Carl Tieke	"Old Comrades"
	Serge Prokofiev	"March," Op. 99
	Johannes Hanssen	"Valdres March"
	D. Delle Cese	"Inglesia"
	Eric Coates	"Knights Bridge"
MG50220/SR90220		*American Masterpieces for Concert Band*
	Ralph Vaughan Williams	Fanfare and Allegro
	Morton Gould	West Point Symphony
	Julian Work	Autumn Walk
	Robert Russell Bennett	Symphonic Songs
MG50221/SR90221		*Diverse Winds*
	Aram Khatchaturian	Armenian Dances
	Vincent Persichetti	Symphony No. 6
	Percy Grainger	Hill Song No. 2
	Walter Hartley	Concerto for 23 Winds

(continued)

Record Number	Composer	Titles
50245/90245		*Music of Andrea and Giovanni Gabrieli*
	Andrea Gabrieli	Aria della Battaglia
	Giovanni Gabrieli	Sonata Octavi Toni Sonata Pian e Forte Canzon Duodecimi Toni Canzon Noni Toni Canzon Septimi Toni, No. 1 Canzon Quarti Toni
MG50256/SR90256		*Ballet for Band*
	Charles Gounod	Ballet Music from *Faust*
	Gioacchino Rossini	Suite from the ballet *La Boutique Fantasque*
	Arthur Sullivan	Suite from the ballet *Pineapple Roll*
MG50264 /SR90264		*Sound Off!*
	John Philip Sousa	"High School Cadets" "The Picadore" "Our Flirtation" "Ballets and Bayonets" "Nobles of the Mystic Shrine" "The Gallant Seventh" "The Invincible Eagle" "Sound Off" "Riders for the Flag" "Sabre and Spurs" "Solid Man to the Front" "Liberty Bell"
MG50276/SR90276		*Wagner for Band*
	Richard Wagner	Prelude to Act III and Bridal Chorus from *Lohengrin* "Good Friday Spell" from *Parsifal*

Record Number	Composer	Titles
MG50276/SR90276	Richard Wagner	"Elsa's Procession to the Cathedral" from *Lohengrin* "Entry of the Gods into Valhalla" from *Das Reingold*
MG50284/SR90284		*Sousa on Review*
	John Philip Sousa	"Ancient and Honorable Artillery Company" "Sesquicentennial Exposition" "Golden Jubilee" "National Game" "Kansas Wildcats" "Rifle Regiment" "Pride of the Wolverines" "Black Horse Troop" "Glory of the Yankee Navy" "New Mexico" "Gridiron Club" "Manhattan Beach"
MG50314/SR90314		*Screamers! A Collection of Exciting Marches from the Circus Ring*
	John Held	"In Storm and Sunshine"
	Karl L. King	"Invictus"
	Henry Fillmore	"Bones Trombones" "The Circus Bee"
	Julius Fucile	"Thunder and Blazes"
	Karl K. King	"Circus Days"
	Will Huff	"The Squealer"
	John H. Ribble	"Bennett's Triumphal"
	Thomas S. Allen	"Whip and Spur"
	Karl L. King	"The Big Cage"
	Getty H. Huffine	"Them Basses"

(continued)

Record Number	Composer	Titles
	Fred Jewell	"The Screamer"
	Karl L. King	"Robinson's Grand Entree"
	Orion R. Farrar	"Bombasto"
	Henry Fillmore	"Rolling Thunder"
	Charles E. Duble	"Bravura"
LPS2–501/LPS2–901		*Civil War, Volume 1*[d]
LPS2–502/LPS2–902		*Civil War, Volume 2*[d]

[a] The camp duty of the United States Army, traditional regimental music for fifes and drums, traditional marching tunes for fifes and drums.

[b] Excerpts from the official U.S. Army manual *Bugle Calls of the Army*, music for rendering honors (bugles, drums, and cymbals), traditional marches, and inspection pieces.

[c] Recoupling of previous march albums.

[d] Two-volume set of band, fife and drum, and bugle music from the American Civil War.

Bibliography

Primary Sources

A. Sibley Music Library

Ruth T. Watanabe Special Collections and Eastman School of Music Archives. References in footnotes to individual, unpublished papers from the Sibley Music Library are indicated by the letters SML.

Individual Collections

Robert Freeman Papers. Robert Freeman served as director of the Eastman School of Music from 1972 to 1996. The collection includes various papers including material dating from the administration of his predecessor, Walter Hendl (served 1964 to 1972).

Howard Hanson Papers. Howard Hanson served as director of the Eastman School of Music from 1924 to 1964. The collection contains various papers including correspondence, drafts of speeches, and reports. Additional material for this collection has recently been acquired by the Sibley Music Library, including an unpublished autobiography written by Hanson following his retirement. In addition to undated multiple versions of various chapters, there exists what appears to be a complete text contained in several black binders. There is continuous pagination for about half of the text, but then each individual chapter is separately paginated. The author has made the assumption, in the absence of any contradictory evidence, that the complete text in the black binders is a later version than any of the other versions contained in separate folders.

Official Publications

Eastman School of Music Board of Managers. Minutes and other documents (1919–85).

Eastman School of Music Magazines. Includes various alumni publications.

Eastman School of Music Programs. A collection of programs of major recitals and concerts sponsored by the Eastman School of Music (1922–).

Eastman School of Music Publications for Alumni. A complete collection of the *Alumni Bulletin* of the Eastman School of Music (1929–) and its successor publications, *Notes from Eastman* (beginning in 1966) and *Eastman Notes* (since 1976).

Eastman School of Music/University of Rochester Publications. Includes Eastman School of Music annual catalogs (1921–) and reports of the president and treasurer.

Eastman School of Music Yearbooks. A complete collection of student yearbooks (1925–).

Faculty File. Sundry documents on almost all individuals who have held teaching positions at the Eastman School of Music.

Festivals of American Music. Bulletins and programs of the American Composers' Concerts and the Festivals of American Music (1925–71), including a cumulative repertoire list compiled by Ruth T. Watanabe (Rochester, NY, 1972).

Rochester Scrapbooks. Approximately 200 scrapbooks compiled by the Sibley Music Library containing newspaper clippings (1921–79) on musical life and events relating to the Eastman School of Music.

B. Rush Rhees Library

Department of Rare Books, Special Collections, and Preservation. References in footnotes to individual, unpublished material from Ruth Rhees Library are identified with the letters RRL.

Rush Rhees Papers. Correspondence of Rush Rhees during his tenure as president of the University of Rochester.

Robert Sproull Papers. Correspondence of Robert Sproull during his tenure as provost and president of the University of Rochester.

W. Allen Wallis Papers. Correspondence of W. Allen Wallis during his tenure as president and chancellor of the University of Rochester.

C. Private Papers of Walter Hendl

A collection of private papers of Walter Hendl, the third director of the Eastman School of Music, at his home in Erie, Pennsylvania, consisting of letters, news clippings, photographs, and other material.

D. *Private Collection of the Author*

The author maintains a large collection of publications, programs, correspondence, photographs, and other material pertaining to the general history of music in Rochester, including material pertinent to the history of the Eastman School of Music and the Eastman Theatre.

Secondary Sources

Ackerman, Carl W. *George Eastman.* Boston: Houghton Mifflin, 1930.

Brayer, Elizabeth. *George Eastman: A Biography.* Baltimore: Johns Hopkins University Press, 1996.

Cahn, William L. *Rochester's Orchestra: A History of the Rochester Philharmonic Orchestra and Its Educational Programming.* Rochester, NY: Citizens for a Quality Philharmonic, 1989.

Fennell, Frederick. *The Wind Ensemble.* Arkadelphia, AK: Delta, 1988.

Lenti, Vincent A. *For the Enrichment of Community Life: George Eastman and the Founding of the Eastman School of Music.* Rochester, NY: University of Rochester Press, 2004.

May, Arthur J. *A History of the University of Rochester 1850–1962.* Rochester, NY: University of Rochester, 1977.

McQuaid, Donald. *Walter Hendl: The Early Years.* Erie, PA: Ruth S. Jageman, 2003.

Oja, Carol J. (editor). *American Music Recordings: A Discography of 20th Century Composers.* Brooklyn, NY: Brooklyn College of CUNY, 1982.

Rickson, Roger E. *Fortissimo: A Bio-Discography of Frederick Fennell.* Cleveland: Ludwig Music Publishing, 1993.

Riker, Charles. *The Eastman School of Music: Its First Quarter Century 1921–46.* Rochester, NY: University of Rochester, 1948.

———. *The Eastman School of Music 1947–62: A Supplement to the Eastman School of Music: Its First Quarter Century.* Rochester, NY: University of Rochester, 1963.

Ruppli, Michel, and Ed Novitsky. *The Mercury Labels: A Discography, Volume IV: The 1969–1991 Era and Classical Records.* Westport, CT: Greenwood, 1993.

Yancich, Milan. *An Orchestral Musician's Odyssey.* Rochester, NY: Wind Music, 1995.

Index

Page numbers with an *f* indicate figures.